Authors' notes

Our freedom of opinion and expression
- Article 220 of the Constitution of the Federative Republic of Brazil. Chapter V of tl manifestation of thought, creation, expression and information in any form, process or vehicle shall not be subject to any restrictions, in compliance with the provisions of this Constitution.
Paragraph 2 - Any censorship of a political, ideological and artistic nature is prohibited.

Copyright
This work is in the public domain. Publication according to Law nº 9,610 of February 19, 1998. ©2018 - Sociedade Armônica. ISBN: 9781981006434.

Photos from the book
Photos are on this site: https://sites.google.com/view/sociedadearmonica

Index

Introduction to the study of the Spiritist Doctrine	2
1st book - Primary causes	14
Chapter 1 - God	14
Chapter 2 - General Elements of the Universe	16
Chapter 3 - Creation	19
Chapter 4 - The vital principle	23
2nd book - The spirit-world or world of spirits	26
Chapter 1 - Spirits	26
Chapter 2 - Incarnation of spirits	34
Chapter 3 - Return from the corporeal to the spirit life	38
Chapter 4 - Plurality of existences	41
Chapter 5 - Plurality of existences	49
Chapter 6 - Spirit - Life	53
Chapter 7 - Return to corporeal life	67
Chapter 8 - Emancipation of the soul	76
Chapter 9 - Intervention of spirits in the corporeal world	84
Chapter 10 - Occupations and missions of spirits	96
Chapter 11 - The three reigns	99
3rd book - Moral laws	104
Chapter 1 - Divine or natural law	104
Chapter 2 - The law of adoration	108
Chapter 3 - The law of labor	112
Chapter 9 - Law of reproduction	114
Chapter 5 - The law of preservation	116
Chapter 6 - The law of destruction	119
Chapter 7 - Social law	124
Chapter 8 - The law of progress	126
Chapter 9 - The law of equality	131
Chapter 10 - The law of liberty	134
Chapter 11 - The law of justice, of love and of charity	141
Chapter 12 - Moral perfection	144
4th book - Hopes and consolations	149
Chapter 1 - Earthly joys and sorrows	149
Chapter 2 - Future joys and sorrows	156
Conclusion	167

Introduction to the study of the Spiritist Doctrine
On the immortality of the soul, the nature of the spirits and their relations with men, moral laws, present life and the future of Humanity, according to the teachings given by superior spirits, with the aid of various mediums, received and coordinated by Allan Kardec.

1 - Spiritism and Spiritualism

For new things, we need new words, for thus it requires the clarity of language, to avoid the confusion inherent in the multiple senses of the words themselves. The words Spiritual, Spiritualist and Spiritualism have a definite meaning, let us give them another, to apply them to the Doctrine of Spirits, would be to multiply the already numerous causes of amphibology. Indeed, Spiritualism is the opposite of Materialism, whoever believes that there is anything in himself other than matter is spiritual, but it doesn't follow that he believes in the existence of the spirits or in his communications with the visible world.

In place of the words Spiritual and Spiritualism, we'll use the words Spiritism and Spiritism to designate this last belief, in which the form resembles the origin and the radical sense and that therefore have the advantage of being perfectly intelligible, leaving to Spiritualism its own significance. We'll say, therefore, that the Spiritist Doctrine or Spiritism has in principle the relations of the material world with the spirits or the beings of the invisible world. The adepts of Spiritism will then be the spirits or if you'll, the Spiritists. As a specialty, *The Spirits' Book* contains the Spiritist Doctrine, as a generality it's linked to Spiritualism, of which it presents one of the phases. That's why it brings about the title the words, Spiritualist Philosophy.

2 - Soul, vital principle and vital fluid

There's another word that we must understand because it's one of the keys of all moral doctrine and has aroused numerous controversies, for lack of a well-defined meaning, it's the word soul. The divergence of opinions about the nature of the soul stems from the particular application that each makes of that word. A perfect language, in which each idea had its representation by a proper term, would avoid many discussions, with a word for each thing, everyone would understand.

According to some, the soul is the principle of material organic life, doesn't have its own existence and is extinguished with life, is pure materialism. In this sense and by comparison, they say of a broken instrument, which produces no sound, that it has no soul. According to this view, the soul would be an effect and not a cause. Others think that the soul is the principle of intelligence, the universal agent of which each being absorbs a portion. According to these, there would be in the whole Universe but a single soul, distributing sparks to the various intelligent beings, during life, after death, each spark returns to the common source, confusing itself in the whole, as the streams and the rivers return to the sea from where they left.

This view differs from the precedent in which, according to this hypothesis, there's in us something more than matter, leaving anything after death, but it's almost as if nothing remained, for not subsisting individuality we'd no longer be aware of ourselves. According to this view, the universal soul would be God and each being a portion of the Godhead, this is a variety of Pantheism. According to others, finally, the soul is a moral being, distinct, independent of matter and retains its individuality after death. This conception is undoubtedly the most common, because, under one name or another, the idea of this being that survives the body is in a state of instinctive belief, and independent of any degree of civilization, among all peoples.

This doctrine, for which the soul is cause and not effect, is that of Spiritualists. Without discussing the merits of these opinions and considering only the linguistic side of the question, we'll say that these three applications of the word soul constitute three distinct ideas, who would each claim a different term. This word has, therefore, threefold meaning, and each one is right, according to his point of view in giving him a definition, the fault lies in the language, which has no more than one word for three ideas. To avoid confusion, it would be necessary to restrict the meaning of the word soul to one of its ideas. Choosing this or that is indifferent, simple matter of convention, and what matters is clarifying.

We think that the most logical thing is to take it in its most vulgar meaning, and therefore we call soul to the immaterial and individual being that exists in us and survives the body. Although this being didn't exist and was only a product of the imagination, it would take a term to designate it. In the absence of a special word for each of the other two ideas, we shall call the principle of material and organic life, whatever its source, which is common to all living beings, from plants to man. Life can exist, without the faculty of thinking; the vital principle is something distinct and independent.

The word vitality would not give the same idea. For some, the vital principle is a property of matter, an effect that is produced when matter finds itself in given circumstances, according to others, and this is the most common idea, it finds himself in a special, universally dispersed fluid from which each being absorbs and assimilates a part during life as we see inert bodies absorbing light. This would then be the vital fluid, which, according to certain opinions, would be nothing other than the animated electric fluid, also called magnetic fluid, nervous fluid, etc.

Be that as it may, there's an undeniable fact, for it results from observation, that organic beings possess an intimate force that produces the phenomenon of life, while that force exists, that material life is common to all organic beings, and that it's independent of intelligence and thought, that intelligence and thought are faculties proper to certain organic species, that, among organic species endowed with intelligence and thought, there's one endowed with a special moral sense which gives it undeniable superiority to the others and that is the human species.

It's understood that, with a multiple meaning, the soul doesn't exclude materialism, nor pantheism. Even the Spiritualist can very well understand the soul according to one or other of the first two definitions, without prejudice to the distinct material being, to which it'll give any other name. So this word doesn't represent an opinion, it's a Proteus, which each one arranges in its own way, which gives rise to so many endless disputes. We'd also avoid confusion, even if we used the word soul in all three cases, as long as we added a qualifier to specify the way we look at it or the application we give it. It would then be a generic term, representing at the same time the principle of material life, intelligence and moral sense, which would be distinguished by the attribute, as gas, for example, which is distinguished by the addition of the words hydrogen, oxygen and nitrogen.

We could say, and perhaps be the best, the vital soul to designate the principle of material life, the intellectual soul for the principle of intelligence, and the spirit soul for the principle of our individuality after death. As you can see, all this is a question of words, but a very important question for us to understand. In this way, the vital soul would be common to all organic beings, plants, animals and men, the intellectual soul would belong to animals and men, and the spirit soul would belong only to man. We believe that we must insist more on these explanations, since the Spiritist Doctrine rests naturally on the existence in us of a being independent of matter and surviving the body. Often he must repeat the word soul in the course of this work; we must fix the sense in which we take it, in order to avoid any mistake.

3 - The Doctrine and its contradictors

The Spiritist Doctrine, like all novelties, has its adherents and its contradictors. We'll try to respond to some of the objections of the latter by examining the value of the reasons on which they're based, without terms, however, the pretense of convincing everyone, for there are people who believe that the light was made only for them. We address people of good faith, without preconceived ideas or signed positions, but sincerely desirous of being instructed, and we'll show them that most of the objections they make to doctrine come from an incomplete observation of the facts and from a very lightly and precipitously judged judgment.

We'll remember initially, in short, the progressive series of phenomena that gave rise to this doctrine. The first observed fact was the movement of objects, have commonly termed it the name of spinning tables or table-dancing. This phenomenon, which seems to have been first observed in America, or better, which would have been repeated in this country because history proves that it dates back to the highest antiquity, it was accompanied by strange circumstances, such as unusual noises and blows without an ostensible, known cause. From there, it spread rapidly across Europe and other parts of the world, at first it provoked much disbelief, but the multiplicity of experiences soon allowed it no longer to doubt its reality. If this phenomenon had been restricted to the movement of material objects, it could be explained by a purely physical cause.

We far from know all the occult agents of Nature and even all the properties of which we already know, electricity, by the way, daily multiplies to the infinite the resources that it offers to the man and seems to be to illuminate the science with a new light. There would be, therefore, nothing impossible in that electricity, modified by certain circumstances, or any other unknown agent, was the cause of this movement. The meeting of many people, increasing the power of action, seemed to support this theory because one could consider this meeting as a multiple stack, where the power corresponds to the number of elements.

The circular movement was nothing extraordinary, it belongs to Nature. All the stars move around, we could, because, being in the face of a small reflection of the general movement of the Universe, or, rather, a cause hitherto unknown could accidentally produce, in small objects and under certain circumstances, a chain analogous to that which drives the worlds. But the movement was not always circular. Often it was abrupt, disorderly, the object violently shaken, knocked over, driven in any direction, and contrary to all the laws of static, suspended and held in space.

Nevertheless, there was nothing in these facts that could not be explained by the power of an invisible physical agent. Don't we see electricity knocking down buildings, tearing trees, throwing away heavier bodies, luring them, or repelling them? Assuming that unusual noises and blows were not common effects of wood dilation or any other accidental cause, they could still very well be produced by accumulation of the hidden fluid. Does electricity not produce the most violent noise? Up to this point, as can be seen, everything can be considered in the realm of purely physical and physiological facts, and without leaving this order of ideas; there would still be serious study material worthy of the attention of the sages. Why didn't this happen?

It's painful to say, but the fact is linked to causes that prove, among a thousand others similar, the levity of the human spirit. At first the vulgarity of the main object that served as the basis for the first experiences is perhaps not strange to him. What influence didn't have a simple word, often, about more serious things? Without considering that the movement could be transmitted to any object, the idea of the table prevailed, no doubt because it's the most comfortable object and because everyone sits more naturally around a table than any other piece of furniture. The superior men are sometimes so childish that it would not be impossible for some elite spirits to think themselves diminished, if they had to deal with what would be called the dance of the tables.

It's likely that, if the phenomenon observed by Galvani had been by vulgar men and characterized by a burlesque name, was still relegated to the side of the magic wand. What wise man would not have thought himself diminished by the frogs? Some, however, modest enough to accept that Nature could not have said the last word, wanted to see for tranquility of conscience, but it happened that the phenomenon didn't always correspond to their expectation, and not to have been produced constantly, at their will and according to their mode of experimentation, they concluded by refusal. However, his sentence, the tables, because there are tables, they continue to turn, and we can say with Galileo: - *However, they move.*

We'll say that the facts have multiplied in such a way that they have the right of citizenship today and that it's only a question of finding a rational explanation for them. One can induce anything against the reality of the phenomenon by the fact that it doesn't always occur in an identical way, according to the will and demands of the observer? Are the phenomena of electricity and chemistry subordinate to certain conditions, and must we deny them because they don't occur outside of them?

We must wonder that the phenomenon of the movement of objects by the human fluid also has its conditions and ceases to occur when the observer, established in his point of view, intends to make him follow his whim or subject him to the laws of ordinary phenomena, without considering that, for new facts, can and should there be new laws? Now, in order to know these laws, it's necessary to study the circumstances in which the facts occur and this study can't be done without persevering, attentive, and sometimes quite prolonged observation, but some people object, there are often visible frauds. We'll ask at first if they're quite sure that there are frauds and if they didn't take by fraud effects that they failed to seize, more or less like the peasant who took a wise professor of physics, experimenting, by a reckless destroyer, and even supposing that the frauds have occurred sometimes, would that be reason to deny the fact?

Must physics be denied because there are prestidigitators who adorn themselves with the title of physicists? It's necessary, in addition, to consider the character of the people and the interest they could have in deceiving. Was it all then simple jokes? One might well play for a moment, but an indefinitely prolonged play would be as annoying to the mystifier as to the mystified. There would be, moreover, a mystification that spreads from one end of the world to the other and among the most serious, venerable and enlightened people, something at least as extraordinary as the phenomenon itself.

4 - Intelligent manifestations

If the phenomena we were dealing with were restricted to the movement of objects, they would have remained in the realm of the physical sciences, but it was not so, they were destined to put us on the track of the facts of a strange order. It was believed to have been discovered, we don't know by initiative of whom, that the impulse given to objects was not only the product of a blind mechanical force, but that there was in this movement the intervention of an intelligent cause. This way, once opened, offered a whole new field of observations, it was the veil that arose over many mysteries, but is there really a clever power in this case? That is the question. If this power exists, what is it, what is its nature, its origin? And is it superior to Humanity? Such are the other issues arising from the first.

The first intelligent manifestations were verified by means of tables that moved and gave certain blows, hitting one foot, and so they answered, according to what had been agreed, by "yes" or "no" to the proposed question. Until here, nothing surely convincing to the skeptics, because one could believe in an effect of chance. Then, more developed answers were obtained through the letters of the alphabet, giving the mobile an order number of each letter, words and phrases that answered the proposed questions were formed. The correctness of the answers and their correspondence with the question provoked admiration. The mysterious being, who thus answered, questioned about its nature, declared that it was a spirit or Gemo, gave his name and provided various information about him. This is a very important circumstance to note.

No one had ever thought of the spirits as a means of explaining the phenomenon, it was the very phenomenon that revealed the word. Hypotheses are frequently made in the exact sciences in order to obtain a basis for reasoning, but in this case it was not what happened. This medium of correspondence was time consuming and uncomfortable. The spirit is this and also a noteworthy circumstance, he said another. It was one of those invisible beings who advised to adapt a pencil to a basket or another object. The basket, placed on a sheet of paper, is moved by the same occult power that turns the tables, but, instead of a simple regular movement, the pencil writes itself, forming words sentences entire discourses of many pages, dealing with the higher questions of philosophy, morals, metaphysics, psychology, etc., and this as quickly as if it were written by hand. This council was given simultaneously in America, in France and in several countries. This is the terms given to one of the most fervent adherents of the Doctrine, who for many years since 1849, had been engaged in the evocation of the spirits in Paris on June 10, 1853: - *Go to the room next to the basket, attach a pencil to it, place it on the paper and put your fingers on the edge.*

After a few moments, the basket began to move, and the pencil legibly wrote this sentence: - *That which I told you, I expressly forbid you to tell anyone, the first time you write, I'll write better.*

The object to which the pencil fits, being no more than simple instrument its nature and its form doesn't matter, looked for the more comfortable disposition and that was how many people began to use a drawing board. The basket or drawing board can't be set in motion unless under the influence of certain persons, endowed with a special power and is called by the name of mediums, that's, intermediaries between spirits and men. The conditions which produce this power are linked to causes which are at the same time physical and spiritual yet imperfectly known because there are mediums of all ages, of both sexes, and in all degrees of intellectual development. This faculty, however, develops through exercise.

5 - Development of psychography

Later it was recognized that the basket were nothing more than appendages of the hand, and the medium, taking the pencil directly, began to write by an involuntary and almost feverish impulse. By this means communications have become faster, easier and more complete; it's this today, the most common means, so much that the number of people endowed with this aptitude is quite considerable and multiplies day by day. Experience, finally, made many other varieties of the mediumistic faculty known, and it was discovered that communications could also be verified through the direct writing of the spirits, that's, without the assistance of the medium's hand or the pencil.

Having verified the fact, an essential point remained to consider, the role of the medium in the responses and the part that took them, mechanically and spiritually. Two capital circumstances, which would not escape an attentive observer, can solve the question. The first is the manner in which the basket moves under its influence by the simple imposition of the fingers on the edge, the examination demonstrates the impossibility of a medium printing a direction to the basket. This impossibility becomes especially evident when two or three people play simultaneously in the same basket, it would be necessary between them a really phenomenal concordance of movements, it would still be necessary the agreement of thoughts so that they could be understood on the answer to give.

Another fact, not less original, still comes to increase the difficulty. It's the radical change of the letter, according to the spirit that manifests itself and each time the same spirit returns, repeating it. Would be, because, it's necessary that the medium should have exercised himself in modifying his own letter in twenty different ways, and above all that he could remember the calligraphy of this or that spirit. The 2nd circumstance arises from the very nature of the replies, that are, in most cases, especially when it comes to abstract or scientific issues, notoriously out of the knowledge and at times of the intellectual reach of the medium. The latter, in general, isn't aware of what he writes and on the other hand doesn't even understand the proposed question, which can be made in a foreign language or mentally, the answer being given in that language. It turns out, finally, that the basket writes spontaneously, without any question proposed, on an absolutely unexpected subject.

The answers, in certain cases, reveal a content of wisdom, depth and opportunity, thoughts so high and so sublime that can only come from a superior intelligence impregnated with the purest morality. At other times they're so frivolous and even so trivial that reason refuses to admit that they can come from the same source. This diversity of language can only be explained by the diversity of intelligences that manifest themselves. Are these intelligences human or not? This is the point to be clarified and upon which the full explanation, as given by the spirits themselves, will be found in this work.

Here, then, are the evident effects which are produced outside the usual circle of our observations, which don't happen in a mysterious way, but in the light of day, which all can see and see, which are not the privilege of any individual and which thousands of People repeat at will every day. These effects necessarily have a cause and, as long as they reveal the action of intelligence and a will, they come out purely physical. Many theories have been made about it. We'll examine them shortly and see if they can make all the facts produced understandable. Let us assume, for a while, the existence of beings distinct from Humanity, for this is the explanation given by the intelligences and let us see what they tell us.

6 - Summary of the doctrine of the spirits

The beings that manifest themselves designate themselves, as we said by the name of spirits or geniuses, and say, some at least, who lived as men on Earth. They constitute the spiritual world, as we have constituted during our life, the corporeal world. Let us briefly summarize the main points of the doctrine which we have been given, in order to more easily answer certain objections, God is eternal, immutable, immaterial, unique, all-powerful, sovereignty just and good. He created the Universe, which comprises all animate and inanimate beings, material and immaterial. Material beings constitute the visible or corporeal world and immaterial beings the invisible or spiritist world, that is, the spirits. The spirit world is the normal world, primitive, eternal, preexisting and survivable to everything.

The corporeal world is secondary, it may cease to exist or never have existed, without altering the essence of the spiritist world. Spirits temporarily coat a perishable material envelope and their destruction by death returns them to freedom. Among the different species of corporeal beings, God chose the human species for the incarnation of spirits who have reached a certain degree of development, which gives them moral and intellectual superiority over others. The soul is an incarnate spirit and the body is only its envelope. There are three things in man: 1 - The body or material being, similar to that of animals and animated by the same vital principle; 2 - The soul or immaterial being, spirit embodied in the body; and 3 - The link that binds the soul to the body, the intermediate principle between matter and spirit.

Man thus has two natures, by the body he participates in the nature of animals, of which he possesses the instincts, by the soul participates in the nature of the spirits. The bond or perispirit that unites body and spirit is a kind of semi-material envelope. Death is the destruction of the coarsest shell. The spirit preserves the second, which constitutes for him an ethereal body, invisible to us in its normal state, but that it can make it accidentally visible and even tangible, as in the phenomena of appearance. The spirit isn't, therefore, an abstract being, indefinite, which only thought can conceive. It's a real being, defined, which in certain cases can be appreciated by our senses of sight, hearing and touch. Spirits belong to different classes, not being equal in power and intelligence, knowledge or morality. Those of the first order are the superior spirits who are distinguished by perfection, by knowledge and by the closeness of God, the purity of the feelings and the love of the good, are the pure angels or spirits.

The other classes distance themselves more and more from this perfection. Those of the lower classes are inclined to our passions, hatred, envy, jealousy, pride, etc., and enjoy evil. In this number there are those who are neither very good nor very bad, rather disturbing and intriguing than evil, malice and inconsequence seem to be their characteristics, are spirits mad or frivolous. Spirits don't belong eternally to the same order. All improve, going through the different degrees of the spiritist hierarchy. This improvement is verified by the incarnation, which is imposed on some as atonement and for others as a mission. The material life is a proof to which they must submit repeatedly until they reach absolute perfection; it's a kind of sieve or purifier from which they come out more or less purified.

Leaving the body, the soul returns to the world of the spirits, that he had left to resume a new material experience after a more or less lengthy period of time during which he'll remain in the state of wandering spirit. Because the spirit goes through many incarnations, one concludes that we all had many existences and that we'll have still others more or less perfected, whether on Earth or on other worlds. The incarnation of spirits always occurs in the human species. It would be a mistake to believe that it could incarnate in an animal body. The different bodily existences of spirit are always progressive and never retrograde, but the speed of progress depends on the efforts we make to attain perfection. The qualities of the soul are the same as the incarnate spirit. Thus the good man is the incarnation of a good spirit and the wicked man, the impure spirit. The soul had its individuality before the incarnation and it preserves it after the separation of the body.

On its return to the world of spirits, the soul rediscovers all that she knew on Earth and all its previous existences are outlined in its memory with the remembrance of all the good and all the evil it has done. The incarnate spirit is under the influence of matter. The man, who overcomes this influence, by the elevation and purification of his soul, is approaching the good spirits with which it'll one day be. He, who lets himself be dominated by bad passions and puts all his joys in the satisfaction of gross appetites, approaches the impure spirits, giving preference to the animal nature. The incarnated spirits inhabit the different globes of the Universe. Spirits who are not incarnate or wandering don't occupy any particular or circumscribed region. They're everywhere, in space and beside us, seeing and jostling us without ceasing. It's an entire invisible population that is agitating around us.

The spirits exercise on the moral world and even on the physical world an incessant action. They act upon matter and thought, and constitute one of Nature's forces, an efficient cause of a multitude of hitherto unexplained or ill-explained phenomena which find no rational solution. The relations of spirits with men are constant. Good spirits invite us to the good, sustain us in the trials of life and help us endure them with courage and resignation, the bad ones invite us to evil, for them it's a pleasure to see us succumb and fall into their state. The hidden communications are verified by the good or bad influence that they exert on us without us knowing, being in our judgment to discern the bad and good inspirations. Ostensible communications are carried out through writing, speaking or other material manifestations, most of the time through the mediums that serve as instruments.

Spirits manifest themselves spontaneously or by evocation. We can evoke all spirits, those who animated dark men and those of the most illustrious characters, whatever the time they may have lived, those of our kinsmen, our friends or enemies, and obtain, by written or verbal communications, advice, information about the situation in which they're in space, their thoughts about us, as well as the revelations they're allowed to make to us. Spirits are attracted by reason of their sympathy for the moral nature of the evocative medium. Superior spirits like serious meetings in which the love of good prevails and the sincere desire of education and improvement. His presence drives away the lower spirits; that they find, instead, free access and can act with complete freedom between frivolous people or guided only by curiosity and everywhere where they find bad instincts.

Far from obtaining good advice and useful information from these spirits, we should expect nothing but trifles, lies, games of bad taste, or mystifications, for they often use venerable names to better mislead us. Distinguishing good and evil spirits is extremely easy. The language of the higher spirits is constantly dignified, noble, full of the highest morality, free from any inferior passion; his counsels reveal the purest wisdom and always aim for our progress and the good of Humanity. The language of the inferior spirits is inconsequential, almost banal and even gross, if they sometimes say good and true things, they say more often falsities and absurdities, out of malice or ignorance, they mock credulity and amuse themselves at the expense of those who question them, flattering their vanity and lulled their desires with false hopes. In short, serious communications, in the perfect sense of the term, are found only in the sine centers, whose members are united by an intimate communion of thoughts directed toward the good. The morality of the higher spirits is summed up, as that of the Christ in this evangelical maxim: - *To do to others what we wish others to do to us, that is, to do good and not evil.*

Man finds in this principle the universal rule of conduct, even for the smallest actions. They teach us that selfishness, pride, and sensuality are passions that bring us closer to the animal nature, attaching ourselves to matter, that the man who, from this world, is liberated from matter by the contempt of worldly futilities and the cultivation of love of neighbor, is approaching the spiritual nature, that each one of us must become useful according to the faculties and means that God has put us in the hands to prove to us, that the Strong and the Mighty owe support and protection to the weak because he who abuses his strength and power to oppress his fellowman, violates the law of God.

They teach that in the spirit world nothing can be hidden, the hypocrite will be unmasked and all his foibles revealed, the inevitable and incessant presence of those we harm is one of the punishments that are reserved for us, to the state of inferiority and superiority of the spirits correspond feathers and joys that are unknown to us on Earth. But they also teach us that there are no irretrievable faults that can't be erased by the atonement. Man finds the necessary means in the different existences that allow him to advance, on the path of progress toward perfection which is his ultimate goal. This is the summary of the Spiritist Doctrine, as it appears in the teaching of the higher spirits. Let us now turn to the objections that are made to it.

7 - Science and Spiritism

The opposition of scientific corporations is, for many people, but at least strong evidence to the contrary. We're not the ones who raise their voices against the wise, for we don't want to give reason to be called astonished, but we fear them, and we'd be very honored if we were numbered among them. However, his opinion could not in any circumstances represent an irrevocable judgment. When Science comes out of the material observation of facts and tries to appreciate and explain them, scientists are opened up to the field of conjectures, each one constructing its own system, which wishes to make it prevail and sustains it.

Do we not daily see the most contradictory opinions being praised and rejected, repelled as absurd errors and then proclaimed as incontestable truths? The facts, this is the true criterion of our judgments, the argument without reply. In the absence of facts, doubt is the opinion of the prudent man. Concerning the evident things, the opinion of the wise is justly worthy of faith, because they know them more and better than the common people, but in regard to new principles, to things unknown, the way they see it's no more than hypothetical, because they're no more free from prejudice than others.

I'll even say that the wise man will have, perhaps, more prejudices than any other, because a natural propensity leads him to subordinate everything to the point of view of his specialty, the mathematician sees no proof at all except through an algebraic demonstration, the chemist relates everything to the action of the elements and so on. Every man who engages in a specialty enslaves his ideas. Keep him from the subject and he'll almost always be confused, because he wishes to submit everything to his way of seeing, it's a consequence of human fragility. I'll therefore willingly and absolutely confidently consult a chemist on a matter of analysis, a physicist, on the electric force, a mechanic, on the driving force, but they'll permit me, without this affecting the esteem which they I owe it for his specialization that he doesn't take better account of his negative opinion of Spiritism than of an architect on matters of music.

The common sciences rely on the properties of matter, which can be tried and manipulated at will, the spirit phenomena rely on the action of intelligences who have a will of their own and prove to us at all times not to be subjected to our whim. The observations, therefore, can't be made in the same way, in either case. In Spiritism, they require special conditions and another way of looking at them, wanting to subject them to ordinary processes of inquiry would be to establish analogies that don't exist. Science itself, as Science, is incompetent to pronounce on the question of Spiritism, it's not for it to take care of the subject and its pronouncement on it, whatever, favorable or not, no weight would have. Spiritism is the result of a personal conviction that the wise can have as individuals, regardless of their condition of sages. However, wanting to defer the question to Science would be to give an assembly of physicists or astronomers the solution to the problem of the existence of the soul.

In fact, Spiritism rests entirely on the existence of the soul and its state after death. Now it's supremely illogical to think that a man should be a great psychologist simply because he is a great mathematician or anatomist. The anatomist, dissecting the human body, seeks the soul and, because he doesn't find it with his scalpel, as if he found a nerve, or because he doesn't see her wrapping herself like a gas, concludes that it doesn't exist. This is because of being placed in an exclusively material point of view. Does it follow that he's right, against universal opinion? No. It's seen, therefore, that Spiritism isn't the domain of Science.

When Spiritist beliefs are vulgarized, when they're accepted by the masses, what, to judge by the speed with which they spread, would not be very far, it'll be given to them what has been given with all new ideas that have found opposition, the wise will surrender to the evidence. They'll accept individually, by force of circumstances. Until this happens, it would be inopportune to divert them from their special labors to embarrass them in dealing with a strange thing, which isn't in their assignments or in their programs. Meanwhile, those who, without previous and in depth study of the matter, they pronounce themselves in the negative and mock those who don't agree with their opinion; they forget that the same thing happened with most of the great discoveries that have honored Humanity.

They risk seeing their names by increasing the list of illustrious deniers of new ideas, inscribed next to the members of the learned assembly who, in 1752, received with loud laughter Franklin's report on the lightning bolts, deeming it unworthy to appear among the communications of agenda, and of the other that made France lose the advantages of steam navigation by declaring Fulton's system an impractical dream. Nevertheless, they were questions of Science. If these meetings, who counted on the greatest sages of the world, they only had mockery and sarcasm for ideas they didn't yet understand and that, some years later, they were supposed to revolutionize science, and customs and industry, how do you expect that a matter foreign to your work can be better accepted?

These regrettable errors would not, however, deprive the scholars of the titles with which in other respects they have earned our respect, but do we need an official diploma to have common sense? And out of the academic chairs will there be no more than fools and imbeciles? One has only to look at the adherents of the Spiritist doctrine to see if there are only among them ignorant and if the immense number of men of merit who embraced it allows us to relegate it to the role of simple creeds. The character and knowledge of these men authorize us to say, for if they affirm it, there must at least be something.

We also repeat that, if the facts of which we're concerned were reduced to the mechanical movement of bodies, the search for the physical cause of the phenomenon would be in the domain of Science, but since it's a manifestation outside the realm of human laws, escapes the competence of material Science because it can't be explained by numbers or mechanical forces. When a new fact arises, which doesn't fit into any known Science, the wise man, to study it, must make abstraction of his science and say to himself that it's a new study, which can't be done through preconceived ideas.

The man who considers his infallible reason is very close to error, even those who have the most false ideas rely on reason itself and that are why they reject everything that seems impossible to them. Those who yesterday repelled the admirable discoveries that humanity today is proud of, appealed to this judge to reject them. What we call reason is almost always masked pride and whoever thinks he is infallible places himself as equal to God. We're therefore directed to those who are very thoughtful to doubt what they have not seen, and, judging the future by the past, they don't believe that man has reached the apogee or that Nature has turned the last page of his book.

8 - Perseverance and seriousness

Let us add that the study of a doctrine such as the spiritist, which throws us suddenly in such a new and great order of things, can't be done profitably, except by serious, persevering men, free from prejudices and animated by a firm and sincere desire to reach a result. We can't classify thus those who judge a priori, lightly, without having seen everything, which don't impart to their studies or continuity, nor the necessary regularity and payment, and even less so to those who, so as not to diminish their reputation as men of the spirit, strive to find a burlesque side in the truest things or thus considered by people whose knowledge, character and convictions, deserve the consideration of those who value urbanity.

That they abstain, therefore, those who don't judge the facts worthy of their attention; no one intends to violate their beliefs, but that they also know how to respect others. What characterizes a serious study is continuity. We should be amazed not to get sensible answers to naturally serious questions, when we do them at random abruptly, amid preliminary or supplementary questions. Those who want to acquire a science should study it in a methodical way, beginning at the beginning and following its chain of ideas. The one who proposes to a wise man, at random, a question about Science that ignores the rudiments, will he gain some benefit? Can the wise man himself, with the greatest good will, give him a satisfactory answer?

This isolated response is necessarily incomplete and, for that very reason, it'll almost be unintelligible, or it may seem absurd and contradictory, the same thing happens in our relations with spirits. If we wish to learn from them, we must follow the course, but, as among us, it's necessary to choose the teachers and to work with assiduity. We have said that the superior spirits only attend serious meetings, those, above all, where the perfect communion of thoughts and good feelings reigns. The levity and the idle questions keep them away, as among men, push away ponderous creatures, the field is then free to the mob of liars and frivolous spirits, always on the lookout for opportunities to mock us and have fun at our expense.

What would become a serious question at such a meeting? Would he have an answer? From who? It'd be the same as throwing these questions into a meeting of gaiates, what's the soul? What is death? And other fun things. If you want serious answers, be serious yourselves, to the fullest extent of the term and keep yourselves in the necessary conditions, only then will you obtain great things. Be more diligent and persevering in your studies, so that the higher spirits don't abandon you, as a teacher does with neglected students.

9 - Monopolizers of common sense

The movement of objects is a proven fact, it remains to know whether there is any intelligent manifestation in this movement and, if so, what its origin. We don't speak of the intelligent movement of certain objects, nor of verbal communications or of those written directly by mediums. This kind of manifestation, so evident to those who have seen and deepened the subject, isn't, at first glance, quite independent of the will to convince a novice observer. We'll therefore treat only the writing obtained with the aid of an object with a pencil, a basket, a drawing board, etc.

The way in which the medium's fingers are placed on the object challenges, as we have already said, the most consummate skill in participating in any form of letter formation, but let us further admit that by a marvelous skill it may deceive the most attentive eyes. How can one explain the nature of the answers, when they surpass the ideas and knowledge of the medium? And it should be noted that these are not monosyllabic answers, but almost always of many pages written with admirable rapidity, either spontaneously or on a determined subject. By the hand of the medium less versed in literature, poetry emerges of sublimity and of impeccable purity, which would not detract from the best human poets, and what still increases the strangeness of these facts is that they're produced and that mediums multiply to infinity.

Are these facts real or not? To this question we can only answer, see and observe, you'll not lack opportunities, but above all, observe with conscience, for a long time and obeying the necessary conditions. For example, what do the antagonists respond to? You are victims of charlatanism, they say, or toys of an illusion. We'll respond, from start, that the word charlatanism must be removed from where there are no profits, for charlatans don't act gratuitously. Would be, at most, a mystification. But why strange coincidence would the mystifiers have understood, from one end of the world to the other, to act in the same way, produce the same effects and give, on the same subjects and in the various languages, identical answers, but as for words, at least as to meaning?

How serious are people, honored and educated would lend themselves to such maneuvers, and for what purpose? How would they have found the necessary patience and skill among the children? Because, if the mediums are not passive instruments, of course, they need skill and knowledge incompatible with certain ages and social positions. Then they add that, if there is no hoax, of the two sides may be blurred by an illusion. In good logic, the quality of the witnesses has a certain weight, is the case of asking if the spiritist doctrine, which today has millions of fans, it only recruits them among the ignorant.

The phenomena on which it rests are so extraordinary that we conceive of doubt, but one can't admit the pretension of some unbelievers to a monopoly of common sense, or that, without regard to the conveniences and moral value of their opponents, they call them inept at all those who don't agree with their opinions. In the eyes of every wise person, the opinion of enlightened men who have seen a certain fact for a long time and who studied and meditated it'll always be a proof or at least a favorable presumption, for having been able to catch the attention of serious men, who had no interest in propagating mistakes or time to waste with trifles.

10 - The language of the spirits and the devilish power

Among the objections, some are more ponderable at least in appearance, because they're based on the observation of serious people. One of these remarks refers to the language of certain spirits, which doesn't seem worthy of the elevation attributed to supernatural beings. If we want to refer to the summary of the doctrine presented above, we'll see that the spirits themselves teach that they're not equal in knowledge or in moral qualities, and that one should not take literally everything they say. It's up to wise people to separate the good from the bad. Surely, those who deduce from this fact that we deal with evil beings whose only intention is to mystify us, don't know the communications given at meetings in which higher spirits are manifested, otherwise they'd not think so.

It's a pity that chance has served so badly to these people, showing them only the evil side of the spirit world; because we don't want to suppose that a sympathetic tendency attracts to them the evil spirits instead of the good ones, the lying spirits or those whose language is of revolting rudeness. We could conclude, at most, that the solidity of its principles isn't strong enough to preserve them from evil, is that, finding some pleasure in satisfying his curiosity, the evil spirits, for your side, they take advantage of it to enter between them, while the good ones move away. To judge the question of the spirits by these facts would be as unreasonable as to judge the character of a people by what is said and done in a meeting of some incoherent or people of bad reputation, to which wise men and wise men don't attend. Those who so judge are in the situation of a foreigner who, arriving at a great capital for its worse suburb, to judge the entire population of the city by the habits and language of this petty neighborhood.

In the world of spirits, there are also social gaps, if those people wanted to study the relations between the high spirits; they'd be convinced that the celestial city contains not only the popular scum. But, they ask, do the high spirits come to us? We'll respond, don't stay in the suburbs, see, observe and judge, the facts are there for everyone. Unless these people apply these words of Jesus: - *They have eyes and they don't see, they have ears and they don't listen.*

A variant of this opinion isn't to see in the spirit communications and in all the material facts to which they give place but the intervention of a diabolical power, new Proteus that would take all the forms to better deceive to us. We don't consider it to be subject to serious examination and so we'll not dwell on the case, it's already refuted by what we said earlier. We'll add only that, if it were so, we would have to agree that the devil is sometimes very clever, quite judicious and above all very moral, or that there are good deeds.

How to believe, indeed, that God will not allow, but the spirit of evil to manifest himself to lose us, without giving us as a counterweight the counsels of the good spirits? If he can't, this is impotence, if he can and doesn't, this is incompatible with his goodness and both would be blasphemy. Let us emphasize that to admit the communication of evil spirits is to recognize the principle of manifestations. However, since they exist, it'll be with the permission of God. How to believe, without committing ungodliness, that he only allows evil, to the exclusion of good? Such a doctrine is contrary to common sense and the simplest notions of religion.

11 - Big and small

Is weird, they add, that they speak only of spirits of known personalities and ask why they only manifest themselves. It's a mistake, like many others, of superficial observation. Among the spirits who manifest themselves spontaneously, there are more unknown than illustrious. They're designated by any name, often by allegorical or characteristic names. As for the evocados, provided they're not relatives or friends, it's very natural that they're preferably those known. The names of distinguished personalities draw more attention because they're more prominent.

They find it strange that the spirits of eminent men attend to our appeal familiarly, occupying, sometimes, of insignificant things compared to the ones they dealt with during life. This is nothing strange to those who know that the power or consideration that these men enjoyed in the world doesn't give them any supremacy in the spirit world. The spirits thus confirm the words of the Gospel, the great ones will be humiliated and the little ones will be exalted, that must be understood in relation to the category that each of us will occupy between them. This is how the one who was first on Earth may be among the last, the one who makes us bow our heads in this life can come back as the most humble craftsman, because, on leaving life, he lost all his greatness, and the most powerful monarch may be there below the last of his soldiers.

12 - Of the identification of spirits

A fact demonstrated by observation and confirmed by the spirits themselves is that the lower spirits often present themselves with well-known and respected names. Who can, therefore, to ensure that those who claim to have been Socrates, Julius Caesar, Charlemagne, Fenelon, Napoleon, Washington, etc., actually animated these characters? This doubt exists among some very fervent adherents of the Spiritist Doctrine. They admit the intervention and manifestation of the spirits, but ask what control we can have of their identity. Such control is indeed quite difficult to accomplish, but if it can't be done as authentically as by a civil registration certificate, it can be done by presumption, by certain clues.

When the spirit of a person we know personally, of a relative or a friend, especially if he died a short time ago, it usually happens that his language corresponds perfectly to the characteristics we knew. This is already a sign of identity. But doubt will no longer be possible when this spirit speaks of particular things; it recalls familiar cases that only the interlocutor knows. A son will not deceive himself, for right, with the language of his father or mother, nor the parents with the language of the child. It happens a few times, in these intimate evocations, awesome things, capable of convincing the most unbelieving. The most hardened skeptic is often terrified by the unexpected revelations that are made to him.

Another quite characteristic circumstance favors identity. We have said that the medium's calligraphy usually changes with the evoked spirit, reproducing exactly the same, each time the same spirit is manifested. It has been found over and over again that, for people who have recently died, writing shows blatant similarity to what it had in life, there have been perfectly identical signatures. However, we're far from citing this fact as a rule, especially as constant, we mention it as something worthy of registration. Spirits who have reached a certain degree of purification are the only freedmen of all bodily influence, but when they're completely dematerialized, they retain most of the ideas, inclinations, and even the manias they had on Earth, and this is still a means by which we can recognize them, but we come to recognition, above all, through a multitude of details that only a close and continuous observation can reveal.

We see writers discussing their own works or doctrines, approving or condemning certain parts of them, other spirits recall unknown or little-known circumstances of their lives or their deaths. All things, at least, which are at least moral proofs of identity, the only ones that can be invoked when dealing with abstract things. If, then, the identity of the spirit evoked may be, to a certain extent, established in some cases, there's no reason why it can't be in others. And if, for people of more remote death, we don't have the same means of control, we always dispose of those that refer to language and character, because surely the spirit of a good man will never speak as a perverse or immoral one. As for the spirits who use respectable names, they're betrayed by their language and their maxims. Anyone who said Fenelon, for example, and even if he accidentally hurt common sense and morals, would show his deception.

If, on the other hand, the thoughts he expresses are always pure, without contradictions, constantly up to the character of Fenelon, there is no reason to doubt his identity. Otherwise, we'd have to suppose that a spirit who preaches well can consciously employ the lie without any use. Experience teaches us that spirits of the same degree, of the same character and animated by the same feelings, come together in groups and in families. Now, the number of spirits is incalculable and we far from know them all, most of them have no names for us. A spirit of the Fenelon category may, therefore, come in your place, sometimes even with your name, because it's identical to it and can replace it and because we need a name to fix our ideas, but what does it matter, actually, that a spirit really is that of Fenelon? As long as he only says good things and says nothing like Fenelon himself, he's a good spirit, the name under which he presents himself is indifferent and is often nothing more than a means for fixing our ideas. The same would not be true in intimate evocations, for in these, as we have already said, identity can be established by means of evidence which is somehow evident.

Finally, it's certain that the substitution of spirits can cause a lot of mistakes, result in errors and often in mystifications. This is one of the difficulties of practical Spiritism, but we have never said that this Science is easy or that one can learn it by joking, as it doesn't happen with any other Science. It'll never be too much to repeat that it requires constant and almost always lengthy study. If it's not possible to provoke the facts, it's necessary to wait for them to present themselves, and often they're brought to us by the circumstances in which we least expected it. To the attentive and patient observer, facts become abundant because he discovers thousands of characteristic nuances that appear to him as rays of light. The same is true of the ordinary sciences, while the superficial man sees only a flower in its elegant form; the sage discovers true wonders for his thought.

13 - The divergences of language

These observations lead us to say a few words about another difficulty, referring to the divergence of language of the spirits. Since spirits are very different from one another in regard to knowledge and morality, it's evident that the same question can be resolved by them in a contradictory way, according to their respective categories, as would a wise man, an ignorant man or a joke in bad taste. The key is to know whom we're addressing. But, they add, how do you explain that the spirits recognized as superior are not always in agreement? We'll say, initially, that in addition to the cause already mentioned, there are others that may exert some influence on the nature of the answers, regardless of the quality of the spirits. This is a key point, the explanation of which we shall get from the study.

This is why we say that these studies require continuous attention, profound observation and above all, as indeed all human sciences, continuity and perseverance. We need years to make a mediocre doctor and three quarters of life to make a sage, but if you want to get in a few hours the science of infinity. That nobody, therefore, be deceived, the study of Spiritism is immense, it binds itself to all questions of metaphysics and social order, it's a whole world that opens before us. Is it any wonder that it requires time and a lot of time for its fulfillment? The contradiction, moreover, isn't always as real as it may seem. Don't we see men who profess the same science every day diverge in their definitions, whether they employ different terms or differences of point of view, although the fundamental idea is always the same? Let it count, if possible, the number of definitions given about grammar.

Let us add that the form of the answer almost always depends on the form of the question. It would be puerile, therefore, to see a contradiction where there is usually no more than a difference of words. The higher spirits don't care at all about form, for them, the essence of thought is everything. Let us take, for example, the definition of soul. Since this word doesn't have a single definition, spirits can, like us, diverge in its application, one may say that it's the principle of life, another, call it soul spark, a third, say that its internal, a room, which is external, etc., and all will be right according to their points of view. We might even believe that some of them profess materialistic theories, and yet they don't.

The same is true of God, he'll be the principle of all things, the creator of the Universe, the supreme intelligence, the infinite, the great spirit, etc., but in definitive will always be God. Let us also mention the classification of spirits. They form an uninterrupted series from the lowest to the highest grade and their classification is therefore arbitrary, one can establish it in three classes, another in five, ten or twenty, at will, without being in error. All human sciences offer the same example, every sage has his system, systems vary, but Science is always the same. Whether you learn botany from the Lineu, Jussieu, or Tournefort systems, you'll not know less botany. Let us, therefore, stop giving purely conventional things more importance than they deserve, in order to hold on to what is truly serious, and not infrequently, reflection will make us discover, in what seems most absurd, a similarity that escaped us at the first examination.

14 - The spelling questions

We'd pass slightly on the objection of some skeptics to the spelling errors of some spirits, if it didn't give us an opportunity to make an essential observation. This spelling, it must be said, isn't always flawless, but only the lack of arguments can make it the object of serious criticism, with the claim that if spirits know everything, they must know spelling. We could oppose to them numerous sins of this kind committed by wise men of the Earth, without having diminished their merit, but there is in this fact a more serious question. For spirits, especially for superiors, the idea is everything, form is nothing. Free from matter their language is quick as thought, for it's the very thought which communicates among them without intermediates.

They must, therefore, feel bad when they're obliged to communicate with us to use the slow and embarrassing forms of human language and, above all, their insufficiency and imperfection, to express all their ideas. This is what they themselves say; being curious to observe the means they use to mitigate this inconvenience. The same would happen to us if we were to express ourselves in a language of words and phrases longer and poorer in expression than ours. It's the difficulty experienced by the man of genius impatient with the slowness of the pen, always late in relation to thought.

It's understood, therefore, that spirits attach little importance to orthographic puerilities, especially when dealing with a deep and serious teaching. Is it not, moreover, marvelous that they express themselves indifferently in all languages, all understanding? It should not be concluded, however, that the conventional correction of language is unknown to them, since they observe it when necessary. For example, the poetry dictated by them almost always defies the criticism of the most demanding purist, and this despite the ignorance of the medium.

15 - Madness and its causes

There are still creatures that see danger everywhere, in all that they don't know, not missing those who draw unfavorable conclusions to the Spiritism of the fact that some people, who gave themselves to these studies, lost the reason. How can wise men accept this objection? Isn't the same with all intellectual concerns when the brain is weak? Are we aware of the number of madmen and maniacs produced by mathematical, medical, musical, philosophical, and other studies? And should we, therefore, ban such studies? What do these effects prove?

In physical works, the arms and legs that are the instruments of material action are clogged, in intellectual works, the brain, which is the instrument of thought, is clogged, but if the instrument has broken, so has not spirit, it remains intact, and when you free yourself from matter, you'll not enjoy less of the fullness of your faculties. It was in his sector, as a man, a martyr of work. All great intellectual preoccupations can lead to madness; the sciences, the arts and religion provide their contingents. Madness has as its primary cause an organic predisposition of the brain, which makes it more or less accessible to certain impressions. Having this predisposition to madness, it'll manifest itself with the character of the main concern of the individual, which will become a fixed idea.

This idea may be that of spirits, angels, the Devil, fortune, power, art, science, motherhood or a political or social system. It's possible that the religious madman presents himself as a spiritist madman, if Spiritism was his dominant concern, as the crazy Spiritist would present himself in another way, according to the circumstances. I say, therefore, that Spiritism has no privilege in this matter and I go further, I say Spiritism well understood is a preservative of madness. Among the most frequent causes of cerebral over excitation, we must mention the disappointments, the misfortunes, the annoyed affections, which are also the most frequent causes of suicide.

Now! The true Spiritist looks at the things of this world from such a high point of view, they seem so small, so petty, in the face of the future that awaits him, and life is so short, so fugitive that tribulations don't seem to him any more than unpleasant incidents of a trip. That which for any other would produce violent emotion, has little effect on him, for he knows that the bitterness of life is proof for his advance, as long as he suffers it without murmuring, for he'll be rewarded according to his courage in bearing them. His convictions give him a resignation that preserves him from despair and consequently from a constant cause of madness and suicide.

Moreover, he knows by the example of the communications of the spirits the fate of those who voluntarily abbreviate their days, and that picture is enough to make him meditate. Thus, the number of those who have been detained on the brink of this dreadful cliff is considerable. This is one of the results of Spiritism. That the unbelievers should laugh as much as they want, I desire the consolations he gives to all who bother to probe the mysterious depths. Among the causes of madness, we must still include dread, and the fear of the Devil has already unbalanced some brains.

One knows the number of victims that he has done to shake weak imaginations with this threat, which is increasingly sought to become more dreadful through hideous details? The devil, they say, just scares the kids, is a means of making them more judicious. Yes, like the bogeyman and the werewolf, but when they cease to fear him, are worse than before and to achieve such a beautiful result don't take into account the epilepsy caused by the concussion of delicate brains. The religion would be very weak, if, for not using fear, his power was compromised. Fortunately, it doesn't. It has other means to act upon souls and Spiritism provides it with the most effective and most serious, as long as they know how to take advantage of them. It shows things in their reality and thereby neutralizes the baneful effects of exaggerated fear.

16 - The magnetic theory and the environment
It remains for us to examine two objections, the only ones that really deserve this name because they rely on rational theories. Both admit the reality of all material and moral phenomena, but exclude the intervention of spirits. For the first of these theories, all manifestations attributed to spirits would be merely magnetic effects. The mediums would be in a state that could be called awakened sleepwalking, a phenomenon known to all who have studied magnetism.

In this state, the intellectual faculties acquire an abnormal development; the circles of intuitive perception extend beyond the limits of our ordinary perception. In this way the medium would take from himself and by effect of his lucidity everything he says and all the notions he conveys, even on the things that are stranger to him in the normal state. It'll not be us who will contest the power of sleepwalking, whose prodigies we have witnessed, studying all facets for more than 35 years. We agree that, in fact, many Spiritist manifestations can be explained by this means, but a prolonged and attentive observation shows a multitude of facts in which the participation of the medium, except as a passive instrument, is materially impossible. To those who participate in this opinion, we'll say as we have already said to others: - *Watch and observe, for surely you have not yet seen everything*.

And then we shall present to you two considerations drawn from your own doctrine. Where did the Spiritist theory come from? Is it a system imagined by some men to explain the facts? Not at all, but then who revealed it? Precisely these mediums that exalt the lucidity. If, therefore, this lucidity is just as you suppose it, why should they have attributed to the spirits what they would have taken from themselves? How would they have given such precise teachings, so logical, so sublime about the nature of extra human intelligences? Of two, one, or they're lucid or they're not. If they're and if we can trust their truth, we can't admit without contradiction that they're not true.

In 2nd place, if all phenomena come from the medium, should be identical for the same individual, and one would not see the same person speaking different languages, nor to express alternately the most contradictory things. This lack of unity in the manifestations of the same medium proves the diversity of the sources. If, because, we can't find them all in the medium, it's necessary to seek them out of it. According to the other theory, the medium is still the source of the manifestations, but, instead of taking them from himself, take them out of the environment. The medium would be a kind of mirror reflecting all ideas, all the thoughts and all the knowledge of the people that surround him, would not say that he was not known at least of some of them.

It could not be denied, and even in it a principle of the doctrine, the influence exerted by the assistants on the nature of the demonstrations, but this influence is quite different from what is intended and, between her and what would make the medium an echo of the thoughts of others, there is great distance, because thousands of facts peremptorily demonstrate the contrary. There is, therefore, a serious error in this theory, which again proves the danger of premature conclusions. Those people, unable to deny the existence of a phenomenon that ordinary science can't explain, and not wanting to admit the intervention of the spirits; explain it in their own way.

The theory they hold would be seductive, if it could cover all the facts, but this doesn't happen, and when it's shown, until the evidence, that some communications from the medium are quite foreign to the thoughts, to knowledge, to the very opinions of all those present, and that these communications are often spontaneous and contradict preconceived ideas, they don't give up for so little. The irradiation, respond, extends far beyond the immediate circle that surrounds us, the medium is the reflection of all Humanity and in this way, if you don't find the inspirations around you, will seek them out in the city, in the country, throughout the world and even in other spheres.

I don't believe that this theory contains a simpler and more probable explanation than that of Spiritism, because it supposes a much more wonderful cause. The idea that beings from space, in permanent contact with us, tell us your thoughts, nothing has to shock reason more than the assumption of these universal radiations, coming from all parts of the Universe to focus on an individual's brain. We'll say it once again and this is the capital point, on which it'll never be too much to insist, that the somnambulistic theory and what one might call reflective were imagined by some men, are individual opinions, formulated to explain a fact, while the Doctrine of Spirits isn't a human conception, was dictated by the very intelligences that manifest themselves, when nobody imagined it and general opinion even repelled it. Now! We asked, where did the mediums seek a doctrine that didn't exist in anyone's thinking on Earth? We also asked why strange coincidence thousands of mediums, scattered all over the globe, without ever having seen each other, agreed to say the same thing?

If the first medium that appeared in France was influenced by opinions already accepted in America, why was it strange that he sought his ideas 2 thousand leagues beyond the sea, in the bosom of a strange people by their customs and their language, instead to take what was around him? But there's still one circumstance in which one didn't think enough. The first manifestations, in France as in America, were not by writing or by word, but by strokes corresponding to the letters of the alphabet, forming words and phrases. It was by this means that the demonstrating intelligences declared themselves to be spirits. If, therefore, we could suppose the intervention of the medium's thought in verbal or written communications, the same could not be done in relation to blows, whose significance could not be known previously.

We could cite numerous facts that demonstrate in the manifesting intelligence an evident individuality and an absolute independence of will. We'll therefore send our contradictors to a closer observation, and if they wish to study well, without prejudices, concluding nothing before they have seen what is necessary, they'll recognize the importance of their theories to explain all the facts. We shall confine ourselves to proposing the following questions, why the intelligence that manifests itself, whatever it's, refuses to answer some questions on perfectly known subjects, as, for example, the name and age of the question, what he brings in his hand, what he did the day before, what do you intend to do tomorrow and so on? If the medium is the mirror of the thoughts of the present, nothing would be easier for him to answer.

Opponents respond to this argument by asking, in its turn, why the spirits, who should know everything, can't say such simple things, according to the axiom: "Who can the more, can or less". And they conclude that they're not spirits. Whether an ignorant or a joker, presenting himself before another assembly, I asked myself, for example, why is it a full day at noon, it would be credible if it bothered to respond seriously and it would be logical to conclude, of his silence or of the mockery that he addressed to the interpellant, that its members were fools?

Now it's precisely because they're superior that spirits don't respond to idle or ridiculous questions, they don't want to enter the ring, that's why they're silent or say that they only deal with more serious things. We'll ask, after all, why spirits come and go, oftentimes, at any given time, it's because, passing this moment, are there no prayers or supplications to make them return? If the medium acted only by the mental impulse of the assistants, of course, in this circumstance, the contest of all the gathered wills should stimulate his clairvoyance. If, however, he doesn't yield to the wishes of the assembly, supported by his own will, it's because it obeys a strange influence, both to him and to others, and this influence demonstrates its independence and individuality.

17 - Filling the empty spaces

The skepticism regarding the Spiritist Doctrine, when it's not the result of a systematic opposition, selfish, almost always comes from an incomplete knowledge of the facts, which doesn't prevent some people from settling the issue as if they knew it perfectly. One can have a lot of spirit and even a lot of education and not have common sense, now, the first clue to the lack of sense is the belief in one's infallibility. Many people also don't see in the manifestations spiritist more than a reason of curiosity. We hope that by reading this book you'll find in these strange phenomena something more than a simple pastime.

The Spiritist Science contains two parts, an experimental, on the manifestations in general, another philosophical, about the intelligent manifestations. Whoever has not observed but the first will be in the position of one who knows only physics for recreational experiences, without having penetrated in Science. If this book were to be more than to show the serious side of the matter, provoking studies on it, this would be enough and we would congratulate ourselves for being chosen to carry out a work about which we don't want to have any personal merit, since the principles here exposed are not of our creation, the merit is therefore entirely of the spirits who dictated it.

We hope that it'll have another result, that of guiding men who wish to become enlightened by showing them in these studies a grand and sublime goal of individual and social progress and indicating the way forward for their attainment. We'll conclude with a final consideration. Astronomers, probing the spaces, found in the distribution of celestial bodies, unjustifiable gaps and in disagreement with the laws of the whole. They suspected that these gaps had to correspond to bodies that had escaped observation. On the other hand, they observed certain effects whose cause was unknown to them and said to themselves: - *There must be a world there, because that gap can't exist and these effects must have a cause.*

Judging then on the cause by the effects, they were able to calculate the elements and later the facts came to justify their predictions. Let us apply this reasoning to another order of ideas. If we look at the series of beings, we'll see that they form a chain without a solution of continuity, from gross matter to the most intelligent man, but between man and God, who are the alpha and omega of all things, what a huge gap. Is it reasonable to think that man is the last ring in this chain?

May he transpose, without transition, the distance that separates him from infinity? Reason tells us that there must be other links between man and God, as astronomers said that among the known worlds there must be other worlds. What philosophy has filled this gap? Spiritism doesn't present it filled by beings of all categories of the invisible world and these beings are no more than the spirits of men in the different degrees that lead to perfection. And so everything connects, everything chains, from alpha to omega. You who deny the existence of the spirits fill the emptiness that they occupy, and you, who run away, dare to laugh at the works of God and his omnipotence. Allan Kardec

Prolegomena

Phenomena that escape the laws of common science are everywhere manifested and reveal as a cause the action of a free and intelligent will. Reason tells us that an intelligent effect must be the cause of an intelligent force, and the masses have proved that this force can enter into communication with men through material signals. This Force, questioned about its nature, declared that it belonged to the world of the spiritual beings that were stripped of the corporal wrapping of the man. This is how the Spirits' Doctrine was revealed. Communications between the spirit world and the corporeal world belong to nature and constitute no supernatural stalk. That's why we find its traits among all peoples and in all ages. Today they're general and evident throughout the world.

The spirits announce that the times marked by Providence for a universal manifestation are arrived at that, being the ministers of God and the agents of his will; it's their mission to instruct and enlighten men, opening a new era for the regeneration of Humanity. This book is the compendium of his teachings. It was written by order and under the dictation of the higher spirits to establish the foundations of a rational philosophy, free from the prejudices of the systemic spirit.

Nothing is contained that isn't the expression of his thought and has not been under his control. The order and methodical distribution of the material as well as the notes and the form of some parts of the essay constitute the only work of the one who has been given the task of publishing it. In the number of the spirits who competed for this work, there are many who lived at different times on earth, where they preached and practiced virtue and wisdom.

Others don't belong, by their names, to any person of whom history has kept the memory, but its elevation is attested by the purity of its doctrine and by the union with those who have venerated names. These are the terms in which they gave us, in writing and through many mediums, the mission of writing this book. Take care, with zeal and perseverance, of the work you have undertaken with our competition, because this work is ours. In it we laid the foundations of the new edifice that rises and one day will bring all men together in the same feeling of love and charity, but before you divulge it, we'll review it together in order to control all the details. We'll be with you whenever you ask, to help you in other jobs, because this is no more than a part of the mission entrusted to you and one of us has already revealed to you. Among the teachings that are given to you, there are some that you must keep only for yourself, until further notice, we'll let you know when it's time to publish them. In the meantime, meditate on them, in order to be ready when we let you know.

You'll put in the book header the vine branch we designed for you because it's the emblem of the work of the Creator. All the material principles that can best represent the body and the spirit in it are reunited, the body is the branch, the spirit is the sap, the soul or the spirit connected to matter is the grain. Man 5th essence the spirit by the work and you know that it's only by the work of the body that the spirit acquires knowledge. Don't be discouraged by criticism. You'll find fierce contradictions, especially among people interested in cheating. You'll find even among the spirits, for those who are not completely dematerialized seek, often, to sow doubt, malice or ignorance, but continue always, believe in God and walk confidently, here we'll be to sustain you and the a time when truth will shine everywhere.

1st book - Primary causes
Chapter 1 - God

1 - God and the infinite

1 - What is God?
- God is the supreme intelligence, the primary cause of all things.

2 - What should we understand by infinity?
- That which has neither beginning nor end, the unknown, the whole unknown is infinite.

3 - Could we say that God is the infinite?
- Incomplete definition. Poverty of the language of men, insufficient to define the things that are beyond their intelligences.

Kardec's opinion: > The spirits referred logically to the Universe. Everything we know about it has a beginning and an end.

2 - Evidence of the existence of God

4 - Where can we find proof of God's existence?
- In an axiom that you apply to your sciences, there's no effect without cause. Seek the cause of all that isn't the work of man, and your reason will answer you.

5 - What consequence can we draw from the intuitive feeling that all men bring with them from the existence of God?
- That God exists, for where would this feeling come from, if he didn't lean on anything? It's a consequence of the principle that there's no effect without cause.

6 - The intimate feeling of the existence of God, which we bring with us, would not be the effect of education and the product of acquired ideas?
- If that were so, why would your savages also have this feeling?

> If the feeling of the existence of a supreme being were nothing more than the product of a teaching, it would not be universal and would not exist, like scientific notions, but among those who could have received this teaching.

7 - Could we find the primary cause of the formation of things in the intimate properties of matter?
- But then what would be the cause of these properties? And a primary cause is always necessary.

> To attribute the primary formation of things to the intimate properties of matter would be to take effect for the cause, for these properties are in themselves an effect, which must have a cause.

8 - What to think of the opinion that attributes primary education to a random combination of matter, that is, random?
- Another nonsense! What man of good sense can regard chance as an intelligent being? And besides, what is chance? Anything!

> The harmony that regulates the forces of the Universe reveals combinations and determined ends, and for that reasons an intelligent power. To attribute primary education to chance would be a lack of sense, because chance is blind and can't produce intelligent effects. Smart chance would no longer be a coincidence.

9 - Where you can see, in the primary cause, a supreme intelligence, superior to all others?
- You have a proverb that says the following, by the work you know the author. Well, look at the work and look for the author. It's pride that breeds unbelief. The proud man admits nothing outside himself and that's why he considers himself a strong spirit. Poor being, that a breath of God can bring down.

> The power of an intelligence is judged by its works. Since no human being can create what Nature produces, the primary cause must be in an intelligence superior to Humanity. Whatever the wonders of human intelligence, this intelligence also has a cause and the greater its realization, the greater the primary cause must be. This higher intelligence is the primary cause of all things whatever the name by which man designates it.

3 - Attributes of divinity

10 - Can man understand the intimate nature of God?
- No, it's missing you, therefore, a sense.

11 - Is it a day allowed for man to understand the mystery of the Godhead?
- When your spirit is no longer obscured by matter, and by its perfection has approached it, then he'll see and understand it.

> The inferiority of man's faculties doesn't allow him to understand the intimate nature of God. In the infancy of mankind, man often confuses him with the creature, whose imperfections he attributes to him, but as his moral sense develops, his thought penetrates the depths of things better, and he makes an idea about himself more just and more in accordance with good reason although always incomplete.

12 - If we can't understand the intimate nature of God, can we have an idea of some of his perfections?
- Yes, some. Man understands himself better, as he rises above matter, he sees through thought.

13 - When we say that God is eternal, infinite, immutable, immaterial, unique, all-powerful, sovereignly just and good, do we not have a complete idea of his attributes?
- From your point of view, yes, because you believe to cover everything, but I know that there are things above the intelligence of the most intelligent man, and for which your language, limited to your ideas and your sensations, has no expressions. The reason tells you that God must have these perfections in a supreme degree, because if he had one of less or that was not to an infinite degree, he would not be superior to everything and therefore would not be God. To be above all things, God must not be subject to vicissitudes and can't have any of the imperfections that the imagination is able to conceive.

> God is eternal. If he had had a beginning, it would have come out of nowhere or would have been created by an earlier being. This is how, little by little, we go back to infinity and eternity. He's unchangeable. If he were subject to change, the laws governing the Universe would have no stability. He's immaterial. That is to say, his nature differs from everything we call matter; otherwise it would not be immutable, being subject to the transformations of matter. He's unique. If there were many Gods, there would be no unity of sight or power in the organization of the Universe. He's all-powerful because he's unique. If he didn't have the sovereign power, there would be something more powerful or powerful than he; that he'd not have done all things, and those that he had not done would be works of another God. He's sovereignty just and good. The providential wisdom of the divine laws is revealed in the least as in the greatest things and this wisdom doesn't allow us to doubt its justice or its goodness.

4 - Pantheism
14 - God is a distinct being, or would be, according to the opinion of some, the resultant of all the forces and all the intelligences of the Universe united?
- If so, God would not exist, because he'd be effect and not the cause, he can't be, at the same time, one and the other. God exists, you can't doubt him, and that's the bottom line. Believe what I tell you and don't want to go further. Don't get lost in a labyrinth from which you could not leave.

15 - What is to be thought of the opinion according to which all natural bodies, all the beings, all the globes of the Universe are parts of the divinity, and constitute in their totality the divinity itself, in other words the Pantheistic theory?
- Man, not being able to make himself God, would fain make himself out to be, at least, a part of God.

16 - Those who hold this theory profess to find in it the demonstration of some of the attributes of God. The worlds of the Universe being infinitely numerous, God is thus seen to be infinite, vacuum, or nothingness, being nowhere, God is everywhere. God being everywhere, since everything is an integral part of God, he's thus seen to be the intelligent cause of all the phenomena of the Universe. What can we oppose to this argument?
- The dictates of reason. Reflect on the assumption in question, and you'll have no difficulty in detecting its absurdity.

> The Pantheistic theory makes of God a material being, who, though endowed with a supreme intelligence, would only be on a larger scale what we're on a smaller one. But, as matter is incessantly undergoing transformation, God, if this theory were true, would have no stability. He'd be subject to all the vicissitudes, and even to all the needs, of humanity he would lack one of the essential attributes of the divinity, unchangeableness. The properties of matter can't be attributed to God without degrading our idea of the Divinity and all the subtleties of sophistry fail to solve the problem of His essential nature.
We don't know what God is but we know that it's impossible that he should not be and the theory just stated is in contradiction with his most essential attributes. It confounds the Creator with the creation, precisely as though we should consider an ingenious 'machine to be an integral portion of the mechanican who invented it. The intelligence of God is revealed in his works, as is that of a painter in his picture but the works of God are no more God himself than the picture is the artist who conceived and painted it.

Chapter 2 - General Elements of the Universe

1 - Knowledge of the first principles of things

17 - Is it given to mankind to know the first principle of things?
- No. There are things that can't be understood by man in this world.

18 - Will man ever be able to penetrate the mystery of things now hidden from him?
- The veil will be raised for him in proportion as he accomplishes his purification, but, in order to understand certain things, he'd need faculties which he doesn't yet possess.

19 - Can't man, through scientific investigation, penetrate some of the secrets of nature?
- The faculty of scientific research has been given to him as a means by which he may advance in every direction, but he can't overstep the limits of his present possibilities.

> The farther man advances in the study of the mysteries around him, the greater should be his admiration of the power and wisdom of the Creator. But, partly through pride, partly through weakness, his intellect itself often renders him the sport of illusion. He heaps systems upon systems, and every day shows him how many errors he has mistaken for truths, how many truths he has repelled as errors. Ail this should be a lesson for his pride.

20 - Is man permitted to receive communications of a higher order in regard to matters which, not being within the scope of his senses, are beyond the pale of scientific investigation?
- Yes. When God judges such revelations to be useful, he reveals to man what science is incompetent to teach him.

> It's through communications of this higher order that man is enabled, within certain limits, to obtain knowledge of his past and of his future destiny.

2 - Spirit and matter

21 - Has matter existed from all eternity, like God, or has it been created at some definite period of time?
- God only knows. There is, nevertheless, one point which your reason should suffice to show you, that God, the prototype of love and beneficence, can never have been inactive. However far off in the past you may imagine the beginning of his action, can you suppose him to have been for a single moment inactive?

22 - Matter is generally defined as being that which has extension, that which can make an impression upon our senses, that which possesses impenetrability. Are these definitions correct?
- From your point of view they're correct, because you can only define in accordance with what you know. But matter exists in states which are unknown to you. It may be, for instance, so ethereal and subtle as to make no impression upon your senses; and yet it's still matter, although it would not be such for you.
- What definition can you give of matter?
- Matter is the element which enchains spirit, the instrument which serves it, and upon which, at the same time, it exerts its action.

> From this point of view it may be said that matter is the agent, the intermediary, through which, and upon which, spirit acts.

23 - What is spirit?
- The intelligent principle of the Universe.
- And what is the essential nature of spirit?
- It's not possible to explain the nature of spirit in your language. For you it's not a thing, because it's not palpable, but for us it's a thing.

24 - Is spirit synonymous with intelligence?
- Intelligence is an essential attribute of spirit, but both merge in a unitary principle, so that, for you, they may be said to be the same thing.

25 - Is spirit independent of matter, or is it only one of the pro properties of matter, as colors are a property of light and as sound is a property of the air?
- Spirit and matter are distinct from one another, but the union of spirit and matter is necessary to give intelligent activity to matter.
- Is this union equally necessary to the manifestation of spirit?
- It's necessary for you, because you're not organized for perceiving spirit apart from matter. Your senses are not formed for that order of perception.

26 - Can spirit be conceived of without matter and matter without spirit?
- Undoubtedly, as objects of thought.

27 - There are, then, two general elements of the Universe matter and spirit?

- Yes, and above them both is God, the Creator and Parent of all things. These three elements are the principle of all that exists, the universal trinity, but to the material element must be added the universal fluid which plays the part of intermediary between spirit and matter, the nature of the latter being too gross for spirit to be able to act directly upon it. Although, from another point of view, this fluid may be classed as forming part of the material element, it's, nevertheless, distinguished from that element by certain special properties of its own.

If it could be classed simply and absolutely as matter, there would be no reason why spirit also should not be classed as matter. It's intermediary between spirit and matter. It's fluid, just as matter is matter, and is susceptible of being made, through its innumerable combinations with matter, under the directing action of spirit, to produce the infinite variety of things of which you know as yet but a very small portion. This universal, primitive, or elementary fluid, being the agent employed by spirit in acting upon matter is the principle without which matter would remain forever in a state of division, and would never acquire the properties given to it by the state of ponderability.

- Is this fluid what we designate by the name of electricity?
- We have said that it's susceptible of innumerable combinations. What you call the electric fluid, the magnetic fluid, etc., are modifications of the universal fluid, which, properly speaking, is only matter of a more perfect and more subtle kind, and that may be considered as having an independent existence of its own.

28 - Since spirit itself is something, would it not be more correct and clearer to designate these two general elements by the terms inert matter and intelligent matter?
- Questions of words are of little importance for us. It's for you to formulate your definitions in such a manner as to make yourselves intelligible to one another. Your disputes almost always arise from the want of a common agreement in the use of the words you employ, owing to the incompleteness of your language in regard to all that doesn't strike your senses.

> One fact, patent to all observers, dominates all our hypotheses. We see matter which isn't intelligent; we see the action of an intelligent principle independent of matter. The origin and connection of these two things are unknown to us. Whether they have, or have not a common source and points of contact preordained in the nature of things. Whether intelligence has an independent existence of its own or is only a property or an effect, or even whether it's an emanation of the Divinity, are points about which we know nothing. Matter and intelligence appear to us to be distinct and we therefore speak of them as being two constituent elements of the Universe. We see, above these, a higher intelligence which governs all things, and is distinguished from them all by essential attributes peculiar to itself. It's this supreme intelligence that we call God.

3 - Properties of matter
29 - Is density an essential attribute of matter?
- Yes, of matter as understood by you, but not of matter considered as the universal fluid. The ethereal and subtle matter which forms this fluid is imponderable for you, and yet it's none the less the principle of your ponderable matter.

> Density is a relative property. Beyond the sphere of attraction of the various globes of the Universe, there is no such thing as weight, just as there is neither up nor down.

30 - Is matter formed of one element or of several elements?
- Of one primitive element. The bodies which you regard as simple are not really elementary; they're transformations of the primitive matter.

31 - Whence come the different properties of matter?
- From the modifications undergone by the elementary molecules, as the result of their union and of the action of certain conditions.

32 - According to this view of the subject, savors, odors, colors, sounds, the poisonous or salutary qualities of bodies, are only the result of modifications of one and the same primitive substance?
- Yes, undoubtedly; and that only exist in virtue of the disposition of the organs destined to perceive them.

> This principle is proved by the fact that the qualities of bodies are not perceived by all persons in the same manner. The same thing appears agreeable to the taste of one person, and disagreeable to that of another. What appears blue to one person appears red to another. That which is a poison for some, is wholesome for others.

33 - Is the same elementary matter susceptible of undergoing all possible modifications and of acquiring all possible qualities?
- Yes, and it's, this fact which is implied in the saying that everything is in everything.
- Doesn't this theory appear to bear out the opinion of those who admit only two essential properties in matter, force and movement, and who regard all the other properties of matter as being merely secondary effects of these, varying according to the intensity of the force and the direction of the movement?
- That opinion is correct, but you must also add, according to the mode of molecular arrangement, as you see exemplified, for instance, in an opaque body, that may become transparent, and vice versa.

> Oxygen, hydrogen, nitrogen, carbon and all the other bodies which we regard as simple, are only modifications of one primitive substance. But the impossibility, in which we have hitherto found ourselves, of arriving at this primitive

matter otherwise than as an intellectual deduction, causes these bodies to appear to us to be really elementary and we may, therefore, without Impropriety, continue for the present to regard them as such.

34 - Have the molecules of matter a determinate form?
- Those molecules undoubtedly have a form, but one which isn't appreciable by your organs.
- Is that form constant or variable?
- Constant for the primitive elementary molecules, but variable for the secondary molecules, which are themselves only agglomerations of the primary ones, for what you term a molecule is still very far from being the elementary molecule.

4 - Universal space
35 - Is universal space infinite or limited?
- Infinite. Suppose the existence of boundaries, what would there be beyond them? This consideration confounds human reason, and nevertheless your reason itself tells you that it can't be otherwise. It's thus with the idea of infinity, under whatever aspect you consider it. The idea of infinity can't be comprehended in your narrow sphere.

> If we imagine a limit to space, no matter how far off our thought may place this limit, our reason tells us that there must still be something beyond It and so on, step by step, until we arrive at the idea of infinity, for the "something beyond", the existence of which is recognized by our thought as necessity, were it only an absolute void, would still be space.

36 - Does an absolute void exist in any part of space?
- No there is no void. What seems like a void to you is occupied by matter in a state in which it escapes the action of your senses and of your instruments.

> All these principles are now proven by scientific research, even in the field of most orthodox materialism.

Chapter 3 - Creation

The Universe comprises the infinity of worlds, both of those we see and those we don't see all animate and inanimate beings all the stars that revolve in space and all fluids with which space is filled.

1 - Creation of the worlds

37 - Has the Universe been created, or has it existed from all eternity, like God?
- Assuredly the Universe can't have made itself and if it had existed from all eternity, like God, it could not be the work of God.

> Reason tells us that the Universe can't have made itself, and that, as it could not be the work of chance, it must be the work of God.

38 - How did God create the Universe?
- To borrow a well-known expression, by his will. Nothing can give a better idea of the action of that all-powerful will than those grand words of *Genesis*, God said: - *Let there be light and there was light.*

39 - Can we know how worlds are formed?
- All that can be said on this subject, within the limits of your comprehension, is this, worlds are formed by the condensation of the matter disseminated in space.

40 - Are comets, as is now supposed, a commencement of condensation of the primitive matter-worlds in course of formation?
- Yes, but it's absurd to believe in the influence attributed to them. I mean, the influence which is commonly attributed to them; for all the heavenly bodies have their share of influence in the production of certain physical phenomena.

41 - Is it possible for a completely formed world to disappear, and for the matter of which it's composed to be again disseminated in space?
- Yes. God renews worlds as he renews the living beings that inhabit them.

42 - Can we know the length of time employed in the formation of worlds, of the Earth, for instance?
- This is a matter in regard to which I can tell you nothing, for its only known to the Creator and foolish indeed would he be who should pretend to possess such knowledge, or to number the ages of such a formation.

2 - Production of living beings

43 - When did the Earth begin to be peopled?
- In the beginning all was chaos, the elements were mixed up in a state of confusion. Gradually those elements settled into their proper places and then appeared the orders of living beings appropriate to the successive e states of the globe.

44 - Whence came the living beings that appeared upon the Earth?
- The germs of these were contained in the earth itself, awaiting the favorable moment for their development. The organic principles came together on the cessation of the force which held them asunder, and those principles formed the germs of all the living beings that have peopled the earth. Those germs remained latent and inert, like the chrysalis and the seed of plants, until the arrival of the proper moment for the vivification of each species. The beings of each species then came together and multiplied.

45 - Where were the organic elements before the formation of the Earth?
- They existed, so to say in the fluidic state, in space, in the midst of the spirits, or in other planets, awaiting the creation of the earth in order to begin a new existence on a new globe.

> Chemistry shows us the molecules of inorganic bodies uniting to produce crystals of regular forms that are invariable for each species, as soon as those molecules find themselves in the conditions necessary to their combination. The slightest disturbance of those conditions suffices to prevent the union of the material elements, or, at least, to prevent the regular arrangement of the latter which constitutes the crystal. Why should not the same action take place among the organic elements? We preserve for years the seeds of plants and of animals, which are only vivified at a certain temperature and under certain conditions, grains of wheat have been seen to germinate after the lapse of centuries.
That is, then, in seeds a latent principle of vitality, which only awaits the concourse of favorable circumstances to develop itself. May not that which takes place under our eyes every day have also taken place at the origin of the globe? Does this view of the formation of living beings brought forth out of chaos by the action of the forces of nature itself detract in any way from the glory of God? So far from doing this, the view of creation thus presented to us is more consonant than any other with our sense of the vastness of his power exerting its sway over all the worlds of infinity through the action of universal laws. This theory, it's true, doesn't solve the problem of the origin of the vital elements, but nature has mysteries which it's as yet impossible for us to explain.

46 - Do any living beings come into existence spontaneously at the present day?
- Yes, but the primal germs of these already existed in a latent state. You're constantly witnesses of this phenomenon. Don't the tissues of the human body and of animals contain the germs of a multitude of parasites; that only await for their

development the occurrence of the putrid fermentation necessary to their life? Each of you contains a slumbering world of microscopic beings in process of creation.

47 - Was the human species among the organic elements contained in the terrestrial globe?
- Yes, and it made its appearance at the time appointed by the Creator. Hence the statement that man was formed out of the dust of the ground.

48 - Can we ascertain the epoch of tile appearance of man and the other living beings on the Earth?
- No, all your calculations are chimerical.

49 - If the germs of the human race were among the organic elements of the globe, why are human beings not produced spontaneously at the present day, as they were at the time of its origin?
- The first beginning of things is hidden from us nevertheless; it may be asserted that the earliest progenitors of the human race, when once brought into existence, absorbed in themselves the elements necessary to their formation in order to transmit those elements according to the laws of reproduction. The same may be said in regard to all the different species of living beings.

3 - Peopling of the Earth - Adam
50 - Did the human race begin with one man only?
- No, he whom you call Adam was neither the first nor the only man who peopled the Earth.

51 - Is it possible to know what Adam lived?
- About the period which you assign to him; that is to say, about 4000 years before Christ.

> The man of whom, under the name of Adam, tradition has preserved the memory, was one of those who, in some one of the countries of the globe survived one of the great cataclysms which at various epochs have changed its surface, and who became the founder of one of the races that people the earth at the present day. The laws of nature render it impossible that the amount of progress which we know to have been accomplished by the human race of our planet long before the time of Christ could have been accomplished so rapidly as must have been the case if it had only been In existence upon the globe since the period assigned as the date of Adam. The opinion most consonant with reason is that which regards the story of Adam as a myth, or as an allegory personifying the earliest ages of the world.

4 - Diversity of Human Races
52 - What is the cause of the physical and moral differences that distinguish the various races of men upon the Earth?
- Climate, modes of life, and social habits. The same differences would be produced in the case of two children of the same mother, if brought up far from one another, and surrounded by different influences and conditions, for the children thus diversely brought up would present no moral resemblance to each other.

53 - Did the human race come into existence on various points of the globe?
- Yes, and at various epochs and this is one of the causes of the diversity of human races. The people of the primitive periods, being dispersed abroad in different climates, and forming alliances with those of other countries than their own, gave rise perpetually to new types of humanity.
- Do these differences constitute distinct species?
- Certainly not. All of them constitute but a single family. Do the differences between the varieties of the same fruit prevent their all belonging to the same species?

54 - If the human species don't all proceed from the same progenitor, should they, on that account, cease to regard one another as brothers?
- All men are brothers in virtue of their common relation to the Creator, because they're animated by the same spirit and tend towards the same goal. The human mind is always prone to attach too literal a meaning to statements which are necessarily imperfect and incomplete.

5 - Plurality of worlds
55 - Are all the globes that revolve in space inhabited?
- Yes, and the people of the Earth are far from being, as you suppose, the first in intelligence, goodness, and general development. There are many men having a high opinion of themselves who even imagine that your little globe alone, of all the countless myriads of globes around you, has the privilege of being inhabited by reasoning beings. They fancy that God has created the Universe only for them. Insensate vanity!

> God has peopled the globes of the Universe with living beings, all of whom concur in working out the aims of his providence. To believe that the presence of living beings is confined to the one point of the Universe inhabited by us is to cast a doubt on the wisdom of God, who has made nothing in vain, and who must therefore have assigned to all the other globes of the Universe a destination more important than that of gratifying our eyes with the spectacle of a starry night. Moreover, there is nothing in the position, size, or physical constitution of the Earth to warrant the supposition that it alone, of the countless myriads of globes disseminated throughout the infinity of apace has the privilege of being inhabited.

56 - Is the physical constitution of all globes the same?

- No, they don't at all resemble one another.

57 - The physical constitution of the various worlds not being the same for all does it follow that the beings who inhabit them have different organizations?
- Undoubtedly it does, just as, in your world; fishes are organized for living in the water, and birds for living in the air.

58 - Are the planets furthest removed from the Sun stinted in light and heat, the Sun only appearing to them of the size of one of the fixed stars?
- Do you suppose that there are no other sources of light and heat than the Sun? And do you count for nothing the action of electricity which, in certain worlds, plays a very much more important part than in your Earth? Besides, how do you know that the beings of those worlds see in the same manner as you do, and with the aid of organs such as yours?

> The conditions of existence for the beings that inhabit the various worlds must be supposed to be appropriate to the sphere in which they're destined to live. If we had never seen fishes, we should be at a loss to understand how any living beings could exist in the sea. So in regard to all the other worlds, which doubtless contain elements that are unknown to us? In our own Earth, are not the long polar nights illumined by the electrical displays of the aurora borealis? Is it impossible that in certain worlds, electricity may be more abundant than in ours, and may subserve, in its general economy, various important uses not imaginable by us? And may not those worlds contain in themselves the sources of the heat and light required by their inhabitants?

6 - The biblical account of the creation
59 - The different nations of the Earth have formed to them-selves widely divergent ideas of the creation, ideas always in harmony with their degree of scientific advancement. Reason and science concur in admitting the fantastic character of certain theories. The explanation of the subject now given through spirit communication is confirmatory of the opinion which has long been adopted by the most enlightened exponents of modern science.

This explanation will no doubt be objected to, on the ground that it's in contradiction with the statements of the *Bible*, but a careful examination of those statements shows us that this contradiction is more apparent than real, and that it results from the interpretation which has been given to expressions whose meaning is allegorical rather than historical. The question of the personality of Adam, regarded as the first man, and sole progenitor of the human race, isn't the only one in regard to which the religious convictions of the world have necessarily undergone modification. The hypothesis of the rotation of the earth round the sun appeared, at one time, to be in such utter opposition to the letter of the *Bible*, that every species of persecution was directed against it, and against those who advocated it.

Yet the Earth continued to move on in its orbit in defiance of anathemas; and no one, at the present day, could contest the fact of its movement without doing violence to his own powers of reasoning. The *Bible* also tells us that the world was created in six days, and fixes the epoch of this creation at about 4000 years before the Christian era. Previously to that period the Earth did riot exist? At that period it was produced out of nothing. Such is the formal declaration of the sacred text, yet science, positive, inexorable steps in with proof to the contrary.

The history of the formation of the globe is written in indestructible characters in the worlds of fossils, proving beyond the possibility of denial that the six lays of the creation arc successive periods, each of which may have been of millions of ages. This isn't a mere matter of statement or of opinion. It's a fact as incontestably certain as is the motion of the Earth, and one that theology itself can no longer refuse to admit, although this admission furnishes another example of the errors into which we are led by attributing literal truth to language which is often of a figurative nature. Are we therefore to conclude that the *Bible* is a mere tissue of errors? No, but we must admit that men have erred in their method of interpreting it.

Geology, in its study of the archives written in the structure of the globe itself, has ascertained the order of succession in which the different species of living beings have appeared on its surface, and this order is found to be in accordance with the sequence indicated in the book of *Genesis*, with this difference, viz., that the Earth, instead of issuing miraculously from the hand of God in the course of a few days, accomplished its formation under the impulsion of the Divine will, but according to the laws and through the action of the forces of nature, in the course of periods incalculable by us.

Does God appear less great and less powerful for having accomplished the work of creation through the action of forces, and according to laws, of his own ordaining? And is the result of the creative energy less sublime for not having been accomplished instantaneously? Evidently not, and puerile indeed must he the mind that doesn't recognize the grandeur of the Almighty Power implied in this evolution of the worlds of the Universe through the action of eternal laws. Science, so far from diminishing the glory of the divine action, displays that action under an aspect still more sublime, and more consonant with our intuitive sense of the power and majesty of God, by showing that it has been accomplished without derogation from the laws which are the expression of the Divine will in the realm of nature.

Modern science, in accordance with the Mosaic record, proves that man was the last in the order of creation of living beings, but Moses puts the universal deluge at the year of the world 1654, while geology seems to show that the great diluvium cataclysm occurred before the appearance of man, because, up to the present time, the primitive strata contain no traces of his presence, nor of that of the animals contemporaneous with him, but this point is far from being decided.

Various recent discoveries suggest the possibility of our being destined to ascertain that the antiquity of the human race is much greater than has been hitherto supposed, and should this greater antiquity become a matter of certainty, it would prove that the letter of the *Bible*, in regard to the date assigned by it to the creation of man, as in regard to so many other matters, can only be understood in an allegorical sense. That the geological deluge isn't that of Noah is evident from the lapse of time required for the formation of the fossiliferous strata; and, if traces should eventually be discovered of the existence of the human race before the geological deluge, it would be evident either that Adam was not the first man, or that his creation dates back from a period indefinitely remote.

There is no arguing against fact; and the antiquity of the human race, if proved by geological discovery, would have to be admitted, just as has been done in regard to the movement of the Earth and the six days of the creation. The existence of the human race before the geological deluge, it may be objected, is still doubtful, but the same objection can't be urged against the following considerations. Admitting that man first appeared upon the Earth 4000 years before Christ, if the whole of the human race, with the exception of a single family, were destroyed 1650 years afterwards, it follows that the peopling of the Earth dates only from the time of Noah-that is to say, only 2500 years before Christ.

But when the Hebrews immigrated to Egypt in the eighteenth century before Christ, they found that country densely populated, and already in possession of an advanced civilization. History also shows that, at the same period, India and various other countries were equally populous and flourishing, to say nothing of the chronological tables of other nations, which claim to go back to periods yet more remote.

We must, therefore, suppose that, from the 24th to the 16th century before Christ, that's to say, in the space of 600 years the posterity of a single individual was able to people all the immense countries which had then been discovered, not to speak of those which were then unknown, but which we have no reason to conclude were destitute of inhabitants; and we must suppose, still further, that the human race, during this brief period, was able to raise itself from the crass ignorance of the primitive savage state to the highest degree of intellectual development sup positions utterly irreconcilable with anthropological laws.

The diversity of the various human races confirms this view of the subject. Climate and modes of life undoubtedly modify the physical characteristics of mankind, but we know the extent to which these modifications can be carried, and physiological examination conclusively proves that there are between the different races of men constitutional differences too profound to have been produced merely by differences of climate. The crossing of races produces intermediary types, it tends to efface the extremes of characteristic peculiarities, but it doesn't produce these peculiarities, and, therefore, creates only new varieties. But the crossing of races presupposes the existence of races distinct from each other, and how is the existence of these to be explained if we attribute their origin to a common stock especially if we restrict the production of these various races to so brief a period?

How is it possible to suppose, for example, that the descendants of Noah could have been, in so short a time, transformed into Ethiopians? Such a metamorphosis would be as inadmissible as that of a wolf into a sheep, of a beetle into an elephant, of a bird into a fish. No preconceived opinion can withstand, in the long run, the evidence of opposing facts. But, on the contrary, all difficulty disappears if we assume that man existed at a period anterior to that which has hitherto been commonly assigned to his creation; that Adam commenced, some 6000 years ago, the peopling of a country until then uninhabited; that the deluge of Noah was a local catastrophe, erroneously confounded with the great geological cataclysm; and, finally, if we make due allowance for the allegorical form of expression characteristic of the Oriental style, and common to the sacred books of every people.

It's unwise to insist upon a literal interpretation of figurative statements of which the inaccuracy may, at any moment, be rendered evident by the progress of scientific discovery; but the fundamental propositions of religion, so far from having anything to fear from the discoveries of science, are strengthened and ennobled by being brought into harmony with those discoveries. And it's only when the religious sentiment shall have been en lightened by its union with scientific truth that religious belief, thus rendered invulnerable to the attacks of skepticism, will take the place of skepticism in the minds and hearts of men.

Chapter 4 - The vital principle

1 - Organic and inorganic beings

Organic beings are those which have in themselves a source of activity that produces the phenomena of life. They're born, grow, reproduce their own species, and die. They're provided with organs specially adapted to the accomplishment of the different acts of their life, to the satisfaction of their needs, and to their preservation. They include men, animals, and plants. Inorganic beings are those which possess neither vitality nor the power of spontaneous movement, and are formed by the mere aggregation of matter, as minerals, water, air, etc.

60 - Is the force which unites the elements of matter in organic and inorganic bodies the same?
- Yes, the law of attraction is the same for all.

61 - Is there any difference between the matter of organic and inorganic bodies?
- The matter of both classes of bodies is the same, but in organic bodies it's animalized.

62 - What is the cause of the animalization of matter?
- Its union with the vital principle.

63 - Does the vital principle reside in a special agent, or is it only a property of organized matter, in other words, is it an effect or a cause?
- It's both. Life is an effect produced by the action of an agent upon matter; this agent, without matter, isn't life, just as matter can't become alive without this agent. It gives life to all beings that absorb and assimilate it.

64 - We have seen that spirit and matter are two constituent elements of the Universe; does the vital principle constitute a third element?
- It's, undoubtedly, one of the elements necessary to the constitution of the Universe, but it has its source in a special modification of the universal matter, modified to that end. For you, it's an elementary body, like oxygen or hydrogen, which, nevertheless, isn't primitive elements, for all the bodies known to you, though appearing to you to be simple, are modifications of the primal fluid.
- This statement seems to imply that vitality isn't due to a distinct primitive agent, but is a special property of the universal matter resulting from certain modifications of the latter.
- Your conclusion is the natural consequence of what we have stated.

65 - Does the vital principle reside in any one of the bodies known to us?
- It has its source in the universal fluid; it's what you call the magnetic fluid, or the electric fluid, animalized. It's the intermediary, the link between spirit and matter.

66 - Is the vital principle the same for all organic beings?
- Yes, but modified according to species. It's that principle which gives them the power of originating movement and activity, and distinguishes them from inert matter; for the movement of matter isn't spontaneous. Matter is moved; it doesn't originate movement.

67 - Is vitality a permanent attribute of the vital principle, or is vitality only developed by the play of the organs in which it's manifested?
- It's only developed in connection with a body. Have we not said that this agent, without matter, isn't life? The union of the two is necessary to the production of life.
- Would it be correct to say that vitality is latent when the vital agent isn't united with a body?
- Yes, that is the case.

> The totality of the organs of a body constitutes a sort of mechanism which receives its impulsion from the active or vital principle that resides in them. The vital principle is the motive power of organized bodies, and while the vital principle gives impulsion to the organs in which it resides, the play of those organs develops and keeps up the activity of the vital principle, somewhat as friction develops heat.

2 - Life and death

68 - What is the cause of the death of organic beings?
- The exhaustion of their bodily organs.
- Would it be correct to compare death to the cessation of movement in a machine that had got out of gear?
- Yes, when the machine gets out of order, its action ceases. When the body falls ill, life withdraws from it.

69 - Why is death caused more certainly by a lesion of the heart than by that of any other organ?
- The heart is a life-making machine. But the heart isn't the only organ of which the lesion causes death; it's only one of the wheels essential to the working of the machine.

70 - What becomes of the matter and the vital principle of organic beings after their death?
- The inert matter is decomposed, and serves to form other bodies; the vital principle returns to the general mass of the universal fluid.

> On the death of an organic being, the elements of which its body was composed undergo new combinations that form new beings. These, in their turn, draw the principle of life and activity from the universal source they absorb and assimilate it, and restore it again to that source when they cease to exist. The organs of organic beings are, so to say, impregnated with the vital fluid. This fluid gives to every part of an organized being the activity which brings its parts into union after certain lesions, and reestablishes functions that have been temporarily suspended. But when the elements essential to the play of the organism have been destroyed, or too deeply injured, the vital fluid is powerless to transmit to them the movement which constitutes life, and the being dies.

The organs of a body necessarily react, more or less powerfully, upon one another their reciprocity of action results from their harmony among themselves. When from any cause this harmony is destroyed, their functions cease just as a piece of machinery comes to a stand-still when the essential portions of its mechanism get out of order, or as a clock stops when its works are worn out by use, accidentally broken, so that the spring is no longer able to keep it going. We have an image of life and death still more exact in the electric battery. The battery, like all natural bodies, contains electricity in a latent state but the electrical phenomena are only manifested when the fluid is set in motion by a special cause.

When this movement is super induced, the battery may be said to become alive but when the cause of the electrical activity ceases, the phenomena cease to occur, and the battery relapses into a state of inertia. Organic bodies may thus be said to be a sort of electric battery, in which the movement of the fluid produces the phenomena of life, and in which the cessation of that movement produces death. The quantity of vital fluid present in organic beings isn't the same all; it varies in the various species of living beings, and isn't constantly the same, either in the same individual or in the individuals of the same species. There are some which may be said to be saturated with it, and others in which it exists in very small proportions. Hence certain species are endowed with a more active and more tenacious life, resulting from the superabundance of the vital fluid present in their organism.

The amount of vital fluid contained in a given organism may be exhausted and may thus become insufficient for the maintenance of life, unless it be renewed by the absorption and assimilation of the substances in which that fluid resides. The vital fluid may be transmitted by one individual to another individual. An organization in which it exists more abundantly may impart it to another in which it's deficient and may thus, in certain cases, rekindle the vital flame when on the point of being extinguished.

3 - Intelligence and instinct

71 - Is intelligence an attribute of the vital principle?
- No, for the plants live and don't think; they have only organic life. Intelligence and matter are independent of one another, for a body may live without intelligence, but intelligence can only manifest itself by means of material organs. Animalized matter can only be rendered intelligent by its union with spirit.

> Intelligence is a faculty which is proper to certain classes of organic beings, and which gives to these the power to think, the will to act, the consciousness of their existence and individuality, and the means of establishing relations with the external world and providing for the needs of their special mode of existence. We may therefore distinguish: 1st, Inanimate beings, formed of matter alone, without life or intelligence the bodies of the mineral world; 2nd, Animated non-thinking beings, formed of matter and endowed with vitality, but without intelligence; and 3rd, Animated and thinking beings, formed of matter, endowed with vitality, and possessed of an intelligent principle which gives them the faculty of thought.

72 - What is the source of intelligence?
- We have already told you, the universal intelligence.
- Would it be correct to say that every intelligent being draws a portion of intelligence from the universal source and assimilates it as it draws and assimilates the principle of material life?
- Such a comparison would be far from exact, for intelligence is a faculty that is proper to each being, and constitutes its moral individuality. Besides, we have told you that there are things which man is unable to fathom; and this, for the present, is one of them.

73 - Is instinct independent of intelligence?
- No, not precisely so, for it's a species of intelligence. Instinct is an unreasoning intelligence, by means of which the lower orders of beings provide for their wants.

74 - Is it possible to establish a line of demarcation between instinct and intelligence, that's, to say, to define precisely where the one ends and the other begins?
- No, for they often blend into one another. But the actions which belong to instinct and those which belong to intelligence are easily distinguished.

75 - Is it correct to say that the instinctive faculties diminish in proportion with the growth of the intellectual faculties?
- No, instinct always continues to exist, but man neglects it. Instinct, as well as reason, may lead us in the right direction. Its guidance almost always makes itself felt, and sometimes more surely than that of reason. It never goes astray.
- Why reason isn't always an infallible guide?
- It would be infallible if it were not perverted by a false education, by pride, and by selfishness. Instinct doesn't reason. Reason leaves freedom to choice, and gives man free-will.

> Instinct is a rudimentary intelligence, differing from intelligence properly so called in this particular, that its manifestations are almost always spontaneous, whereas those of intelligence are the result of combination and of deliberation. The manifestations of instinct vary according to the differences of species and of their needs. In beings that possess self-consciousness and the perception of things external to themselves, it's allied to intelligence, that is to say, to freedom of will and of action.

2nd book - The spirit-world or world of spirits
Chapter 1 - Spirits

1 - Origin and nature of spirits

76 - What definition can be given of spirits?
- Spirits may be defined as the intelligent beings of the creation. They constitute the population of the Universe, in contradistinction to the forms of the material world.

77 - Are spirits beings distinct from the Deity, or are they only emanations from or portions of the Deity, and called, for that reason, "sons" or "children" of God?
- Spirits are the work of God, just as a machine is the work of the mechanician, who made it, the machine is the man's work, but it's not the man. You know that when a man has made a fine or useful thing, he calls it his child of his creation. It's thus with us in relation to God. We're His children in this sense, because we're his work.

78 - Have spirits had a beginning, or have they existed, like God, from all eternity?
- If spirits had not had a beginning, they would be equal with God; whereas they're his creation and subject to his will. That God has existed from all eternity is incontestable, but as to when and how he created us, we know nothing. You may say that we have had no beginning in this sense, that, God being eternal, he must have incessantly created, but as to when and how each of us was made, this, I repeat, is known to no one. It's the great mystery.

79 - Since there are two general elements in the Universe, the intelligent element and the material element, would it be correct to say that spirits are formed from the intelligent element as inert bodies are formed from the material element?
- It's evident that such is the case. Spirits are the individualization of the intelligent principle, as bodies are the individualization of the material principle. It's the epoch and mode of this formation that are unknown to us.

80 - Is the creation of spirits always going on, or did it only take place at the beginning of time?
- It's always going on; that is to say, God has never ceased to create.

81 - Are spirits formed spontaneously, or do they proceed from one another?
- God creates them as he creates all other creatures, by his will, but we must again repeat that their origin is a mystery.

82 - Is it correct to say that spirits are immaterial?
- How is it possible to define a thing in regard to which no terms of comparison exist and which your language is incompetent to express? Can one who is born blind define light? Immaterial isn't the right word; incorporeal would be nearer the truth, for you must understand that a spirit, being a creation, must be something real. Spirit is quintessentialised matter, but matter existing in a state which has no analogue within the circle of your comprehension, and so ethereal that it could not be perceived by your senses.

> We say that spirits are immaterial because their essence differs from everything that we know under the name of "matter". A nation of blind people would have no terms for expressing light and its effects. One who are born blind imagines that the only modes of perception are hearing, smell, taste, and touch, he doesn't comprehend the other ideas that would be given him by the sense of sight which he lacks. So, in regard to the essence of superhuman beings, we're really blind. We can only define them by means of comparisons that are necessarily imperfect or by an effort of our imagination.

83 - Is there an end to the duration of spirits? We can understand that the principle from which they emanate should be eternal, but what we desire to know is, whether their individuality has a term, and whether, after a given lapse of time, longer or shorter, the element from which they're formed isn't disseminated, doesn't return to the mass from which they were produced, as is the case with material bodies? It's difficult to understand that what has had a beginning should not also have an end.
- There are many things that you don't understand, because your intelligence is limited, but that is no reason for rejecting them. The child doesn't understand all that is understood by its father, nor does an ignorant man understand all that is understood by a learned one. We tell you that the existence of spirits has no end; that is all we can say on the subject at present.

2 - Primitive and normal world

84 - Do spirits constitute a world apart from that which we see?
- Yes, the world of spirits or incorporeal intelligences.

85 - Which of the two, the spirit-world or the corporeal world, is the principal one in the order of the Universe?
- The spirit-world. It's pre-existent to, and survives, everything else.

86 - Might the corporeal world never have existed, or cease to exist, without changing the essentiality of the spirit-world?

- Yes, they're independent of each other, and yet their correlation is incessant, for they react incessantly upon each other.

87 - Do spirits occupy a determinate and circumscribed region in space?
- Spirits are everywhere; the infinitudes of space are peopled with them in infinite numbers. Unperceived by you, they're incessantly beside you, observing and acting upon you, for spirits are one of the powers of Nature and are the instruments employed by God for the accomplishment of his providential designs, but all spirits don't go everywhere, there are regions of which the entrance is interdicted to those who are less advanced.

88 - Have souls a determinate, circumscribed, and unvarying form?
- Not for eyes such as yours, but, for us, they have a form though one only to be vaguely imagined by you as a flame a gleam, or an ethereal spark.
- Is this flame or spark of any color?
- If you could see it, it would appear to you to vary from a dull grey to the brilliancy of the ruby, according to the degree of the spirit's purity.

> Genie is usually represented with a flame or a star above their foreheads-a sort of allegorical allusion to the essential nature of spirits. The flame or star is placed upon the head because the head is the seat of intelligence.

89 - Do spirits employ any time in transporting themselves through space?
- Yes, but their motion is as rapid as that of thought.
- Isn't thought the movement of the soul itself, a transportation of the soul itself to the place or the object thought of by it?
- Wherever the thought is, there the soul is, since it's the soul that thinks. Thought is an attribute.

90 - When a spirit travels from one place to another, is he conscious of the distance he traverses and of the extent of space through which he passes; or is he suddenly transported to the place to which he wishes to go?
- A spirit can travel in either way. He can, if he'll, take cognizance of the distance he passes through, or he can rid himself entirely of the sense of distance. This depends on the spirit's will, and also on his degree of purity.

91 - Does matter constitute an obstacle to the movement of a spirit?
- No, spirits pass through everything, the air, the Earth, water, fire even, are equally accessible to them.

92 - Have spirits the gift of ubiquity? In other words, can a spirit divide itself, or exist at several points of space at the same time.
- There can be no division of any given spirit, but every spirit is a centre which radiates in all directions, and it's thus that a spirit may appear to be in several places at once. The Sun is only one body, yet it radiates in all directions, and sends out its rays to great distances, but it's not divided.
- Have all spirits the same power of radiation?
- There is a great difference between them in this respect; it depends on the degree of their purity.

> Each spirit is an indivisible unity, but each has the power of extending his thought on all aides without thereby dividing himself. It's only in this sense that the gift of ubiquity attributed to spirits is to be understood. It's thus that a spark sends out its brightness far and wide, and may be perceived from every point of the horizon. It's thus, also, that a man, without changing his place, and without dividing himself, may transmit orders, signals, etc., to many distant points in many different directions.

4 - Perispirit

93 - Is the spirit, properly so called, without a covering, or is it, as some declare, surrounded by a substance of some kind?
- The spirit is enveloped in a substance which would appear to you as mere vapour, but which, nevertheless, appears very gross to us, thought it's sufficiently vaporous to allow the spirit to float in the atmosphere, and to transport himself through space at pleasure.

> As the germ of a fruit is surrounded by the perisperm so the spirit, properly so called, is surrounded by an envelope which, by analogy, may be designated as the perispirit.

94 - Whence does the spirit draw its semi-material envelope?
- From the universal fluid of each globe. For this reason the perispirit isn't the same in all globes. In passing from one globe to another, the spirit changes its envelope as you change a garment.
- When spirits who inhabit worlds of a higher degree than ours come among us, are they obliged to take on a grosser order of perispirit?
- Yes, they're obliged to clothe themselves with your matter in order to be able to enter your world.

95 - Does the semi-material envelope of the spirit assume determinate forms, and can it become perceptible for us?
- Yes, it can assume any form that the spirit may choose to give to it. It's thus that a spirit is able sometimes to make himself visible to you, whether in dreams or in your waking state, and can take a form that may be visible, and even palpable, for your senses.

5 - Different orders of spirits
96 - Are all spirits equal or does there exist among them a hierarchy of ranks?
- They're of different degrees according to the degree of purification to which they have attained.

97 - Is there a fixed number of order or degrees of purification among spirits?
- The number of such orders is unlimited, because there is nothing like a barrier or line of demarcation between the different degrees of elevation, and, therefore, as there are no fixed or arbitrary divisions among spirits, the number of orders may be increased or diminished according to the point of view from which they're considered. Nevertheless, if we consider the general characteristics of spirits, we may reduce them to three principal orders or degrees.

We may place in the 1st or highest rank those who have reached the degree of relative perfection which constitutes what may be called pure spirits. We may place in the 2nd rank those who have reached the middle of the ascensional ladder, those who have achieved the degree of purification in which aspiration after perfection has become the ruling desire. We may place in the 3rd or lowest rank all those imperfect spirits who are still on the lower rungs of the ladder. They're characterized by ignorance, the love of evil, and all the low passions that retard their progress upwards.

98 - Have spirits of the second order only the aspiration after perfection, have they also the power to achieve it?
- They have that power in degrees proportionate to the degree of purification at which they have severally arrived. Some of them are distinguished by their scientific knowledge, others by their wisdom and their kindness, but all of them have still to undergo the discipline of trial through temptation and suffering.

99 - Are all spirits of the third order essentially bad?
- No. Some of them are inactive and neutral, not doing either good or evil, others, on the contrary, take pleasure in evil, and are delighted when they find an opportunity of doing wrong. Others, again, are frivolous, foolish, fantastic, mischievous rather than wicked, tricky rather than positively malicious; amusing themselves by mystifying the human beings on whom they're able to act, and causing them various petty annoyances for their own diversion.

6 - Spirit - Hierarchy
100 - Preliminary Observations. The classification of spirits is based upon the degree of their advancement, upon the qualities which they have acquired, and upon the imperfections from which they have still to free themselves. This classification, however, is by no means absolute. It's only in its totality that the character of each category is distinctly marked, for each category merges in the one above it by imperceptible gradations, the peculiarities of the successive categories shading off into one another at their extremities, as is the case in the various reigns of nature, in the colors of the rainbow, in the phases of a human life.

Spirits may, therefore, be divided into a number of classes more or less considerable, according to the point of view from which we consider the subject. It's in this matter as in all other systems of scientific classification. The systems adopted may be more or less complete, more or less rational, more or less convenient for the understanding, but, whatever may be their form, they change nothing in regard to the facts of the science which employs them. That the answers of spirits, when questioned on this point, should vary as to the number of the categories into which they're divided is, therefore, a matter of no practical importance.

Too much weight has been attributed to this apparent contradiction by those who forget that disincarnate intelligences attach no importance whatever to mere conventionalities. For them, the meaning of a statement is the only important point about it. They leave to us the question of its form, the choice of terms and of classification, in a word, all that belongs to the making of systems. Another thing that should never be lost sight of is the fact that there are among spirits, as well as among men, some who are very ignorant, and that we can't be too much on our guard against a tendency to believe that all spirits know everything simply because they're spirits. The work of classification demands method. Analysis, and a thorough knowledge of the subject investigated.

But those who, in the spirit-world, possess only a small amount of knowledge, are as incompetent as are ignorant human beings to embrace the whole of any subject or to formulate a system. They have no idea, or but a very imperfect one, of any sort of classification. All spirits superior to themselves appear to them to be of the highest order, for they are as incapable of discriminating the various shades of knowledge, capacity, and morality by which they're distinguished, as one of our savages would be to discriminate the various characteristics of civilized men.

And even those who are capable of this discrimination may vary, in their appreciation of details, according to their special point of view, especially in regard to a matter which, from its very nature, has nothing fixed or absolute about it. Linnaeus, Jussieu, Tournefort, have each their special system of classification, but the nature of botany has not been changed by this diversity of system among botanists. The latter have not invented either plants or their characteristics, they have merely observed certain analogies, according to which they have formed certain groups or classes. We have proceeded in the same way. We have not invented either spirits or their characteristics. We have seen and observed them, we have judged them by their own words and acts, and we have classed them by order of similitude, basing our classification on the data furnished by themselves.

The higher spirits generally admit the existence of three principal categories, or main divisions, among the people of the other world. In the lowest of these, at the bottom of the ladder, are the imperfect spirits who are characterized by the predominance of the instincts of materiality over the moral nature, and by the propensity to evil. Those of the 2nd degree are characterized by the predominance of the moral nature over the material instincts, and by the desire of good. They constitute the category of good spirits. The 1st or highest category consists of those who have reached the state of pure spirits, and have thus attained to the supreme degree of perfection imaginable by us.

This division of spirits into three well-marked categories appears to us to be perfectly rational, and, having arrived at this general classification, it only remained for us to bring out, through a sufficient number of subdivisions, the principal shades of the three Great Spirit categories thus established. And this we have done with the aid of the spirits themselves, whose friendly instructions have never failed us in the carrying out of the work upon which we have been led to enter. With the aid of the following table it'll be easy for us to determine the rank and degree of superiority or inferiority of the spirits with whom we may enter into communication, and, consequently, the degree of esteem and confidence to which they're entitled.

The power of determining these points may be said to constitute the key to spiritist investigation; for it alone, by enlightening us in regard to the intellectual and moral inequalities of spirits, can explain the anomalies presented by spirit-communications. We have, however, to remark that spirits don't, in all cases belonged exclusively to such and such a class. Their progress in knowledge and purity being only accomplished gradually, and often, for a time, more in the one than in the other, they may unite the characteristics of several subdivisions; a point which is easily settled by observing their language and their acts.

3rd order - Imperfect spirits

101 - General characteristics. Predominant influence of matter over spirit. Propension to evil, ignorance, pride, selfishness, and all the evil passions which result from these. They have the intuition of the existence of God, but they have no comprehension of him. They're not all of them thoroughly bad; in many of them there is more of frivolity, want of reasoning power, and love of mischief, than of downright wickedness. Some of them do neither good nor evil, but the very fact that they do no good denotes their inferiority. Others, on the contrary, take pleasure in evil, and are gratified when they find an opportunity of doing wrong.

Among spirits of this order, a certain amount of intelligence is often allied with malice and the love of mischief, but, whatever may be their intellectual development, their ideas are wanting in elevation, and their sentiments are more or less abject. Their knowledge of the things of the spirit-world is narrow, and the little they know about them is confused with the ideas and prejudices of the corporeal life. They can give only false and incomplete notions of the spirit-world, but the attentive observer may always find in their communications, however imperfect, the confirmation of the great truths proclaimed by spirits of the higher orders. Their character is revealed by their language. Every spirit who, in his communications, betrays an evil intention, may be ranged in the third order, consequently every evil thought suggested to our mind comes to us from a spirit of that order.

Their character is revealed by their language. Every spirit who, in his communications, betrays an evil intention, may be ranged in the third order, consequently every evil thought suggested to our mind comes to us from a spirit of that order. They see the happiness enjoyed by good spirits, and this sight causes them perpetual torment, for they experience all the agonies produced by envy and jealousy. They preserve the remembrance and the perception of the sufferings of corporeal life; and this impression is often more painful than the reality. They suffer, in fact, both from the ills they have themselves endured, and from those which they have caused to be endured by others. And as these sufferings endure for a very long time, they believe themselves to be destined to suffer forever. God, for their punishment, wills that they should believe this. They may be subdivided into five principal classes:

102 - 10th class - Impure Spirits: They're inclined to evil, and make it the object of all their thoughts and activities. As spirits, they give to men perfidious counsels, stir up discord and distrust, and assume every sort of mask in order the more effectually to deceive. They beset those whose character is weak enough to lead them to yield to their suggestions, and whom they thus draw aside from the path of progress, rejoicing when they're to retard their advancement by causing them to succumb under the appointed trials of the corporeal life. Spirits of this class may be recognized by their language, for the employment of coarse or trivial expressions by spirits, as by men, is always an indication of moral, if not of intellectual, inferiority.

Their communications show the baseness of their inclinations and though they may try to impose upon us by speaking with an appearance of reason and propriety, they're unable to keep up that false appearance, and end by betraying their real quality. Certain nations have made of them infernal deities, others designate them by the name of demons, evil genie evil spirits. The human beings in whom they're incarnated are addicted to all the vices engendered by vile and degrading passions-sensuality, cruelty, roguery, hypocrisy, cupidity, avarice. They do evil for its own sake, without any definite motive, and, from hatred to all that is good, they generally choose their victims from among honest and worthy people. They're the pests of humanity, to whatever rank of society they belong and the varnish of a civilized education is ineffectual to cure or to hide their degrading defects.

103 - 9th class - Frivolous Spirits: They're ignorant, mischievous, unreasonable and addicted to mockery. They meddle with everything, and reply to every question without paying any attention to truth. They delight in causing petty annoyances, in raising false hopes of petty joys, in misleading people by mystifications and trickery. The spirits vulgarly called hobgoblins, the wisps, gnomes, etc., belong to this class. They're under the orders of spirits of a higher category, who make use of them as we do of servants. In their communications with men their language is often witty and facetious, but shallow. They're quick to seize the oddities and absurdities of men and things, on which they comment with sarcastic sharpness. If they borrow distinguished names, as they're fond of doing, it's rather for the fun of the thing than from any intention to deceive by so doing.

104 - 8th class - Spirits who pretend to more Science than they possess: Their knowledge is often considerable, hut they imagine themselves to know a good deal more than they know in reality. Having made a certain amount of progress from various points of view, their language has an air of gravity that may easily give a false impression as to their capacities and enlightenment, but their ideas are generally nothing more than the reflection of the prejudices and false reasoning of their terrestrial life. Their statements contain a mixture of truths and absurdities, in the midst of which traces of presumption, pride, jealousy, and obstinacy, from which they have not yet freed themselves, are abundantly perceptible.

105 - 7th class - Neutral Spirits: They're not sufficiently advanced to take an active part in doing good, nor are they bad enough to be active in doing wrong. They incline sometimes to the one, sometimes to the other; and don't rise above the ordinary level of humanity, either in point of morality or of intelligence. They're strongly attached to the things of this world, whose gross satisfactions they regret.

106 - 6th class - Noisy and Scouts Spirits: Spirits of this kind don't, strictly speaking, form a distinct class in virtue of their personal qualities; they may belong to all the classes of the third order. They often manifest their presence by the production of phenomena perceptible by the senses, such as raps, the movement and a normal displacing of solid bodies, the agitation of the air, etc. They appear to be, more than any other class of spirits, attached to matter; they seem to be the principal agents in determining the vicissitudes of the elements of the globe, and to act upon the air, water, fire, and the various bodies in the entrails of the Earth.

Whenever these phenomena present a character of intention and intelligence, it's impossible to attribute them to a mere fortuitous and physical cause. All spirits are able to produce physical phenomena, but spirits of elevated degree usually leave them to those of a lower order, more apt for action upon matter than for the things of intelligence, and, when they judge it to be useful to produce physical manifestations, employ spirits of subaltern degree as their auxiliaries.

2nd order - Good spirits

107 - General Characteristics - Predominance of spirit over matter, desire of excellence. Their qualities and their power for good are proportionate to the degree at which they have arrived. Some of them possess scientific knowledge, others have acquired wisdom and charity, the more advanced among them combine knowledge with moral excellence. Not being yet completely dematerialized, they preserve the traces of their corporeal existence, more or less strongly marked, according to their rank-traces which are seen either in their mode of expressing themselves, in their habits, or even, in some cases, in the characteristic eccentricities and hobbies still retained by them. But for these weaknesses and imperfections they'd be able to pass into the category of spirits of the first order.

They have acquired the comprehension of the idea of God and of infinity, and already share the felicity of the higher spheres. They find their happiness both in the accomplishment of good and in the prevention of evil. The affection by which they're united affords them ineffable delight, troubled neither by envy, remorse nor any other of the evil passions which make the torment of spirits of lower degree, but they have still to undergo the discipline of trial until they have completed the work of their purification.

As spirits, they infuse good and noble thoughts into the minds of men, turn them from the path of evil, protect those whose course of life renders them worthy of their aid, and neutralize by their suggestions, the influence of lower spirits on the minds of those who don't willingly yield to the evil counsels of the latter. The human beings in whom they're incarnated are upright and benevolent, they're actuated neither by pride, selfishness, nor ambition; they feel neither hatred, rancor, envy, nor jealousy, and do good for its own sake. To this order belong the spirits commonly designated in the popular beliefs by the names of good genie protecting genie, good spirits. In periods of ignorance and superstition, men have regarded them as beneficent divinities. They may be divided into four principal groups:

108 - 5th class - Benevolent Spirits: Their dominant quality is kindness. They take pleasure in rendering service to men and in protecting them, but their knowledge is somewhat narrow. They have progressed in morality rather than in intelligence.

109 - 4th class - Learned Spirits: They're specially distinguished by the extent of their knowledge. They're less interested in moral questions than in scientific investigation, for which they have a greater aptitude; but their scientific studies are always prosecuted with a view to practical utility, and they're entirely free from the base passions common to spirits of the lower degrees of advancement.

110 - 3rd class - Wise Spirits: The most elevated moral qualities form their distinctive characteristics. Without having arrived at the possession of unlimited knowledge, they have reached a development of intellectual capacity that enables them to judge correctly of men and of things.

111 - 2nd class - High Spirits: They unite, in a very high degree, scientific knowledge, wisdom and goodness. Their language, inspired only by the purest benevolence, is always noble and elevated, often sublime. Their superiority renders them more apt than any others to impart to us just and true ideas in relation to the incorporeal world, within the limits of the knowledge permitted to mankind. They willingly enter into communication with those who seek for truth in simplicity and sincerity, and who are sufficiently freed from the bonds of materiality to be capable of understanding it; but they turn from those whose inquiries are prompted only by curiosity, or who are drawn away from the path of rectitude by the attractions of materiality. When, under exceptional circumstances, they incarnate themselves in this Earth, it's always for the accomplishment of a mission of progress, and they thus show us the highest type of perfection to which we can aspire in the present world.

1st order - Pure spirits

112 - General characteristics. The influence of matter null, a superiority, both intellectual and moral, so absolute as to constitute what, in comparison with the spirits of all the other orders, may be termed perfection.

113 - 1st and only Class: They have passed up through every degree of the scale of progress and have freed themselves from all the impurities of materiality. Having attained the sum of perfection of which created beings are susceptible, they have no longer to undergo either trials or expiations. Being no longer subject to reincarnation in perishable bodies, they

enter on the life of eternity in the immediate presence of God. They're in the enjoyment of a beatitude which is unalterable, because they're no longer subject to the wants or vicissitudes of material life, but this beatitude isn't the monotonous idleness of perpetual contemplation. They're the messengers and ministers of God, the executors of his orders in the maintenance of universal harmony.

They exercise a sovereign command over all spirits inferior to themselves, aid them in accomplishing the work of their purification, and assign to each of them a mission proportioned to the progress already made by them. To assist men in their distresses, to excite them to the love of good or to the atonement of the faults which keep them back on the road to the supreme felicity, are for them congenial occupations. They're sometimes spoken of as angels, archangels or seraphim. They can, when they choose to do so, enter into communication with men; but presumptuous indeed would he be who should pretend to have them at his orders.

7 - Progression of spirits
114 - Are spirits good or bad by nature, or are they the same spirits made better through their own efforts?
- The same spirits made better through their own efforts. In growing better they pass from a lower to a higher order.

115 - Are some spirits created good and others created bad?
- God has created all spirits in a state of simplicity and ignorance, that is to say, without knowledge. He has given to each of them a mission, with a view to enlighten them and to make them gradually arrive at perfection through the knowledge of the truth, and thus to bring them nearer and nearer to himself. This perfection is, for them, the condition of eternal and unalloyed happiness. Spirits acquire knowledge by passing through the trials imposed on them by God. Some of them accept these trials with submission, and arrive more quickly at the aim of their destiny others undergo them with murmuring, and thus remain, through their own fault, at a distance from the perfection and the felicity promised to them.
- According to this statement, it'd appear that spirits, a their origin, are like children, ignorant and without experience, but acquiring, little by little, the knowledge which they lack, by passing through the different phases of human life?
- Yes, the comparison is correct. The child, if rebellious, remains ignorant and faulty; he profits more or less according to his docility, but the life of man has a term, whereas that of spirits stretches out into infinity.

116 - Do any spirits remain forever in the lower ranks?
- No, all become perfect. They change in course of time, however long may be the process of amendment; for, as we have already said, a just and merciful parent can't condemn his children to eternal banishment. Can you suppose that God, so great, so good, so just, is less kind than you are?

117 - Does it depend on the spirits themselves to hasten their progress towards perfection?
- Certainly, they reach the goal more or less quickly according to the strength of their desire and the degree of their submission to the will of God. Doesn't a docile child learn faster than one who is obstinate and idle?

118 - Can spirits degenerate?
- No, in proportion as they advance, they understand what has retarded their progress. When a spirit has finished with any given trial, he has learned the lesson of that trial, and never forgets it. He may remain stationary, but be never degenerates.

119 - Could God exonerate spirits from the trials which they have to undergo in order to reach the highest rank?
- If they had been created perfect, they'd not have merited the enjoyment of the benefits of that perfection. Where would be the merit without the struggle? Besides, the inequality which exists between spirits is necessary to the development of their personality, and, moreover, the mission which each spirit accomplishes at each step of his progress is an element of the providential plan for ensuring the harmony of the Universe.

> Since, in social life all men may reach the highest posts. We might as well ask why the sovereign of a country doesn't make a general of each of his soldiers, why all subaltern functionaries are not made heads of departments, why all scholars are not schoolmasters, but there's this difference between the life of the social and the spirit worlds, that the first is limited, and doesn't afford to everyone the possibility of raising himself to the highest rank whereas the second is unlimited, and ensures to everyone the possibility of attaining to supreme degree.

120 - Do all spirits pass by the road of evil to arrive at good?
- Not by the road of evil, but by that of ignorance.

121 - How is it that some spirits have followed the road of good, and others the road of evil?
- Have they not their free-will? God has not created any spirits bad; he has created them simple and ignorant, that is to say, possessing an equal aptitude for good and for evil. Those who become bad become so of their own free-will.

122 - How can spirits, at their origin, when they have not yet acquired self-consciousness, possess freedom of choice between good and evil? Is there in them any principle, any tendency, which inclines them towards either road rather than towards the other?
- Free-will is developed in proportion as the spirit acquires the consciousness of himself. Freedom would not exist for the spirit if his choice were solicited by a cause independent of his will. The cause which determines his choice isn't in him, but is exterior to him, in the influences to which he voluntarily yields in virtue of the freedom of his will. It's this

choice that is represented tinder the grand figure of the fall of man and of original sin. Some spirits have yielded to temptation, others have withstood it.
- Whence come the influences that act upon him?
- From the imperfect spirits, who seek to take possession of him and to dominate him, and who are happy to see him succumb. It's this temptation that is allegorically pictured as Satan.
- Does this influence act upon a spirit only at its origin?
- It follows him through all the phases of his existence as a spirit, until he has acquired such thorough self-command that evil spirits renounce the attempt to obsess him.

123 - Why has God permitted it to be possible for spirits to take the wrong road?
- The wisdom of God is shown in the freedom of choice which he leaves to every spirit, for each has thus the merit of his deeds.

124 - Since there are spirits who, from the beginning, follow unswervingly the right path and others who wander into the lowest depths of evil, there are, no doubt, many degrees of deviation between these two extremes?
- Yes, certainly, and these degrees constitute the paths of the great majority of spirits.

125 - Will the spirits who have chosen the wrong road be able to reach the same degree of elevation as the others?
- Yes, but the eternities will be longer in their case.

> This expression, "the eternities", must be understood as referring to the belief of spirits of inferior degree in the perpetuity their sufferings, resulting from the fact that it's not given to them to foresee the termination of those sufferings, and that this conviction of the perpetuity of the latter is renewed after every new trial to which they have succumbed.

126 - Are spirits who have reached the supreme degree after wandering into the wrong road less meritorious than the others in the sight of God?
- God regards the wanderers who have returned to the right road with the same approval and the same affection as the others. They have been classed, for a time, as evil spirits, because they succumbed to the temptation of evil, but, before their fall, they were merely neutral in regard to good and evil, like all other spirits.

127 - Are all spirits created equal in point of intellectual capacity?
- They're all created equal, but not knowing from whence they come, for their free-will must have its fling. They progress more or less rapidly in intelligence as in morality.

> The spirits, who, from the beginning, follow the right road, don't thereby attain at once to the state of perfection for, although they're free from evil tendencies, they have none the less to acquire the experience and the varied knowledge indispensable to their perfection. They may be compared to children who, however good their natural instincts, need to be developed and enlightened, and who can't attain to maturity without transition. But, just as some men are good and others bad from their infancy, so some spirits are good and others bad from their beginning, with this radical difference, however, that the child possesses instincts already formed, whereas the spirit, at his formation, is neither bad nor good, but possesses all possible tendencies, and strikes out his path, in the direction of good or evil through the action of his own free-will.

8 - Angels and Demons
128 - Do the beings that we call angels, archangels, seraphim, form a special category of a different nature from that of other spirits?
- No, the spirits who have purified themselves from all imperfection, have reached the highest degree of the scale of progress, and united in themselves all species of perfection.

> The word angel is generally supposed to imply the idea of moral perfection but it's often applied, nevertheless, to all beings, good or bad, beyond the pale of humanity. We say, a good angel, a bad angel, an angel of light, the angel of darkness, etc. In those cases, it's synonymous with spirit or genius. It's employed here in its highest sense.

129 - Have the angels passed up through all the degrees of progress?
- They have passed up through all those degrees, but with the difference which we have already mentioned. Some of them, accepting their mission without murmuring, have reached the goal more quickly; others have been longer in reaching the same goal.

130 - If the opinion which admits that some beings have been created perfect and superior to all others be erroneous, how is it that this opinion is to be found in the tradition of almost every people?
- Your world has not existed from all eternity. Long before it was called into being hosts of spirits had already attained to the supreme degree, and, therefore, the people of your Earth naturally supposed those perfected spirits to have always been at the same degree of elevation.

131 - Are there any demons in the usual acceptation of that term?
- If demons existed, they'd be the work of God, but would it he just on the part of God to have created beings condemned eternally to evil and to misery? If demons exist, it's in your low world, and in other worlds of similar degree,

that they're to be found. They're the human hypocrites who represent a just God as being cruel and vindictive, and who imagine that they make themselves agreeable to him by the abominations they commit in his name.

> It's only in its modern acceptation that the word demon implies the idea of evil spirits, for the Greek work daimôn from which it's derived, signifies genius, intelligence, and is applied indiscriminately to all incorporeal beings, whether good or bad. Demons or devils, according to the common acceptation of these words are supposed to be a class of beings essentially bad. If they exist, they must necessarily be, like everything else, a creation of God but God, who is sovereignly just and good, can't have created beings predestined to evil by their very nature, and condemned beforehand to eternal misery.

If, on the contrary, they're not a creation of God, they must either have existed, like him, from all eternity, or there must be several creators. The first requisite of every theory is to be consistent with itself, but that which asserts the existence of demons, in the popular acceptation of the term, lacks this essential condition of theoretic soundness. It was natural that the religious belief of peoples who, knowing nothing of the attributes of God, were backward enough to admit the existence of maleficent deities, should also admit the existence of demons but, on the of those who acknowledge the goodness of God to be his distinguishing quality, it's illogical and contradictory to suppose that he can have created beings doomed to evil, and destined to do evil forever, for such a supposition is the negation of his goodness.

The partisans of the belief in devils appeal to the words of Christ in support of their doctrine and it's certainly not we who would contest the authority of his teachings, which we would faint, see established, not merely on the lips of men, but also in their hearts, but are those partisans quite sure of the meaning attached be him to the word "devil"? Is it not fully admitted that the allegorical form is one of the distinctive characteristics of his utterances, and that the Gospels contain many things which are not to be taken literally? To prove that such is the case, we need only quote the following passage.

Immediately after the tribulation of those days the Sun shall be darkened, and the Moon shall not give her light, and the stars shall fall from Heaven, and the powers of the Heavens shall be shaken and then shall appear the sign of the Son of Man in Heaven. Verily I say unto you. This generation shall not pass till all these things are fulfilled. Have we not seen that the form of the biblical text, in reference to the creation and movement of the Earth, is contradicted by the discoveries of science? May it not be the same in regard to certain figurative expressions employed by Christ in order to adapt his teachings to the time and the scene of his mission?

Christ could not have made a statement knowing it to be false. If, therefore, his sayings contain statements which appear to be contrary to reason, it's evident either that we don't understand their meaning or that we have interpreted them erroneously. Men have done in regard to devils what they have done in regard to angels. Just as they have imagined that there are beings that were created perfect from all eternity, so they have imagined that spirits of the lower degrees were beings essentially and eternally bad. The words demon, devil, ought, therefore, to be understood as indicating impure spirits who are often no better that the imaginary beings designated by those names, but with this difference, that their state of impurity and inferiority is only transitory.

They're the imperfect spirits who rebel against the discipline of trial to which they're subjected, and who, therefore, have to undergo that discipline for a longer period, but who will, nevertheless, reach the goal in time, when they shall have made up their minds to do so. The words demon, devil, might accordingly be employed in this sense but as they have come to be understood exclusively as conveying the meaning now shown to be false. Their employment might lead into error by seeming to recognize the existence of beings specially created for evil.

As regards the term Satan, it's evidently a personification of the principle of evil under an allegorical form for it's impossible to admit the existence of a being who fights against God as an independent and rival power, and whose sole business in life is to contravene his designs. As images and figures are necessary in order to strike the human imagination, men have pictured to themselves the beings of the incorporeal world under a material form, with attributes indicative of their good or bad qualities. It's thus that the ancients, wishing to personify the idea of time, represented it under the figure of an old man with a scythe and an hour-glass.

To have personified it under the figure of a youth would have been contrary to common sense. The same may be said of the allegories of Fortune, Truth, etc. The moderns have represented the angels or pure spirits under the form of radiant beings with white wings-emblem of purity Satan, with horns, claws, and the attributes of bestiality-emblems of the lowest passions, and the vulgar, prone to understand such representations literally, have taken these allegorical embodiments of abstract ideas for real personalities, as they formerly did in regard to the allegorical personifications of the old mythology.

Chapter 2 - Incarnation of spirits

1 - Aim of incarnation

132 - What is the aim of the incarnation of spirits?
- It's a necessity imposed on them by God, as the means of attaining perfection. For some of them it's an expiation, for others, a mission. In order to attain perfection, it's necessary for them to undergo all the vicissitudes of corporeal existence. It's the experience acquired by expiation that constitutes its usefulness. Incarnation has also another aim, that of fitting the spirit to perform his share in the work of creation, for which purpose he's made to assume a corporeal apparatus in harmony with the material state of each world into which he's sent, and by means of which he is enabled to accomplish the special work, in connection with that world which has been appointed to him by the divine ordering. He's thus made to contribute his quota towards the general weal, while achieving his own advancement.

> The action of corporeal beings is necessary to the carrying on of the work of the Universe, but God in his wisdom has willed that this action should furnish them with the means of progress and of advancement towards himself. And thus, through an admirable law of his providence, all things are linked together, and solidarity is established between all the realms of nature.

133 - Is incarnation necessary for the spirits who, from the beginning, have followed the right road?
- All are created simple and ignorant; they gain instruction in the struggles and tribulations of corporeal life. God, being just, could not make some of them happy, without trouble and without exertion and consequently without merit.
- But it so, what do spirits gain by having followed the right road, since they're not thereby exempted from the pains of corporeal life?
- They arrive more quickly at the goal, and besides, the sufferings of life are often a consequence of the imperfection of the spirit; therefore, the fewer his imperfections, the less will be his sufferings. He, who is neither envious, jealous, avaricious, nor ambitious, will not have to undergo the torments which are a consequence of those defects.

2 - The soul

134 - What is the soul?
- An incarnate spirit.
- What was the soul before its union with a body?
- A spirit.
- Souls and spirits are, then, the very same thing?
- Yes, souls are only spirits. Before uniting itself with a body, the soul is one of the intelligent beings who people the invisible world, and who temporarily assume a fleshly body in order to effect their purification and enlightenment.

135 - Is there in man anything else than a soul and a body?
- There's the link which unites the soul and the body.
- What is tile nature of that link?
- It's semi-material, that is to say, of a nature intermediate between soul and body, as it must necessarily be, in order that they may be enabled to communicate with each other. It's by means of this link that the spirit acts upon matter, and that matter acts reciprocally upon the spirit.

> Man is thus formed of three essential elements or parts: 1st - The body, or material being, analogous to the animals, and animated by the same vital principle. 2nd - The soul, or incarnated spirit, of which the body is the habitation; and 3rd - The intermediary principle, or perispirit, a semi-material substance, which constitutes the innermost envelope of the spirit and unites the soul with the body. This triplicity is analogous to that of the fruit, which consists of the germ, the perisperm, and the rind or shell.

136 - Is the soul independent of the vital principle?
- The body is only the envelope of the soul, as we have repeatedly told you.
- Can a body exist without a soul?
- Yes, but it's only when the body ceases to live that the soul quits it, previous to birth, the union between the soul and the body isn't complete, but, when this union is definitively established, it's only the death of the body that can sever the bonds that unite it to the soul, and thus allow the soul to withdraw from it. Organic life may vitalize a body without a soul, but the soul can't inhabit a body deprived of organic life.
- What would our body be if it had no soul?
- A mass of flesh without intelligence, anything you choose to call it, excepting a man.

137 - Can the same spirit incarnate itself in two different bodies at the same time?
- No, the spirit is indivisible and can't simultaneously animate two different beings.

138 - What is to be thought of the opinion of those who regard the soul as being the principle of material life?
- That's a question of definition, we attach but slight importance to mere words. You should begin by agreeing among yourselves as to the exact meaning of the expressions you employ.

139 - Certain spirits and certain philosophers before them have defined the soul as an animated spark that has emanated from the Great Whole, why this contradiction?

- There's nothing contradictory in such a definition. Everything depends on the meaning you attribute to the words you use. Why have you not a word for each thing?

> The word soul is employed to express very different things. Sometimes it's used to designate the principle of life and in this sense it's correct to say, figuratively, that the soul is an animated spark that has emanated from the Great Whole. These latter words designate the universal source of the vital principle, of which each being absorbs a portion that returns to the general mass after its death. This Idea doesn't exclude that of a moral being, a distinct personality, independent of matter, and preserving its own individuality it's this being which, at other times, is called the soul, and it's in this sense that we speak of the soul as an incarnate spirit. In giving different definitions of soul, the spirits who have given them have spoken according to their various ways of applying that word, and also according to the terrestrial ideas with which they're more or less imbued. This apparent confusion results from the insufficiency of human language, which doesn't possess a specific word for each idea an insufficiency that gives rise to a vast number of misapprehensions and discussions. It's for this reason that the higher spirits tell us to begin by distinctly defining the meaning of the words we employ.

140 - What is to be thought of the theory according to which the soul is subdivided into as many parts as there are muscles in the body, and thus presides over each of the bodily functions?
- That, again, depends on the meaning attached to the word soul. If by soul is meant the vital fluid, that theory is right; if the word is used to express an incarnate spirit, it's wrong. We have already told you that a spirit is indivisible; it transmits movement to the bodily organs through the intermediary fluids, but it undergoes no division.
- Nevertheless, there are spirits who have given this definition.
- Spirits who are ignorant may mistake the effect for the cause.

> The soul acts through the intermediary of the bodily organs and those organs are animated by the vital fluid which is distributed among them, arid more abundantly in those which constitute the centers or foci of movement for each organism, but this explanation becomes Inadmissible when the term soul is employed to designate the spirit which inhabits the body during life and quits it at death.

141 - Is there any truth in the opinion of those who suppose that the soul is exterior to the body and environs it?
- The soul isn't shut up in the body like a bird in a cage. It radiates in all directions, and manifests itself outside the body as a light radiates from a glass globe, or as a sound is propagated from a sonorous centre. In this sense the soul may be said to be exterior to the body, but it's not therefore to be considered as enveloping the body. The soul has two envelopes; the first, or innermost, of these, of a light and subtle nature, is what you call the perispirit the other, gross, material, heavy, is the body. The soul is the centre of both these envelopes, like the germ in the stone of the fruit, as we have already said.

142 - What is to be thought of that other theory according to which the formation of the soul of the child is carried on to completion during the successive periods of the human lifetime?
- The spirit is a unit and is as entire in the child as in the adult. It's only the bodily organs, or instruments of the manifestations of the soul, that are gradually developed and completed in the course of a lifetime. Here, again, you mistake the effect for the cause.

143 - Why don't all spirits define the soul in the same way?
- All spirits are not equally enlightened in regard to these matters. Some are still so little advanced intellectually as to be incapable of understanding abstract ideas; they're like children in your world. Other spirits are full of false learning, and make a vain parade of words in order to impose their authority upon those who listen to them. They, also, resemble too many in your world. And besides, even spirits who are really unenlightened may express themselves in terms which appear to be different, but which, at bottom, mean the same thing, especially in regard to matters which your language is incapable of expressing dearly, and which can only he spoken of to you by means of figures and comparisons that you mistake for literal statements of fact.

144 - What is to be understood by the soul of the world?
- The universal principle of life and intelligence from which individualities are produced, but, very often, they who make use of these terms don't know what they mean by them. The word soul is so elastic that every one interprets it according to his own imaginings. Certain persons have also attributed a soul to the Earth, which must he understood as indicating the assemblage of devoted spirits who direct your actions in the right direction when you listen to them, and who are, as it were, the lieutenants of God in the administration of your globe.

145 - How is it that so many philosophers both ancient and modern have so long been discussing psychological questions without having arrived at the truth?
- Those men were precursors of the eternal truths of the true Spiritist Doctrine, for which they have prepared the way. They were men, and therefore subject to error, because they often mistook their own ideas for the true light, but their very errors have served the cause of truth by bringing into relief both sides of the argument. Moreover, among those errors are to be found many great truths which a comparative study of the various theories thus put forth would enable you to discover.

146 - Has the soul a circumscribed and determinate seat in the body?

- No, but it may be said to reside more especially in the head, in the case of men of great genius and of all who think much, and in the heart, in the case of those who feel much, and whose actions have always a humanitarian aim.
- What is to be thought of the opinion of those who place the soul in a centre of organic life?
- The spirit may be said to inhabit more especially such a part of your organism, because it's to such a part that all the sensations converge, but those who place it in what they consider to be the centre of vitality confound it with the vital fluid or principle. Nevertheless, it may be said that the soul is more especially present in the organs which serve for the manifestation of the intellectual and moral qualities.

3 - Materialism

147 - Why is it that anatomists physiologists, and in general those who apply themselves to the pursuit of the natural sciences, are so apt to fall into materialism?
- The physiologist refers everything to the standard of his senses. Human pride imagines that it knows everything, and refuses to admit that there can be anything which transcends the human understanding. Science itself inspires some minds with presumption; they think that nature can have nothing hidden from them.

148 - Is it not regrettable that materialism should be a consequence of studies which ought, on the contrary, to show men the superiority of the intelligence that governs the world?
- It's not true that materialism is a consequence of those studies it's a result of the imperfection which leads men to draw a false conclusion from their studies, for men may make a bad use of the very best things. The idea of annihilation, moreover, troubles those who profess to hold it more than they'll allow to seen; and those who are the loudest in proclaiming their materialistic convictions are often more boastful than brave the greater number of the so-called materialists are only such because they have no rational ground of belief in a future life. Show a firm anchor of rational belief in a future state to those who see only a yawning void before them, and they'll grasp it with the eagerness of drowning men.

> There are those who, through an aberration of the intellect, can see nothing in organized beings but the action of matter, and attribute to this action alt the phenomena of existence. They have seen, in the human body. Only the action of an electrical machine they have studied the mechanism of life only in the play of the bodily organ; they have often seen life extinguished by the rupture of a filament, and they have seen nothing but this filament. They have looked to see whether anything stilt remained, and as they have found nothing but matter that has become inert, as they have neither seen the soul escape from the body nor been able to take hold of it, they have concluded that everything is reducible to the properties of matter, and that death is consequently the annihilation of all thought.

A melancholy conclusion, if such were really the case for, were it so, good and evil would be alike devoid of aim every man would be justified in thinking only of himself, and in subordinating every other consideration to the satisfaction of his material instincts. Thus all social ties would be broken, and the holiest affections would be destroyed forever. Happily for mankind, these ideas are far from being general. Their area may even be said to be a narrow one, limited to the scope of invidious opinions, for nowhere have they been erected into a system of doctrine. A state of society founded on such a basis would contain within itself the seeds of its own dissolution; and its members would tear each other to pieces like so many ferocious beasts of prey. Man has an intuitive belief that, for him, everything doesn't end with the life of his body; he has a horror of annihilation. No matter how obstinately men may have set themselves against the idea of a future life, there are very few who, on the approach of death.

Don't anxiously ask themselves what is going to become of them for the thought of bidding an eternal adieu to life is appalling to the stoutest heart. Who, indeed could look with indifference on the prospect of an absolute and eternal separation from all that he has loved? Who, without terror, could behold, yawning beneath him, the bottomless abyss of nothingness in which all his faculties and aspirations are to be swallowed up forever? Who could calmly say to himself, after my death there will be nothing for me but the void of annihilation, all will be ended. A few days hence, all memory of me will have been blotted out from the remembrance of those who survive me, and the Earth itself will retain no trace of my passage. Even the good that I have done will be forgotten by the ungrateful mortals whom I have benefited. And there is nothing to compensate me for all this loss, no other prospect, beyond this ruin, than that of my body devoured by worms. Is there not something horrible in such a picture, something that sends an icy chill through the heart?

Religion teaches us that such can't be our destiny and reason confirms the teachings of religion, but the vague, indefinite assurance of a future existence, which is all that is given us either by religion or by reason, can't satisfy our natural desire for some positive proof in a matter of such paramount importance for us and it's just the lack of such proof, In regard to a future life, that, in so many cases, engenders doubt as to its reality. Admitting that we have a soul, many very naturally ask, what is our soul? Has it a form, an appearance of any kind? Is it a limited being or is it something undefined and impersonal? Some say that it's a breath of God, others, that it's a spark others, again, declare it to be part of the Great Whole, the principle of life and of Intelligence.

But what do we learn from these statements? What is the good of our possessing a soul, if our soul is to be merged in immensity like a drop of water in the ocean? Isn't the loss of our individuality equivalent, so far as we're concerned, to annihilation? The soul is said to be immaterial, but that which is immaterial can have no defined proportions and therefore can have no reality for us. Religion also teaches that we shall be happy, or unhappy. According to the good or the evil we have done, but of what nature is the happiness or unhappiness thus promised us in another life? Is that happiness a state of beatitude in the bosom of God, an external contemplation, with no other employment than that of singing the praises of the Creator? And the flames of Hell are they a reality or a figure of speech? The Church itself attributes to them a figurative meaning but of what nature are the sufferings thus figuratively shadowed forth? And where is the scene of those sufferings? In short, what shall we be, what shall we do, what shall we see, in that other world which is said to await us all?

No one, it's averred, has ever come back to give us an account of that world, but this statement is erroneous, and the mission of Spiritism is precisely to enlighten us in regard to the future which awaits us to enable us, within certain limits, to see and to touch it, not merely as a deduction of our reason, but through the evidence of facts. Thanks to the communications made to us by the people of that other world, the latter is no longer a mere presumption, a probability, which each one pictures to himself according to his own fancy, which poets embellish with fictitious and allegorical images that serve only to deceive us it's that other world itself, in its reality, which is now brought before us, for it's the beings of the life beyond the grave who come to us, who describe to us the situations in which they find themselves, who tell us what they're doing, who allow us to become.

So to say, the spectators of the details of their new order of life, and who thus show us the inevitable fate which is reserved for each of us according to our merits or our misdeeds. Is there anything anti-religious in such a demonstration? Assuredly not since it furnishes unbelievers with a ground of belief, and inspires lukewarm believers with renewed fervor and confidence. Spiritism is thus seen to be the most powerful auxiliary of religion. And, if it be such, it must be acknowledged to exist by the permission of God, for the purpose of giving new strength to our wavering convictions, and thus of leading us back into the right road by the prospect of our future happiness.

Chapter 3 - Return from the corporeal to the spirit life

1 - The soul after death

149 - What becomes of the soul at the moment of death?
- It becomes again a spirit; that's to say, it returns into the world of spirits, which it had quitted for a short time.

150 - Does the soul, after death, preserve its individuality?
- Yes, it never loses its individuality. What would the soul be if it didn't preserve it?
- How does the soul preserve the consciousness of its individuality, since it no longer has its material body?
- It still has a fluid peculiar to itself, which it draws from the atmosphere of its planet, and which represents the appearance of its last incarnation-its perispirit.
- Does the soul take nothing of this life away with it?
- Nothing but the remembrance of that life and the desire to go to a better world. This remembrance is full of sweetness or of bitterness according to the use it has made of the earthly life it has quitted. The more advanced is the degree of its purification, the more clearly does it perceive the futility of all that it has left behind it upon the Earth.

151 - What is to be thought of the opinion that the soul after death returns to the universal whole?
- Doesn't the mass of spirits, considered in its totality, constitute a whole? Does it not constitute a world? When you are in an assembly you form an integral part of that assembly, and yet you still retain your individuality.

152 - What proof can we have of the individuality of the soul after death?
- Is not this proof furnished by the communications which you obtain? If you were not blind, you would see; if you were not deal you would hear; for you are often spoken to by a voice which reveals to you the existence of a being exterior to yourself.

> Those who think that the soul, with death, returns to the universal whole, will be wrong, if by this they understand that it loses its individuality, like a drop of water that fell of the ocean. They'll be right, however, if they understand the universal whole the incorporeal beings of each soul or spirit is an element. If souls were blended together into a mass, they would possess only the qualities common to the totality of the mass there would be nothing to distinguish them from one another, and they would have no special, intellectual, or moral qualities of their own.

But the communications we obtain from spirits give abundant evidence of the possession by each spirit of the consciousness of the me, and of a distinct will, personal to itself; the infinite diversity of characteristics of all kinds presented by them is at once the consequence and the evidence of their distinctive personal individuality. If, after death, there were nothing but what is called the Great Whole, absorbing all individualities, this whole would be uniform in its characteristics and, in that case, all the communications received from the invisible world would be identical.

But as among the denizens of that other world we meet with some who are good and some who are bad, some who are learned and some who are ignorant, some who are happy and some who are unhappy, and as they present us with every shade of character, some being frivolous and other, serious, etc., it's evident that they're different individualities, perfectly distinct from one another. This individuality becomes still more evident when they're able to prove their identity by unmistakable tokens, by personal details relating to their terrestrial life, and susceptible of being verified, and it can't be a matter of doubt when they manifest themselves to our sight under the form of apparitions. The individuality of the soul has been taught theoretically as an article of faith; Spiritism renders it patent, as an evident, and, so to say, a material fact.

153 - In what sense should we understand eternal life?
- It's the life of the spirit that is eternal; that of the body is transitory and fleeting. When the body dies, the soul re-enters the eternal life.
- Would it not be more correct to apply the term eternal life to the life of the purified spirits, of those who, having attained to the degree of relative perfection, have no longer to undergo the discipline of suffering?
- The life of that degree might rather be termed eternal happiness, but this is a question of words. You may call things as you please, provided you are agreed among yourselves as to your meaning.

2 - Separation of soul and body

154 - Is the separation of the soul from the body a painful process?
- No, the body often suffers more during life than at the moment of death, when the soul is usually unconscious of what is occurring to the body. The sensations experienced at the moment of death are often a source of enjoyment for the spirit, who recognizes them as putting an end to the term of his exile.

> In cases of natural death, where dissolution occurs as a consequence of the exhaustion of the bodily organs through age, man passes out of life without perceiving that he is doing so. It's like the flame of a lamp that goes out for want of aliment.

155 - How is the separation of soul and body effected?
- The bonds which retained the soul being broken, it disengages itself from the body.
- Is this separation effected instantaneously, and by means of an abrupt transition? Is there any distinctly marked line of demarcation between life and death?

- No, the soul disengages itself gradually. It doesn't escape at once from the body, like a bird whose cage is suddenly opened. The two states touch and run into each other, and the spirit extricates himself, little by little, from his fleshly bonds, which are loosed, but not broken.

> During life, a spirit is held to the body by his semi-material envelope or perispirit. Death is the destruction of the body only, but not of this second envelope, which separates itself from the body when the play of organic life ceases in the latter. Observation shows us that the separation of the perispirit from the body is not suddenly completed at the moment of death, but is only effected gradually and more or less slowly in different Individuals. In some cases it's affected so quickly that the perispirit is entirely separated from the body within a few hours of the death of the latter, but in other cases, and especially in the case of those whose life has been grossly material and sensual, this deliverance is much less rapid, and sometimes takes days, weeks and even months, for its accomplishment.

This delay doesn't imply the slightest persistence of vitality in the body nor any possibility of its return to life, but is simply the result of a certain affinity between the body and the spirit which affinity is always more or less tenacious in proportion to the preponderance of materiality in the affections of the spirit during his earthly life. It's, in fact, only rational to suppose that the more closely a spirit has identified himself with matter, the greater will be his difficulty in separating himself from his material body, while, on the contrary, intellectual and moral activity, and habitual elevation of thought, effect a commencement of this separation even during the life of the body, and therefore, when death occurs, the separation is almost instantaneous. The study of a great number of individuals after their death has shown that affinity which, in some cases, continues to exist between the soul and the body is sometimes extremely painful for it causes the spirit to perceive all the horror of the decomposition of the latter. This experience is exceptional, and peculiar to certain kinds of life and to certain kinds of death. It sometimes occurs in the case of those who have committed suicide.

156 - Can the definitive separation of the soul and body take place before the complete cessation of organic life?
- It sometimes happens that the soul has quitted the body before the last agony comes on, so that the latter is only the closing act of merely organic life. The dying man has no longer any consciousness of himself and nevertheless there still remains in him a faint breathing of vitality. The body is a machine that is kept in movement by the heart. It continues to live as long as tile heart causes the blood to circulate in the veins and has no need of the soul to do that.

157 - Does the soul sometimes at the moment of death, experience an aspiration or an ecstasy that gives it a fore glimpse of the world into which it's about to return?
- The soul often feels the loosening of the bonds that attach it to the body, and does its utmost to hasten and complete the work of separation. Already partially freed from matter, it beholds the future unrolled before it, and enjoys, in anticipation, the spirit-state upon which it's about to re-enter.

158 - Do the transformations of the caterpillar, which, first of all, crawls upon the ground, and then shuts itself up, in its chrysalis in seeming death, to be reborn there from into a new and brilliant existence, give us anything like a true idea of the relation between our terrestrial life, the tomb, and our new existence beyond the latter?
- An idea on a very small scale. The image is good, hut; nevertheless, it would not do to accept it literally, as you so often do in regard to such images.

159 - What sensation is experienced by the soul at the moment when it recovers its consciousness in the world of spirits?
- That depends on circumstances. He who has done evil from the love of evil is overwhelmed with shame for his wrong doing. With the righteous it's very different. His soul seems to be eased of a heavy load, for it doesn't dread the most searching glance.

160 - Does the spirit find himself at once in company with those whom he knew upon the Earth and who died before him?
- Yes, and more or less promptly according to the degree of his affection for them and of theirs for him. They often come to meet him on his return to the spirit world and help to free him from the bonds of matter. Others whom he formerly knew, but whom he had lost sight of during his sojourn on the Earth, also come to meet him. He sees those who are in erraticity and he goes to visit those who are still incarnated.

161 - In cases of violent or accidental death, when the organs have not been weakened by age or by sickness, does the separation of the soul take place simultaneously with the cessation of organic life?
- It does so usually, and, at any rate, the interval between them, in all such cases, is very brief.

162 - After decapitation, for instance, does a man retain consciousness for a longer or shorter time?
- He frequently does so for a few minutes, until the organic life of the body is completely extinct, but, on the other hand, the fear of death often causes a man to lose consciousness before the moment of execution.

> The question here proposed refers simply to the consciousness which the victim may have of himself as a man, through the intermediary of his bodily organs and not as a spirit. If he hasn't lost this consciousness before execution, he may retain it for a few moments afterwards, but this persistence of consciousness can only be of very short duration and must necessarily cease with the cessation of the organic life of the brain. The cessation of the human consciousness, however, by no means implies the complete separation of the perispirit from the body. On the contrary, in all cases in which death has resulted from violence, and not from a gradual extinction of the vital forces, the bonds which unite the body to the perispirit are more tenacious and the separation is effected more slowly.

3 - Temporarily - Confused state of the soul after death

163 - Does the soul, on quitting the body, find itself at once in possession of its self-consciousness?
- Not at once. It's for a time in a state of confusion which obscures all its perceptions.

164 - Do all spirits experience, in the same degree and for the same length of time, the confusion which follows the separation of the soul from the body?
- No, this depends entirely on their degree of elevation. He who has already accomplished a certain amount of purification recovers his consciousness almost immediately, because he had already freed himself from the thralldom of materiality during his bodily life, whereas the carnally minded man, he whose conscience is not clear, retains the impression of matter for a much longer time.

165 - Does knowledge of Spiritism exercise any influence on the duration of this state of confusion?
- It exercises a very considerable influence on that duration, because it enables the spirit to understand beforehand the new situation in which it's about to find itself, but the practice of rectitude during the earthly life, and a clear conscience, are the conditions which conduce most powerfully to shorten it.

> At the moment of death, everything appears confused. The soul takes some time to recover its self-consciousness, for it's as though stunned, and in a state similar to that of a man walking out of a deep sleep, and trying to understand his own situation. It gradually regains clearness of thought and the memory of the past in proportion to the weakening of the influence of the material envelope from which it has just freed itself, and the clearing away of the sort of fog that obscured its consciousness. The duration of the state of confusion that follows death varies greatly in different cases. It may be only of a few hours, and it may be of several months or even years. Those with whom it lasts the least are they who, during the earthly life, have identified themselves most closely with their future state, because they're soonest able to understand their pew situation.

This state of confusion assumes special aspects according to characterial peculiarities, and also according to different modes of death. In all cases of violent or sudden death, by suicide, by capital punishment, accident, apoplexy, etc., the spirit is surprised, astounded, and doesn't believe himself to be dead. He obstinately persists in asserting the contrary, and, nevertheless, he sees the body he has quitted as something apart from himself he knows that body to be his own, and he can't make out how it should be separated from him. He goes about among the persons with whom he is united by the ties of affection, speaks to them, and can't conceive why they don't hear him. This sort of illusion lasts until the entire separation of the perispirit from the earthly body, for its only when this is accomplished that the spirit begins to understand his situation, and becomes aware that he no longer forms part of the world of human beings.

Death having come upon him by surprise, the spirit is stunned by the suddenness of the change that has taken place in him. For him, death is still synonymous with destruction, annihilation and he thinks, sees, hears, it seems to him that he can't be dead. And this illusion is still further strengthened by his seeing himself with a body similar in form to the one he has quitted for he doesn't at first perceive its ethereal nature, but supposes it to be solid and compact like the other and when his attention has been called to this point, he is astonished at finding that it's not palpable. This phenomenon is analogous to that which occurs in the case of somnambulists, who, when thrown for the first time into the magnetic sleep, can't believe that they're not awake. Sleep, according to their idea of it, is synonymous with suspension of the perceptive faculties, and as they think freely, and see, they appear to themselves not to be as sleep.

Some spirits present this peculiarity; even in cases where death hasn't supervened unexpectedly but it more frequently occurs in the case of those who, although they may have been ill, had no expectation of death. The curious spectacle is then presented of a spirit attending his own funeral as though it were that of someone else, and speaking of it as of something which in no way concerns him, until the moment when at length he comprehends the true state of the case. In the mental confusion which follows death, there is nothing painful for him who has lived an upright life. He is calm, and his perceptions are those of a peaceful awaking out of sleep, but for him whose conscience is not clean, it's full of anxiety and anguish that become more and more poignant in proportion as he recovers consciousness. In cases of collective death, in which many persons have perished together in the same catastrophe, it has been observed that they don't always see one another immediately afterwards. In the state of confusion which follows death, each spirit goes his own way, or concerns himself only with those in whom he takes an interest.

Chapter 4 - Plurality of existences

1 - Reincarnation

166 - How can the soul that has not attained to perfection during the corporeal life complete the work of its purification?
- By undergoing the trial of a new existence.
- How does the soul accomplish this new existence? Is it through its transformation as a spirit?
- The soul, in purifying itself, undoubtedly undergoes a transformation, but, in order to effect this transformation, it needs the trial of corporeal life.
- The soul has then, many corporeal existences?
- Yes, we all have many such existences. Those who maintain the contrary wish to keep you in the same ignorance in which they're themselves.
- It'd seem to result from this statement that the soul, after having quitted one body, takes another one, in other words, that it reincarnates itself in a new body. Is it thus that this statement is to be understood?
- Evidently so.

167 - What is the aim of reincarnation?
- Expiation, progressive improvement of mankind. Without this aim, where would be its justice?

168 - Is the number of corporeal existences limited, or does a spirit go on reincarnating himself forever?
- In each new existence, a spirit takes a step forwards in the path of progress; when he has stripped himself of all his impurities, he has no further need of the trials of corporeal life.

169 - Is the number of incarnations the same for all spirits?
- No, he who advances quickly spares himself many trials. Nevertheless, these successive incarnations are always very numerous, for progress is almost infinite.

170 - What does the spirit become after its last incarnation?
- It enters upon the state of perfect happiness, as a purified spirit.

2 - Justice of reincarnation

171 - What foundation is there for the doctrine of reincarnation?
- The justice of God, and revelation, for, as we have already remarked, an affectionate father always leaves a door of repentance open for his erring children. Doesn't reason itself tell you that it would be unjust to inflict an eternal privation of happiness on those who have not had the opportunity of improving themselves? Are not all men God's children? It's only among selfish human beings that injustice, implacable hatred, and irremissibly punishments are to be found.

> All spirits tend towards perfection and are furnished by God with the means of advancement through the trials of corporeal life, but the divine justice compels them to accomplish, in new existences, that which they have not been able to do, or to complete, in a previous trial. It'd not be consistent with the justice or with the goodness of God to sentence to eternal suffering those who may have encountered obstacles to their improvement independent of their will, and resulting from the very nature of the conditions in which they found themselves placed. If the fate of mankind were irrevocably fixed after death, God would not have weighed the actions of all in the same scales and would not have treated them with impartiality.

The doctrine of reincarnation-that is to say, the doctrine which proclaims that men have many successive existence, is the only one which answers to the idea we form to ourselves of the justice of God in regard to those who are placed, by circumstances over which they have no control, in conditions unfavorable to their moral advancement, the only one which can explain the future, and furnish us with a sound basis for our hopes, because it offers us the means of redeeming our errors through new trials.

This doctrine is indicated by the teachings of reason, as well as by those of our spirit instructors. He who is conscious of his own inferiority derives a consoling hope from the doctrine of reincarnation. If he believes in the justice of God, he can't hope to be placed, at once and for all eternity, on a level with those who have made a better use of life than he has done, but the knowledge that this inferiority will not exclude him forever from the supreme felicity, and that he'll be able to conquer this felicity through new efforts, revives his courage and sustains his energy. Who doesn't regret, at the end of his career. That the experience he has acquired should have come too late to allow of his turning it to useful account? This tardily acquired experience will not be lost for him; he'll profit by it in a new corporeal life.

3 - Incarnation in different worlds

172 - Do we accomplish all our different corporeal existences upon this Earth?
- Not all of them, for those existences take place in many different worlds. The world in which you now are is neither the first nor the last of these, but is one of those that are the most material, and the furthest removed from perfection.

173 - Does the soul, at each new corporeal existence, pass from one world to another or can it accomplish several existences on the same globe?
- It may live many times on the same globe, if it be not sufficiently advanced to pass into a higher one.
- We may, then, re-appear several times upon the Earth?
- Certainly.

- Can we come back to it after having lived in other worlds?
- Assuredly you can; you may already have lived elsewhere as upon the Earth.

174 - Is it necessary to live again upon this Earth?
- No, but if you don't advance, you may go into a world no better than this one or even worse.

175 - Is there any advantage in coming back to inhabit this Earth?
- No special advantage, unless it's the fulfillment of a mission, in that case the spirit advances, whether incarnated in this Earth or elsewhere.
- Would it not be happier to remain as a spirit?
- No, no! For we should remain stationary and we want to advance towards God.

176 - Can spirits come to this world, for the first time, after having been incarnated in other worlds?
- Yes, just as you may go into other ones. All the worlds of the Universe are united by the bonds of solidarity; that which is not accomplished in one of them is accomplished in another.
- Some of those who are now upon this Earth are here, then, for the first time?
- Many of them are so and at various degrees of advancement.
- Is there any sign by which we can know the spirits who are here for the first time?
- Such knowledge would not be of the slightest use to you.

177 - In order to arrive at the perfection and the supreme felicity which are the final aim of mankind, is it necessary for a spirit to pass through all the worlds that exist in the Universe?
- No, for there are a great number of worlds of the same degree, in which a spirit would learn nothing new.
- How, then, are we to explain the plurality of his existences upon the same globe?
- He may find himself, each time he comes back, in very different situations, which afford him the opportunity of acquiring new experience.

178 - Can spirits live corporeally in a world relatively inferior to the one in which they have already lived?
- Yes, when they have to fulfill a mission in aid of progress and in that case they joyfully accept the tribulations of such an existence, because these will furnish them with the means of advancement.
- May this not occur also as an expiation and may not rebellious spirits be sent by God into worlds of lower degree?
- Spirits may remain stationary, but they never retrograde; those who are rebellious are punished by not advancing, and by having to recommence their misused existences under the conditions suited to their nature.
- Who're they that are compelled to recommence the same existence?
- They who fail in the fulfillment of their mission or in the endurance of the trial appointed to them.

179 - Have all the human beings who inhabit any given world arrived at the same degree of perfection?
- No, it's in the other worlds as upon the Earth, there are some who are more advanced, and others who are less so.

180 - In passing from this world into another one, does a spirit retain the intelligence which he possessed in this one?
- Undoubtedly he does, intelligence is never lost, but he may not have the same means of manifesting it for that depends both on his degree of advancement and on the quality of the body he'll take.

181 - Have the human beings who inhabit the other worlds bodies like ours?
- They undoubtedly have bodies, because it's necessary for the spirit to be clothed with matter in order to act upon matter, but this envelope is more or less material according to the degree of purity at which each spirit has arrived, and it's these gradations of purity that decide the different worlds through which we have to pass; for in our father's house are many mansions, and therefore many degrees among those mansions. There are some who know this, and possess the consciousness of this fact, while upon the Earth, and there are others who have no such intuition.

182 - Can we obtain any exact knowledge of the physical and moral state of the different worlds?
- We, spirits, can only reply according to the degree at which you have arrived; that's to say, that we must not reveal these things to all, because some are not in the state which would enable them to understand such revelations, and would be confused by them.

> In proportion as a spirit becomes purified, the body with which he clothes himself also approaches more nearly to the spirit-nature. The matter of which his body is composed is less dense he no longer crawls heavily on the surface of the ground; his bodily needs are less gross and the various living beings in those higher worlds are no longer obliged to destroy one another in order to feed themselves.

A spirit incarnated in those worlds enjoys a greater degree of freedom, and possesses, in regard to objects at a distance, orders of perception of a nature unknown to us; he sees with his eyes what we see only in thought. The purification of spirits determines the moral excellence of the corporeal beings in which they're incarnated. The animal passions become weaker, and selfishness gives place to the sentiment of fraternity. Thus, in worlds of higher degree than our Earth, wars are unknown, because no one thinks of doing harm to his fellow-beings, and there is consequently no motive for hatred or discord.

The foresight of their future, which is intuitive in the people of those worlds, and the sense of security resulting from a conscience void of remorse, cause them to look forward to death without fear, as being simply a process of transformation, the approach of which they perceive without the slightest uneasiness. The duration of a lifetime, in the different worlds, appears to be proportionate to the degree of moral and physical superiority of each world and this is perfectly consonant with reason. The less material is the body, the less subject is it to the vicissitudes which disorganize it, the purer the spirit, the less subject is it to the passions which undermine and destroy it. This correspondence between moral and physical conditions is a proof of the beneficence of providential law, even in worlds of low degree; as the duration of the suffering which is the characteristic of life in those worlds is thus rendered proportionally shorter.

183 - In passing from one world to another, does the spirit pass through a new infancy?
- Infancy is, in all worlds, a necessary transition, but it's not, in all of them, as stupid as it in yours.

184 - Has a spirit the choice of the new world which lie is to inhabit?
- Not always, but he can make his demand, and it may be granted, but only if he have deserved it, for the various worlds are only accessible to spirits according to the degree of their elevation.
- If a spirit makes no such demand, what is it that decides as to the world in which he'll be reincarnated?
- The degree of his elevation.

185 - Is the physical and moral state of the living beings of each globe always the same?
- No, worlds, like the beings that live in them, are subject to the law of progress. All have begun, like yours, by being in a state of inferiority, and the Earth will undergo a transformation similar to that which has been accomplished by the others. It'll become a terrestrial paradise, when the men by whom it's inhabited have become good.

> The races which now people the Earth will gradually disappear, and will be succeeded by others more and more perfect. Those transformed races will succeed the races now upon the Earth, as these have succeeded earlier races, still more gross than the present ones.

186 - Are there worlds in which the spirit, ceasing to inhabit a material body, has no longer any other envelope than the pen spirit?
- Yes, and this envelope itself becomes so etherealized that, for you, it's as though it didn't exist. This is the state of the fully purified spirits.
- It'd seem, from this statement, that there's no clearly marked line of demarcation between the state of the latter incarnations and that of pure spirit?
- No such demarcation exists. The difference between them growing gradually less and less, they blend into one another as the darkness of night melts into the dawn.

187 - Is the substance of the perispirit the same in all globes?
- No, it's more or less ethereal. On passing from one world to another, a spirit clothes himself with the matter proper to each, changing his envelope with the rapidity of lightning.

188 - Do the pure spirits inhabit special worlds, or are they in universal space without being attached to any particular globe?
- The pure spirits inhabit certain worlds, but they're not confined to them as men are confined to the Earth, they possess, in a higher degree than any others, the power of instantaneous locomotion, which is equivalent to ubiquity.

> Of all the globes constituting our planetary system, according to the spirits, the Earth is of those whose inhabitants are less advanced, physically and morally. Mars would still be lower and Jupiter far superior in every way. The Sun would not be a world inhabited by corporeal beings, but a place of meeting of higher spirits, who from there radiate their thought to other worlds, which they direct through lesser spirits, with which they communicate through the universal fluid. As a physical constitution, the Sun would be a focus of electricity. All suns, it would seem, would be in the same condition.
The volume and spacing of the Sun has no necessary relation to the degree of development of the worlds, for it seems that Venus is ahead of Earth and Saturn less than Jupiter. Many spirits who have animated people known on Earth have said that they're reincarnated in Jupiter, one of the worlds closest to perfection, and it's marvelous that in such an early globe are found men whom earthly opinion didn't consider so high. This, however, is not surprising, if we consider that certain spirits inhabiting that planet could have been sent to Earth, in fulfillment of a mission which, in our eyes, would not put them in the foreground; secondly, between their earthly existence and that of Jupiter, there could have been other intermediaries in which they had improved; thirdly, in that world, as in ours, there are different degrees of development, and between these degrees there may be the distance between us the savage of civilized man.
Thus the fact that they inhabit Jupiter doesn't follow that they're at the level of the most evolved beings, just as a person is not at the level of a scholar of the Institute for the simple reason of living in Paris. Longevity conditions are not everywhere the same on Earth and it's not possible to compare ages. One person, who died a few years ago when he was mentioned, said that he had incarnated, six months earlier, in a world whose name is unknown. Asked about her age in the world, she replied: - *I can't calculate, because we don't count the time like you, and our livelihood is not the same, we develop much faster, so much so that there are only six of your months I'm in it, and I can say that when I am intelligent, I'm 30 years of age on Earth.*
Many similar answers have been given by other spirits, and nothing is improbable. Don't we see on Earth so many animals get a normal development in a few months? Why could it not be the same with man in other spheres? Let us note, on the other hand, that the development attained by man on Earth, at the age of 30, may be no more than a kind of childhood compared to what he must attain. It's necessary to have a very short vision to consider ourselves the prototypes of creation, and it would be to lower the Deity, to believe that besides us, he could create nothing more.

4 - Progressive transmigrations

189 - Does the spirit enjoy the plenitude of his faculties from the beginning of his formation?
- No, for the spirit, like the man, has his infancy. Spirits at their origin have only an instinctive existence, and have scarcely any consciousness of themselves or of their acts; it's only little by little that their intelligence is developed.

190 - What is the state of the soul at its first incarnation?
- A state analogous to that of infancy, considered in its relation to a human life. Its intelligence is only beginning to unfold itself; it may be said to he essaying to live.

191 - Are the souls of our savage's souls in a state of infancy?
- Of relative infancy, but they're souls that have already accomplished a certain amount of development, for they have passions.
- Passions, then, are a sign of development?
- Of development, yes, but not of perfection. They're a sign of activity, and of the consciousness of the me, while, on the contrary, in the primitive state of the soul, intelligence and vitality exist only as germs.

> The life of a spirit in his totality goes through successive phases similar to those of a corporeal lifetime. He passes gradually from the embryonic state to that of infancy, and arrives, through a succession of periods, at the adult state, which is that of his perfection, with this difference, however, that it's not subject either to decrepitude or to decline, like the corporeal life that the life of a spirit, though it has had a beginning, will have no end, that he takes what appears from our point of view to be an immense length of time in passing from the state of spirit infancy to the attainment of his complete development, and that he accomplishes this progression, not in one and the same sphere, but by passing through different worlds. The life of a spirit is thus composed of a series of corporeal existences, each of which affords him an opportunity of progress, as each of his corporeal existences is composed of a series of days, in each of which he acquires a new increment of experience and of knowledge, but just as in a human lifetime there are days which bear no fruit, so in the life of a spirit there are corporeal existences which are barren of profitable result, because he has failed to make a right use of them.

192 - Is it possible for us, by leading a perfect life in our present existence, to overleap all the intervening steps of the ascent, and thus to arrive at the state of pure spirits, without passing through the intermediate degrees?
- No, for what a man imagines to be perfect is very far from perfection, there are qualities which are entirely unknown to him, and which he could not now be made to comprehend. He may be as perfect as it's possible for his terrestrial nature to be, but he'll still be very far from the true and absolute perfection. It's just as with the child, who, however precocious he may he, must necessarily pass through youth to reach adult life, or as the sick man, who must pass through convalescence before arriving at the complete recovery of his health. And besides, a spirit must advance in knowledge as well as in morality, if he has advanced in only one of these directions, he'll have to advance equally in the other, in order to reach the top of the ladder of perfection, but it's none the less certain that the more a man advances in his present life the shorter and the less painful will be the trials he'll have to undergo in his subsequent existences.
- Can a man, at least, insure for himself, after his present life, a future existence less full of bitterness than this one?
- Yes, undoubtedly, he can abridge the length and the difficulties of the road. It's only he who doesn't care to advance that remains always at the same point.

193 - Can a man in his new existences descend to a lower point than that which he has already reached?
- As regards his social position, yes, but not as regards his degree of progress as a spirit.

194 - Can the soul of a good man, in a new incarnation, animate the body of a scoundrel?
- No, because a spirit can't degenerate.
- Can the soul of a bad man become tile soul of a good man?
- Yes, if he have repented, and, in that case, his new incarnation in the reward of his efforts at amendment.

> The line of march of all spirits is always progressive, never retrograde. They raise themselves gradually in the hierarchy of existence they never descend from the rank at which they have once arrived. In the course of their different corporeal existences they may descend in rank as men, but not as spirits. Thus the soul of one who has been at the pinnacle of earthly power may, in a subsequent incarnation, animate the humblest day-laborer, and vice versa, for the elevation of ranks among men is often in the inverse ratio of that of the moral sentiments. Herod was a king, and Jesus, a carpenter.

195 - Might not the certainty of being able to improve oneself in a future existence lead some persons to persist in evil courses, through knowing that they'll always be able to amend at some later period?
- He, who could make such a calculation, would have no real belief in anything; and such a one would not be any more restrained by the idea of incurring eternal punishment, because his reason would reject that idea, which leads to every sort of unbelief. An imperfect spirit, it's true, might reason in that way during his corporeal life, but when he's freed from his material body, he thinks very differently; for he soon perceives that he has made a great mistake in his calculations, and this perception causes him to carry an opposite sentiment into his next incarnation. It's thus that progress is accomplished and it's thus also that you have upon the Earth some men who are farther advanced than others, because some possess experience that the others have not yet acquired, but that will be gradually acquired by them. It depends upon each spirit to hasten his own advancement or to retard it indefinitely.

> The man who has an unsatisfactory position desires to change it as soon as possible. He, who is convinced that the tribulations of the present life are the consequences of his own imperfections, will seek to insure for himself a new existence of a less painful character and this conviction will draw him away from the wrong road much more effectually than the threat of eternal flames, which he doesn't believe in.

196 - As spirits can only be ameliorated by undergoing the tribulations of corporeal existence, it would seem to follow that the material life is a sort of sieve or strainer, by which the beings of the spirit-world are obliged to pass in order to arrive at perfection?
- Yes, that is the case. They improve themselves under the trials of corporeal life by avoiding evil, and by practicing what is good. But it's only through many successive incarnations or purifications that they succeed, after a lapse of time which is longer or shorter according to the amount of effort put forth by them, ill reaching the goal towards which they tend.
- Is it the body that influences the spirit for its amelioration or is it the spirit that influences's the body?
- Your spirit is everything; your body is a garment that rots, and nothing more.

> A material image of the various degrees of purification of the soul is furnished by the juice of the grape. It contains the liquid called spirit or alcohol, but weakened by the presence of various foreign elements which change its nature, so that it's only brought to a state of absolute purity after several distillations, at each of which it is cleared of some portion of its impurity. The still represents the corporeal body into which the spirit enters for its purification the foreign elements represent the imperfections from which the perispirit is gradually freed, in proportion as the spirit approaches the state of relative perfection.

5 - Fate of children after death
197 - Is the spirit of a child who dies in infancy as advanced as that of an adult?
- He is sometimes much more so, for he may previously have lived longer and acquired more experience, especially if he be a spirit who has already made considerable progress.
- The spirit of a child may, then, be more advanced than that of his father?
- That is very frequently the case. Do you not often see examples of this superiority in your world?

198 - In the case of a child who has died in infancy, and without having been able to do evil, does his spirit belong to the higher degrees of the spirit-hierarchy?
- If he has done no evil, he has also done nothing good, and God doesn't exonerate him from the trials which he has to undergo. If such a spirit belongs to a high degree, it's not because he was a child, but because he had achieved that degree of advancement as the result of his previous existences.

199 - Why is it that life is so often cut short in childhood?
- The duration of the life of a child may be, for the spirit thus incarnated, the complement of an existence interrupted before its appointed term and his death is often a trial or an expiation for his parents.
- What becomes of the spirit of a child who dies in infancy?
- He recommences a new existence.

> If man had but a single existence, and if, after this existence, his future state were fixed for all eternity, by what standard of merit could eternal felicity be adjudged to that half of the human race which dies in childhood, and by what would it be exonerated from the conditions of progress, often so painful, imposed on the other half? Such an ordering could not be reconciled with the justice of God. Through the reincarnation of spirits the most absolute justice is equally meted out to all. The possibilities of the future are open to all, without exception, and without favor to any. Those who are the last to arrive have only themselves to blame for the delay. Each man must merit happiness by his own right action, as he has to bear the consequences of his own wrong-doing.

It's, moreover, most irrational to consider childhood as a normal state of innocence. Do we not see children endowed with the vilest instincts at an age at which even the most vicious surroundings can't have begun to exercise any influence upon them? Do we not see many who seem to bring with them at birth cunning, falseness, perfidy, and even the instincts of thieving and murder, and this in spite of the good examples by which they're surrounded? Human law absolves them from their misdeeds, because it regards them as having acted without discernment and its right in doing so, for they really act
Instinctively rather than from deliberate intent, but whence proceed the instinctual differences observable in children of the same age, brought up amidst the same conditions, and subjected to the same influences? Whence comes this precocious perversity, if not from the inferiority of the spirit himself, since education has had nothing to do with producing it? Those who are vicious are so because their spirit has made less progress and, that being the case, each will have to suffer the consequences of his inferiority, not on account of his wrong-doing as a child, but as the result of his evil courses in his former existences. And thus the action of providential law is the same for each, and the justice of God reaches equally to all.

7 - Sex in spirits
200 - Have spirits sex?
- Not as you understand sex; for sex, in that sense, depends on the corporeal organization. Love and sympathy exist among them, but founded on similarity of sentiments.

201 - Can a spirit, who has animated the body of a man, animate the body of a woman in a new existence, and vice versa?
- Yes, the same spirits animate men and women.

202 - Does a spirit, when existing in the spirit-world, prefer to be incarnated as a man or as a woman?
- That is a point in regard to which a spirit is indifferent, and which is always decided in view of the trials which he has to undergo in his new corporeal life.

> Spirits incarnate themselves as men or as women, because they're of no sex and, as it's necessary for them to develop themselves in every direction, both sexes, as well as every variety of social position. Furnish them with special trials and duties, and with the opportunity of acquiring experience. A spirit who had always incarnated itself as a man would be only known by men and vice versa.

7 - Relationship - Filiation
203 - Do parents transmit to their children a part of their soul, or do they only give them the animal life to which another soul afterwards adds the moral life?
- The animal life only is given by the parents, for the soul is indivisible. A stupid father may have clever children, and vice versa.

204 - As we have had many existences, do our relationships extend beyond our present existence?
- It can't be otherwise. The succession of their corporeal existences establishes among spirits a variety of relationships which date back from their former existences; and these relationships are often the cause of the sympathies or antipathies which you sometimes feel towards persons whom you seem to meet for the first time.

205 - The doctrine of reincarnation appears, to some minds, to destroy family ties, by carrying them back to periods anterior to our present existence.
- It extends those ties, but it doesn't destroy them, on the contrary, the conviction that the relationships of the present life are based upon anterior affections renders the ties between members of the same family less precarious. It makes the duties of fraternity even more imperative, because in your neighbor, or in your servant, may be incarnated some spirit who has formerly been united to you by the closest ties of consanguinity or of affection.
- It nevertheless diminishes the importance which many persons attach to their ancestry, since we may have had for our father a spirit who has belonged to a different race, or who has lived in a different social position.
- That is true, but this importance is usually founded on pride, for what most people honor in their ancestors is title, rank, and fortune. Many a one, who would blush to have an honest shoemaker for his grandfather, boasts of his descent from some debauchee of noble birth, but no matter what men may say or do, they'll not prevent things from going on according to the divine ordering, for God has not regulated the laws of nature to meet the demands of human vanity.

206 - If there be no filiations among the spirits successively incarnated as the descendants of the same family, does it follow that it's absurd to honor the memory of one's ancestors?
- Assuredly, not, for one ought to rejoice in belonging to a family in which elevated spirits have been incarnated. Although spirits don't proceed from one another, their affection for those who are related to them by family-ties is none the less real, for they're often led to incarnate themselves in such and such a family by pre-existing causes of sympathy and by the influence of attractions due to relationships contracted in anterior lives, but you may be very sure that the spirits of your ancestors are in no way gratified by the honors you pay to their memory from a sentiment of pride. Their merits, however great they may have been, can only add to your deserts by stimulating your efforts to follow the good examples they may have given you; and it's only through this emulation of their good qualities that your remembrance can become for them not only agreeable but useful also.

8 - Physical and moral likeness
207 - Parents often transmit physical resemblance to their children; do they also transmit to them moral resemblance?
- No, because they have different souls or spirits. The body proceeds from the body, but the spirit doesn't proceed from any other spirit. Between the descendants of the same race there is no other relationship than that of consanguinity.
- What is the cause of the moral resemblance that sometimes exists between parents and children?
- They're sympathetic spirits, attracted by the affinity of their inclinations.

208 - Are the spirits of the parents without influence upon the spirit of their child after its birth?
- They exercise, on the contrary, a very great influence upon it. As we have already told you, spirits are made to conduce to one another's progress. To the spirits of the parents is confided the mission of developing those of their children by the training they give to them; it's a task which is appointed to them and which they can't without guilt fail to fulfill.

209 - How is it that good and virtuous parents often give birth to children of perverse and evil nature? In other words, how is it that the good qualities of tile parents don't always attract to them, through sympathy, a good spirit to animate their child?
- A wicked spirit may ask to be allowed to have virtuous parents, in the hope that their counsels may help him to amend his ways; and God often confides such a one to the care of virtuous persons, in order that he may be benefited by their affection and care.

210 - Can parents, by their intentions and their prayers, attract a good spirit into the body of their child, instead of an inferior spirit?
- No, but they can improve the spirit of the child whom they have brought into the world, and is confided to them for that purpose. It's their duty to do this; but bad children are often sent as a trial for the improvement of the parents also.

211 - What is the cause of the similarity of character so often existing among brothers, especially between twins?
- The sympathy of two spirits who are attracted by the similarity of their sentiments, and who are happy to be together.

212 - In children whose bodies are joined together, and who have some of their organs in common, are there two spirits, that's to say, two souls?
- Yes, but their resemblance to one another often makes them seem to you as though there were but one.

213 - Since spirits incarnate themselves in twins from sympathy whence comes the aversion that is sometimes felt by twins for one another?
- It's not a rule that only sympathetic spirits are incarnated as twins. Bad spirits may have been brought into this relation by their desire to struggle against each other on the stage of corporeal life.

214 - In what way should we interpret the stories of children fighting in their mother's womb?
- As a figurative representation of their hatred to one another, which, to indicate its inveteracy, is made to date from before their birth. You rarely make sufficient allowance for the figurative and poetic element in certain statements.

215 - What is the cause of the distinctive character which we observe in each people?
- Spirits constitute different families, formed by the similarity of their tendencies, which are more or less purified according to their elevation. Each people are a great family formed by the assembling together of sympathetic spirits. The tendency of the members of these families to unite together is the source of the resemblance which constitutes the distinctive character of each people. Do you suppose that good and benevolent spirits would seek to incarnate themselves among a rude and brutal people? No, spirits sympathize with masses of men as they sympathize with individuals. They go to the region of the Earth with which they're most in harmony.

216 - Does a spirit, in his new existence, retain any traces of the moral character of his former existences?
- Yes, he may do so, but, as he improves, he changes. His social position, also, may be greatly changed in his successive lives. If, having been a master in one existence, he becomes a slave in another, his tastes will be altogether different, and it'd be difficult for you to recognize him. A spirit being the same in his various incarnations, there may be certain analogies between the manifestations of character in his successive lives, but these manifestations will, nevertheless, be modified by the change of conditions and habits incident to each of his new corporeal existences, until, through the ameliorations thus gradually effected, his character has been completely changed, he who was proud and cruel becoming humble and humane through repentance and effort.

217 - Does a man, in his different incarnations, retain any traces of the physical character of his preceding existences?
- The body is destroyed and the new one has no connection with the old one. Nevertheless, the spirit is reflected in the body, and although the body is only matter, yet, being modeled on the capacities of the spirit, the latter impresses upon it a certain character that is more particularly visible in the face, and especially in the eyes, which have been truly declared to be the mirror of the soul, that is to say, that the face reflects the soul more especially than does the rest of the body. And this is so true that a very ugly face may please when it forms part of the envelope of a good, wise, and humane spirit, while, on the other hand, very handsome faces may cause you no pleasurable emotion, or may even excite a movement of repulsion. It might seem, at first sight; that only well-made bodies could be the envelopes of good spirits and yet you see every day virtuous and superior men with deformed bodies. Without there being any very marked resemblance between them, the similarity of tastes and tendencies may, therefore, give what is commonly called a family-likeness to the corporeal bodies successively assumed by the same spirit.

> The body with which the soul is clothed in a new incarnation not having any necessary connection with the one which it has quitted, it would be absurd to infer a succession of existences from a resemblance which may be only fortuitous, but, nevertheless, the qualities of the spirit often modify the organs which serve for their manifestations, and impress upon the countenance, and even on the general manner, a distinctive stamp. It's thus that an expression of nobility and dignity may be found under the humblest exterior, while the fine clothes of the grandee are often unable to hide the baseness and ignominy of their wearer. Some persons, who have risen from the lowest position, adopt without effort the habits and manners of the higher ranks, and seem to have returned to their native element while others, notwithstanding their advantages of birth and education, always seem to be out of their proper place in refined society. How can these facts be explained unless as a reflex of what the spirit has been in his former existences?

9 - Innate ideas
218 - Does a spirit retain, when incarnated, any trace of the perceptions he has had, and the knowledge he had acquired, in its former existences?
- There remains with him a vague remembrance, which gives him what you call innate ideas.
- Then the theory of innate ideas is not a chimera?

- No, the knowledge acquired in each existence is not lost. A spirit, when freed from matter, always remembers what he has learned. He may, during incarnation, forget partially and for a time, but the latent intuition which he preserves of all that he has once known aids him in advancing. Were it not for this intuition of past acquisitions, he'd always have to begin his education over again. A spirit, at each new existence, takes his departure from the point at which he had arrived at the close of his preceding existence.

219 - If that be the case, there must be a very close connection between two successive existences?
- That connection is not always so close as you might suppose it to be; for the conditions of the two existences are often very different, and, in the interval between them, the spirit may have made considerable progress.

220 - What is the origin of the extraordinary faculties of those individuals who, without any preparatory study, appear to possess intuitively certain branches of knowledge, such as languages, arithmetic, etc.?
- The vague remembrance of their past, the result of progress previously made by the soul, but of which it has no present consciousness. From what else could those intuitions be derived? The body changes, but the spirit doesn't change, although he changes his garment.

221 - In changing our body, can we lose certain intellectual faculties, as, for instance, the taste for an art?
- Yes, if you have sullied that faculty, or made a bad use of it. Moreover, an intellectual faculty may be made to slumber during an entire existence, because the spirit wishes to exercise another faculty having no connection with the one which, in that case, remains latent, but will come again into play in a later existence.

222 - Is it to a retrospective remembrance that are due the instinctive sentiment of the existence of God, and the presentiment of a future life, which appear to be natural to man, even in the savage state?
- Yes, to a remembrance which man has preserved of what he knew as a spirit before he was incarnated, but pride often stifles this sentiment.
- Is it to this same remembrance that is due certain beliefs analogous to Spiritist Doctrine, which is found among every people?
- That Doctrine is as old as the world, and is, therefore, to be found everywhere, a ubiquity which proves it to be true. The incarnate spirit, preserving the intuition of his state as a spirit, possesses an instinctive consciousness of the invisible world, but this intuition is often perverted by prejudices, and debased by the admixture of superstitions resulting from ignorance.

Chapter 5 - Plurality of existences

223 - The dogma of reincarnation, it's sometimes objected, is not new, it's a resuscitation of the doctrine of Pythagoras. We have never said that Spiritist Doctrine was of modern invention, on the contrary, as the inter-communication of spirits with men occurs in virtue of natural law, it must have existed from the beginning of time, and we have always endeavored to prove that traces of this inter-communication are to be found in the earliest annals of antiquity. Pythagoras, as is well known, was not the author of the system of metempsychosis; he borrowed it from the philosophers of Hindustan and of Egypt, by whom it had been held from time immemorial.

The idea of the transmigration of soul was, therefore, in the earliest ages of the world, a general belief, equally admitted by the common people and by the most eminent thinkers of that period. By what road did this idea come to them? Did it reach them through revelation or through intuition? In regard to this point we know nothing; but it may be safely assumed that no idea could thus have traversed the successive ages of the worlds, and have commanded the assent of the highest intellects of the human race, if it had not been based on some solid ground of truth and reason.

The antiquity of this doctrine should therefore be considered as an argument in its favor, rather than as an objection. But, at the same time, it must not be forgotten that there is, between the antique doctrine of metempsychosis and the modern doctrine of reincarnation, this capital difference, that the spirits who inculcate the latter reject absolutely the idea that the human soul can pass into an animal, and vice versa. The spirits, therefore, who now proclaim the dogma of the plurality of our corporeal existences reassert a doctrine which had its birth in the earliest ages of the world, and which has maintained its footing to the present day in the convictions of many minds, but they present this dogma under an aspect which is more rational, more conformable with the natural law of progress, and more in harmony with the wisdom of the Creator, through the stripping away of accessories added to it by superstition.

A circumstance worthy of notice is the fact that it's not in this book alone that the doctrine in question has been inculcated by them of late years; for, even before its publication, numerous communications of a similar nature had already been obtained in various countries, and their number has since been greatly increased. It may here be asked, why it's that the statements of all spirits are not in unison in regard to this subject? To this question we shall recur elsewhere. Let us, for the present, examine the matter from another point of view, entirely irrespective of any assumed declarations of spirits in regard to it. Let us put the latter entirely aside for the moment; let us suppose them to have made no statement whatever in regard to it; let us even suppose the very existence of spirits not to have been surmised. Placing ourselves a moment on neutral ground, and admitting, as equally possible, the hypotheses of the plurality and of the unity of corporeal existences, let us see which of these hypotheses is most in harmony with the dictates of reason and with the requirements of our own interest.

There are persons who reject the idea of reincarnation simply because they don't like it, declaring that their present existence has been quite enough for them, and that they have no wish to recommence a similar one. Of such persons we would merely inquire whether they suppose that God has consulted their wishes and opinions in regulating the Universe? Either the law of reincarnation exists, or it doesn't exist. If it exists, no matter how displeasing it may be to them, they'll be compelled to submit to it; for God will not ask their permission to enforce it. It's as though a sick man should say: - *I have suffered enough today; I don't chose to suffer tomorrow.*

No matter what may be his unwillingness to suffer, he'll nevertheless be obliged to go on suffering, not only on the morrow, but day after day, until he is cured. In like manner, if it be their destiny to live again corporeally, they'll thus live again, they'll be reincarnated.

In vain will they rebel against necessity, like a child refusing to go to school, or a condemned criminal refusing to go to prison? They'll be compelled to submit to their fate, no matter how unwilling they may be to do so. Such objections are too puerile to deserve a more serious examination. Let us say, however, for the consolation of those who urge them, that the Spiritist Doctrine of reincarnation is by no means so terrible as they imagine it to be, that the conditions of their next existence depend on themselves and will be happy or unhappy according to the deeds done by them in this present life, and that they may even, by their action in this life, raise themselves above the danger of falling again into the mire of expiation. We take it for granted that those whom we are addressing believe in some sort of future after death, and that they don't look forward either to annihilation or to a drowning of their soul in a universal whole, without individuality, like so many drops of rain in the ocean; which comes to much the same thing.

But, if you believe in a future state of existence, you probably don't suppose that it'll be the same for all; for, in that case, where would be the utility of doing right? Why should men place any restraint upon themselves? Why should they not satisfy all their passions, all their desires, even at the expense of the rest of the world, if the result is to be the same in all cases? On the contrary, you no doubt believe that our future will be more or less happy according to what we have done in our present life; and you have doubtless the desire to be as happy as possible in the future to which you look forward, since it'll be for all eternity!

Do you, perchance, consider yourself to be one of the most excellent of those who have ever existed upon the Earth, and therefore entitled to supreme felicity? No. You admit, then, that there are some who are better than you, and who have consequently a right to a higher place, although you don't deserve to be classed among the reprobate. Place yourself, then, in thought, for a moment, in the medium condition which, according to your own admission, will properly be yours, and suppose that someone comes to you and says: - *You suffer; you're not so happy as you might be and meanwhile you see others in the enjoyment of unmixed happiness. Would you like to exchange your position for theirs?*

- *Undoubtedly, what must I do to bring about such a result?*
- *Something very simple, you have only to begin again what you have done badly, and try to do it better.*
- *Would you hesitate to accept the offer, even at the cost of several existences of trial?*

Let us take another illustration, still more prosaic. Suppose that someone comes to a man who, though not in a state of absolute destitution, has to endure many privations through the smallness of his means, and says to him: - *Here is an immense fortune, of which you may have the enjoyment, on condition that you work hard during one minute.*

The laziest of men, in response to such an offer, would say, without hesitation: - *I'm ready to work for one minute, for two minutes, for an hour, for a whole day if necessary! What is a day's labor in comparison with the certainty of ease and plenty for all the rest of my life?*

But what is the duration of a corporeal life in comparison with eternity? Less than a minute, less than a moment. We sometimes hear people bring forward the following lug argument: - *God, who is sovereignty good, can't impose upon man the hard necessity of recommencing a series of sorrows and tribulations.*

But would there be more kindness in condemning a man to perpetual suffering for a few moments of error than in giving him the means of repairing his faults? Two manufacturers had each a workman no might hope to become someday the partner of his employer. But it happened that both workmen made so very bad a use of their day that they merited dismissal. One of the manufacturers drove away his unfaithful workman, despite his supplications; and this workman, being unable to obtain any other employment, died of want. The other said to his workman: - *You have wasted a day; you owe me compensation for the loss you have thus caused me. You have done your work badly; you owe me reparation for it. I give you leave to begin it over again. Try to do well, and I'll keep you in my employ, and you may still aspire to the superior position which I had promised you.*

Need we ask which of the manufacturers, as shown himself to be the most humane? And would God, who is clemency itself, be more inexorable than a just and compassionate man? The idea that our fate is decided forever by a few years of trial, and notwithstanding the fact that it was not in our power to attain to perfection while we remained upon the Earth, fills the mind with anguish; while the contrary idea is eminently consoling, for it leaves us hope. Thus, without pronouncing for or against the plurality of existences, without admitting either hypothesis in preference to the other, we assert that, if the matter were left to our own choice, there is no one who would prefer incurring a sentence against which there should be no appeal.

A philosopher has said that "if God didn't exist, it would be necessary to invent him for the happiness of the human race"; the same might be said in regard to the plurality of existences, but, as we have already remarked, God doesn't ask our permission in the establishment of providential ordering; he doesn't consult our preferences in the matter. Either the law of reincarnation exists, or it doesn't exist; let us see on which side is the balance of probabilities, considering the matter from another point of view, but still leaving out of sight all idea of any statements that have been made by spirits in regard to it, and examining the question merely as matter of philosophic inquiry.

If the law of reincarnation don't exist, we can have but one corporeal existence and if our present corporeal life be our only one, the soul of each individual must have been created at the same time as his body, unless, indeed, we assume the anteriority of the soul, in which case we should have to inquire what was the state of the soul before its union with the body, and whether this state didn't constitute an existence of some kind or other. There's no middle ground. Either the soul existed before its union with the body, or it didn't. If it existed, what was its condition? Was it possessed of self-consciousness? If not, its state must have been nearly equivalent to non-existence. If possessed of individuality, it must have been either progressive or stationary; in either case, what was its degree of advancement on uniting itself to the body? If, on the contrary, it be assumed, according to the general belief, that the soul is born into existence at the same time as the body-or that, previous to the birth of the body, it possesses only negative faculties-we have to propose the following questions:

1 - Why do souls manifest so great a diversity of aptitudes independently of the ideas acquired by education?

2 - Whence comes the extra-normal aptitude for certain arts and sciences displayed by many children while still very young, although others remain in a state of inferiority, or of mediocrity, all their life?

3 - Whence do some individuals derive the innate or intuitive ideas that are lacking in others?

4 - Whence do some children derive the precocious instincts of vice or of virtue, the innate sentiments of dignity or of baseness, which often contrast so strikingly with the situation into which they're born?

5 - Why is it that some men, independently of education, are more advanced than others?

6 - Why is it that among the races which people the globe some are savage and others civilized? If you took a Hottentots baby from its mother's breast, and brought it up in our most renowned schools, could you succeed in making of it a Laplace or a Newton? What is the philosophy or the theosophy that can solve these problems? Either the souls of men are equal at their birth, or they're unequal. If they're equal, why these inequalities of aptitude? Will it be said that these inequalities depend on the corporeal organization of each child? But such a doctrine would be the most monstrous and the most immoral of hypotheses; for, in that case, man would be a mere machine, the sport of matter; he would not be responsible for his actions, but would have the right to throw all the blame of his wrongdoing on the imperfections of his physical frame.

If, on the other hand, souls are created unequal, God must have created them so; but, in that case, why is this innate superiority accorded to some and denied to others? And would such partiality be consistent with the justice of God, and the equal love he bears to all His creatures? Admit, on the contrary, a succession of existences, and everything is explained. Men bring with them, at their birth in flesh, the amount of intuition they have previously acquired. They're more or less advanced, according to the number of existences they have previously accomplished, according as they're nearer to or farther from the common starting-point; exactly as, in a company made up of individuals of different ages, each will possess a degree of development proportionate to the number of years he has already lived; the succession of years being, to the life of the body, what the succession of existences is to the life of the soul.

Bring together in the same place, at the same time, a thousand individuals of all ages, from the new-born babe to the patriarch of eighty. Suppose that a veil is thrown over their past, and that you, in your ignorance of that past, imagine them all to have been born on the same day. You'd naturally wonder how it's that some are winkled and others little; that some are wrinkled and others fresh; that some are learned and others ignorant; but if the cloud which hid their past were dispersed, and you discovered that some had lived longer than others, all these differences would be explained. God, in his justice, could not create souls more or less perfect. But granting the plurality of our corporeal existences, there is nothing in the differences of quality that we see around us in any way inconsistent with the most rigorous equity; for what we see around us is then perceived to have its roots, not in the present, but in the past.

Is this argument based on any pre-conceived system or gratuitous supposition? No. We start from a fact that is patent and incontestable, the inequality of natural aptitudes and of intellectual and moral development; and we find this fact to be inexplicable by any of the theories in vogue, while the explanation of this fact afforded by another theory is at once simple, natural, and rational. Is it reasonable to prefer a theory which doesn't explain this fact to one which does? In regard to the sixth question, it'll doubtless be replied that the Hottentots is of an inferior race; in which case we beg to inquire whether a Hottentots is or is not a man? If he be not a man, why try to make him a Christian? If he be a man, why has God refused to him and to his race the privileges accorded to the Caucasian race?

Spiritist philosophy is too broad to admit the existence of different species of men; it recognizes only men whose spiritual part is more or less backward, but who are all capable of the same progress. Is not this view of the human race more conformable with the justice of God? We have considering the soul in regard to its past and its present; if we consider it in regard to the future; we are met by difficulties which the theories in vogue are equally unable to explain:

1 - If our future destiny is to be decided solely by our present existence, what will be in the future the respective positions of the savage and of the civilized man? Will they be on the same level, or will there be a difference in the sum of their eternal felicity?

2 - Will the man who has labored diligently all his life to advance his moral and intellectual improvement be placed in the same rank with the man who, not through his own fault, but because he has had neither the time nor the opportunity for advancing, has remained at a lower point of moral and intellectual improvement?

3 - Can the man who has done wrong because the means of enlightenment have been denied to him be justly punished for wrong-doing which has not been the result of his own choice?

4 - We endeavor to enlighten, moralize, and civilize mankind; but, for one whom we are able to enlighten, there are millions who die every year without the light having reached them. What is to be the fate of these millions? Are they to be treated as reprobates? And, if they're not to be so treated, how have they deserved to be placed in the same category with those who have become enlightened and moralized?

5 - What is to be the fate of children who die before they have been able to do either good or evil? If they're to be received among the supremely happy, why should this favor be granted to them without their having done anything to deserve it? And in virtue of what privilege are they exempted from undergoing the tribulations of the earthly life? Which of the doctrines hitherto propounded can solve these problems? But, if we admit the fact of our consecutive existences all these problems are solved in conformity with the divine justice. What we are not able to do in one existence we do in another. None are exempted from the action of the law of progress; everyone is rewarded progressively, according to his deserts, but no one is excluded from the eventual attainment of the highest felicity, no matter what may be the obstacles he has to encounter on the road.

The questions growing out of the subject we are considering might be multiplied indefinitely, for the psychologic and moral problems which can only find their solution in the plurality of existences are innumerable. In the present considerations we have restricted our inquiry to those which are most general in their nature. But, it may still be urged by some objectors, "whatever may be the arguments in its favor, the doctrine of reincarnation is not admitted by the Church; its acceptance would therefore be the overthrow of religion."

It's not our intention to treat of the question, in this place, under the special aspect suggested by the foregoing objection; it's sufficient for our present purpose to have shown the eminently moral and rational character of the doctrine we are considering, but it may be confidently asserted, that a doctrine which is both moral and rational can't be antagonistic to a religion which proclaims the divine being to be the most perfect goodness and the highest reason. What, we may ask in our turn, would have become of the Church if, in opposition to the convictions of mankind and the testimony of science, it had persisted in rejecting overwhelming evidence, and had cast out from its bosom all who didn't believe in the movement of the sun or in the six days of creation?

What would be the credit or authority possessed among enlightened nations by a religious system that should inculcate manifests errors as articles of belief? Whenever any matter of evidence has been established, the Church has wisely sided with the evidence. If it be proved that the facts of human life are irreconcilable, on ally other supposition, with a belief in the justice of God, if various points of the Christian dogma can only be explained with the aid of this doctrine, the Church will be compelled to admit its truth, and to acknowledge that the apparent antagonism between them is only apparent.

We shall show, elsewhere, that religion has no more to fear from the acceptance of this doctrine than from the discovery of the motion of the Earth and of the periods of geologic formation, which, at first sight, appear to contradict the statements of the *Bible*. Moreover, the principle of reincarnation is implied in many passages of holy writ, and is explicitly formulated in the Gospels. When they came down from the mountain, Jesus gave this commandment, and said to them: - *Speak to no one of what you have just seen, until the Son of Man shall have been resuscitated from among the dead.*

His disciples thereupon began to question him, and inquired: - *Why, then, do the Scribes say that Elias must first come?*

But Jesus replied to them: - *It's true that Elias must come, and that he'll re-establish all things.*

But I declare to you that Elias has already come, and they didn't know him, but have made him suffer as they listed. It's thus that they'll put to death the Son of Man.

Then his disciples understood that he spoke to them of John the Baptist. Since John the Baptist is declared by Christ to have been Elias, it follows that the spirit or soul of Elias must have been reincarnated in the body of John the Baptist. But whatever may be our opinion in regard to reincarnation whether we accept it or whether we reject it, it's certain that we shall have to undergo it, if it really exists, notwithstanding any belief of ours to the contrary. The point which we here desire to establish is this, that the teaching of the spirits who proclaim it's eminently Christian, that it's founded on the doctrines of the immortality of the soul, of future rewards and punishments, of the justice of God, of human free-will, and the moral code of Christ, and that, therefore, it can't be anti-religious.

We have argued the matter, as we remarked above, without reference to statements made by spirits, such statements being, for many minds, without authority. If we, and so many others, have adopted the hypothesis of the plurality of existences, we have done so not merely because it has been proclaimed by spirits, but because it has appeared to us to be eminently rational, and because it solves problems that are insoluble by the opposite hypothesis. Had it been suggested to us by a mere mortal, we should, therefore, have adopted it with equal confidence, renouncing, with equal promptitude, our preconceived opinions on the subject; for when an opinion has been shown to be erroneous, even self-love has more to lose than to gain by persisting in holding it. In like manner, we should have rejected the doctrine of reincarnation, even though proclaimed by spirits, if it had appeared to us to be contrary to reason, as, indeed, we have rejected many other ideas which spirits have sought to inculcate, for we know, by experience, that we can no more give a blind acceptance to ideas put forth by spirits than we can to those put forth by men.

The principal merit of the doctrine of reincarnation is, then, to our minds, that it's supremely rational. But it has also in its favor the confirmation of facts-facts positive and, so to say, material, which are apparent to all who study the question with patience and perseverance, and in presence of which all doubt as to the reality of the law in question is impossible. When the appreciation of these facts shall have become popularized, like those which have revealed to us the formation and rotation of the Earth, they who now oppose this doctrine will be compelled to renounce their opposition. To sum up: - *We assert the doctrine of the plurality of existences is the only one which explains what, without this doctrine, is inexplicable; that it's at once eminently consolatory and strictly conformable with the most rigorous justice; and that it's the anchor of safety which God in his mercy has provided for mankind.*

The words of Jesus himself are explicit as to the truth of this last assertion, for we read in the 3rd chapter of the Gospel according to St John that Jesus, replying to Nicodemus, thus expressed himself: - *Verily, verily, I tell thee that, if a man be not born again, he can't see the kingdom of God.*

And when Nicodemus inquires: - *How can a man be born when he is old? Can he enter again into his mother's womb and be born a second time?*

Jesus replies: - *Except a man be born of water and of the spirit, he can't enter the kingdom of God. What is born of the flesh is flesh and what is born of the spirit is spirit. Be not amazed at what I have told thee, you must be born again.*

> Reincarnation is now proven, through cases of memories of previous lives in children, of hypnotic searches of memory regression, of mediumistic revival notices with signs and conditions subsequently verified. Although the Official Sciences still reluctant to accept these tests, the Spiritist Science considers them valid and hopes for its official acceptance soon.

Chapter 6 - Spirit - Life

1 - Wandering spirits

223 - Is the soul reincarnated immediately after its separation from the body?
- Sometimes immediately, but more often after intervals of longer or shorter duration. In the higher worlds, reincarnation is almost always immediate. Corporeal matter in those worlds being less gross than in the worlds of lower advancement, a spirit, while incarnated in them, retains the use of nearly all his spirit faculties, his normal condition being that of your somnambulists in their lucid state.

224 - What becomes of the soul in the intervals between successive incarnations?
- It becomes an errant or wandering spirit, aspiring after a new destiny. Its state is one of waiting and expectancy.
- How long may these intervals last?
- From a few hours to thousands of ages. Strictly speaking, there are no fixed limits to the period of erraticity or wandering, which may be prolonged for a very considerable time, but which, however, is never perpetual. A spirit is always enabled, sooner or later, to commence a new existence which serves to effect the purification of its preceding existences.
- Does the duration of the state of erraticity depend on the will of the spirit or may it be imposed as an expiation?
- It's a consequence of the spirit's free-will. Spirits act with full discernment, but, in some cases, the prolongation of this state is a punishment inflicted by God, while in others, it has been granted to them at their own request, to enable them to pursue studies which they can prosecute more effectually in the disincarnate state.

225 - Is erraticity necessarily a sign of inferiority on the part of spirits?
- No, for there are errant spirits of every degree. Incarnation is a transitional state, as we have already told you. In their normal state, spirits are disengaged from matter.

226 - Would it be correct to say that all spirits who aren't incarnated are errant?
- Yes, as regards those who are to be reincarnated, but the pure spirits who have attained to perfection are not errant, their state is definitive.

> In virtue of their special qualities, spirits are of different orders or degrees of advancement, through which they pass successively as they become purified. As regards their state, they may be, incarnated, that is to say, united to a material body. Errant or wandering, that is to say disengaged from the material body and waiting a new incarnation for purposes of improvement, and pure pints, that is to say, perfected, and having no further need of incarnation.

227 - In what way do wandering spirits obtain instruction, it can hardly be in the same way as men?
- They study their past, and seek out the means of raising them-selves to a higher degree. Possessed of vision, they observe all that is going on in the regions through which they pass. They listen to the discourse of enlightened men and to the counsels of spirits more advanced than themselves and they thus acquire new ideas.

228 - Do spirits retain any human passion?
- Elevated spirits, on quitting their bodily envelope, leave behind them the evil passions of humanity, and retain only the love of goodness. But inferior spirits retain their earthly imperfections. Were it not for this retention, they'd be of the highest order.

229. How is it that spirits, on quitting the Earth, don't leave behind them all their evil passions, since they're then able to perceive the disastrous consequences of those passions?
- You have among you persons who are, for instance, excessively jealous; do you imagine that they lose this defect at once on quitting your world? There remains with spirits, after their departure from the earthly life, and especially with those who have had strongly marked passions, a sort of atmosphere by which they're enveloped, and which keeps up all their former evil qualities; for spirits are not entirely freed from the influence of materiality. It's only occasionally that they obtain glimpses of the truth, showing them, as it were, the true part which they ought to follow.

230 - Do spirits progress in the state of erraticity?
- They may make a great advance in that state, in proportion to their efforts and desires after improvement, but it's in the corporeal life that they put in practice the new ideas they have thus acquired.

231 - Are wandering spirits happy or unhappy?
- More or less so according to their deserts. They suffer from the passions of which they have retained the principle, or they're happy in proportion as they're more or less dematerialized. In the state of erraticity, a spirit perceives what he needs in order to become happier, and he is thus stimulated to seek out the means of attaining what he lacks. But he's not always permitted to reincarnate himself when he desires to do so and the prolongation of erraticity then becomes a punishment.

232 - Can spirits in the state of erraticity enter all the other worlds?
- That depends on their degree of advancement. When a spirit has quitted the body, he is not necessarily disengaged entirely from matter, and he still belongs to the world in which he has lived, or to a world of the same degree, unless he has raised himself during his earthly life to a world of higher degree; and this progressive elevation should be the

constant aim of every spirit, for without it lie would never attain to perfection. A spirit, however, may enter worlds of higher degree; but, in that case, he finds himself to be a stranger in them. He can only obtain, as it were, a glimpse of them, but such glimpses often serve to quicken his desire to improve and to advance, that he may become worthy of the felicity which is enjoyed in them, and may thus be enabled to inhabit them in course of time.

233 - Do spirits who are already purified ever come into worlds of lower degree?
- They come into them very frequently in order to help them forward. Unless they did so, those worlds would be left to them-selves, without guides to direct them.

2 - Transitional worlds

234 - Are there, as has been stated, worlds which serve as stations and resting-places for errant spirits?
- Yes, there are worlds which are specially adapted for the reception of wandering beings, worlds which they may temporally inhabit; a sort of camping-ground in which they may bivouac for a time, and repose after a too lengthened erraticity-a state which is always somewhat wearisome. Those worlds constitute intermediary stations between the worlds of other orders, and are graduated according to the nature of the spirits who are to come into them, and who'll find in them the conditions of a rest more or less enjoyable.
- Can the spirits who occupy these worlds quit them at pleasure?
- Yes, they can leave them for any other region to which they may have to go. They're like birds of passage alighting on an island in order to rest and recover strength for reaching their destination.

235 - Do spirits progress during their sojourns in the transitional worlds?
- Certainly, those who thus come together do so with a view to their instruction, and in order more readily to obtain permission to enter a higher region, and thus to advance their progress towards the perfection which is their aim.

236 - Are the transitional worlds of a special nature, and destined to be forever the sojourn of wandering spirits.
- No, their position in the hierarchy of worlds is only temporary.
- Are they, at the same time, inhabited by corporeal beings?
- No, their surface is sterile. Those who inhabit them have no corporeal wants.
- Is this sterility permanent, and does it result from anything special in their nature?
- No, their sterility is only transitional.
- Such worlds are, then, void of everything like the beauties of nature?
- The inexhaustible richness of creation is manifested by beauties of immensity that are no less admirable than the terrestrial harmonies which you call the beauties of nature.
- Since the state of those worlds is only transitory, will the state of our Earth, at some future time, be of that character?
- Such has already been its state.
- At what epoch?
- During its formation.

> Nothing in nature is useless everything has its purpose, its destination. There's no void every portion of immensity is inhabited. Life is everywhere. Thus, during the long series of ages which preceded man's appearance upon the Earth, during the vast periods of transition attested by the superposition of the geologic strata, before even the curliest formation of organized beings, upon that formless mass, in that arid chaos in which the elements existed in a state of fusion, there was no absence of life. Beings who had neither human wants nor human sensations found therein a welcome refuge. The will of God had ordained that the Earth, even in that embryonic state, should be useful. Who, then, would Venture to say that, of the innumerable orbs which circulate in immensity, one only, and one of the smallest of them all, lost in the crowd, has the exclusive privilege of being inhabited?

What, in that case, would be the use of the others? Would God have created them merely to regale our eyes? Such a supposition, of which the absurdity is incompatible with the wisdom that appears in all his works, becomes still more evidently inadmissible when we reflect on the myriads of heavenly bodies which we are unable to perceive. On the other hand, no one can deny the grandeur and sublimity of the idea that worlds in course of formation, and which are still unfitted for the habitation of material life, are, nevertheless, peopled with living beings appropriate to its condition-an idea which may possibly contain the solution of more than one problem as yet obscure.

3 - Perceptions, sensations and suffering of spirits

237 - Does the soul, when it has returned into the world of spirits, still possess the perceptions it possessed in the earthly life?
- Yes, and others which it didn't possess in that life, because its body acted as a veil which obscured them. Intelligence is an attribute of spirit, but it's manifested more freely when not hindered by the trammels of flesh.

238 - Are the perceptions and knowledge of in a word, do they know everything?
- The nearer they approach to perfection, the more they know spirits of the higher orders possess a wide range of knowledge; those of the lower orders are more or less ignorant in regard to everything.

239 - Do spirits comprehend tile first principle of things?
- That depends on their degree of elevation and of purity inferior spirits know no more than men.

240 - Do spirits perceive duration as we do?

- No, and this is why you don't always understand us when you seek to fix dates and epochs.

> Spirits live out of time, as we understand it, the duration, for them, practically doesn't exist, and the centuries, so long for us, are in their eyes only moments that disappear in eternity, just as inequalities of the soil fade and disappear, to the one that rises in space.

241 - Do spirits take a truer and more precise view of present than we do?
- Their view, in comparison with yours, is pretty much what eyesight is in comparison with blindness. They see what you don't see; they judge, therefore, otherwise than you do, but we must remind you that this depends on their degree of elevation.

242 - How do spirits acquire the knowledge of the past, and is this knowledge without limits for them?
- The past, when we turn our attention to it, is perceived by us as though it were present, exactly as is the case with you, when you call to mind something which may have struck you in the course of your present exile, with this difference, however, that, as out view is no longer obscured by the material veil which covers your intelligence, we remember things that are at present effaced from your memory, but spirits don't know everything, for example, their creation.

243 - Do spirits foresee the future?
- That, again, depends on their degree of advancement. Very often, they foresee it only partially, but, even when they foresee it more clearly, they're not always permitted to reveal it. When they foresee it, it appears to them to be present. A spirit sees the future more clearly in proportion as he approaches God. After death, the soul sees and embraces at a glance all its past emigrations, but it can't see what God has in store for it. This foreknowledge is only possessed by the soul that has attained to entire union with God, after a long succession of existences.
- Do spirits, arrived at absolute perfection; possess the complete knowledge of the future?
- Complete is not the word, for God alone is the sovereign master, and none can attain to equality with him.

244 - Do spirits see God?
- Only spirits of the highest order see and understand him, spirits of lower order feel and divine him.
- When a spirit of lower degree says that such and such a thing is permitted to him or forbidden by God, how does he know that such ordering is really by him?
- He doesn't see God, but he feels his sovereignty; and when anything is not to be done or said, he feels a sort of intuition, an invisible warning, which commands him to abstain. Are not you yourselves sometimes conscious of a secret impression, enjoining on you to do or not to do, as the case may be? It's the same thing with us, but in a higher degree, for you can easily understand that, the essence of spirits being suppler than yours, they're better able to receive the divine monitions.
- Are the divine commands transmitted to each spirit directly by God, or through the intermediary of other spirits?
- Those commands don't come direct from God; in order to communicate directly with God, a spirit must have made himself worthy of such communication. God transmits his orders through spirits of higher degrees of wisdom and purity.

245 - Is spirit-sight circumscribed, as is tile sight of corporeal beings?
- No, it resides in them.

246 - Do spirits require light in order to see?
- They sec of themselves and have no need of any exterior light. There is, for them, no other darkness than those in which they may be made to find themselves as expiation.

247 - Do spirits need to travel in order to see two different points? Can they, for instance, see the two hemispheres of the globe at the same time?
- As spirits transport themselves from point to point with the rapidity of thought, they may be said to see everywhere at the same time. A spirit's thought may radiate at the same moment on many different points, but this faculty depends on his purity. The more impure the spirit, the narrower is his range of sight. It's only the higher spirits who can take in a whole at a single glance.

> The faculty of vision, among spirits, is a property inherent in their nature, and which resides in their whole being, as light resides in every part of a luminous body. It's a sort of universal lucidity, which extends, to everything, which embraces at once time, space, and things, and in relation to which, darkness or material obstacles has no existence, and a moment's reflection shows us that this must necessarily be the case. In the human being, sight being produced by the play of an organ acted upon by light, it follows that, without light, man finds himself in darkness but the faculty of vision being an attribute of the spirit himself, independently of any exterior agent, spirit-sight is independent of light.

248 - Do spirits see things as distinctly as we do?
- More distinctly, for their sight penetrates what yours can't penetrate, nothing obscures it.

249 - Do spirits perceive sounds?
- Yes, they perceive sounds that your obtuse senses can't perceive
- Does the faculty of hearing reside in tile whole of a spirit's being, like the faculty of sight?

- All the perceptive faculties of a spirit are attributes of his nature, and form part of his being. When he is clothed with a material body, his perceptions reach him only through the channel of his bodily organs, but the perceptions of a spirit, when restored to the state of freedom, are no longer localized.

250 - The perceptive faculties being attributes of a spirit's nature, is it possible for him to withdraw himself from their action?
- A spirit only sees and hears what he chooses to see and hear. This statement, however, is to he taken in a general sense, and mainly as regards spirits of the higher orders, for imperfect spirits are compelled to see and hear, and often against their will, what, ever may be useful for their amelioration.

251 - Are spirits affected by music?
- Do you mean the music of your Earth? What is it in comparison with the music of the celestial spheres, of that harmony of which nothing in your Earth can give you any idea? The one is to the other as is the howl of the savage to the loveliest melody. Spirits of low degree, however, may take pleasure in hearing your music, because they're not yet able to appreciate anything more sublime. Music has inexhaustible charms for spirits, owing to the great development of their sensitive qualities; I mean, celestial music, than which the spiritual imagination can conceive of nothing more exquisitely sweet and beautiful.

252 - Are spirits sensible of the beauties of nature?
- The beauties of nature are so different in the different globes, that spirits far from know them all. They're sensible of them in proportion to their aptitude for appreciating and comprehending them, but, for spirits of a high degree of advancement, there are beauties of general harmony in which beauties of detail are, so to say, lost sight of.

253 - Do spirits experience our physical needs and sufferings?
- They know them, because they have undergone them, but they don't, like you, experience them materially, they're spirits.

254 - Do spirits experience fatigue and the need of rest?
- They can't feel fatigue as you understand it, and consequently they have no need of your corporeal rest, because they have no organs whose strength requires to be restored, but a spirit may be said to take rest, inasmuch as he's not constantly in a state of activity. He doesn't act materially; his action is altogether intellectual, and his resting is altogether moral; that is to say, that there are moments when his thought becomes less active, and is no longer directed to any special object, and this constitutes for him a state which is really one of repose, but a kind of repose which can't be likened to that of the body. The sort of fatigue which may be felt by spirits is proportionate to their inferiority, for, the higher their degree of elevation; the less is their need of rest.

255 - When a spirit says that he suffers, what is the nature of the suffering he feels?
- Mental anguish, which causes him tortures far more painful than any physical sufferings.

256 - How is it, then, that spirits sometimes complain of suffer mg from cold or heat?
- Such sensations on their part are caused by the remembrance of sufferings endured by them in the earthly life, and are sometimes as painful as though they were real, but complaints of that nature are often only figures by which, for lack of any better means of description, they endeavor to express the situation in which they find themselves. When they remember their earthly body, they experience the same sort of impression which makes you feel for a few moments, when you have taken off a cloak, as though you had it still upon your shoulders.

4 - Theoretic explanation of the nature of sensation in spirits
257 - The body is the instrument of pain, of which, if not the primary cause, it's, at least, the immediate cause. The soul possesses the faculty of perceiving the pain thus caused, the perception of pain is, therefore, the effect of this action of the soul. The remembrance of pain retained by a spirit may be very painful; hut can't exercise any physical action. The tissues of the soul can't be disorganized either by cold or heat; the soul can neither freeze nor burn. But do we not constantly see that the remembrance or the apprehension of physical pain may produce all the effect of reality, and may even occasion death? We know that recently-amputated patients often complain of felling pain in the limb they have lost, yet it's evident that the amputated limb can't really be the seat, nor even the point of departure, of the pain feel, which is due solely to the action of the brain, that has retained and reproduces the impression of the pain formerly experienced by them.

It may therefore be inferred that the suffering felt by spirits after death is of a similar nature. A careful study of the perispirit, which plays so important a part in all spirit phenomena, the indications afforded by apparitions, whether vaporous or tangible, the state of the spirit at the moment of death, the striking pictures presented by the victims of suicide and of capital punishment, by the spirits of those who have been absorbed in carnal enjoyments, and a great variety of other facts, hayed thrown new light on this question, and have given rise to the explanations of which we offer the following summary. The perispirit is the link which unites the spirit with the material body. It's drawn from the surrounding atmosphere, from the universal fluid; it participates at once in the nature of electricity of the magnetic fluid, and of inert matter.

It may be said to he the quintessence of matter; it's the principle of organic life, but it's not that of intellectual life, the principle of which is in the spirit. It's also the agent of all the sensations of the outer life. Those sensations are localized in the earthly body by the organs which serve as their channels. When the body is destroyed, those sensations become general. This explains why a spirit never says that he suffers in his head or in his feet, but we must take care not to confound the sensations of the perispirit, rendered independent by the death of the body, with the sensations experienced through the body; for the latter can only be understood as offering a means of comparison with the former, but not as being analogous to them.

When freed from the body, a spirit may suffer, but this suffering is not the suffering of the body. And yet it's not a suffering exclusively moral, like remorse, for example, for he complains of feeling cold or hot, although he suffers no more in summer than in winter, and we have seen spirits pass through flames without feeling any painful effect therefore, temperature making no impression upon them. The pain which they feel is therefore not a physical pain in the proper sense of that term; it's a vague feeling perceived in himself by a spirit and which he himself is not always able to account for, precisely because his pain is not localized, and is not produced by any exterior agents: it's a remembrance rather than a reality, but a remembrance as painful as though it were a reality.

Nevertheless, spirit-suffering is sometimes more than a remembrance, as we shall see. Observation has shown us that the perispirit, at death, disengages itself more or less slowly from the body. During the first few moments which follow dissolution, a spirit doesn't clearly understand his own situation. He doesn't think himself dead, for he feels himself living. He sees his body beside him, he knows that it's his, and he doesn't understand that he is separated from it; and this state of indecision continues as long as there remains the slightest connection between the body and the perispirit. One who had committed suicide said to us: - *No, I'm not dead and yet I feel the worms that are devouring my body.*

Now, most assuredly, the worms were not devouring his perispirit, still less could they be devouring the spirit himself, but, as the separation between the body and the perispirit was not complete, a sort of moral repercussion transmitted to the latter the sensation of what was taking place in the former. Repercussion is perhaps hardly the word to be employed in this case, as it may seem to imply an effect too nearly akin to materiality; it was rather the sight of what was going on in the decaying body, to which he was still attached by his perispirit; that produced in him an illusion which he mistook for reality.

Thus, in his case, it was not a remembrance, for he had not, during his earthly life, been devoured by worms. It was the feeling of something which was actually taking place. We see, by the examination of the case here alluded to, the deductions that may be drawn from an attentive observation of facts. During life, the body receives external impressions and transmits them to the spirit through the intermediary of the perispirit, which constitutes, probably, what is called the nervous fluid. The body, when dead, no longer feels anything, because there is in it no longer either spirit or perispirit. The perispirit, when disengaged from the body, still experiences sensation, but, as sensation no longer reaches it through a limited channel, its sensation is general.

Now, as the perispirit is, in reality, only an agent for the transmission of sensations to the spirit, by whom alone they're perceived, it follows that the perispirit, if it could exist without a spirit, would no more be able to feel any sensation than is the body when it's dead; and it also follows that the spirit, if it had no perispirit, would be inaccessible to any painful sensation, as is the case with spirits who are completely purified. We know that, in proportion as the spirit progresses, the essence of its perispirit becomes more and more etherealized; whence it follows that the influence of matter diminishes in proportion to the advancement of the spirit, that is to say, in proportion as his perispirit becomes less and less gross.

But, it may be urged, it's through the perispirit that agreeable sensations are transmitted to the spirit, as well as disagreeable ones; therefore, if the purified spirit be inaccessible to the latter, he must also be to the former. Yes, undoubtedly so, as far as regards those which proceed solely from the influence of the matter which is known to us. The sound of our instruments, the perfume of our flowers, produce no impression upon spirits of the highest orders; and yet they experience sensations of the most vivid character, of a charm indescribable for us, and of which it's impossible for us to form any idea, because we are, in regard to that order of sensations, in the same position as that in which men, born blind, are in regard to light.

We know that they exist; but our knowledge is inadequate to explain their nature or the mode in which they're produced. We know that spirits possess perception, sensation, hearing, sight, and that these faculties are attributes of their whole being, and not, as in men, of a part of their being. But we seek in vain to understand by what intermediary these faculties act, of this we know nothing. Spirits themselves can give us no explanation of the matter, because our language can no more be made to express ideas which are beyond the range of our comprehension than the language of savages can be made to furnish terms for expressing our arts, our sciences, or our philosophic doctrines.

In saying that spirits are inaccessible to the impressions of earthly matter, we must be understood as speaking of spirits of very high order, to who's etherealized envelope there is nothing analogous in our lower sphere. It's different with spirits whose perispirit is of denser quality, for they perceive our sounds and our odors, though no longer through special parts of their personality, as they did during life. The molecular vibrations may be said to be felt by them throughout their whole being, reaching thus their common sensorium, which is the spirit himself, although in a different manner, and causing, perhaps, a different impression, which may produce a modification of the resulting perception.

They hear the sound of our voice, and yet are able to understand us, without the help of speech, by the mere transmission of thought, and this penetration are the easier for them in proportion as they're more dematerialized. Their sight is independent of our light. The faculty of vision is an essential attribute of the soul, for whom darkness has no existence, but it's more extended, more penetrating, in those whose purification is more advanced. The soul or spirit, therefore, possesses in itself the faculty of all perceptions, during our corporeal life these are deadened by the grossness of our physical organs, but, in the extra-corporeal life, they become more and more vivid as our semi material envelope becomes more and more etherealized.

This envelope is drawn from the atmosphere in which the spirit finds himself for the time being, and varies according to the nature of the different worlds. In passing from one world to another, spirits change their envelope as we change a garment when we pass from summer to winter or from the pole to the equator. The most elevated spirits, when they come to visit us, assume a terrestrial perispirit, which they retain during their stay among us, and their perceptions are therefore produced, while they're thus clothed upon, in the same way as those of the lower spirits, of whom this grosser order of perispirit is the appropriate envelope, but all spirits, whether high or low, only hear and feel what they choose to hear and to feel.

Without possessing organs of sensation, spirits are able to render their perceptions active or to prevent their action, there is but one thing which they're compelled to hear, and that is the counsels of their guides. The sight of spirits is always active, but they're able, nevertheless, to render themselves invisible to one another, according to the rank they occupy, those of a higher rank having the power of hiding themselves from those who are below them, although a spirit of lower rank can't hide himself from those who are above him. In the first moments after death, the sight of a spirit is always dim and confused; it becomes cleared as he becomes freed from the body, acquiring not only the same clearness which it possessed during rife, but also the power of penetrating bodies which is opaque for us. As for the extension of a spirit's vision through space, and into the future and the past, that depends entirely on his degree of purity and of consequent elevation.

This theory, it'll be said, is anything but encouraging. We had thought that, once freed from our gross bodily envelope, the instrument of all our sufferings, we should suffer no more, and now you tell us that we shall still suffer in the other life, although not in the same way as we do here. But suffering is none the less painful, whatever its nature; and this prospect are by no means an agreeable one. Alas, yes! We may still have to suffer, to suffer much, and for a long time, but we may also have no more to suffer, even from the very moment of quitting the corporeal life.

The sufferings of our present existence are sometimes independent of ourselves, but they're often the consequences of our own volition. If we trace our sufferings back to their source, we see that the greater number of them is due to causes which we might have avoided. How many ills, how many infirmities, does man owe to his excesses, his ambition in a word, to the indulgence of his various passions. He, who should live soberly in all respects, who should never run into excesses of any kind, who should be always simple in his tastes, modest in his desires, would escape a large proportion of the tribulations of human life.

It's the same with regard to spirit-life, the sufferings of which are always the consequence of the manner in which a spirit has lived upon the Earth. In that life undoubtedly, he'll no longer suffer from gout or rheumatism, but his wrong-doing down here will cause him to experience other sufferings no less painful. We have seen that those sufferings are the result of the links which exist between a spirit and matter, that the more completely he is freed from the influence of matter-in other words, the more dematerialized he is the fewer are the painful sensations experienced by him. It depends, therefore, on each of us to free ourselves from the influence of matter by our action in this present life. Man possesses free-will, and, consequently, the power of electing to do or not to do.

Let him conquer his animal passions, let him rid himself of hatred, envy, jealousy, pride, let him throw off the yoke of selfishness, let him purify his soul by cultivating noble sentiments, let him do good, let him attach to the things of this world only the degree of importance which they deserve, and he'll, even under his present corporeal envelope, have affected his purification, and achieved his deliverance from the influence of matter, which will cease for him on his quitting that envelope. For such a one the remembrance of physical sufferings endured by him in the life he has quitted has nothing painful, and produces no disagreeable impression, because they affected his body only, and left no trace in his soul. He is happy to be relieved from them; and the calmness of a good conscience exempts him from all moral suffering.

We have questioned many thousands of spirits having belonged to every class of society; we have studied them at every period of their spirit-life, from the instant of their quitting the body. We have followed them step by step in that life beyond the grave, with a view to ascertaining the changes that should take place in their ideas and sensations; and this examination-in which it has not always been the most commonplace spirits that have furnished us the least valuable subjects of study has invariably shown us, on the one hand, that the sufferings of spirits are the direct result of the misconduct of which they have to undergo the consequences, and, on the other hand, that their new existence is the source of ineffable happiness for those who have followed the right road. From which it follows that those who suffer do so because they have so willed it, and have only themselves to thank for their suffering, in the other world, as in this one.

5 - Choice of trials

258 - In the state of erraticity, and before taking on a new corporeal existence, does a spirit foresee the things which will happen to him in that new existence?

- He chooses for himself the kind of trials which he'll undergo, and it's in this freedom of choice that his free-will consists.

- It's not God, then, who imposes upon him the tribulations of life as a chastisement?

- Nothing comes to pass without the permission of God, for it's he who has established all the laws that rule the Universe. You'd have to inquire why he has made such and such a law, instead of taking some other way. In giving to a spirit the liberty of choice, he leaves to him the entire responsibility of his acts and of their consequences. There is nothing to bar his future; the right road is open to him as freely as the wrong road. But if he succumbs, there still remains to him the consoling fact that all is not over with him, and that God in his goodness allows him to recommence the task which he has done badly. You must, moreover, always distinguish between what is the work of God's will and what is the work of man's will. If a danger threatens you, it's not you who have created this danger, but God, but you have voluntarily elected to expose yourself to this danger, because you have seen in so doing a means of advancement, and God has permitted you to do so.

259 - If the spirit has the choice of the kind of trials which he'll undergo, does it follow that all the tribulations we experience in the earthly life have been foreseen and chosen by us?

- It'd not be correct to say that such has been the case with all of them, for you can't be said to have chosen and foreseen all the things which happen to you in this life, and all their details. You have chosen the kind of trial to which you are subjected; the details of this trial are a consequence of the general situation which you have chosen, and are often the result of your own actions. If, for instance, a spirit has chosen to he born among male-factors, he knew to what kind of temptations he was exposing himself, but not each one of the actions which he would accomplish; those actions are the effect of his volition, of his free-will.

A spirit knows that, in choosing such and such a road, he'll have such and such a kind of struggle to undergo, he knows, therefore, the nature of the vicissitudes which he'll encounter, but he doesn't know whether these will present themselves under one form or under another. The details of events spring from circumstances and the force of things. It's only the leading events of his new life, those which will exercise a determining effect on his destiny, that are foreseen by him. If you enter upon a road full of ruts, you know that you must walk very warily, because you run a risk of stumbling; hut you don't know the exact place where you'll stumble, and it may be that, if you are sufficiently on your guard, you'll not stumble at all. If, when you are passing along a street, a tile falls upon your head, you must not suppose that 'it was written,' as the common saying is.

260 - How can a spirit choose to be born among those who are leading a bad life?
- It's necessary for him to be sent into the conditions which will furnish the elements of the trial he has demanded. To this end, there must be a correspondence between the imperfection of which he desires to free himself, and the social surroundings into which he is born. For example, if he have to struggle against the instinct of brigandage, it's necessary for him to be thrown among brigands.
- If, then, there were no evil livers upon the Earth, spirits couldn't find in it the conditions necessary to certain kinds of trial?
- Would there be any reason for complaining, if such were the case? The cases you suppose is that of the worlds of higher order, to which evil has no access, and which are therefore inhabited only by good spirits. Try to bring about such a state of things as soon as possible in your Earth.

261 - Is it necessary for the spirit, in the course of the trials to which he has to submit in order to arrive at perfection, to undergo every sort of temptation? Must he encounter all the circumstances that can excite in him pride, jealousy, avarice, sensuality, etc?
- Certainly, not, since there are, as you know, many spirits who take from the beginning a road which spares them the necessity of undergoing many of those trials, but he who suffers himself to be drawn into the wrong road, exposes himself to all the dangers of that road. A spirit, for instance, may ask for riches, and his demand may he granted, and, in that case, he'll become, according to his character, avaricious or prodigal, selfish or generous, and will make a noble use of his wealth, or waste it on vanity or sensuality, but this doesn't imply that he'll be compelled to run the gauntlet of all the evil tendencies that may be fostered by the possession of riches.

262 - As a spirit, at its origin, is simple, ignorant and without experience, how can he make an intelligent choice of an existence, and how can he be responsible for such a choice?
- God supplies what is lacking through his inexperience, by tracing out for him the road which he has to follow, as you do for the infant in its cradle, but he allows him, little by little, to become the master of his choice, in proportion as his free-will becomes developed, and it's then that he often loses his way and takes the wrong road, if he don't listen to the advice of the good spirits, who endeavor to instruct him; it's this which may be called the fall of man.
- When a spirit is in possession of his free-will, does the choice of his corporeal existence always depend solely on his own volition, or is this existence sometimes imposed on him by God as an expiation?
- God can afford to wait; he never hurries the work of expiation. Nevertheless, God does sometimes impose an existence upon a spirit, when the latter, through his ignorance or his obstinacy, is incapable of perceiving what would be to his advantage, and when he sees that this existence may sub serve his purification and advancement, while furnishing him also with the conditions of expiation.

263 - Do spirits make their choice immediately after death?
- No, many of them believe their sufferings to be eternal; you have already been told that this is a chastisement.

264 - What is it that decides a spirit's choice of the trials which he determines to undergo?
- He chooses those which may serve to expiate faults and at the same time help him to advance more quickly. In view of these ends, some may impose upon themselves a life of poverty privations, in order to exercise themselves in bearing them with courage; others may wish to test their powers of resistance by the temptations of fortune and of power, much more dangerous, because of the bad use that may be made of them, and the evil passions that may be developed by them; others, again, may desire to strengthen their good resolutions by having to struggle against the influence of vicious surroundings.

265 - If some spirits elect to expose themselves to the contact of vice as a trial of their virtue, may it not be that others make a similar choice from a desire to live amidst surroundings in unison with their depraved tastes, and in which they may give free course to their sensual tendencies?
- Such instances undoubtedly occur, but only among those whose moral sense is still but imperfectly developed. In such cases, the needed trial occurs spontaneously, and they're subjected to it for a longer time. Sooner or later, they'll understand that indulgence of the animal instincts leads to disastrous consequences, which they'll undergo during a period so long that it'll seem to them to be eternal, and God sometimes leaves them in this state until they have comprehended the gravity of their fault, and demand of their own accord, to be allowed to repair it by undergoing trials of a profitable nature.

266 - Does it not seem natural to make choice of such trials as are least painful?

- From your point of view, it would seem to be so, but not from that of the spirit, when he is freed from materiality, his illusions cease and he thinks differently.

> Man, while upon the Earth, and subjected to the influence of carnal ideas, sees only the painful aspect of the trials he's called upon to undergo and it therefore appears to him to be natural to choose the trials that are allied to material enjoyments, but when he has returned to spirit-life, he compares those gross and fugitive enjoyments with the unchangeable felicity of which he obtains occasional glimpses, and judges that such felicity will be cheaply purchased by a little temporary suffering. A spirit may therefore, make choice of the hardest trial, and consequently of the most painful existence, in the hope of thereby attaining more rapidly to a happier state, just as a sick man often chooses the most unpalatable medicine in the hope of obtaining a more rapid cure.

He, who aspires to immortalize his name by the discovery of an unknown country doesn't seek a flowery road. He takes the road which will bring him most surely to the aim he has in view, and he's not deterred from following it even by the dangers it may offer. On the contrary, he braves those dangers for the sake of the glory he'll win if he succeeds. The doctrine of our freedom in the choice of our successive existences and of the trials which we have to undergo ceases to appear strange when we consider that spirits, being freed from matter, judge of things differently from men. They perceive the ends which these trials are intended to work out ends far more important for them than the fugitive enjoyments of Earth.

After each existence, they see the steps they have already accomplished, and comprehend what they still lack for the attainment of the purity which alone enables them to reach the goal and they willingly submit to the vicissitudes of corporeal life, demanding of their own accord to be allowed to undergo those which will aid them to advance most rapidly. There's, therefore, nothing surprising in a spirit making choice of a hard or painful life. He knows that he can't, in his present state of imperfection, enjoy the perfect happiness, to which he aspires, but he obtains glimpses of that happiness, and he seeks to effect his own improvement, as the sole means to its attainment. Do we not, every day, witness examples of a similar choice?

What is the action of the man who labors, without cessation or repose, to amass the property which will enable him eventually to live in comfort, but the discharge of a task which he has voluntarily assumed as the means of insuring for himself a more prosperous future? The soldier who offers himself for the accomplishment of a perilous mission, the traveler who braves dangers no less formidable in the interest of science or of his own fortune, are examples of the voluntary incurring of hardships for the sake of the honor or profit that will result from their successful endurance.

What will not men undergo for gain or for glory? Is not every sort of competitive examination a trial to which men voluntarily submits in the hope of obtaining advancement in the career they have chosen? He who would gain a high position in science, art, industry, is obliged to pass through all the lower degrees which lead up to it, and which constitute so many trials. Human life is thus seen to be modeled on spirit-life, presenting the same vicissitudes on a smaller scale. And as in the earthly life we often make choice of the hardest conditions as means to the attainment of the highest ends, why should not a disincarnate spirit, who sees farther than he saw when incarnated in an earthly body, and for whom the bodily life is only a fugitive incident, make choice of a laborious or painful existence, if it may lead him or towards an eternal felicity?

Those who say that, since spirits have the power choosing their existences, they'll demand to be princes and millionaires, are like the purblind, who only see what they touch, or like greedy children, who, when asked what occupation they would prefer to follow, reply that they would like to be pastry-cooks or confectioners. It's with a spirit as with a traveler, who, in the depths of a valley obscured by fog, sees neither the length nor the extremities of his road. When he has reached the top of me hill, and the fog has cleared away, his view takes in both the road along which he has come and that by which he has still to go. He sees the point which he has to reach, and the obstacles he has to overcome in reaching it, and he's thus able to take his measures for successfully accomplishing his journey.

A spirit, while incarnated, is like the traveler at the foot of the hill when freed from terrestrial trammels, he is like the traveler who has reached the top of the hill. The aim of the traveler is to obtain rest after fatigue the aim of the spirit is to attain to perfect happiness after tribulations and trials. Spirits say that, in the state of erraticity, they seek, study, observe, in order to make their choice wisely. Have we not examples of analogous action in corporeal life? Do we not often spend years in deciding on me career upon which, at length, we freely fix our choice, because we consider it to be the one in which we are most likely to succeed?

If, after all, we fail in the one we have chosen, we seek out another and each career thus embraced by us constitutes a phase, a period, of our life. Is not each day employed by us in deciding what we shall do on the morrow? And what, for a spirit, are his different corporeal existences, but so many phases, periods, days, in comparison with his spirit life, which, as we know, is his normal life, the corporeal life being only a transitional passage?

267 - Can a spirit make his choice while in the corporeal state?
- His desire may exercise a certain amount of influence, according to the quality of his intention, but, when he returns to spirit life, he often judges things very differently. It's only as a spirit that he makes his choice, but he may, nevertheless, make it during the material life, for a spirit, even while incarnated, has occasional moments in which he is independent of the matter he inhabits.

- Many persons desire earthly greatness and riches, but not assuredly, either as expiation or as trial.
- Undoubtedly, in such cases it's their material instinct which desires greatness in order to enjoy its satisfactions. The spirit could only desire it in order to understand its vicissitudes.

268 - Until a spirit has reached the state of perfect purity, has he constantly to undergo trials?
- Yes, but not such as you understand by that term. By the term trials, you understand only material tribulations, but when a spirit has reached a certain degree of purification, although he is not yet perfect, he has no more tribulations of

that kind to undergo, lie has, nevertheless, to perform creating duties which advance his own improvement, but there is nothing painful in these, as, for example, the duty of aiding others to work out their own improvement.

269 - Is it possible for a spirit to make a mistake as to the efficacy of the trial he chooses?
- He may choose one which exceeds his strength, and, in that case, he'll succumb, or he may choose one from which he'll reap no profit whatever, as, for instance, if he seeks to lead an idle and useless life, but, in such cases, he perceives, on returning to the spirit-world, that he has gained nothing and he then demands to make up for lost time.

270 - What is the cause of the vocations of some persons, and their spontaneous desire to follow one career rather than another?
- It seems to me that you yourselves might answer this question. Is not the existence of such vocations a necessary consequence of what we have told you concerning the choice of trials, and of the progress accomplished in a preceding existence?

271 - As a spirit in the wandering state studies the various conditions of corporeal life that will aid him to progress, how can he sup pose that lie will do so by being born, for example, among cannibals?
- Those which are born among cannibals are not advanced spirit, but spirits who are still at the cannibal degree, or, it may be, who are even lower than cannibals.

> We know that our anthropophagi are not at the lowest degree of the scale, and that there are worlds in which are found degrees of brutishness and ferocity that have no analogues in our Earth. The spirits of those worlds are, therefore, lower than the lowest of our world, and to come among our savages is, for them, a step in advance, as it would be for our cannibals to exercise, in a civilized community, some profession obliging them to shed blood. If they take no higher aim, it's because their moral backwardness doesn't allow of their comprehending any higher degree of progress. A spirit can only advance gradually he can't clear at a single bound the distance which separates barbarism from civilization. And in this impossibility we see one of the causes that necessitate reincarnation, which is thus seen to be really a consequence of the justice of God for what would become of the millions of human beings who die every day in the lowest depths of degradation, if they had no means of arriving at higher states? And why should God have refused to them the favors granted to other men?

272 - Can spirits, coming from a world of lower degree than the Earth, or from the lowest of our human races, such as our cannibals for instance, be born among our civilized peoples?
- Yes, such spirits sometimes come into your world, through trying to reach a degree too far above them, but they're out of their proper place among you, because they bring with them instincts and habits that clash with the convictions and habits of the society into which they have strayed.

> Such beings present us with the melancholy spectacle of ferocity in the midst of civilization. For them, to return among cannibals is not a going down, but only a resuming of their proper place and they may even gain by so doing.

273 - Might a man belonging to a civilized race be reincarnated, as an expiation, in a savage race?
- Yes, but that would depend on the kind of expiation he bad incurred. A master who had been cruel to his slaves might become a slave in his turn, and undergo the torments he had inflicted on others. He who has wielded authority may, in a new existence, be obliged to obey those who formerly bent to his will. Such an existence may be imposed upon him as an expiation if he have abused his power, but a good spirit may also choose an influential existence among the people of some lower race, in order to hasten their advancement; in that case, such a reincarnation is a mission.

6 - Relationships beyond the grave
274 - Do the different degrees which exist in the advancement of spirits establish among the latter a hierarchy of powers? Are there, among spirits, subordination and authority?
- Yes, the authority of spirits over one another, in virtue of their relative superiority, is very great and gives to the higher ones a moral ascendancy over the lower ones which is absolutely irresistible.
- Can spirits of lower degree withdraw themselves from the authority of those who are higher than themselves?
- I have said that the authority which comes of superiority is irresistible.

275 - Do the power and consideration which a man may have enjoyed in the earthly life give him supremacy in the spirit-world?
- No, for in that world the humble are exalted and the proud abased.
- In what sense should we understand exalting and abasing?
- Do you not know that spirits are of different orders, according to their degree of merit? Therefore, he who has held the highest rank upon the Earth may find himself in the lowest rank in the world of spirits, while his servitor may be in the highest. Is not this clear to you? Has not Jesus said that: - *Whosoever exalteth himself shall be abased, and whosoever humbleth himself shall be exalted?*

276 - When one who has been great upon the Earth finds himself occupying an inferior place in the spirit-world, does he feel humiliated by this change of position?
- Often exceedingly so, especially if he have been haughty and jealous.

277 - When a soldier, after a battle, meets his general in the spirit-world, does he still acknowledge him as his superior?
- Titles are nothing, intrinsic superiority is everything.

278 - Do spirits of different orders mix together in the other?
- Yes, and no, that is to say, they see each other, but they're none the less removed. They shun or approach one another according to the antipathies or sympathies of their sentiments, just as is the case among yourselves. The spirit-life is a whole world of varied conditions and relationships, of which the earthly life is only the obscured reflex. Those of the same rank are drawn together by a sort of affinity, and form groups or families of spirits united by sympathy and a common aim, the good, by the desire to do what is good, and the bad, by the desire to do evil, by the shame of their wrong, doing, and by the wish to find themselves among those whom they resemble.

> The spirit-world is like a great city, in which men of all ranks and conditions see and meet one another without mixing together in which various social circles are formed by similarity of tastes in which vice and virtue elbow each other without speaking to one another.

279 - Are all spirits reciprocally accessible to one another?
- The good go everywhere, as it's necessary that they should do, in order to bring their influence to bear upon the evil-minded, but the regions inhabited by them are inaccessible to inferior spirits, so that the latter can't trouble those happy abodes by the introduction of evil passions.

280 - What is the nature of the relations between good and bad spirits?
- The good ones endeavor to combat the evil tendencies of the others, in order to aid them to raise themselves to a higher degree, this intercourse, is, for the former, a mission.

281 - Why do inferior spirits take pleasure in inducing us to do wrong?
- From jealousy. Not having earned a place among the good, their desire is to prevent, as far as in them lies, other spirits, as yet inexperienced, from attaining to the happiness from which they're excluded. They desire to make others suffer what they suffer themselves. Do you not see the working of the same desire among yourselves?

282 - How do spirits hold communication with one another?
- They see and comprehend one another. Speech is material; it's a reflex of spirit. The universal fluid establishes a constant communication between them; it's the vehicle by which thought is transmitted, as the air, in your world, is the vehicle of sound. This fluid constitutes a sort of universal telegraph, which unites all worlds, and enables spirits to correspond from one world to another.

283 - Can spirits hide their thoughts from each other? Can they hide themselves from one another?
- No, with them everything is open, and especially so with those who have attained to perfection. They may withdraw from one another, but they're always visible to each other. This, however, is not an absolute rule, for the higher spirits are perfectly able to render themselves invisible to the lower ones, when they consider it to he useful to do so.

284 - How can spirits, who have no longer a body, establish their individuality, and cause it to be distinguishable from that of the other spiritual beings by which they're surrounded?
- Their individuality is established by their perispirit, which makes of each spirit a separate personality, distinct from all others, as the body does among men.

285 - Do spirits recognize one another as having lived together upon the Earth? Does the son recognize his father, the friend, his friend?
- Yes, and from generation to generation.
- How do those who have known each other on the Earth recognize one another in the world of spirits?
- We see our past life and read therein as in a hook, on seeing the past of our friends and our enemies; we see their passage from life to death.

286 - Does the soul see, immediately on quitting its mortal remains, the relations and friends who have returned before it into the world of spirits?
- Immediately is not always the right word, for, as we have said, the soul requires some time to resume its self-consciousness, and to shake off the veil of materiality.

287 - How is the soul received on its return to the spirit-word?
- That of the righteous, as a dearly, beloved brother, whose return has been long waited for, that of the wicked, with contempt.

288 - What sentiment is experienced by impure spirits at the sight of another bad spirit, on his arrival among them?
- Such spirits are gratified at seeing others who resemble them, and who, like them, are deprived of the highest happiness, just as a band of scoundrels, upon the Earth, are gratified at meeting with another scoundrel like themselves.

289 - Do our relatives and friends sometimes come to meet us when we are leaving the Earth?

- Yes, they come to meet the soul of those they love; they felicitate it as one who has returned from a journey if it has escaped the dangers of the road, and they aid it in freeing itself from the bonds of the flesh. To be met thus by those they have loved is a favor granted to the souls of the upright; while the soul of the wicked is punished by being left alone, or is only surrounded by spirits like itself.

290 - Are relatives and friends always reunited after death?
- That depends on their elevation and on the road they have to follow for their advancement. If one of them is further advanced, and progresses more rapidly than the other, they can't remain together; they may see one another occasionally, but they can only he definitively reunited when he who was behind is able to keep pace with him who was before, or when both of them shall have reached the state of perfection. Moreover, the privation of the sight of relatives and friends is sometimes inflicted on a spirit as a punishment.

7 - Sympathies and antipathies of spirits - Eternal halves
291 - Have spirits special personal affections among themselves, besides the general sympathy resulting from similarity?
- Yes, just as among men; but the link between spirits is stronger when the body is absent, because it's no longer exposed to the vicissitudes of the passions.

292 - Do spirits experience hatreds among themselves?
- Hatreds only exist among impure spirits. It's they who sow hatreds and dissensions among men.

293 - Do those who have been enemies on Earth always retain their resentment against one another in the spirit-world?
- No, for they often see that their hatred was stupid, and perceives the puerility of the object by which it was excited. It's only imperfect spirits who retain the animosities of the earthly life of which they rid themselves in proportion as they become purified. Spirits whose anger, as men, has been caused by some merely material interest, forget their dissension as soon as they're dematerialized. The cause of their dissension no longer existing, they may, if there be no antipathy between them, see each other again with pleasure.

> Just as two schoolboys, when they have reached the age of reason, perceive the folly of their boyish quarrels, and no longer keep up a grudge against each other on account of them.

294 - Is the remembrance of wrongs they may have done one another, as men, an obstacle to sympathy between two spirits?
- Yes, it tends to keep them apart.

295 - What is the sentiment, after death, of those whom we have wronged?
- If they're good, they forgive you as soon as you repent; if they're bad, they may retain resentment against you, and may even pursue you with their anger in another existence. This may be permitted by God as a chastisement.

296 - Are the individual affections of spirits susceptible of change?
- No, for they can't be mistaken in one another. The mask under which hypocrites hide themselves on Earth has no existence in the world of spirits and their affections, when they're pure, are therefore unchangeable. The love which unites them is a source of supreme felicity.

297 - Does the affection which two spirits have felt for each other upon the Earth always continue in the spirit-world?
- Yes, undoubtedly, if that affection were founded on sympathy, but, if physical causes have had more share in it than sympathy, it ceases with those causes. Affections are more solid and lasting among spirits than among men, because they're not subordinated to the caprices of material interests and self-love.

298 - Is it true that the souls of those who will eventually be united in affection are predestined to this union from their beginning, and that each of us has thus, in some part of the Universe, his other half, to whom he'll someday be necessarily reunited?
- No, there is no such thing as any special and fated union between any two souls. Union exists between all spirits, but in different degrees, according to the rank they occupy, that's to say, according to the degree of perfection they have acquired; and the greater their perfection, the more united they're. It's discord that produces all the ills of human life. The complete and perfect happiness at which all spirits eventually arrive is the result of concord.

299 - In what way should we understand the term other half, sometimes employed by spirits to designate other spirits for whom they have special sympathy?
- The expression is incorrect. If one spirit were the half of another spirit, he would, if separated from that other, be incomplete.

300 - When two perfectly sympathetic spirits are reunited in the other world, are they thus reunited for all eternity, or can they separate from each other and unite themselves with other spirits?
- All spirits are united among themselves. I speak of those who have reached the state of perfection. In the spheres below that state, when a spirit passes from a lower sphere to a higher one, he doesn't always feel the same sympathy for those whom he has quitted.

301 - When two spirits are completely sympathetic, are they, the complement of each other or is that sympathy the result of their perfect identity of character?
- The sympathy which attracts one spirit to another is the result of the perfect concordance of their tendencies and instincts. If one of them were necessary to complete the other, he'd lose his individuality.

302 - Does similarity of thoughts and of sentiments suffice to constitute the kind of identity which is necessary to the production of perfect sympathy, or is uniformity of acquired knowledge also required for its production?
- Perfect sympathy between two spirits results from equality in the degree of their elevation.

303 - May spirits, who are not now sympathetic, become so in the future?
- Yes, all will be sympathetic in course of time. Thus, of two spirits who were once together, one may have advanced more rapidly than the other, but the other, though now in a lower sphere, will by and by have advanced sufficiently to be able to enter the higher sphere in which the former is now residing, and their reunion will take place all the sooner if the one who was most advanced should fail in the trials he has still to undergo, and so should remain for a time just where he now is, without making any further progress.
- May two spirits, who are now sympathetic, cease to be so?
- Certainly, if one of them is wanting in energy, and lags behind, while the other is advancing.

> The hypothesis of twin-souls is merely a figurative representation of the union of two sympathetic spirits and must not be understood literally. The spirits who have made use of this expression are certainly not of high order; and, therefore, as their range of thought is necessarily narrow, they have sought to convey their meaning by using the terms they were accustomed to employ in their earthly life. The idea that two souls were created for each other, and that, after having been separated for a longer or shorter period, they'll necessarily be eventually reunited for all eternity, is, therefore, to be entirely rejected.

8 - Remembrance of corporeal existence
304 - Does spirit remember his corporeal existence?
- Yes, having lived many times as a human being, he remembers what he has been, and often smiles pityingly at the follies of his past.

> As a man, who has reached the age of reason, smiles at the follies of his youth and the silliness of his childhood.

305 - Does the remembrance of his corporeal existence present itself to a spirit, complete, and spontaneously, immediately after his death?
- No, it comes back to him little by little, in proportion as he fixes his attention upon it, as objects gradually become visible out of a fog.

306 - Does a spirit remember the details of all the events of his life? Does he take in the whole of his life at a single retrospective glance?
- He remembers the things of his life more or less distinctly and in detail, according to the influence they have exercised on his state as a spirit, but you can easily understand that there are many things in his life to which he attaches no importance, and which he doesn't even seek to remember.
- Could he remember them if he wished to do so?
- He has the power of recalling the minutest details of every incident of his life, and even of his thoughts; but when no useful purpose would be served by exerting this power, he doesn't exert it.

307 - In what way does his past life present itself to a spirit's memory? Is it through an effort of his imagination, or is it like a picture displayed before his eyes?
- It comes back to him in both ways. All the actions which he has an interest in remembering appear to him as though they were present; the others are seen by him more or less vaguely in his thought, or are entirely forgotten. The more dematerialized he is, the less importance does he attach to material things. It has often happened to you, on evoking some wandering spirit who has just left the Earth, to find that he remembers neither the names of persons whom he liked, nor details which to you appear to be important. He cares but little about them, and they have faded from his memory, but you always find that he perfectly remembers the main facts of his life which have conduced to his intellectual and moral progress.

308 - Does a spirit remember all the existences which have preceded the one he has just quitted?
- His entire past is spread out before him like the stages already accomplished by a traveler, but, as we have told you, he doesn't remember all his past actions with absolute precision; he remembers them more or less clearly in proportion to the influence they have had upon his present state. As to his earliest existences, those which may be regarded as constituting the period of spirit-infancy, they're lost in vagueness, and disappear in the night of oblivion.

309 - How does a spirit regard the body he has just quitted?
- As an uncomfortable garment that hampered him, and that he is delighted to be rid of.
- What feeling is produced in him by seeing the decomposition of his body?
- Almost always that of indifference, as something about which he no longer cares.

310 - After a time, does a spirit recognize the mortal remains, or other objects, that once belonged to him?
- Sometimes he does so, but this depends on the more or less elevated point of view from which he regards terrestrial things.

311 - Is a spirit's attention attracted to the material relics of himself by the respect entertained for those objects by his survivors, and does he see this respect with pleasure?
- A spirit is always gratified at being held in kindly remembrance by those he has left. The objects thus preserved in remembrance of him serve to recall him to the memory of those by whom they're preserved, but it's the action of their thought which attracts him, and not those objects.

312 - Do spirits retain the remembrance of the sufferings endured by them in their last corporeal existence?
- They frequently do so; and this remembrance makes them realize all the more vividly the worth of the felicity they enjoy as spirits.

313 - Does he who has been happy down here regret his terrestrial enjoyments on quitting the Earth?
- Only spirits of inferior degree can regret material satisfactions in harmony with impurity of nature, and which are expiated by suffering. For spirits of higher degrees of elevation, the happiness of eternity is immeasurably preferable to the ephemeral pleasures of the earthly life.

> As the adult despises watch constituted the delights of his infancy.

314 - When a man, who has commenced a series of important labors in view of some useful end, has seen these labors interrupted by death, does he, in the other world, feel regret at having had to leave them unfinished?
- No, because he sees that others are destined to complete them. On the contrary, he endeavors to act upon the minds of other human beings, so as to lead them to carry on what he had begun. His aim while upon the Earth was to be useful to the human race: his aim is the same in the spirit-world.

315. When a man has left behind him works of art or of literature, does he preserve for them in the other life the interest he took in them while living upon the Earth?
- He judges them from another point of view, according to his elevation, and he often blames what he formerly admired.

316 - Does a spirit still take an interest in the labors which are going on upon the Earth, in the progress of the arts and sciences?
- That depends on his degree of elevation, and on the mission he may have to fulfill. What appears magnificent to you often appears a very small matter to spirits, if they take an interest in it, it's only as a man of learning takes an interest in the work of a school-boy. They examine whatever indicates the elevation of incarnated spirits and mark the degree of their progress.

317 - Do spirits, after death; retain any preference for their native country?
- For spirits of elevated degree, their country is the Universe, in regard to the Earth; their only preference is for the place in which there is the greatest number of persons with whom they're in sympathy.

> The situation of spirits, and their way of looking at things, is infinitely varied, according to their various degrees of moral and intellectual development. Spirits of a high order generally make but short sojourns upon the Earth all that goes on here is so paltry in comparison with the grandeurs of infinity, the matters to which men attribute most importance appear to them so puerile, that the things of this Earth have very little interest for them, unless they have been sent to it for the purpose of quickening the progress of its people.
Spirits of lower degree visit our Earth more frequently, but they judge its affairs from a higher point of view than that of their corporeal life. The common ruck of spirits may be said to be sedentary among us they constitute the great mass of the ambient population of the invisible world. They retain very much the same ideas, tastes, and tendencies which they had while clothed with their corporeal envelope, and mix themselves up with our gatherings, our occupation, our amusements in all of which they take a part more or, less active according to their character. Being no longer able to satisfy their material passions, they take delight in witnessing the excesses of those who abandon themselves to their indulgence, to which they excite them by every means in their power. Among their number are some who are better disposed, and who see and observe in order to acquire knowledge and to advance.

318 - Do spirits modify their ideas in the other life?
- Very considerably. A spirit's ideas undergo very great modifications in proportion as he becomes dematerialized, he may sometimes retain the same ideas for a long period, but little by little the influence of matter diminishes, and he sees more clearly. It's then that he seeks for the means of advancing.

319 - As spirits had already lived in the other world before being incarnated, why do they feel astonished on re-entering that world?
- This feeling is only momentary, and results from the confusion that follows their waking; they soon recover their knowledge of themselves, as the memory of the past comes back to them, and the impression of the terrestrial life becomes effaced.

8 - Commemoration of the dead - Funerals

320 - Are spirits affected by the remembrance of those whom they have loved on Earth?
- Very much more so than you are apt to suppose. If they're happy this remembrance adds to their happiness; if they're unhappy, it affords them consolation.

321 - Are spirits specially attracted towards their friends upon the earth by the return of the day which, in some countries, is consecrated to the 'memory of those who have quitted this life? Do they make it a point to meet those who, on that day, go to pray beside the graves where their mortal remains are interred?
- Spirits answer to the call of affectionate remembrance on that (lay as they do on any other day).
- Do they, on that day, go especially to the burial, place of their corporeal body?
- They go to the cemeteries in greater numbers on that day, because called thither by the thoughts of a greater number of persons, but each spirit goes solely for his own friends, and not for the crowd of those who care nothing about him.
- In what form do they come to these places, and what would be their appearance if they could render themselves visible to us?
- The form and appearance by which they were known during their lifetime.

322 - Do the spirits of those who are forgotten, and whose graves no one visits, go to the cemeteries notwithstanding this neglect? Do they feel regret at seeing that no one remembers them?
- What is the Earth to them? They're only linked to it by the heart. If, upon the Earth, no affection is felt for a spirit, there is nothing that can attach him to it; he has the whole Universe before him.

323 - Does a visit made to his grave give more pleasure to a spirit than a prayer offered for him by friends in their own home?
- A visit made to his grave is a way of showing to a spirit that he's not forgotten, it's a sign. As I have told you, it's the prayer that sanctifies the action of the memory; the place where it's offered is of little importance, if it come from the heart.

324 - When statues or other monuments are erected to persons who have quitted this life, are the spirits of those persons present at their inauguration; and do they witness such ceremonies with pleasure?
- Spirits often attend on such occasions, when able to do so; but they attach less importance to the honors paid to them than to the remembrance in which they're held.

325 - What makes some persons desire to be buried in one place rather than in another? Do they go thither more willingly offer their death? And is it a sign of inferiority on the part of a spirit that lie should attribute importance to a matter so purely material?
- That desire is prompted by a spirit's affection for certain places and is a sign of moral inferiority. To an elevated spirit, what is one spot of Earth more than another? Does he not know that his foul will be reunited with those he loves, even though their bones are separated?
- Is it futile to bring together the mortal remains in of all tile members of a family in the same burial-place?
- Such reunion is of little importance to spirits, but it's useful to men, whose remembrance of those who have gone before them is thus strengthened and rendered more serious.

326 - When the soul has returned into spirit-life, is it gratified by the honors paid to its mortal remains?
- When a spirit has reached a certain degree of advancement, he is purified from terrestrial vanities, for he comprehends their futility. But there are many spirits who, in the early period of their return to the other life, take great pleasure in the honors paid to their memory, or are much disturbed at finding themselves forgotten, for they still retain some of the false ideas they held during their earthly life.

327 - Do spirits ever attend their own funeral?
- Spirits very often do so; but, in many cases, without understanding what is going on, being still in the state of confusion that usually follows death.
- Do they feel flattered by the presence of a large concourse of persons at their funeral?
- More or less so, according to the sentiment which has brought them together.

328 - Is a spirit ever present at the meetings of his heirs?
- Almost always. Providence has so ordained it for the spirit's own instruction and for the chastisement of selfishness. The deceased is thus enabled to judge of the worth of the protestations of affection and devotion addressed to him during his life and his disappointment on witnessing the rapacity of those who dispute the property he has left is often very great. But the punishment of greedy heirs will come in due time.

329 - Is the respect which mankind, in all ages and among all peoples, has always instinctively shown to the dead, to be attributed to an intuitive belief in a future state of existence?
- The one is the natural consequence of the other, were it not for that belief, such respect would have neither object nor meaning.

Chapter 7 - Return to corporeal life

1 - Preludes to return

330 - Do spirits foresee the epoch of their next return to corporeal life?
- They have the presentiment of that return, as a blind man feels the heat of the fire he is approaching. They know that they'll be reincarnated, as you know that you'll die, but without knowing when the change will occur.
- Reincarnation, then, is a necessity of spirit-life, as death is a necessity of corporeal life?
- Certainly.

331 - Do all spirits occupy themselves beforehand with their approaching incarnation?
- There are some who never give it a thought, and who even know nothing about it; that depends on their greater or less degree of advancement. In some cases, the uncertainty in which they're left in regard to their future is a punishment.

332 - Can a spirit hasten or retard the moment of his reincarnation?
- He may hasten it by the action of a strong desire; he may also put it off if he shrink from the trial awaiting him (for the cowardly and the indifferent are to be found among spirits as among men), but he can't do so with impunity. He suffers from such delay, as the sick man suffers who shrinks from employing the remedy which alone can cure him.

333 - If a spirit found himself tolerably happy in an average condition among errant Spirits, could he prolong that state indefinitely?
- No, not, indefinitely. The necessity of advancing is one which is felt by every spirit, sooner or later. All spirits have to ascend it's their destiny.

334 - Is the union of a given soul with a given body predestined beforehand, or is the choice of a body only made at the last moment?
- The spirit who is to animate a given body is always designated beforehand. Each spirit, on choosing the trial he elects to undergo, demands to be reincarnated; and Cod, who sees and knows all things, has foreseen and for known that such and such a soul would be united to such and such a body.

335 - Is the spirit allowed to choose the body into which lie will enter, or does he only choose the kind of life which is to serve for his trial?
- He may choose a body also, for the imperfections of a given body are so many trials that will aid his advancement, if he succeeds in vanquishing the obstacles thus placed in his way. This choice doesn't always depend on himself, but he may ask to be allowed to make it.
- Could a spirit refuse, at the last moment, to enter into the body that had been chosen by him?
- If lie refused, he would suffer much more than one who had not attempted to undergo a new trial.

336 - Could it happen that a child about to be born should find no spirit willing to incarnate himself in it?
- God provides for all contingencies. Every child who is predestined to be born viable, is also predestined to have a soul. Nothing is ever created without design.

337 - Is the union of a given soul with a given body ever imposed by God?
- It's sometimes imposed, as well as the different trials to be undergone by a spirit, and especially when the latter is still too backward to be able to choose wisely for himself. A spirit may be constrained, as an expiation, to unite himself with the body of a child that, by the circumstances of its birth, and the position it'll have in the world, will become for him an instrument of chastisement.

338 - If several spirits demanded to incarnate themselves in a body about to be born, in what way would the decision be made between them?
- In such a case, it's God who judges as to which spirit is best fitted to fulfill the destiny appointed for the child; but, as I have already told you, the spirit is designated before the instant in which he is to unite himself with the body.

339 - Is the moment of incarnation accompanied by a confusion similar to that which follows the spirit's separation from the body?
- Yes, but much greater and especially much longer. At death the spirit is emancipated from the state of slavery, at birth, he re-enters it.

340 - Does the moment in which he is to reincarnate himself appear to a spirit as a solemn one? Does he accomplish that act as something serious and important for him?
- He is like a traveler who embarks on a perilous voyager, and who doesn't know whether he may not find his death in the waves among which he is venturing.

> Just as the death of the body is a sort of re-birth for the spirit, so reincarnation is for him a sort of death, or rather of exile and claustration. He quits the world of spirits for the corporeal world just as a man quits the corporeal world for the world of spirits. A spirit knows that he'll be reincarnated, just as a man knows that he will die but, like the latter, he only becomes aware of the change at the moment when it occurs. It's at this moment that the confusion produced by the

change takes possession of him, as is the case with a man in the act of dying and this confusion lasts until his new existence is fully established. The commencement of reincarnation is, for the spirit, a sort of dying.

341 - Is a spirit's uncertainty, in regard to the successful issue of the trials he is about to undergo in his new life, a cause of anxiety to him before his incarnation?
- Yes, of very great anxiety, since those trials will retard or hasten his advancement, according as he shall have borne them ill or well.

342 - Is a spirit accompanied, at the moment of his rein carnation, by spirit-friends who come to be present at his departure from the spirit-world, as they come to receive him when he returns to it?
- That depends on the sphere which the spirit inhabits. If he belongs to a sphere in which affection reigns, spirits who love him remain with him to the last moment, encourage him, and often even follow him in his new life.

343 - Is it the spirit-friends who thus follow us in our earthly life that we sometimes see in our dreams manifesting affection for us, but whose features are unknown to us?
- Yes, in very many cases; they come to visit you as you visit a prisoner in his cell.

2 - Union of soul and body

344 - At what moment is the soul united to the body?
- The union begins at the moment of conception, but is only complete at the moment of birth. From the moment of conception, the spirit designated to inhabit a given body is united to that body by a fluidic link, which becomes closer and closer up to the instant of birth; the cry then uttered by the infant announces that he is numbered among the living.

345 - Is the union between the spirit and the body definitive from the moment of conception? Could the spirit, during this first period of that union, renounce inhabiting the body designed for him?
- The union between them is definitive in this sense namely, that no other spirit could replace the one who has been designated for that body, but, as the links which hold them together are at first very weak, they're easily broken, and may be severed by the will of a spirit who draws back from the trial he had chosen, but, in that case, the child doesn't live.

346 - What becomes of a spirit, if the body he has chosen happens to die before birth?
- He chooses another body.
- What can be the use of premature deaths?
- Such deaths are most frequently caused by the imperfections of matter.

347 - What benefit can a spirit derive from his incarnation in a body which dies a few days after birth?
- In such a case, the new being's consciousness of his existence is so slightly developed that his death is of little importance. As we have told you, such deaths are often intended mainly as a trial for the parents.

348 - Does a spirit know beforehand that tile body he chooses has no chance of living?
- He sometimes knows it, but if he chooses it on this account. It's because he shrinks from the trial he foresees.

349 - When, from any cause, a spirit has failed to accomplish a proposed incarnation, is another existence provided for him immediately?
- Not always immediately. The spirit requires time to make a new choice, unless his instantaneous reincarnation had been previously decided upon.

350 - When a spirit is definitively united to an infant body and it's thus too late for him to refuse this union, does lie sometimes regret the choice he has made?
- If you mean to ask whether, as a man, he may complain of the life he has to undergo, and whether he may not wish it were otherwise, I answer, yes, but if you mean to ask whether he regrets the choice he has made, I answer, no, for he doesn't remember that he has made it. A spirit, when once incarnated, can't regret a choice which he is not conscious of having made, but he may find the burden lie has, assumed too heavy, and, if lie believes it to be beyond his strength, he may have recourse to suicide.

351 - Does a spirit, in the interval between conception and birth enjoy the use of all his faculties?
- He does so more or less according to the various periods of gestation, for he is not yet incarnated in his new body, but only attached to it. From the instant of conception confusion begins to take possession of the spirit, who is thus made aware that the moment has come for him to enter upon a new existence, and this confusion becomes more and denser until the period of birth. In the interval between these two terms, his state is nearly that of an incarnated spirit during the sleep of the body. In proportions as the moment of birth approaches, his ideas become effaced, together with his remembrance of the past, of which, when once he has entered upon corporeal life, he is no longer conscious. But this remembrance comes back to him little by little when he has returned to the spirit-world.

352 - Does the spirit, at the moment of birth, recover the plenitude of his faculties?
- No, they're gradually developed with the growth of his organs. The corporeal life is for him a new existence; he has to learn the use of his bodily instruments. His ideas come back to him little by little, as in the case of a man who, waking out of slumber, should find himself in a different situation from that in which he was before he fell asleep.

353 - The union of the spirit and the body not being completely and definitively consummated until birth has taken place can the fetus is considered as having a soul?
- The spirit who is to animate it exists, as it were, outside of it, strictly speaking, therefore, it has no soul, since the incarnation of the latter is only in course of being effected, but it's linked to the soul which it's to have.

354 - What is the nature of intra-uterine life?
- That of the plant which vegetates. The fetus, however, lives with vegetable and animal life, to which the union of a soul with the child-body at birth adds spiritual life.

355 - Are there, as is indicated by science, children so constituted that they can't live, and if so, for what purpose ore they produced?
- That often happens. Such births are permitted as a trial, either for the parents or for the spirit appointed to animate it.

356 - Are there, among still-born children, some who were never intended for the incarnation of a spirit?
- Yes, there are some who never had a spirit assigned to them, for whom nothing was to be done. In such a case, it's simply as a trial for the parents that the child arrives.
- Can a being of this nature come to its term?
- Yes, sometimes; but it doesn't live.
- Every child that survives its birth has, then, necessarily a spirit incarnated in it?
- What would it be if such were not the case? It'd not he a human being.

357 - What are, for a spirit, the consequences of abortion?
- It's an existence that is null and must be commenced over again.

358 - Is artificial abortion a crime, no matter at what period of gestation it may be produced?
- Every transgression of the law of God is a crime. The mother, or any other, who takes the life of an unborn child, is necessarily criminal; for, by so doing, a soul is prevented from undergoing the trial of which the body thus destroyed was to have been the instrument.

359 - In cases in which the life of the mother would be endangered by the birth of the child, is it a crime to sacrifice the child in order to save the mother?
- It's better to sacrifice the being whose existence is not yet complete than the being whose existence is complete.

360 - Is it rational to treat the fetus with the same respect as the body of a child that has lived?
- In the one, as in the other, you should recognize the will and the handiwork of God, and these are always to be respected.

3 - Moral and intellectual faculties
361 - Whence has man his moral qualities, good or bad?
- They're those of the spirit who is incarnated in him. The purer is that spirit, the more decidedly is the man inclined to goodness. It would seem, then, that a good man is the incarnation of a good spirit, and a vicious man that of a bad spirit?
- Yes, but you should rather say of an imperfect spirit, otherwise it might be supposed that there are spirits who will always remain bad, what you call devils.

362 - What is the character of the individuals in whom light and foolish spirits are incarnated?
- They're hare-brained, prankish, and sometimes mischievous.

363 - Have spirits any passions that don't belong to humanity?
- No, if they had, they would communicate them to you.

364 - Is it one and the same spirit that gives a man both his moral and his intellectual qualities?
- Certainly it's the same. A man has not two spirits in him.

365 - How comes it that some men, who are very intelligent, which shows that they have in them a spirit of considerable advancement, are also extremely vicious?
- It's because the spirit incarnated in a man is not sufficiently purified and the man yields to the influence of other spirits still worse than himself. The upward progress of a spirit is accomplished by slow degrees, but this progress doesn't take place simultaneously in all directions. At one period of his career he may advance in knowledge, at another in morality.

366 - What is to be thought of the opinion according to which a man's various intellectual and moral faculties are the product of so many different spirits incarnated in him, and each possessing a special aptitude?
- The absurdity of such an opinion becomes evident on a moment's reflection. Each spirit is destined to possess all possible aptitudes, but, in order to progress, he must possess one sole and unitary will. If a man were an amalgam of different spirits, this unitary will would not exist, and he would possess no individuality, because, at his death, all the spirits would fly off in different directions, like birds escaped from a cage. Men often complain of not comprehending

certain things and yet how ingenious they're in multiplying difficulties, while they have within reach the simplest and most natural of explanations. I such an opinion is, but another instance of the way in which men so often take the effect for the cause. It does for man what the pagans did for God. They believed in the existence of as many gods as there are phenomena in the Universe, but even among them, the more sensible ones only saw in those phenomena a variety of effects having for their cause one and the same God.

> The physical and moral worlds offer us, in regard to this subject, numerous points of comparison. While the attention of mankind was confined to the appearance of natural phenomena, they believed in the existence of many kinds of matter. In the present day, it's seen that all those phenomena, however varied, may very probably be merely the result of modifications of a single elementary matter. The various faculties of a human being are manifestations of one and the same cause, which is the soul or spirit incarnated in him, and not of several souls just as the different sounds of an organ is the product of one and the same sir and not of as many sorts of air as there are sounds. According to the theory in question, when a man acquires or loses aptitudes or tendencies, such modifications would be the result of the coming or going of a corresponding number of the spirits conjoined with him, which would make of him a multiple being without individuality, and, consequently, without responsibility. This theory, moreover, is disproved by the numerous, manifestations of spirits which conclusively demonstrate their personality and their identity.

4 - Influence of organism
367 - Does a spirit, in uniting itself with a body, identify itself with matter?
- Matter is only the envelope of the spirit, as clothing is the envelope of the body. A spirit, in uniting himself with a body, retains the attributes of his spiritual nature.

368 - Does a spirit exercise his faculties in full freedom after his union with a body?
- The exercise of faculties depends on the organs which serve them for instruments. Their exercise is weakened by the grossness of matter.
- It would appear, then, that the material envelope is an obstacle to the free manifestation of a spirit's faculties, as the opacity of ground glass is an obstacle to the free emission of light?
- Yes, an obstacle which is exceedingly opaque.

> The action exercised upon a spirit by the gross matter of his body may also be compared to that of muddy water, impeding the movements of the objects plunged into it.

369 - Is the free exercise of a spirit's faculties subordinated, during his incarnation, to the development of his corporeal organs?
- Those organs are the soul's instruments for the manifestation of its faculties; that manifestation is, therefore, necessarily subordinated to the degree of development and perfection of those organs, as the perfection of a piece of manual work depends on the goodness of the tool employed.

370 - May we, from the influence of the corporeal organs, infer a connection between the development of the cerebral organs and that of the moral and intellectual faculties?
- Don't confound effect and cause. A spirit always possesses the faculties that belong to him, but you must remember that it's not the organs that give the faculties, but the faculties that incite to the development of the organs.
- According to this view of the subject the diversity of aptitudes in each man depends solely on the state of his spirit?
- To say that it does so solely would not be altogether correct. The qualities of the incarnated spirit are, undoubtedly, the determining principle of those aptitudes, but allowance must be made for the influence of matter, which hinders every man, more or less, in the exercise of the faculties inherent in his soul.

> A spirit, in incarnating himself, brings with him certain characterical predispositions therefore, if we admit the existence, for each of these, of a special organ in the brain the development of the cerebral organs is seen to be an effect, and not a cause. If his faculties were a result of his bodily organs, man would be a mere machine, without free-will, and would not be responsible for his actions. Moreover, if such were the case, we should be forced to admit that the greatest geniuses-men of science, poets, artists-are only such because a lucky chance has given them certain special organs whence it would follow, still further, that, but for the chance-acquisition of those organs, they would not have been geniuses, and that the stupidest of men might have been a Newton, a Virgil, or a Raphael, if he had been provided with certain organs a supposition still more flagrantly absurd, if we attempt to apply it to the explanation of the moral qualities.
For, according to this system, Saint Vincent de Paul, had he been gifted by nature with such and such an organ, might have been a scoundrel and the greatest scoundrel alive, had he only been gifted with an organ of an opposite nature, might have been a Saint Vincent de Paul. If, on the contrary, we admit that our special organs, supposing such to exist, are an effect and not a cause, that they're developed by the exercise of the faculties to which they correspond, as muscles are developed by movement, we arrive at a theory which is certainly not irrational. Let us employ an illustration equally conclusive and commonplace. By certain physiognomic signs we recognize a man who is addicted to drink. Is it those signs that make him a drunkard, or is it his drunkenness that produces those signs? It may be safely asserted that our organs are a consequence of our faculties.

5 - Idiocy - Madness
371 - Is there any foundation for the common belief that the souls of idiots are of a nature inferior to those of others?

- No, they have a human soul, which is often more intelligent than you suppose, and which suffers acutely from the insufficiency of its means of communication, as the dumb man suffers from his inability to speak.

372 - What is the aim of Providence in creating beings so ill-treated by nature as idiots?
- Idiots are incarnations of spirits who are undergoing punishment and who suffer from the constraint they experience, and from their inability to manifest themselves by means of organs which are undeveloped, or out of order.
- Then it's not correct to say that organs are without influence upon faculties?
- We have never said that organs are without influence. They have very great influence on the manifestation of faculties, but they don't give faculties, there is just the difference. A skilful player will not make good music with a bad instrument, but that will not prevent his being a good player.

> It's necessary to distinguish between the normal state and the pathologic state. In the normal state, the moral strength of an Incarnated spirit enables him to triumph over the obstacles which are placed in his way by matter but there are cases in which matter opposes a resistance so powerful that the manifestations of the spirit incarnated in it are hindered or changed from what he intended, as in idiocy and madness. These cases are pathologic and as the soul, in such states, is not in the enjoyment of its full liberty, human law itself exempts such persons from the responsibility of their actions.

373 - What merit can there be in the existence of beings who, like idiots, can do neither good nor evil, and therefore can't progress?
- Such an existence is imposed as an expiation of the abuse which a spirit has made of certain faculties; it constitutes a pause in his career.
- The body of an idiot may, then, contain a spirit that has animated a man of genius in a preceding existence?
- Yes, genius sometimes becomes a scourge when it's abused.

> Intellectual superiority is not always accompanied by an equal degree of moral superiority and the greatest geniuses may have much to expiate. For this reason, they often have to undergo an existence inferior to the one they have previously accomplished, which is a cause of suffering for them the hindrances to the manifestation of his faculties thus imposed upon a spirit being like chains that fetter the movements of a vigorous man. The idiot may be said to be lame in the brain, as the halt is lame in the legs, and the blind, in the eyes.

374 - Is the idiot, in the spirit-state, conscious of his mental condition?
- Yes, very often. He comprehends that the chains which hinder his action are a trial and an expiation.

375 - When a man is mad, what is the state of his spirit?
- A spirit, in the state of freedom, receives his impressions directly and exerts his action directly upon matter, but when incarnated, he is in an altogether different condition and compelled to act only through the instrumentality of special organs. If some or all of those organs are injured, his actions or his impressions, as far as those organs are concerned, are interrupted. If he loses his eyes, he becomes blind, if he loses his hearing; he becomes deaf and so on. Suppose that the organ which presides over the manifestations of intelligence and of will is partially or entirely weakened or modified in its action, and you'll easily understand that the spirit, having at his service only organs that are incomplete or diverted from their proper action, must experience a functional perturbation of which he is perfectly conscious, but is not able to arrest the course.
- It's then always the body and not the spirit that is disorganized?
- Yes, but you must not forget that, just as a spirit acts upon matter, matter, to a certain extent, reacts upon him, and that he may therefore find himself, for the time being, subjected to the influence of the false impressions consequent on the vitiated state of his organs of perception and of action. And it may happen, when this mental aberration has continued for a long time, that the repetition of the same perverted action may exercise upon a spirit an influence from which he is only delivered after his complete separation from all material impressions.

376 - How is it that madness sometimes leads to suicide?
- In such cases, the spirit suffers from the constraint which, he feels and from his inability to manifest himself freely, and he therefore seeks death as a means of breaking his chains.

377 - Does the spirit of a madman continue to feel, after death, the derangement from which he suffered in his corporeal life?
- He may continue to feel it for some time after death, until he is completely freed from matter; just as a man, on waking, continues to feel, for some little time, the confusion in which he has been plunged by sleep.

378 - How can brain-disease act upon a spirit after his death?
- It's an effect of remembrance, which weighs like a burden upon the spirit, and as he was not aware of all that took place during his madness, he always needs a certain amount of time for recovering the hang of his ideas. It's for this reason that the continuance of his uneasiness after death is always proportioned to the longer or shorter continuance of the corporeal insanity from which he has previously suffered. A spirit, when freed from the body, still feels, for a longer or shorter time, the impression of the links that united him with it.

6 - Infancy
379 - Is the spirit who animates the body of a child as developed as that of an adult?

- He may be more so, if before reincarnating himself, he bad progressed farther; it's only the imperfection of his organs that prevents him from manifesting himself. He acts according to the state of the instrument by which alone, when incarnated, he can manifest himself.

380 - During the infancy of his body, and without reference to the obstacle opposed to his free manifestation by the imperfection of his organs, does a spirit think as a child or as an adult?
- While he remains a child, it's evident that his organs of thought, not being developed, can't give him all the intuition of an adult; his range of intellect is therefore only narrow, until increasing age has ripened his reason. The confusion which accompanies incarnation doesn't cease, all at once, at the moment of birth, it's only dissipated gradually with the development of the bodily organs.

> The observation of a fact of human life furnishes us with a confirmation of the preceding reply, that the dreams of childhood have not the character of those of adult age. Their object is almost always childish a characteristic indication of the nature of a spirit's thoughts during the Infancy of his organs.

381 - At the death of a child, does its spirit at once regain his former vigor?
- He should do so, since he is freed from his fleshly envelope, but, in point of fact, he only regains his former lucidity when the separation is complete, that is to say, when there's no longer any connection between the spirit and the body.

382 - Does the incarnated spirit suffer, during the state of childhood, from the constraint imposed on him by the imperfections of his organs?
- No, that state is a necessity. It's a part of the ordination of nature, and of the providential plan. It constitutes a time of repose for the spirit.

383 - What is the use for a spirit of passing through the state of infancy?
- The aim of incarnation is the improvement of the spirit subjected to it and a spirit is more accessible during childhood to the impressions he receives, and which may conduce to his advancement, the end to which all those who are entrusted with his education should contribute.

384 - Why is it that the infant's first utterances are those of weeping?
- It's in order to excite the mother's interest on his behalf, and to ensure to him the care he needs. Can you not understand that if a child, before he's able to speak, uttered only cries of joy, those around him would trouble themselves very little about his wants? In all these arrangements admire the wisdom of Providence.

385 - Whence comes the change which occurs in the character of the young on the approach of manhood, is it the spirit that becomes modified?
- The spirit, regaining possession of himself, shows himself such as he was before his incarnation.
- You know not the secrets hidden under the seeming innocence of children. You know neither what they're, nor what they have been, nor what they'll be, and nevertheless you love and cherish them as though they were a part of yourselves, and to such a degree, that the love of a mother for her children is reputed to be the greatest love that one being canned has for another. Whence comes the sweet affection, the tender benevolence, that even strangers feel for a child? Do you know its origin? No, but I'll now explain it to you. Children are beings sent by God into new existences, and, in order that they may not be able to reproach Him with having been unduly severe to them, He gives them all the external appearances of innocence, even in the case of a child of the worst possible nature, its misdeeds are covered by its unconsciousness of the quality of its acts.

This apparent innocence doesn't constitute for children any real superiority over what they previously were, it's merely the image of what they ought to be, and, if they're not such, it'll be on themselves alone that the punishment will fall. But it's not merely for themselves that God has given to children this appearance of innocence, it's given to them also, and especially, in view of their parents, whose love is so necessary to them in their weakness, for this love would be greatly diminished by the sight of a harsh or cross-grained nature, whereas, believing their children to be good and gentle, they give them all their affection, and surround them with the most minute and delicate care.

But, when children no longer need this protection, this assistance, which has been given them during fifteen or twenty years, their real character and individuality reappears in all its nudity. He who is really good remains good, but, even then, his character reveals many traits and shades that were hidden during his earlier years. You see that God's ways are always for the best; and that, for the pure in heart, they're easily explicable. Get it well into your minds that the spirit of the child who is born among you may have come from a world in which he has acquired habits totally different from yours; how would it be possible for this new being, coming among you with passions, inclinations, tastes, entirely opposed to yours, to accommodate himself to your world, if became among you in any other way than in that which has been ordained by God, that is to say, by passing through the sieve of infancy?

It's through this sifting process of infancy that all the thoughts, all the characteristics, all the varieties of beings engendered by the crowd of worlds in which creatures pursue the work of growth, are eventually mingled. And you, also, on dying, find yourselves in a sort of infancy, and in the midst of a new family of brothers, and in your new non-terrestrial existence you are ignorant of the habits, manners, relations of a world which is new to you, and you find it difficult to express yourselves in a language which you are not accustomed to employ, a language more living than is your thought to-day.

Childhood possesses yet another utility. Spirits only enter into corporeal life in order to effect their improvement, their self-amelioration. The weakness of corporeal youth tends to render them more pliable, more amenable to the counsels of those whose experience should aid their progress. It's thus that evil tendencies are repressed, and faulty characters are gradually reformed; and this repression and reformation constitute the duty confided by God to those who assume the parental relation, a sacred mission of which parents will have to render a solemn account to him.

-You see, therefore, that childhood is not only useful, necessary, indispensable, but that it's, moreover, the natural result of the laws which God has established, and which govern the Universe.

7 - Terrestrial sympathies and antipathies

386 - Could two beings, who have already known and loved each other, meet again and recognize one another, in another corporeal existence?

- They could not recognize one another; but they might be attracted to each other. The attraction resulting from the ties of a former existence is often the cause of the most intimate affection unions of a subsequent existence. It often happens in your world that two persons are drawn together by circumstances which appear to be merely fortuitous, but which are really due to the attraction exercised upon one another by two spirits who are unconsciously seeking each other amidst the crowds by whom they're surrounded.

- Would it not be more agreeable for them to recognize each other?

- Not always, the remembrance of past existences would be attended with greater disadvantages than you suppose. After death they would recognize one another, and would then remember the periods they had passed together.

387 - Is sympathy always the result of anterior acquaintanceship?

- No, two spirits who are in harmony naturally seek one another, without their having been previously acquainted with each other as men.

388 - May it not be that the meetings which sometimes take place between two persons, and which are attributed to chance, are really due to the action of some sort of sympathetic relationship?

- There are, among thinking beings, orders of relationship with which you are not yet acquainted. Magnetism is the pilot of the science that will enable you to understand them at a future period.

389 - What is the cause of the instinctive repulsion sometimes excited in us by persons whom we see for the first time?

- The latent antipathy of two spirits who divine each other's nature, and recognize one another, without the need of speaking together.

390 - Is instinctive antipathy allays the sign of an evil nature on the part of one or both of the parties who feel it?

- Two spirits aren't necessarily evil because they're not sympathetic, for antipathy may spring from a want of similarity in their way of thinking, but in proportion as they ascend, these shades of difference are effaced and their antipathy disappears.

391 - Does the antipathy of two persons take its first beginning on the part of the better or the worse one of the two?

- It may begin simultaneously on the part of both, but, in such a case, its causes and effects are different. A bad spirit feels antipathy against whoever is able to judge and to unmask him. On seeing such a person for the first time, he knows that he'll be disapproved by him, his repulsion changes into hatred or jealousy, and inspires him with the desire of doing harm to the object of his antipathy. A good spirit feels repulsion for a bad one, because he knows that he'll not be understood by him, and that they don't share the same sentiments, but, strong in his own superiority, he feels neither hatred nor jealousy towards him, and contents himself with avoiding and pitying him.

8 - Forgetfulness of the past

392 - Why does the incarnated spirit lose the remembrance of his past?

- Man can't, and may not, know everything. God, in his wisdom, has so ordained. Without the veil which hides certain things from his view, man would be dazzled, like one who passes suddenly from darkness to light. Through the forgetfulness of his past a man is more fully himself.

393 - How can a man be responsible for deeds, and atone for faults, of which he has no remembrance? How can he profit by the experience acquired in existences which he has forgotten? We could understand that the tribulations of life might be a lesson for him if he remembered the wrong-doing which has brought them upon him, but if he forgets his former existences, each new existence is, for him, as though it were his first, and thus the work is always to be begun over again. How is this to be reconciled with the justice of God?

- With each new existence a spirit becomes more intelligent and better able to distinguish between good and evil. Where would be his freedom if he remembered all his past? When a spirit reenters his primitive life, his whole past unrolls itself before him. He sees the faults which he has committed, and which are the cause of his suffering, and he also sees what would have prevented him from committing them; he comprehends the justice of the situation which is assigned to him, and he then seeks out the new existence that may serve to repair the mistakes of the one which has just passed away. He demands new trials analogous to those in which he has failed, or which he considers likely to aid his advancement, and he demands of the spirits who are his superiors to aid him in the new task he is about to undertake, for he knows that the spirit who will be appointed as his guide in that new existence will endeavor to make him cure himself of his faults by giving him a sort of intuition of those he has committed in the past.

This intuition is the evil thought, the criminal desire, which often come to you, and which you instinctively resist, attributing your resistance to the principles you have received from your parents, while it's due in reality to the voice of your conscience, and that voice is the reminiscence of your past, warning you not to fall again into the faults you have already committed. He, who, having entered upon a new existence, undergoes its trials with fortitude and resists its temptations to wrong-doing, rises in the hierarchy of spirits and takes a higher place when he returns into the normal life. If we have not an exact remembrance, during our corporeal life, of what we have been, and of the good or evil we have done, in our preceding existences, we have the intuition of our past, of which we have a reminiscence in the instinctive tendencies that our conscience, which is the desire we have conceived to avoid committing our past faults in the future, warns us to resist.

394 - In worlds more advanced than ours, where the human race is not a prey to our physical wants and infirmities, do men understand that they're better off than we are? Happiness is usually relative; it's felt to be such by comparison with a state that is less happy. As some of those worlds, though better than ours, have not reached perfection, the men by whom they're inhabited must have their own troubles and annoyances. Among us, the rich man, although he has not to endure the physical privations that torture the poor, is none the less a prey to tribulations of other kinds that embitter his life. What I ask is, whether the inhabitants of those worlds don't consider themselves to be just as unhappy, according to their standard of happiness, as we consider ourselves to be according to ours, and whether they don't, like us, complain of their fate, not having the remembrance of an inferior existence to serve them as a standard of comparison?
- To this question two different answers must be given. Three are some worlds among those of which you speak the inhabitants of which have a very clear and exact remembrance of their past existences, and therefore can and do appreciate the happiness which God permits them to enjoy. But there are others, of which the inhabitants, though placed, as you say, in better conditions than yours, are, nevertheless, subject to great annoyances, and even to much unhappiness, and who don't appreciate the more favorable conditions of their life, because they have no remembrance of a state still more unhappy. But if they don't rightly appreciate those conditions as men, they appreciate them more justly on their return to the spirit-world.

> Is there not, in the forgetfulness of our past existences, and especially when they have been painful, a striking proof of the wisdom and beneficence of providential arrangements? It's only in worlds of higher advancement, and when the remembrance of our painful existences in the past is nothing more to us than the shadowy remembrance of an unpleasant dream, that those existences are allowed to present themselves to our memory. Would not the painfulness of present suffering, in worlds of low degree, be greatly aggravated by the remembrance of all the miseries we may have had to undergo in the past? These considerations should lead us to conclude that whatever has been appointed by God is for the best, and that it's not our province to find fault with his works nor to decide upon the way in which he ought to have regulated the Universe.

The remembrance of our former personality would be attended, in our present existence, with many very serious disadvantages. In some cases, it would cause us cruel humiliation in others, it might incite us to pride and vanity in all cases, it'd be a hindrance to the action of our free-will. God gives us for our amelioration just what is necessary and sufficient to that end, the voice of our conscience and our instinctive tendencies. He keeps from us what would be for us a source of injury. Moreover, if we retained the remembrance of our own former personalities and doings, we should also remember those of other people a kind of knowledge that would necessarily exercise a disastrous influence upon our social relations.

Not always having reason to be proud of our past, it's evidently better for us that a veil should be thrown over it. And these considerations are in perfect accordance with the statements of spirits in regard to the existence of higher worlds than ours. In those worlds, in which moral excellence reigns, there is nothing painful in the remembrance of the past, and therefore the inhabitants of those happier worlds remember their preceding existence as we remember today what we did yesterday. As to the sojourns they may have made in worlds of lower degree, it's no more to them, as we have already said, than the remembrance of a disagreeable dream.

395 - Can we obtain any revelations respecting our former existences?
- Not in all cases. There are, however, many who know who they have been and what they have done. If it were permitted to them to speak openly, they'd make curious revelations about the past.

396 - Some persons believe themselves to have a vague remembrance of an unknown past, which comes before them like the fugitive image of a dream that one vainly endeavors to recall. Is this belief only an illusion?
- It's sometimes real, hut it's often an illusion to he guarded against, for it may be merely the effect of an excited imagination.

397 - In corporeal existences of a more elevated nature than ours, is the reminiscence of our anterior existences more exact?
- Yes, in proportion as the body is less material, the spirit incarnated in it remembers them more clearly. The remembrance of the past is always clearer in those who inhabit worlds of a higher order.

398 - A man's instinctive tendencies being a reflex of his past, does it follow that by studying those tendencies, he can ascertain what the faults he has formerly committed are?
- Undoubtedly he can do so up to a certain point, but he would also have to take account of the improvement which may have been effected in his spirit and of the resolutions taken by him in the state of erraticity. His present existence may he very much better than his preceding one.
- Might it be worse? That is to say, might a man commit, in a subsequent existence, faults which he had not committed in the preceding one?
- That depends on his advancement. If he were unable to resist temptation, he might be drawn into new faults as a consequence of the situation chosen by him, but such faults must be considered as indicating a state which is stationary rather than retrograde, for a spirit may advance or remain stationary, but he never goes back.

399 - The vicissitudes of corporeal life being at once an expiation of the faults of the past and lessons for the future, can we, from the nature of those vicissitudes, infer the character of our preceding existence?

- You can do so very frequently, since the nature of the punishment incurred always corresponds to that of the fault committed. Nevertheless, it would not do to consider this as being an absolute rule. The instinctive tendencies furnish a more certain indication, for the trials undergone by a spirit are as much for the future as for the past.

> When a spirit has reached the end of the term assigned by Providence to his errant life, he chooses for himself the trials which he determines to undergo in order to hasten his progress, that is to say, the kind of existence which he believes will be most likely to furnish him with the means of advancing and the trials of this new existence always correspond to the faults which he has to expiate. If he triumphs in this new struggle, he rises in grade, if he succumbs, he has to try again. A spirit always possesses free-will. It's in virtue of this free-will that he chooses, when in the spirit-state, the trials he elects to undergo in the corporeal life, and that he deliberates, when in the incarnate state whether he'll do, or not do, and chooses between good and evil.

To deny a man's free-will would be to reduce him to a machine. When a spirit has re-entered corporeal life, he experiences a temporary forgetfulness of his former existences, as though these were hidden from him by a veil. Sometimes, however, he preserves a vague consciousness of them, and they may, under certain circumstances, be revealed to him but this only occurs as a result of the decision of higher spirits, who make that revelation spontaneously for some useful end, and never for the gratification of idle curiosity.

A spirit's future existences can't, in any case, be revealed to him during the corporeal life, because they'll depend on the manner in which he accomplishes his present existence, and on his own ulterior choice. Temporary forgetfulness of the faults he has committed is no obstacle to a spirit's improvement for if he have not a precise remembrance of them, the knowledge he had of them In the state of erraticity, and the desire he then conceived to repair them, guide him intuitively, and inspire him with the Intention of resisting the evil tendency. This Intention is the voice of his conscience, and is seconded by the spirits who assist him, if he gives heed to the suggestions with which they inspire him.

Although a man doesn't know exactly what may have been his acts in his former existences, he always knows the kind of faults of which he has been guilty, and what has been his ruling characteristic. He has only to study himself, and he'll know what he has been, not by what he is, but by his tendencies the vicissitudes of corporeal life are both an expiation of faults in the past, and trials designed to render us better for the future. They purify and elevate, provided we hear them resignedly and un-repiningly.

The Nature of the vicissitudes and trials that we have to undergo may also enlighten us in regard to what we have been end what we have done, just as we infer the crimes of which a convict has been guilty from the penalty inflicted on him by the law. Thus, he who has sinned through pride will be punished by the humiliations of an inferior position the self-indulgent and avaricious, by poverty the hard-hearted, by the seventies he'll undergo the tyrant, by slavery a bad son, by the ingratitude of his children the idle, by subjection to hard and incessant labor and so on.

Chapter 8 - Emancipation of the soul

1 - Sleep and dreams

400 - Does the incarnated spirit reside willingly in his corporeal envelope?

- You might as well ask whether a prisoner willingly remains locked up in prison. The incarnated spirit aspires incessantly after his deliverance and the grosser his envelope, the more desirous is be to be rid of it.

401 - Does the soul take rest like tile body during sleep?

- No, a spirit is never inactive. The bonds which unite him to the body are relaxed during sleep, and as the body doesn't then need his presence, he travels through space, and enters into more direct relation with other spirits.

402 - How can we ascertain the fact of a spirit's liberty during sleep?

- By dreams. Be very sure that, when his body is asleep, a spirit enjoys the use of faculties of which he is unconscious while his body is awake. He remembers the past, and sometimes foresees the future: he acquires more power, and is able to enter into communication with other spirits, either in this world or in some other.

- You often say, "I have had a strange dream, a frightful dream, without any likeness to reality". You're mistaken in thinking it to be so, for it's often a reminiscence of places and things which you have seen in the past, or a foresight of those which you'll see in another existence, or in this one at some future time. The body being torpid, the spirit tries to break his chain, and seeks, in the past or in the future, for the means of doing so.

Poor human beings! How little do you know of the commonest phenomena of your life? You fancy yourselves to be very learned, and you are puzzled by the most ordinary things. To questions that any child might ask, what do we do when we are asleep? What are dreams? You're incapable of replying. Sleep effects a partial freeing of the soul from the body. When you sleep, your spirit is, for the time being, in the state in which you'll be after your death. The spirits who at death are promptly freed from matter are those who, during their life, have had what may be called intelligent sleep.

Such persons, when they sleep, regain the society of other spirits superior to themselves. They go about with them, conversing with them, and gaining instruction from them; they even work, in the spirit-world, at undertakings which, on dying, they find already begun or completed. From this you see how little death should be dreaded, since, according to the saying of St. Paul, you die daily.

What we have just stated refers to spirits of an elevated degree of advancement. As for those of the common mass of men, who, after their death, remain for long hours in the state of confusion and uncertainty of which you have been told by such, they go, during sleep, into worlds of lower rank than the Earth, to which they're drawn back by old affections, or by the attraction of pleasures still baser than those to which they're addicted in your world; visits in which they gather ideas still viler, more ignoble, and more mischievous than those which they had professed during their waking hours.

And that which engenders sympathy in the earthly life is nothing else than the fact that you feel yourselves, on waking, affectionately attracted towards those with whom you have passed eight or nine hours of happiness or pleasure.

On the other hand, the explanation of the invincible antipathies you sometimes feel for certain persons is also to be found in the intuitive knowledge you have thus acquired of the fact that those persons have another conscience than yours, because you know them without having previously seen them with your bodily eyes. It's this same fact, moreover, that explains the indifference of some people for others; they don't care to make new friends, because they know that they have others by whom they're loved and cherished. In a word, sleep has more influence than you think upon your life.

Through the effects of sleep, incarnated spirits are always in connection with the spirit world, and it's in consideration of this fact that spirits of higher order consent, without much repugnance, to incarnate themselves among you. God has willed that, during their contact with vice, they may go forth and fortify themselves afresh at the source of rectitude, in order that they, who have come into your world to instruct others, may not fall into evil themselves. Sleep is the gate opened for them by God, that they may pass through it to their friends in the spirit-world; it's their recreation after labor, while awaiting the great deliverance, the final liberation, that will restore them to their true place.

Dreams are the remembrance of what your spirit has seen during sleep; but you must remark that you don't always dream, because you don't always remember what you have seen, or all that you have seen. Your dreams don't always reflect the action of your soul in its full development; for they're often only the reflex of the confusion that accompanies your departure or your return, mingled with the vague remembrance of what you have done, or of what has occupied your thoughts, in your waking state.

In what other way can you explain the absurd dreams which are dreamed by the wisest as by the silliest of mankind? Bad spirits, also, make use of dreams to torment weak and timid souls. You'll see, ere long, the development of another kind of dream, a kind which is as ancient as the one you know, but one of which you are ignorant. The dream we allude to is that of Jeanne D'arc, of Jacob, of the Jewish prophets, and of certain Hindoo ascetics, a dream which is the remembrance of the soul's experiences while entirely freed from the body, the remembrance of the second life, of which I spoke just now. You should carefully endeavor to distinguish these two kinds of dreams among those which you are able to recall, unless you do this, you'll be in danger of falling into contradictions and errors that would be prejudicial to your belief.

> Dreams are a product of the emancipation of the soul, rendered more active by the suspension of the active life of relation, and enjoying a sort of indefinite clairvoyance which extends to places at a great distance from us, or that we have never seen, or even to other worlds. To this state of emancipation is also due the remembrance which retraces to our memory the events that have occurred in our present existence or in preceding existences the strangeness of the images of what has taken place in worlds unknown to us, mixed up with the things of the present world, producing the confused and whimsical medleys that seem to be equally devoid of connection and of meaning. The incoherence of dreams is still farther explained by the gaps resulting from the incompleteness of our remembrance of what has appeared to us in our

nightly visions, an incompleteness similar to that of a narrative from which. Whole sentences, or parts of sentences, have been omitted by chance, and whose remaining fragments, having been thrown together again at random, have lost all intelligible meaning.

403 - Why do we not always remember our dreams?
- What you call sleep is only the repose of the body, for the spirit is always in motion. During sleep, he recovers a portion of his liberty, and enters into communication with those who are dear to him, either in this world, or in other worlds, but as the matter of the body is heavy and gross, it's difficult for him to retain, on waking, the impressions he has received during sleep, because those impressions were not received by him through the bodily organs.

404 - What is to be thought of the signification attributed to dreams?
- Dreams are not really indications in the sense attributed to them by fortune-tellers; for it's absurd to believe that a certain kind of dream announces the happening of a certain kind of event. But they're indications in this sense; that they present images which are real for the spirit, though they may have nothing to do with what takes place in his present corporeal life.
Dreams are also, in many cases, as we have said, a remembrance; they may also be sometimes a presentiment of the future, if permitted by God, or the sight of something which is taking place at the time in some other place to which the soul has transported itself. Have you not many instances proving that persons may appear to their relatives and friends in dreams, and give them notice of what is happening to them? What are apparitions, if not the soul or spirit of persons who come to communicate with you? When you acquire the certainty that what you saw has really taken place, is it not a proof that it was no freak of your imagination, especially if what you saw were something which you had not thought of when you were awake?

405 - We often see in dreams things which appear to be presentiments, but which don't come to pass, how is this?
- Those things may take place in the experience of the spirit, though not in that of the body; that is to say, that the spirit sees what he wishes to see because he goes to find it. You must not forget that, during sleep, the spirit is always more or less under the influence of matter; that, consequently, he is never completely free from terrestrial ideas, and that the objects of his waking thoughts may therefore give to his dreams the appearance of what he desires or of what he fears, thus producing what may be properly termed an effect of the imagination. When the mind is much busied with any idea, it's apt to connect everything it sees with that idea.

406 - When, in a dream, we see persons who are well known to us doing things which they're not in any way thinking of, is it not a mere effect of the imagination?
- Of which they're not thinking? How do you know that it's so? Their spirit may come to visit yours, as yours may go to visit theirs, and you don't always know, in your waking state, what they may be thinking of. And besides, you often, in your dreams, apply to persons whom you know, and according to your own desires, reminiscences of what took place, or are taking place, in other existences.

407 - Is it necessary to the emancipation of the soul that the sleep of the body should be complete?
- No, the spirit recovers his liberty as soon as the senses become torpid. He takes advantage, in order to emancipate himself, of every moment of respite left him by the body. As soon as there occurs any prostration of the vital forces, the spirit disengages himself from the body, and the feebler the body, the freer is the spirit.

> It's for this reason that dozing, or a mere dulling of the senses, often presents the same images as dreaming.

408 - We sometimes seem to hear within ourselves words distinctly pronounced, but having no connection with what we are thinking of, what is the cause of this?
- Yes, you often hear words, and even whole sentences, especially when your senses begin to grow torpid. It's sometimes the faint echo of the utterance of a spirit who wishes to communicate with you.

409 - Often, when only half-asleep, and with our eyes closed, we see distinct images, figures of which we perceive the minutest details, is this an effect of vision or of imagination?
- The body being torpid, the spirit tries to break his chain; he goes away and sees, if the sleep were deeper, the vision would be a dream.

410 - We sometimes, when asleep, or half-asleep, have ideas which seem to us to be excellent, but which, despite all the efforts we make to recall them, are effaced from our memory on waking, whence come these ideas?
- They're the result of the freedom of the spirit, who emancipates himself from the body, and enjoys the use of other faculties during this moment of liberty, and they're often counsels given you by other spirits.
- What is the use of such ideas and counsels, since we lose the remembrance of them, and can't profit by them?
- Those ideas often belong rather to the world of spirits than to the corporeal world, but, in general, though the body may forget them, the spirit remembers them, and the idea recurs to him at the proper time, in his waking state, as though it were an inspiration of the moment.

411 - Does the incarnated spirit, when he is freed from matter and acting as a spirit, know the epoch of his death?
- He often has the presentiment of it. He sometimes has a very clear foreknowledge of it, and it's this which gives him the intuition of it in his waking state. It's this, also, which enables some persons to foresee the time of their death with perfect exactness.

412 - Can the activity of the spirit, during the repose or the sleep of the body, cause fatigue to the latter?

- Yes, for the spirit is attached to the body, as the captive-balloon is fastened to the post, and, just as the post is shaken by the movements of the balloon, so the activity of the spirit reacts upon the body and may cause it to feel fatigued.

2 - Visits between the spirits of living persons

413 - The emancipation of the soul during sleep would seem to indicate that we live simultaneously two lives, the life of the body, which is that of exterior relation, and the life of the soul, which is that of occult relation, is this so?

- During the emancipation of the soul, the life of the latter takes precedence of the life of the body, this, however, doesn't, strictly speaking, constitute two lives, but rather two phases of one and the same life, for a man doesn't live a double life.

414 - Can two persons, who are acquainted with each other, visit one another in sleep?

- Yes, and many others, who, in their waking state, don't know that they're acquainted, meet and converse together. You may, without suspecting it, have friends in another country. The fact of going, during sleep, to visit friends, relatives, acquaintances, persons who can be of use to you, is extremely frequent; and you yourselves accomplish these visits almost every night.

415 - What can be the use of these nocturnal meetings, since we don't remember them?

- The intuition of them generally remains with you in your waking state, and is often the origin of ideas which afterwards occur to you, as it were, spontaneously, without your being able to account for them, but which are really those you had obtained in the spirit-intercourse carried on by you during your sleep.

416 - Can a man ensure the making of spirit-visits by the exertion of his will? Can he do so, for example, by saying to himself, on going to sleep, I'll to-night meet such and such a person in spirit and speak with him about such and such a thing?

- This is what takes place. The man falls asleep, and his spirit wakens to the other life, but his spirit is often very far from following out the plan which had been resolved upon by the man, for the life of the man excites but little interest in a spirit when he is emancipated from matter. This statement, however, only applies to men who have already reached a certain degree of elevation. The others pass their spirit-existence very differently. They give free rein to their passions, or remain inactive. It may happen; therefore, according to the aim of the proposed action, that a spirit may go to see the parties he had, as a man, proposed to visit; but it doesn't follow that, because he has willed to do so in his waking state, he'll necessarily do so in his state of freedom.

417 - Can a number of incarnate spirits, during sleep, meet together and form assemblies?

- Undoubtedly, they can. The ties of friendship, old or new, often bring together spirits who are happy to be in each other's company.

> By the term 'old' must be understood the ties of friendship contracted in anterior existences. We bring back with us, on waking, an intuition of the ideas which we have derived from these occult meetings, but of the source of which we are ignorant.

418 - If a person believed one of his friends to be dead who is not dead, could he meet him as a spirit, and thus learn that he is living? Could he, in such a case, preserve the intuition of this fact on waking?

- He could, certainly, as a spirit, see his friend, and know what is his situation; and if the belief in the death of that friend had not been imposed on him as an expiation, he might retain an impression of his existence, as, in the contrary case, he might retain that of his death.

3 - Occult transmission of thought

419 - Whence comes it that the same idea that of a discovery, for instance-so often suggests itself at the same time to several persons, although they may be at a distance from one another?

- We have already said that, during sleep, spirits communicate with one another, well, when his body awakes, a spirit remembers what he has learned and the man thinks he has invented it. Thus several persons may find out the same thing at the same time. When you say that an idea is in the air, you employ a figure of speech that is much nearer the truth than suppose. Every one helps unconsciously to propagate it.

> In this way our spirit often reveals to other spirits, without our being aware of it, that which formed the object of our meditations before we went to sleep.

420 - Can spirits communicate between themselves when the body is awake?

- A spirit isn't enclosed in his body as in a box, but radiates around it in every direction. He can, therefore, hold communication with other spirits even in the waking state, although he does so with more difficulty.

421 - How comes it that two persons, perfectly awake, often have the same thought at the same moment?

- It's because two spirits, who are in sympathy, may communicate their thought to each other even when the body is not asleep.

> There is, between spirits, a communication of thoughts which sometimes enables two persons to see and understand one another without having any need of human speech. They may be said to speak the language of spirits.

4 - Lethargy, catalepsy, apparent death

422 - In lethargy and catalepsy, the patients generally see and hear what takes place around them, but are unable to manifest their impressions. Is it through the eyes and ears of the body that these impressions are received?
- No, they're received by the spirit. The spirit is conscious, but can't express himself.
-Why can he not express himself?
- The state of his body prevents his doing so; an(l this peculiar state of his bodily organs proves that man consists of something more than a body, since the body no longer works, and yet the spirits acts.

423 - Can a spirit, in a state of lethargy, separate himself entirely from his body, so as to give to the latter all the outward appearances of death, and afterwards come back and inhabit it?
- In lethargy, the body is not dead, for it still accomplishes some of its functions. Its vitality is latent, as in the chrysalis hut is not annihilated; and a spirit is united to his body as long as it remains alive. When once the links which keep them together are broken by the death and desegregation of the bodily organs, the separation complete, and the spirit never again comes back to his body. When one who is apparently dead comes to life again, it's because the process of death was not entirely consummated.

424 - Is it possible, by means of timely help, to renew the ties which were ready to break, and to give back life to a person who, but for this help, would have definitively ceased to live?
- Yes, undoubtedly, and you have proofs of this every day. Mesmerism often exercises, in such cases, a powerful restorative action, because it gives to the body the vital fluid which it lacks, and which is necessary to keep up the play of the organs.

> Lethargy and catalepsy proceed from the same cause, the temporary loss of sensibility and power of motion, from some as yet unexplained physiological condition. They differ in this respect; that, in lethargy, the suppression of the vital force is general, and gives to the body an appearances of death, whereas, in catalepsy, that suppression is localized, and may affect a more or less extensive portion of the body, while leaving the intelligence free to manifest itself a fact which doesn't allow it to be confounded with death. Lethargy is always natural catalepsy is sometimes spontaneous, but it may be produced and dissipated artificially by mesmeric action.

5 - Somnambulism

425 - Is there any connection between natural somnambulism and dreaming?
- In somnambulism the independence of the soul is more complete and its functions are more developed than in dreaming, and it has perceptions that it has not in dreaming, which is an imperfect somnambulism. In somnambulism, the spirit is entirely freed from the action of matter; the material organs, being in a sort of catalepsy, are no longer receptive of external impressions. This state most frequently occurs during sleep, because the spirit is then able to absent itself from the body which is given up to the repose that is indispensable to matter. When somnambulism occurs, it's because the spirit of the sleeper, intent upon doing something or other that requires the aid of his body, makes use of it in a manner analogous to that in which spirits make use of a table, or other material object, in producing the phenomena of physical manifestations, or of a human hand, in giving written communications.
In the dreams of which a man is conscious, his organs, including those of memory, are beginning to awaken; and, as they only receive and transmit to the spirit imperfectly the impressions made on them by exterior objects or action, the spirit, who is then in a state of repose, only perceives these impressions through confused and often disconnected sensations, which, in many cases, are still further confused by being mingled with vague remembrances of his present life and anterior existences. It's easy, therefore, to understand why somnambulists don't remember their visions, and why the greater numbers of the dreams you remember have no rational meaning. I say the greater number, for it sometimes happens that dreams are the consequence of a precise remembrance of events that have occurred in one of your former lives, or even a sort of intuition of the future.

426 - Is there any connection between what is called mesmeric somnambulism and natural somnambulism?
- They're the same thing, the only difference between them being that one of them is artificially produced.

427 - What is the nature of the agent called the magnetic or mesmeric fluid?
- It's the vital fluid, animalized electricity, a modification of the universal fluid.

428 - What is the nature of somnambulic clairvoyance?
- We have told you that it's soul-sight.

429 - How can the somnambulist see through opaque bodies?
- It's only to your gross organs that bodies are opaque. Have we not told you that matter is not an obstacle for a spirit, since he passes freely through it? A somnambulist often tells you that he sees through his forehead, his knee, etc., because you, being plunged in matter, don't understand that he can see without the help of organs. He himself, influenced by your ideas, believes that he needs those organs; but, if you left him to himself, he'd understand that he sees through every part of his body, or rather, that he sees independently of his body.

430 - Since the clairvoyance of the somnambulist is that of his soul or of his spirit, why does lie not see everything, and why does he so often make mistakes?
- In the first place, spirits of low degree don't see and comprehend everything, for, as you know, they still share your errors and your prejudices, and, in the next place, as long as they remain more or less attached to matter, they have not the use of all their spirit faculties. God has given the faculty of clairvoyance to man for a serious and useful purpose, and not to inform him of what it's not permitted to him to know; and this is why somnambulists don't know everything.

431 - What is the source of the somnambulist's innate ideas, and how can he speak correctly of things of which he's ignorant in his waking state, and which are even above his intellectual capacity?
- A somnambulist may possess more knowledge than you give him credit for; but this knowledge is latent in his waking state, because his envelope is too imperfect for him to be able to remember all he knows as a spirit, but, in point of fact, what is he? Like all of us, he's a spirit who has been incarnated in matter for the accomplishment of his mission, and his going into the somnambulic state rouses him from the lethargy of incarnation. We have repeatedly told you that we re-live many times. It's this changing of our existences that causes him to lose sight, in a new connection with matter, of what he may have known in a preceding one. On entering into the state which you call a crisis, he recalls what he has formerly known, but not always with completeness. He knows, but he can't tell whence he derives his knowledge, nor in what way he possesses it. The crisis over, his reminiscences fade from his consciousness, and he re-enters the obscurity of corporeal life.

> Experience shows us that somnambulists also receive communications from other spirits, who tell them what they're to say, and supply what is lacking on their part. This supplementing of their insufficiency is often and especially witnessed in medical consultations the spirit of the clairvoyant seeing the malady, and another spirit indicating the remedy required. This double action is often patent to bystanders, and is also frequently revealed by such expressions on the part of the somnambulist as, "I'm told to say", or "I'm forbidden to say", etc. In the latter case, it's always dangerous to persist in the effort to obtain a revelation refused by the clairvoyant, because, by doing so, we open the door to frivolous and unscrupulous spirits, who prate about everything without any regard to veracity.

432 - How do you explain the power of seeing at a distance possessed by some somnambulists?
- Doesn't the soul transport itself to a distance during sleep? It does the same thing in somnambulism.

433 - Does the greater or less degree of somnambulic clairvoyance depend on the Physical organization of the body, or on the nature of the spirit incarnated in it?
- On both, but there are physical qualities that allow the spirit to liberate himself more or less easily from matter.

434 - Are the faculties enjoyed by the somnambulist the same as those possessed by the spirit after death?
- They're the same, but only up to a certain point, for you have to take into account the influence of the matter to which he's still attached.

435 - Can somnambulists see other spirits?
- That depends on the nature and degree of their faculties. The greater number of them see other spirits perfectly well, but they don't always recognize them at once as being such, and thus mistake them for corporeal beings; a mistake that is often made by somnambulists, and especially by those among them who know nothing of Spiritism. Not understanding anything of the essence of spirits, they're astonished at seeing them in human form and suppose them to be living persons.

> The same effect is produced at the moment of death in the consciousness of those who suppose themselves to be still living. Nothing about them appears to them to be changed. The spirits around them seem to have bodies like ours, and they take the appearance of their own body to be that of a real body of flesh.

436 - When a somnambulist sees objects at a distance, does he see them with his body or with his soul?
- Why should you ask such a question, since it's the soul that sees, and not the body?

437 - Since it's the soul that transports itself to a distance, haw is it that the somnambulist feels in his body the sensation of the heat or the cold of the place where his soul is, and which is sometimes very far from the place where his body is?
- His soul has not entirely quitted his body, to which it's still attached by the link which unites them together; it's this link that is the conductor of sensation. When two persons in two different cities correspond with each other by electricity, it's the electricity that constitutes the link between their thoughts, and enables them to communicate with one another as though they were close together.

438 - Is the state of the somnambulist influenced after death by the use he has made of his faculty?
- Very considerably, as is done by the good or bad use of all the faculties that God has given to man.

6 - Trance
439 - What difference is there between trance and somnambulism?
- Trance is more refined somnambulism. The soul, when in trance, is still more independent.

440 - Does the soul of the ecstatic really enter into higher worlds?

- Yes, he sees them, and perceives the happiness of those who are in them, but there are worlds that are inaccessible to spirits who are not sufficiently purified.

441 - When a person in trance expresses the desire to quit the Earth, does he speak sincerely, and is he not retained by the instinct of self-preservation?
- That depends on the degree of the spirit's purification. If he sees that his future situation will be better than his present one, he makes an effort to break the links that bind him to the Earth.

442 - If the ecstatic were left to himself, might his soul definitively quit his body?
- Yes, he might die, and it's therefore necessary to call him back by everything that may attach him to the lower life, and especially by making him see that, if he breaks the chain which keeps him here, he'll have taken the most effectual means of preventing his staying in the world in which he perceives that he'd be happy.

443 - The ecstatic sometimes professes to see things which are evidently the product of an imagination impressed with earthly beliefs and prejudices. What he sees, therefore, is not always real?
- What he sees is real for him, but, as his spirit is always under the influence of terrestrial ideas, he may see it in his own way, or, to speak more correctly, he may express it in a language accommodated to his prejudices, or to the ideas in which he has been brought up, or to your own, in order the better to make himself understood it's in this way that he's most apt to err.

444 - What degree of confidence should be accorded to the revelations of persons in a state of trance?
- The ecstatic may very frequently be mistaken, especially when he seeks to penetrate what must remain a mystery for man; for he then abandons himself to his own ideas, or becomes the sport of deceiving spirits, who take advantage of his enthusiasm to dazzle him with false appearances.

445 - What inductions are to be drawn from the phenomena of somnambulism and of trance? May they not be considered as a sort of initiation into the future life?
- It'd be more correct to say that, in those states, the somnambulist may obtain glimpses of his past and future lives. Let man study those phenomena; he'll find in them the solution of more than one mystery which his unassisted reason seeks in vain to penetrate.

446 - Could the phenomena of somnambulism and trance be made to accord with theoretic materialism?
- He, who should study them honestly, and without preconceived ideas, could not be either a materialist or an atheist.

7 - Second-sight
447 - Is there any connection between the phenomena of what is designated as second-sight and those of dreaming and somnambulism?
- They're all the same thing. What you call second-sight is also a state in which the spirit is partially free, although the body is not asleep. Second-sight is soul-sight.

448 - Is the faculty of second-sight a permanent one?
- The faculty of second-sight is permanent, but its exercise is not. In worlds less material than yours, spirits free themselves from matter more easily, and enter into communication with one another simply by thought, without, however, excluding the use of articulate speech. In those worlds, second-sight is, for the greater part of their inhabitants, a permanent faculty. Their normal state may be compared to that of lucid somnambulism among you; and it's for this reason that they manifest themselves to you more easily than those who are incarnated in bodies of a grosser nature.

449 - Does second-sight occur spontaneously, or through an exertion of the will of those who possess that faculty?
- It generally occurs spontaneously; but the will, nevertheless, often plays an important part in producing this phenomenon. Take, for example, the persons who are called fortune teller sand some of whom really have that power and you'll find that the action of their will helps them to this second-sight, and to what you call vision.

450 - Is second-sight susceptible of being developed by exercise?
- Yes, effort always leads to progress, and the veil which covers things becomes more transparent.
- Is this faculty a result of physical organization?
- Organization has undoubtedly a great deal to do with it; there are organizations with which it's incompatible.

451 - How is it that second-sight appears to be hereditary in certain families?
- This proceeds from similarity of organization which is transmitted like other physical qualities and also from the development of the faculty through a sort of education, which, also, is transmitted from one generation to another.

452 - Is it true that circumstances develop second-sight?
- Illness, the approach of danger, any great commotion, may develop it. The body is sometimes in a state which allows of the spirit's seeing what can't be seen with the fleshly eye.

> Times of crisis and of calamity, powerful emotions all the causes, in short, which excite the moral nature, may develop second-sight. It'd seem as though Providence gave us, when in the presence of danger, the means of escaping it. All sects and all parties subjected to persecution have offered numerous instances of this fact.

453 - Are the persons who are gifted with second-sight always conscious of their faculty?

- Not always, it appears to them to be altogether natural, and many of them suppose that, if everybody observed their own impressions, they'd find themselves to be possessed of the same power.

454 - May we attribute to a sort of second-sight the perspicacity of those persons who, without being remarkably gifted in other ways, possess an unusually clear judgment in relation to the things of everyday life?

- Such clearness of judgment is always due to a freer radiation of the soul, enabling the man to see more correctly than those whose perceptions are more densely veiled by matter.

- Can this lucidity of judgment, in some cases, give the fore knowledge of future events?

- Yes, it may give presentiments; for there are many degrees in this faculty, and the same person may possess all those degrees, as he may possess only some of them.

8 - Explanation of somnambulism, trance and second-sight

455 - The phenomena of natural somnambulism occur spontaneously and independently of any known external cause, but, in persons endowed with a special organization, they may be produced artificially through the action of the mesmeric agent. The only difference between the state designated as mesmeric somnambulism, and natural somnambulism is, that the one is artificially produced, while the other is spontaneous. Natural somnambulism is a notorious fact, the reality of which few now dispute, notwithstanding the marvelous character of the phenomena it presents. Why, then, should mesmeric somnambulism be regarded as more extraordinary or incredible, simply because it's produced artificially, like so many other things? It has been abused by charlatans, some persons will reply, but that fact only affords an additional reason for not leaving it in their hands.

When science shall have taken possession of it, charlatanism will have much less credit with the masses; but, meanwhile, as somnambulism, both natural and artificial, is a fact, and as a fact can't be argued down, it's making its way, despite the ill-will of its adversaries, and obtaining a footing even in the temple of science, which it's entering by a multitude of side-doors, instead of entering by the principal one. Its right to be there will, ere long, be fully recognized. For the Spiritist, somnambulism is more than a physical phenomenon; it's a light thrown on the subject of psychology; it's a state in which we can study the soul, because in it the soul shows itself, so to say, without covering. Now, one of the phenomena which characterize the soul is clear-seeing independently of the ordinary visual organs.

Those who contest this fact do so on the ground that the somnambulist doesn't see at all times, and at the will of the experimentalist, as with the eyes. Need we be astonished if, the means employed being different, the results are not the same? Is it reasonable to demand identical effects in cases in which the instruments employed are not the same? The soul has its properties just as has the eye, and the former must be judged of by themselves, and not by analogy with the latter. The cause of the clairvoyance of the mesmeric and of the natural somnambulist is identically the same: it's an attribute of the soul, a faculty inherent in every part of the incorporeal being which is in us, and has no other limits than those assigned to the soul itself. The somnambulist sees wherever his soul can transport itself, at no matter what distance.

In sight at distance, the somnambulist doesn't see from the point at which his body is, and as though through a telescope. The things he sees are present with him, as though he were at the place where they exist, because his soul is there in reality, and it's for this reason that his body is, as it were, annihilated, and seems to he deprived of sensation, until the moment when the soul comes back and retakes possession of it. This partial separation of the soul and the body is an abnormal state, which may last for a longer or shorter time, but not indefinitely; it's the cause of the fatigue felt by the body after a certain lapse of time, especially when the soul during that partial separation, busies itself with some active pursuit.

The fact that soul sight or spirit-sight is not circumscribed, and has no definite seat, explains why somnambulists are unable to assign to it any special organ or focus. They see, because they see, without knowing why or how; their sight, as spirit-sight, having no special focus. If they refer their perception to their body, this focus seems to them to he in the organic centers in which the vital activity is greatest, especially in the brain, in the epigastric region, or in whatever organ appears to them to be the point at which the bond between the spirit and the body is most tenacious. The scope of somnambulistic lucidity is not unlimited. A spirit, even when completely free, only possesses the faculties and the knowledge appertaining to the degree of advancement at which he has arrived, a limitation which becomes still further narrowed when he is muted with matter, and thus subjected to its influence.

This is the reason why somnambulistic clairvoyance is neither universal nor infallible; and its infallibility is all the less to be counted on when it's turned aside from the aim which has been assigned to it by nature, and made a mere matter of curiosity and experimentation. In the state of comparative freedom in which the somnambulist finds himself, he enters more easily into communication with other spirits, incarnate or disincarnate, and this communication is established through the contact of the fluids which compose their perispirits, and serve, like the electric wire, for the transmission of thought. The somnambulist, therefore, has no need of articulate speech as a vehicle of thought, which he feels and divines, a mode of perception that renders him eminently accessible to, and impressionable by, the influences of the moral atmosphere in which he finds himself.

For the same reason, a numerous concourse of spectators, and especially of those who are attracted by a more or less malevolent curiosity, is essentially unfavorable to the manifestation of his peculiar faculties, which close up, so to say, at the contact of hostile influences, and only unfold freely in intimacy, and under the influence of sympathetic surroundings. The presence of those who are malevolent or antipathetic produces upon him the effect of the contact of the hand upon a sensitive plant. The somnambulist sees, at the same time, his own spirit and his body; they're, so to say, two beings which represent to him his double existence, spiritual and corporeal, and which, nevertheless, are blended into one by the ties which united them together.

The somnambulist doesn't always comprehend this duality, which often leads him to speak of himself as though he were speaking of another person; in such cases, the corporeal being sometimes speaking to the spiritual being, and the spiritual being sometimes speaking to the corporeal being. The spirit acquires an increase of knowledge and experience in each of his corporeal existences. He loses sight of part of these gains during his reincarnation in matter, which is too gross to allow of his remembering them in their entirety; but he remembers them as a spirit. It's thus that some somnambulists give evidence of possessing knowledge beyond their present degree of instruction, and even of their apparent intellectual capacity.

The intellectual and scientific inferiority of somnambulism in his waking state, therefore, proves nothing against his possession of the knowledge he may display in his lucid state. According to the circumstances of the moment and the aim proposed, he may draw this knowledge from the stores of his own experience, from his clairvoyant perception of things actually occurring, or from the counsels which he receives from other spirits, but, in proportion as his own spirit is more or less advanced, he'll make his statements more or less correctly.

In the phenomena of somnambulism, whether natural or mesmeric, Providence furnishes us with undeniable proof of the existence and independence of the soul, by causing us to witness the sublime spectacle of its emancipation from the fetters of the body, and thus enabling us to read our future destiny as in an open book. When a somnambulist describes what is taking place at a distance, it's equally evident that he sees what he describes, and that he doesn't see it with his bodily eyes. He sees himself at that distant point, and he feels himself to be transported thither. Something of himself, therefore, is really present at that distant point; and that something, not being his body, can only be his soul or his spirit.

While man, in search of the causes of his moral being, loses himself in abstract and unintelligible metaphysical subtleties, God places daily before his eyes, and within reach of his hand, the simplest and most certain means for the study of experimental psychology. Trance is the state in which the soul's independence of the body is made most clearly visible, and, so to say, palpable, to the senses of the observer. In dreaming and somnambulism, the soul wanders among terrestrial worlds; in trance, it penetrates into a sphere of existence of another order, into that of the etherealized spirits, with whom it enters into communication, without, however, being able to overstep certain limits which it could not pass without entirely breaking the links that attach it to the body.

Surrounded by novel splendors, enraptured by harmonies unknown to Earth, penetrated by bliss that defies description, the soul enjoys a foretaste of celestial beatitude, and may be said to have placed one foot on the threshold of eternity. In the state of trance, the annihilation of corporeal ties is almost complete. The body no longer possesses anything more than organic life; and we feel that the soul is only held thereto by a single thread, which any further effort on its part would break forever. In this state, all earthly thoughts disappear, and give place to the purified perception that is the very essence of our immaterial being.

Entirely absorbed in this sublime contemplation, the ecstatic regards the earthly life as being merely a momentary halt upon our eternal way; the successes and misfortunes of this lower world, its gross joys and sorrows, appear to him only as the futile incidents of a journey of which he is delighted to foresee the end. It's with ecstatics as with somnambulists; their lucidity may be more or less perfect, and their spirit, according as it's more or less elevated, is also more or less apt to apprehend the truth of things. In their abnormal state, there is sometimes more of nervous excitement than of true lucidity, or, to speak more correctly, their nervous excitement impairs their lucidity, and, for this reason, their revelations are often a mixture of truths and errors, of sublime ideas and absurd or even ridiculous fancies.

Inferior spirits often take advantage of this nervous excitement, in order to subjugate the ecstatic; and to this end they assume to his eyes the appearances which confirm him in the ideas and prejudices of his waking state. This subjugation of clairvoyants by the presentation of false appearances is the "rock ahead" of this order of revilement, but all of them are not equally subject to this dangerous misleading; and it's for us to weigh their statements coolly and carefully, and to judge their revelations by the light of science and of reason. The emancipation of the soul occurs sometimes in the waking state, and gives, to those who are endowed with the faculty designated by the name of second-sight, the power of seeing, hearing, and feeling, beyond the limits of the bodily senses. They perceive things at a distance, at all points to which their soul extends its action; they see them, so to say, athwart their ordinary sight, and as though in a sort of mirage.

At the moment when the phenomenon of second-sight occurs, the physical state of the seer is visibly modified. His glance becomes vague; he looks before him without seeing; his physiognomy reflects an abnormal state of the nervous system. It's evident that his organs of sight have nothing to do with his present perceptions; for his vision continue, even when his eyes are shut. The faculty of second-sight appears to those who are endowed with it to be as natural as ordinary sight. It seems to them to be an attribute of their being; and they're not aware of its exceptional character. They generally forget this fugitive lucidity, the remembrance of which, becoming more and vaguer, disappears at length from their memory like a dream.

The power of second-sight varies from a confused sensation to a clear and distinct perception of things present or distant. In its rudimentary state, it gives to some person's tact, perspicacity, a sort of sureness, in their decisions and actions; that may be styled the rectitude of the moral glance. At a higher degree of development, it awakens presentiments; still further developed, it shows to the seer events that have already happened, or that are about to happen. Natural and artificial somnambulism, trance, and second-sight are only varieties or modifications of the action of one and the same cause. Like dreams, they're a branch of natural phenomena, and have therefore existed in every age. History shows us that they have been known, and even abused, from the remotest antiquity, and they furnish the explanation of innumerable facts which superstitious prejudices have led men to regard as supernatural.

Chapter 9 - Intervention of spirits in the corporeal world

1 - Penetration of our thoughts by spirits

456 - Do spirits see everything that we do?
- They can do so if they choose, since they're incessantly around you, but, practically, each spirit sees only those things to which he directs his attention, for he pays no heed to those which don't interest him.

457 - Can spirits see our most secret thoughts?
- They often see what you'd fain hide from yourselves; neither acts nor thoughts can be hidden from them.
- It'd appear, then, to be easier to hide a thing from a person while living than to hide it from that same person after his death?
- Certainly, and when you fancy yourselves to be hidden from every eye, you have often a crowd of spirits around you, and watching you.

458 - What is thought of us by the spirits who are about us, and observing us?
- That depends on the quality of the spirits themselves. Frivolous spirits enjoy the little annoyances they cause you, and laugh at your fits of impatience. Graver spirits pity your imperfections, and endeavor to aid you to cure yourselves of them.

2 - Occult influence of spirits on our thoughts and actions

459 - Do spirits influence our thoughts and our actions?
- Their influence upon them is greater than you suppose, for it's very often they who direct both.

460 - Have we some thoughts that originate with ourselves, and others that are suggested to us?
- Your soul is a spirit who thinks. You must have observed that many thoughts, and frequently very opposite ones, come into your mind reference to the same subject, and at the same time, in such cases, some of them are your own, and some are ours. This is the cause of your uncertainties, because you have thus in your mind two ideas that are opposed to each other.

461 - How can we distinguish between the thoughts which are our own and those which are suggested to us?
- When a thought is suggested, it's like a voice speaking to you. Your own thoughts are generally those which first occur to you. In point of fact, this distinction is not of much practical importance for you, and it's often better for you not to be able to make it. Man's action is thus left in greater freedom. If he decides for the right road, he does so more spontaneously; if he takes the wrong one, he is more distinctly responsible for his mistake.

462 - Do men of intelligence and genius allays draw their ideas from their own minds?
- Their ideas sometimes come from their own spirit, but they're often suggested to them by other spirits who judge them to be capable of understanding them and worthy of transmitting them. When they don't find the required ideas in themselves, they make an unconscious appeal for inspiration, a sort of evocation that they make without being aware of what they're doing.

> If it were useful for us to be able to distinguish clearly between our own thoughts and those which are suggested to us, God would have given us the means of doing so, as he has given us that of distinguishing between day and night. When a matter has been left by Providence in a state of vagueness, it has been left so because it's better for us.

463 - It's sometimes said that our first thought is always the best, is this true?
- It may be good or bad according to the nature of the incarnated spirit; it's always well to listen to good inspirations.

464 - How can we ascertain whether a suggested thought comes from a good spirit or from an evil one?
- Study its quality. Good spirits give only good counsels. It's for you to distinguish between the good and the bad.

465 - To what end do imperfect spirits incite us to evil?
- To make you suffer as they do themselves.
- Does that lessen their own sufferings?
- No, but they do so from jealousy of those who are happier than themselves.
- What kind of sufferings do they wish to make us undergo?
- Those which result from being of an inferior order, and far removed from God.

466 - Why does God permit spirits to incite us to evil?
- Imperfect spirits are used by Providence as instruments for trying men's faith and constancy in well-doing. You, being a spirit, must advance in the knowledge of the infinite. It's for this end that you're made to pass through the trials of evil in order to attain to goodness. Our mission is to lead you into the right road. When you are acted upon by evil influences, it's because you attract evil spirits to you by your evil desires, for evil spirits always come to aid you in doing the evil you desire to do, they can only help you to do wrong when you give way to evil desires. If you're inclined to commit murder, you'll have about you a swarm of spirits who will keep this inclination alive in you, but you'll also have others about you who will try to influence you for good, which restores the balance and leaves you of your decision. It's

thus that God leaves to our conscience the choice or the road we decide to follow and the liberty of yielding to one or other of the opposing influences that act upon us.

467 - Can we free ourselves from the influence of the spirits who incite us to evil?
- Yes, for they only attach themselves to those who attract them by the evil nature of their thoughts and desires.

468 - Do spirits, whose influence is repelled by our will, renounce their temptations?
- What else can they do? When they see that they can't accomplish their aim, they give up the attempt, but they continue to watch for a favorable moment, as the cat watches for the mouse.

469 - By what means can we neutralize the influence of evil spirits?
- By doing only what is right, and putting all your trust in God, you repel the influence of inferior spirits, and prevent them from obtaining power over you. Take care, not to listen to the suggestions of spirits who inspire you with evil thoughts, stir up discord among you, and excite in you evil passions. Distrust especially those who flatter your pride, for, in so doing, they attack you on your weakest side. This is why Jesus makes you say in the Lord's Prayer: - *Let us not succumb to temptation, but deliver us from evil.*

470 - Have the spirits who seek to lead us into evil, and who thus put our firmness in rectitude to the proof, received a mission to do this, and, is so, are they responsible for the accomplishment of such a mission?
- No spirit ever receives a mission to do evil; when he does it, he does it of his own will, and, therefore, undergoes the consequences of his wrongdoing. God may let him take his evil way, in order to try you; but he doesn't command him to do so, and it's for you to repel him.

471 - When we feel a sensation of vague anxiety, of indefinable uneasiness, or of interior satisfaction, without any assignable cause, do these sensations proceed simply from our physical state?
- They're almost always an effect of the communications which you unconsciously receive from the spirits about you, or which you have received from them during your sleep.

472 - When spirits wish to excite us to evil, do they merely take advantage of the circumstances in which we find ourselves or can they themselves bring about the circumstances which may favor their designs?
- They take advantage of the occurrence of any favorable circumstances, but they also often bring them about, by urging you on, without your being aware of it, towards the object of your unwise desire. Thus, for instance, a man picks up a roll of banknotes by the wayside. You must not imagine that spirits have brought this money to this particular spot, but they may have suggested to the man the idea of going that way, and, when he has found the money, they may suggest to him the idea of taking possession of it, while others suggest to him the idea of restoring it to its rightful owner. It's thus in all other temptations.

3 - Possession
473 - Can a spirit temporarily assume the envelope of a living person--that is to say, can he introduce himself into an animate body, and act in the room and place of the spirit incarnated in it?
- A spirit doesn't enter into a body as you enter into a house. He assimilates himself to an incarnate spirit who has the same defects and the same qualities as himself, in order that they may act conjointly, but it's always the incarnate spirit who acts at his pleasure on the matter with which he is clothed. No other spirit can substitute himself in the place of the spirit who is incarnated in a given body, for a spirit is indissolubly united with his body until the arrival of the hour that has been appointed by Providence for the termination of his material existence.

474 - If there be no such thing as "possession", in the ordinary sense of that term-that is to say, cohabitation of two spirits in the same body, is it possible for one soul to find itself dominated, subjugated, obsessed by another soul to such a point as that it'll is, so to say, paralyzed?
- Yes, and it's this domination which really constitutes what you call possession, but you must understand that this domination is never established without the participation of the spirit who is subjected to it, either through his weakness[1] or his free-will. Men have often mistaken for cases of possession what were really cases of epilepsy or madness, demanding the help of the physician rather than of the exorciser.

> The word 'possession', in its common acceptation, presupposes the existence of demons, that is to say, of a category of beings of a nature essentially evil, and the cohabitation of one of those beings with the soul of a man in the body of the latter. Since there are no such beings as demons in the sense just defined, and since two spirits can't inhabit simultaneously the same body, there's no such thing as possession in the sense commonly attributed to that word. The word possessed should only be understood as expressing the state of absolute subjection to which a soul in flesh may be reduced by the imperfect spirits under whose domination it has fallen.

475 - Can a soul, of its own motion, drive away tile evil spirits by whom it's thus obsessed, and free itself from their domination?
- You can always shake off a yoke if you are firmly resolved to do so.

476 - Might not the fascination exercised by the evil spirit be so complete that the person subjugated should be unaware of it, and, in such a case, might not a third person be able to put an end to the subjection? And what course should be taken by the latter to that end?

- The will-power of an upright man may be useful by attracting the cooperation of good spirits in the work of deliverance, for the more upright a man is, the more power he possesses, both over imperfect spirits to drive them away, and over good ones to draw them nearer. Nevertheless, even the best of men would be powerless in such a case, unless the subjugated person lent himself to the efforts made on his behalf, for there are persons who take delight in a state of dependence which panders to their depraved tastes and desires. In no case can one who is impure in heart exercise any liberating influence, for he is despised by the good spirits and the bad ones stand in no awe of him.

477 - Have formulas of exorcism any power over bad spirits?
- No, when bad spirits see any one seriously endeavoring to act upon them by such means, they laugh at him, and persist in their obsession.

478 - Persons who are well-intentioned arc sometimes obsessed, what are the best means of getting rid of obsessing spirits?
- To tire out their patience, to give no heed to their suggestions, to show them that they're losing their time. When they see that they can do nothing, they go away.

479 - Is prayer efficacious as a means of putting an end to obsession?
- Prayer is always an efficacious means of obtaining help, but you must remember that the muttering of certain words will not suffice to obtain what you desire. God helps those who help themselves, but not those who limit their action to asking for help. It's therefore necessary for the person obsessed to do his utmost to cure himself of the defects which attract evil spirits to him.

480 - What is to be thought of the casting out of devils, spoken of in the Gospels?
- That depends on the meaning you attach to the word devil. If you mean by that term a bad spirit who subjugates a human being, it's evident that, when his influence is destroyed, he'll really be driven away. If you attribute a malady to the devil, you may say, when you have cured the malady, that you have driven the devil away. A statement may be true or false, according to the meaning attributed to certain words. The weightiest truths may appear absurd when you look only at the form under which they're presented, and when an allegory is taken for a fact. Get this principle well into your mind, and keep it there, for it's of universal application.

4 - Convulsionaries

481 - Do spirits play a part in the phenomena exhibited by the individuals designated under the name of convulsionaries?
- Yes, a very important one, as does also the agent that you call magnetism, whether employed by human beings or by spirits, for this agent is the original source of those phenomena, but charlatanism has often exaggerated those effects, and made them a matter of speculation, which has brought them into ridicule.
- What is generally the nature of the spirits who help to produce phenomena of this kind?
- Of slight elevation. Do you suppose that spirits of high degree would waste their time in such a way?

482 - How can a whole population are suddenly thrown into the abnormal state of convulsions and crises.
- Through sympathy. Moral dispositions are sometimes exceedingly contagious. You are not as ignorant of the effects of human magnetism as not to understand this, and also the part that certain spirits would naturally take in such occurrences, through sympathy with those by whom they're produced.

> Among the strange peculiarities remarked in convulsionaries, several are evidently identical with those of which somnambulism and mesmerism offer numerous examples, physical insensibility, thought reading, sympathetic transmission or sensations, etc. It's therefore impossible to doubt that these crisiacs are in a sort of waking somnambulism, determined by the influence which they unwittingly exercise upon each other. They're at once mesmerized and mesmerized, unconsciously to themselves.

483 - What is the cause of the physical insensibility sometimes remarked in convulsionaries, and sometimes, also, in other persons, when subjected to the most atrocious tortures?
- In some cases it's simply an effect of human magnetism, which acts upon the nervous system in the same manner as do certain substances. In other cases, mental excitement deadens the sensibility of the organism, the life seeming to retire from the body in order to concentrate itself in the spirit. Have you not observed that, when the spirit is intensely occupied with any matter, the body neither feels, nor sees, nor hears?

> The excitement of fanaticism and enthusiasm often offer, on the part of persons subjected to a violent death, examples of a calmness and coolness that could hardly triumph over excruciating pain unless the sensibility of the patient were neutralized by a sort of moral anesthesia. We know that, in the heat of battle, a severe wound is often received without being perceived; whilst, under ordinary circumstances, a mere scratch is felt acutely. Since the production of these phenomena is due, in part, to the action of physical causes, in part to that of spirits, it may be asked how it can have been possible for the civil authorities, in certain cases, to put a stop to them? The reason of this is, however, very simple. The action of spirits, in these cases, is only secondary they do nothing more than take advantage of a natural tendency. The public authorities didn't suppress this tendency, but the cause which kept up and stimulated it, thus reducing it from a state of activity to one of latency and they were right in so doing, because the matter was giving rise to abuses and scandal. Such intervention, nevertheless, is powerless in cases where the action of spirits is direct and spontaneous.

3 - This reply from the spirits reminds Kardec of the magnetic studies he had devoted himself to before Spiritism, and which served him, as it turns out, as preparation for the performance of his mission as researcher and codifier.

5 - Affection of certain spirits for certain persons
484 - Do spirits affectionately prefer certain persons?
- Good spirits sympathize with all men who are good or susceptible of amelioration, inferior spirits, with men who are bad or who may become such. The attachment, in both cases, is a consequence of the similarity of sentiment.

485 - Is the affection of certain spirits for certain persons exclusively one of sentiment?
- True affection has nothing of carnality, but, when a spirit attaches himself to a living person, it's not always through affection only; for there may also be in that attachment a reminiscence of human passions.

486 - Do spirits take an interest in our misfortunes and our prosperity? Those who wish us well, are they grieved by the ills we undergo during life?
- Good spirits do you all the good they can, and rejoice with you in all your joys. They mourn over your afflictions when you don't bear them with resignation, because in that case affliction produces no beneficial result, for you are like the sick man who rejects the disagreeable draught that would cure him.

487 - What is the kind of ills that causes most grief to our spirit-friends? Is it cur physical sufferings, or our moral imperfections?
- What grieve them most are your selfishness and your hard heartedness, for these are the root of all your troubles. They smile at the imaginary sorrows that are born of pride and ambition; they rejoice in those which will shorten your term of trial.

> Our spirit-friends, knowing that corporeal life is only transitory, and that the tribulations by which it's accompanied are the means that will enable us to reach a happier state, are more grieved for us by the moral imperfections which keep us back, than by physical ills, which are only transitory. Spirits attach as little importance to misfortunes which affect us only in our earthly ideas, as we do to the trilling sorrows of childhood. Seeing the afflictions of life to be the means of our advancement, they regard them only as the passing crisis which will restore the sick man to health. They're grieved by our sufferings, as we are grieved by those of a friend but, judging the events of our lives from a truer point of view, they appreciate them differently. While inferior spirits try to drive us to despair, in order to hinder our advancement, the good ones seek to inspire us with the courage that will turn our trials into a source of gain for our future.

488 - Have the relatives and friends who have gone before us into the other life more sympathy for us than spirits who are strangers to us?
- Undoubtedly they have, and they often protect you as spirits, according to their power.
- Are they sensible of the affection we preserve for them?
- Very sensible, but they forget those who forget them.

6 - Guardian, angels, protecting, familiar and sympathetic spirits
489 - Are there spirits who attach themselves to a particular individual, in order to protect and help him?
- Yes, the spirit-brother, what you call the- spirit-protector, or tile good genius.

490 - What is to be understood by the expression, guardian-angel?
- A spirit-protector of high degree.

491 - What is the mission of a spirit-protector?
- That of a father towards his children-to lead the object of his protection into the right road, to aid him with his counsels, to console him in his afflictions, and to sustain his courage under the trials of his earthly life.

492 - Is a spirit-protector attached to an individual from his birth?
- From his birth to his death, and he often follows him after death in the spirit-life, and even in several successive corporeal existences, for these existences are hut every short phases of his existence as a spirit.

493 - Is the mission of a spirit-protector voluntary or obligatory?
- Your spirit-protector is obliged to watch over you because he has accepted that task, but a spirit is allowed to choose his ward among the beings that are sympathetic to him. In some cases this office is a pleasure; in others, it's a mission or a duty.
- In attaching himself to a person, is a spirit obliged to refrain from protecting other individuals?
- No, but he does so less exclusively.

494 - Is the spirit-protector indissolubly attached to the person confided to his guardianship?
- It often happens that spirits quit their position in order to fulfill various missions, but, in that case, an exchange of wards takes place.

495 - Does a spirit-protector sometimes abandon his ward when the latter persists in neglecting his counsels?
- He withdraws from him when he sees that his counsels are useless and that there is a stubborn determination to yield to the influence of inferior spirits, but he doesn't abandon him entirely, and continues to make himself heard. It's

not the spirit who quits the man, but the man who closes his ears against the spirit. As soon as the man calls him back, the spirit returns to him. If there be a doctrine that should win over the most incredulous by its charm and its beauty, it's that of the existence of spirit-protectors, or guardian-angels. To think that you have always near you beings who are superior to you, and who are always beside you to counsel you, to sustain you, to aid you in climbing the steep ascent of self-improvement, whose friendship is truer and more devoted than the most intimate union that you can contract upon the Earth, is not such an idea most consoling?

Those beings are near you by the command of God. It's he who has placed them beside you. They're there for love of him and they fulfill towards you a noble but laborious mission. They're with you wherever you may be, in the dungeon, in solitude, in the lazar-house, even in the haunts of debauchery. Nothing ever separates you from the friend whom you can't see, hut whose gentle impulsions are felt, and whose wise monitions are heard, in the innermost recesses of your heart. Would that you were more fully impressed with this truth! How often would it aid you in your moments of need! How often would it save you from the snares of evil spirits.

But, at the great day of account, how often will your guardian-angel have to say to you, "did I not urge you, and yet you'd not follow my leading"? Did I not show you the abyss, and yet you persisted in throwing yourself into it? Did I not cause your con-science to hear the voice of truth, and have you not followed lying counsels?' Question your guardian-angels; establish between yourselves and them the affectionate intimacy which exists between tried and loving friends. Don't think to hide anything from them, for they're the eye of God, and you can't deceive them. Think of the future; seek to advance on the upward road: your trials will be shorter, your existences happier. Men, take courage! Cast far from you all prejudices and mental reservations; enter resolutely upon the new road that opens before you! You have guides, follow them; your goal can't fail you, for that goal is God himself.

To those who may think it impossible that spirits of high degree should bind themselves to a task so laborious and demanding so much patience on their part, we reply, that we influence your souls while at many millions of leagues from you. To us, space is nothing; and, while living in another world, our spirits preserve their connection with yours. We possess qualities of which you can form no idea, but be sure that God has not imposed upon us a task above our strength, and that He has not abandoned you upon the Earth without friends and without support. Every guardian-angel has his ward, over whom he watches as a father watches over his child, he rejoices when he sees him following the right road, he mourns when his counsels are neglected.

Don't fear to weary us with your questions. Remain; on the contrary, always in connection with us, you'll thus be stronger and happier. It's this communication between each man and his familiar spirit that will eventually make all men mediums, and drive out incredulity from your world. You, who have received instruction, instruct in your turn: you who are possessed of talents, raise your brethren. You know not how great a work you accomplish by so doing; it's the work of Christ, the work imposed on you by God. Why has God given you intelligence and knowledge, if not to share them with your brethren, to aid them to advance on the road that leads to eternal felicity?

The doctrine of guardian-angels watching over their wards, notwithstanding the distance which separates different worlds, has in it nothing that should excite our surprise it's as natural as it's grand and sublime. Do we not see a father, upon the Earth, watch over his child even though at a distance from him, and aid him by the wise counsels of his letters? Why, then, should it be deemed surprising that spirits should guide, from one world to another, those whom take under their protection, since, to them, the distance which separates worlds is less than that which, on Earth, separates continents? Besides, have they not the universal fluid which binds together all the worlds of the Universe, and makes them part and parcel of each other, the universal vehicle of the transmission of through, as the air is, for us, the vehicle of the transmission of sound?

496 - If a spirit abandons his ward and no longer does him good, can he do him harm?
- Good spirits never do harm to anyone. They leave that to those who take their place and you, then, accuse fate of the misfortunes which overwhelm you, while these are, in reality, the result of your own wrong doing.

497 - Can a spirit-protector leave his ward at the mercy of a spirit who should desire to do him harm?
- Evil spirits unite together to neutralize the action of the good ones, but the will of the ward suffices to give back all his power to the spirit-protector. The latter may find elsewhere another person whose goodwill renders it easy to help him; in such a case, he takes advantage of the opportunity of doing good, while awaiting the return of his ward.

498 - When the spirit-protector allows his ward to wander into wrong paths, is it because he is unable to cope with tile malevolent spirits who mislead him?
- It's not because he's unable, but because he doesn't choose to do so; he knows that his ward will become wiser and better through the trials he'll have brought upon himself. The spirit-protector assists his ward through the sage counsels he suggests to his mind, hut which unhappily are not always heeded. It's only the weakness, carelessness, or pride of men that gives strength to bad spirits, their power over you comes solely from your not opposing sufficient resistance to their action.

499 - Is the spirit-protector constantly with his ward? Are there no circumstances under which, without abandoning him, he may lose sight of him?
- There are circumstances under which the presence of the spirit-protector is not necessary to the ward.

500 - Does a time arrive when tile spirit no longer needs a guardian-angel?
- Yes, when he has reached the degree of advancement which enables him to guide himself, as a time arrives when the scholar bas no longer need of a master. But this doesn't take place upon your Earth.

501 - Why is the action of spirits upon our existence occult? And why, when they're protecting us, do they not do so ostensibly?

- If you counted on their support, you'd not act of yourselves, and your spirit would not progress. In order to advance, each man needs to acquire experience, and often at his own expense. He needs to exercise his powers; otherwise he'd be like a child, who is not allowed to walk alone. The action of the spirits who desire your welfare is always regulated in such a way as to leave you your free-will; for, if you had no responsibility, you'd not advance on the road that is to lead you to God. Man, not seeing his supporter, puts forth his own strength; his guide, however, watches over him, and calls to him from time to time, to bid him beware of danger.

502 - When the spirit-protector succeeds in leading his ward on tile right road, does he thereby gain any benefit for himself?

- It's a meritorious work, which will he counted to him either for his advancement or for his happiness. He rejoices when he sees his care crowned by success, and triumphs as a teacher triumphs in the success of his pupil.
- Is he responsible if he doesn't succeed?
- No, since he has done everything that depended on him.

503 - Does tile spirit-protector feel sorrow on seeing a ward taking tile wrong road? And doesn't such sight disturb his own felicity?

- He's grieved at his errors, and pities him, but this affliction has none of the anguish of terrestrial paternity, because he knows that there is a remedy for the evil and that what is not done today will be done tomorrow.

504 - Can we always know the name of our guardian-angel?

- How is it possible for you to know names which have no existence for you? Do you suppose there are no spirits but those whom you know of?
- But how can we invoke him if we don't know who he is?
- Give him any name you please-that of any superior spirit for whom you feel sympathy or veneration. Your spirit-guardian will answer this appeal, for all good spirits are brothers, and assist each other.

505 - Are the spirit-guardians who take well-known names always the persons who bore those names?

- No, but they're spirits who are in sympathy with them, and who, in many cases, come by their order. You require names; they therefore take a name that will inspire you with confidence. When you are unable to execute a commission in person, you send someone in your place, who acts in your name.

506 - When we are in the spirit-life, shall we recognize our spirit-guardian?

- Yes, for it is often a spirit whom you knew before being incarnated.

507 - Do all spirit-guardians belong to the higher classes of spirits? Are they sometimes found among those of average advancement? Can a father, for example, become the spirit-guardian of his child?

- He may do so, but such guardianship presupposes a certain degree of elevation, and, in addition, a power of virtue granted by God. A father who watches over his child may himself be assisted by a spirit of more elevated degree.

508 - Can all spirits who have quitted the Earth under favorable conditions become the protectors of those whom they love among their survivors?

- Their power is more or less narrowed by their position, which doesn't always leave them full liberty of action.

509 - Have savages, and men who are very low as regards their moral state, their spirit-guardians? And if so, are these spirits of as high an order as those of men who are more advanced?

- Every man has a spirit who watches over him, but missions are always proportional to their object. You don't give a professor of philosophy to a child who is only learning to read. The advancement of the familiar spirit is always proportioned to that of the spirit he protects. While you yourself have a spirit of higher degree who watches over you, you may, in your turn, become the protector of a spirit who is lower than you and the progress you help him to make will contribute to your own advancement. God doesn't demand of any spirit more than is consistent with his nature and with the degree at which he has arrived.

510 - When a father who watches over his child is reincarnated, does he still continue to watch over him?

- His task, in that case, becomes more difficult, but, in a moment of freedom, he asks some sympathetic spirit to assist him in accomplishing it, but spirits don't undertake missions which they can't carry on to the end.
- A spirit, when incarnated, especially in worlds in which existence is grossly material, is too much fettered by his body to be able to devote himself entirely to another, that is to say, to give him personally all the help he needs. For this reason, those who are not sufficiently elevated to suffice for the work of guardianship are themselves assisted by spirits of higher degree, so that if, from any cause, the help of one spirit should fail, his place is supplied by another.

511 - Is there, besides the spirit-guardian, an evil spirit attached to each individual for the purpose of exciting him to evil, thus of furnishing him with the opportunity of struggling between good and evil?

- It'd not be correct to say 'attached.' It's very true that bad spirits endeavor to draw you out of the right road when they find an opportunity of doing so, but when one of them attaches himself to an individual, he does so of his own accord, because he hopes to be listened to. In such a case, there's a struggle between the good and the evil spirit, and the victory remains with the one to whose influence the man has voluntarily subjected himself.

512 - May we have several protecting spirits?
- Every man has always about him a number of sympathetic spirits of more or less elevation, who interest themselves in him from affection, as he also has others who help him to do evil.

513 - Do spirits who are sympathetic to an individual act upon him in virtue of a mission to that effect?
- In some cases they may have a temporary mission; but, in general, they're only drawn to an individual by similarity of sentiments in good or in evil.
- It'd seem, then, that sympathetic spirits may be either good or bad?
- Yes, a man is always surrounded by spirits who are in sympathy with him, whatever may be his character.

514 - Are familiar-spirits the same as sympathetic-spirits and spirit-guardians?
- There are very many shades in guardianship and in sympathy, you may give to these whatever names you please, but the familiar spirit is rather the general friend of the family.

> From the above explanations and from observation of the nature of spirits who attach themselves to men, we draw the following inferences: The spirit-protector, good genius or guardian-angel, is the one whose mission it's to follow each man through the course of his life and to aid him to progress. His degree of advancement is always superior to that of his ward. Familiar spirits attach themselves to certain persons, for a longer or shorter period, in order to be useful to them within the limits of their possibilities they're generally well-intentioned, but sometimes rather backward, and even frivolous. They busy themselves with the everyday details of human life and only act by order, or with the permission, of the spirit-guardians. Sympathetic spirits are those who are drawn to us by personal affection and by a similarity of tastes in good or in evil. The duration of their relationship with us is almost always dependent on circumstances. An evil genius is an imperfect or wicked spirit who attaches himself to a man for the purpose of perverting him but he acts of his own motion, and not in virtue of a mission. His tenacity is proportionate to the more or less easy access accorded to him. A man is always free to listen to the suggestions of an evil genius, or to repel them.

515 - What is to be thought of those persons who seen to attach themselves to certain individuals in order to urge them on to their injury, or to guide them on the right road?
- Some persons do, in fact, exercise over others a species of fascination which seems irresistible. When this influence is used for evil, it's to be attributed to evil spirits, who make use of evil men in order the more effectually to subjugate their victim. God may permit this in order to try you.

516 - Could our good or our evil genius incarnate himself in order to accompany us more closely in our earthly life?
- That sometimes occurs; but they more frequently entrust this mission to incarnated spirits who are in sympathy with them.

517 - Are there spirits who attach themselves to all the members of a family in order to watch over and aid them?
- Some spirits attach themselves to the members of a family who live together and who are united by affection, but don't attribute pride of race to spirit-guardians.

518 - Spirits being attracted to individuals by their sympathies, are they similarly attracted to companies of persons united in view of special ends?
- Spirits go by preference to the places where they meet their similars; they're more at ease among such, and more sure of being listened to. Every one attracts spirits to himself according to his tendencies, whether as an individual or as an element of a collective whole, such as a society, a city, or a nation. Societies, towns, and nations are therefore assisted by spirits of more or less elevated degree, according to the character and passions which predominate in them. Imperfect spirits withdraw from those who repel them, from which it follows that the moral excellence of collective wholes, like that of individuals, tends to keep away bad spirits and to attract good ones, who rouse and keep alive the sense of rectitude in the masses, as others may sow among them the worst passions.

519 - Have agglomerations of individuals-such as societies, cities, nations, their special spirit-guardians?
- Yes, for those assemblages constitute collective individualities, who are pursuing a common end, and who have need of a higher direction.

520 - Are the spirit-guardians of masses of men of a higher degree of advancement than those who are attached to individuals?
- Their advancement is always in proportion with the degree of advancement of masses as of individuals.

521 - Can certain spirits advance the progress of the arts by protecting those who cultivate them?
- There are special spirit-protectors who assist those by whom they're invoked when they judge them to be worthy of their help; but what could they do with those who fancy themselves to be what they're not? They can't make the blind to see nor the deaf to hear.

> The ancients converted these spirit-guardians into special deities. The Muses were nothing else than the allegoric personification of the spirit-protectors of arts and sciences, just as the spirit-protectors of the family-circle designated by the name of lares or of penates. Among the moderns, the arts, the various industries, cities, countries, have also their protecting patrons, who are no other than spirit-guardians of a higher order, but under different names. Each man

having his sympathetic spirit, it follows that, in every collective whole, the generality of sympathetic spirits corresponds to the generality of individuals that stranger-spirits are attracted to it by identity of thoughts, in a word, that these assemblages, as well as individuals, are more or less favorably surrounded, influenced, assisted, according to the predominant character of the thoughts of those who compose them.

Among nations, the conditions which exercise an attractive action upon spines are the habits, manners, dominant characteristics, of their people, and. above all, their legislation, because the character of a nation is reflected in its laws. Those who uphold the reign of righteousness, among themselves combat the influence of evil spirits. Wherever the laws consecrate injustice, inhumanity, good spirits are in the minority and the mass of bad ones who flock in, attracted by that state of things, keep the people in their false ideas, and paralyze the good influences which, being only partial, are lost in the crowd, like a solitary wheat, ear in the midst of tares. It's therefore easy, by studying the characteristics of nations or of any assemblage of men, to form to oneself an idea of the invisible population which is mixed up with them in their thoughts and in their actions.

7 - Presentiments

522 - Is a presentiment always a warning from the spirit-guardian?

- A presentiment is a counsel privately addressed to you by a spirit who wishes you well. The same may be said of tile intuition which decides the choice of his flew existence by a spirit about to reincarnate himself, the voice of instinct is of the same nature. A spirit, before incarnating himself, is aware of the principal phases of his new existence, that's to say, of the kind of trials to which he is about to subject himself. When these are of a very marked character, he preserves, in his inner consciousness, a sort of impression respecting them; and this impression, which is the voice of instinct, becoming more vivid as the critical moment draws near, becomes presentiment.

523 - Presentiments and the voice of instinct are always some-what vague; what should we do when in a state of uncertainty?

- When you're in doubt, invoke your spirit-guardian, or implore our common Master, God, to send you one of his messengers, one of us.

524 - Are the warnings of our spirit-guardians given solely for our moral guidance, are they also given for our guidance in regard to our personal affairs?

- They're given in reference to everything that concerns you. Your spirit-guardians endeavor to lead you to take, in regard to everything that you have to do, the best possible course, but you often close your ears to their friendly counsels, and thus get yourselves into trouble thorough your own fault.

> Our protecting-spirits aid us by their counsels and by awakening the voice of our conscience but as we don't always attach sufficient importance to these hints, they give us more direct warnings through the persons about us. Let a man reflect upon the various circumstances of his life, fortunate or unfortunate, and he'll see that, on many occasions, he received advice which, had he followed it, would have spared him a good deal of annoyance.

8 - Influence of spirits en the events of human life

525 - Do spirits exercise an influence over the events of our lives?

- Assuredly they do, since they give you advice.
- Do they exercise this influence in any other way than by means of the thoughts they suggest to us, that's to say, have they any direct action on the course of earthly events?
- Yes, but their action never oversteps the laws of nature.

> We erroneously imagine that the action of spirits can only be manifested by extraordinary phenomena we'd have spirits come to our aid by means of miracles, and we imagine them to be always armed with a sort of magic wand. Such is not the case, all that is done through their help being accomplished by natural means; their intervention usually takes place without our being aware of it. Thus, for instance, they bring about the meeting of two persons who seem to have been brought together by chance they suggest to the mind of someone the idea of going in a particular direction. They call your attention to some special point, if the action on your part thus led up to by their suggestion, unperceived by you, will bring about the result they seek to obtain. In this way, each man supposes himself to be obeying only his own impulse, and thus always preserves the freedom of his will.

526 - As spirits possess the power of acting upon matter, can they bring about the incidents that will ensure tile accomplishment of a given event? For example, a man is destined to perish in a certain way, at a certain time. He mounts a ladder, the ladder breaks, and he's killed. Have spirits caused the ladder to break, in order to accomplish the destiny previously accepted by or imposed upon this man?

- It's very certain that spirits have the power of acting upon matter, but for the carrying out of the laws of nature, and not for derogating from them, by causing the production at a given moment of some unforeseen event, in opposition to those laws. In such a case as the one you have just supposed, the ladder breaks because it's rotten, or is not strong enough to bear the man's weight, but, as it was the destiny of this man to be killed in this way, the spirits about him will have put into his mind the idea of getting upon a ladder that will break down under his weight, and his death will thus have taken place naturally, and without any miracle having been required, to bring it about.

527 - Let us take another example, one in which the ordinary conditions of matter would seem, to be insufficient to account for the occurrence of a given event. A man is destined to be killed by lightning. He's overtaken by a storm and

seeks refuge under a tree, the lightning strikes the tree and he's killed. Is it by spirits that the thunderbolt has been made to fall, and to fall upon this particular man?

- The explanation of this case is the same as that of the former one. The lightning has fallen on the tree at this particular moment, because it was in accordance with the laws of nature that it should do so. The lightning was not made to fall upon the tree because the man was under it, but the man was inspired with the idea of taking refuge under a tree upon which the lightning was about to fall, for the tree would have been struck all the same, whether the man had been under it or not.

528 - An ill-intentioned person hurls against someone a projectile which passes close by him, but doesn't touch him. Has the missile, in such a case, been turned aside by some friendly spirit?

- If the individual aimed at were not destined to be struck, a friendly spirit would have suggested to him the thought of turning aside from the path of the missile, or would have acted on his enemy's sight in such a way as to make him take a bad aim; for a projectile, when once impelled on its way, necessarily follows the line of its projection.

529 - What is to be thought of the magic bullets which figure in certain legends, and which, by a mysterious fatality, infallibly reach their mark?

- They're purely imaginary. Man delights in the marvelous, and is not contented with the marvels of nature.

- May the spirits who direct the events of our lives be thwarted by other spirits who desire to give to our lives a different direction?

- What God has willed must need take place. If delay or hindrances occur, it can only be by his appointment.

530 - Can't frivolous and mocking spirits give rise to the various little difficulties that defeat our projects and upset our calculations? In a word, are they not the authors of what may be termed the petty troubles of human life?

- Such spirits take pleasure in causing vexations which serve as trials for the exercise of your patience; but they tire of this game when they see that they don't succeed in ruffling you, but it would neither be just nor correct to charge them with all your disappointments, the greater number of which is caused by your own heedlessness. When your crockery is broken, the breakage is much more likely to have been caused by your own awkwardness than by spirit action.

- Do the spirits who bring about petty vexations act from personal animosity, or do they direct their attacks against the first person who comes handy, without any fixed aim, and simply to gratify their malice?

- They act from both these motives. In some cases, they're enemies whom you have made during your present life, or in some former one, and who pursue you accordingly, in others, they act without any fixed motive.

531 - In the case of those who have done us harm in the earthly life is their malevolence extinguished when they return to the spirit-world?

- In many cases, they perceive the injustice of their action, and regret the wrong they have done you; but, in other cases, they continue to pursue you with their animosity, if God permits them to do so, as a continuation of your trial.

- Can we put an end to this sort of persecution, and by what means?

- You can do so, in many cases, by praying for them, because, by thus rendering them good for evil, you gradually bring them to see that they're in the wrong, and, in all cases, if you can show them, by your patience, that you are able to raise superior to their machinations, they'll cease to attack you, seeing that they gain nothing by so doing.

> Experience proves that imperfect spirits follow up their vengeance from one existence to another, and that we are thus made to expiate sooner or later, the wrongs we may have done to others.

532 - Are spirits able to avert misfortunes from some persons, and to bring them upon others?

- Only to a certain extent; for there are misfortunes that come upon you by the decrees of Providence, but spirits can lessen your sufferings by helping you to bear them with patience and resignation.

- Know, also, that it often depends on yourselves to avert misfortunes, or, least, to attenuate them. God has given you intelligence in order that you may make use of it, and it's especially by so doing that you enable friendly spirits to aid you most effectually, by suggesting useful ideas; for they only help those who help themselves: a truth implied in the words, Seek, and yet shall find; knock, and it shall be opened unto you.

- Besides, you must remember that what appears to you to be a misfortune is not always such; for the good which it's destined to work out is often greater than the seeming evil. This fact is not always recognized by you, because you are too apt to think only of the present moment, and of your own immediate satisfaction.

533 - Can spirits obtain for us the gifts of fortune, if we entreat them to do so?

- They may sometimes accede to such a request as a trial for you; but they often refuse such demands, as you refuse the inconsiderate demands of a child.

- When such favors are granted, is it by good spirits or by bad ones?

- By both, for the quality both, of the request and of the grant depends on the intention by which they're prompted, but such acquiescence is more frequent on the part of spirits who desire to lead you astray, and who find an easy means of doing this through the material pleasures procured by wealth.

534 - When obstacles seem to be placed, by a sort of fatality, in the way of our projects, is it always through the influence of spirits?

- Such obstacles are sometimes thrown in your, way by spirits, but they're more often attributable to your own bad management, position and character have much to do with your successes or failures. If you persist in following a path which is not your right one, you become your own evil genius, and have no need to attribute to spirit action the disappointments that result from your own obstinacy or mistake.

535 - When anything fortunate happens to us, ought we to thank our spirit-guardian for it?
- Let your thanks be first for God, without whose permission anything takes place, and, next, for the good spirits who have been his agents.
- What would happen if we neglected to tank them?
- That which happens to the ungrateful.
- Yet there are persons who neither pray nor give thanks, and who nevertheless succeed in everything they do?
- Yes, but wait to see the end of their lives. They'll pay dearly for this passing prosperity, which they have not deserved; for, the more they have received, the more they'll have to answer for.

9 - Action of spirits in the production of the phenomena of nature
536 - Are the great phenomena of nature, those which we consider as perturbations of the elements, due to fortuitous cause, or have they all a providential aim?
- There's a reason for everything, nothing takes place without the permission of God.
- Have these phenomena always some reference to mankind?
- They have sometimes a direct reference to man, but they have often no other object than the re-establishment of the equilibrium and harmony of the physical forces of nature.
- We fully admit that the will of God must be the primal cause of these phenomena, as of everything else, but, as we know that spirits exercise an action upon matter, and that they're the agents of the divine will, we ask whether some among them don't exert an influence upon the elements, to rouse, calm or direct them?
- It's evident that they must do so, it could not be otherwise. God doesn't exercise a direct action upon matter; he has his devoted agents at every step of the ladder of worlds.

537 - The mythology of the ancients is entirely based on spiritist ideas with this difference that they regarded spirits as divinities. They represented those gods or spirits with special attributes; thus, some of them had charge of the winds, others of the lightning; others, again, presided over vegetation, etc. Is this belief entirely devoid of foundation?
- It's so far from being devoid of foundation; that it's far below the truth.
- May there, in the same way, be spirits inhabiting the interior of the Earth and presiding over the development of geological phenomena?
- Those spirits don't positively inhabit the Earth, but they preside over and direct its developments according to their various attributions. You'll someday have the explanation of all these phenomena and you'll then understand them better.

538 - Do the spirits who preside over the phenomena of nature form a special category in the spirit-world; are they beings apart or spirits who have been incarnated like us?
- They're spirits who will be incarnated, or who have been so.
- Do those spirits belong to the higher or lower degrees of the spirit-hierarchy?
- That's according as their post is more or less material or intelligent; some command, others execute; those who discharge material functions are always of an inferior order, among spirits as among men.

539 - In the production of certain phenomena, of storms, for example, is it a single spirit that acts, or a mass of spirits?
- A mass of spirits; or, rather, innumerable masses of spirits.

540 - Do the spirits who exert an action over the phenomena of nature act with knowledge and intention, in virtue of their free-will, or from an instinctive end unreasoning impulse?
- Some act in the one way, others in the other. To employ a comparison, figure to yourself the myriads of animalcule that build up islands and archipelagos in the midst of the sea; do you believe that there can be, in this process, no providential intention, and that this transformation of the surface of the globe is not necessary to the general harmony? Yet all this is accomplished by animals of the lowest degree, in providing for their bodily wants, and without any consciousness of their being instruments of God.
In the same way, spirits of the most rudimentary degrees are useful to the general whole; while preparing to live, and prior to their having the full consciousness of their action and free-will, they're made to concur in the development of the various departments of nature, in the production of the phenomena of which they're the unwitting agents. They begin by executing the orders of their superiors; subsequently, when their intelligence is more developed, they command in their turn, and direct the processes of the material world; still later, again, they're able to direct the things of the moral world. It's thus that everything in nature is linked together, from the primitive atom to the archangel, who himself began at the atom; an admirable law of harmony, which your mind is, as yet, too narrow to seize in its generality.

10 - Spirits during a battle
541 - When a battle is being fought, are there spirits who assist and support each party?
- Yes, and who stimulate their courage.

> The ancients represented the gods as taking part with such and such a people. Those gods were nothing else than spirits represented under allegorical figures.

542 - In every war, the right is only on one side. How can spirits take the part of the one which is in the wrong?

- You know very well that there are spirits who seek only discord and destruction; for them war is war; they care little whether it be just or unjust.

543 - Can spirits influence a general in the planning of a campaign?
- Without any doubt spirits can use their influence for this object, as for all other conceptions.

544 - Could hostile spirits suggest to him unwise combinations in order to ruin him?
- Yes, but has he not his free-will? If his judgment don't enable him to distinguish between a good idea and a bad one, he'll have to bear the consequences of his blindness, and would do better to obey than to command.

545 - May a general sometimes be guided by a sort of second-sight, an intuitive perception that shows him, beforehand, the result of his combinations?
- It's often thus with a man of genius; this kind of intuition is what is called inspiration, and causes him to act with a sort of certainty. It comes to him from the spirits who direct him, and who act upon him through the faculties with which he is endowed.

546 - In the tumult of battle, what becomes of the spirits of those who succumb? Do they continue to take an interest in the struggle after their death?
- Some of them do so; others withdraw from it.

> In the case of those who are killed in battle, as in all other cases of violent death, a spirit, during the first few moments, is in a state of bewilderment, and as though he were stunned. He doesn't know that he is dead and seems to be taking part in the action. It's only little by little that the reality of his situation becomes apparent to him.

547 - Do the spirits of those who had fought against each other while alive still regard one another as enemies after death and arc they still enraged against one another?
- A spirit, under such circumstances, is never calm. At the first moment, he may still be excited against his enemy, and even pursue him; but, when he has recovered his self-possession, he sees that his animosity has no longer any motive, but he may, nevertheless, retain some traces of it for a longer or shorter period, according to his character,
- Does he still perceive the clang of the battle field?
- Yes, perfectly.

548 - When a spirit is coolly watching a battle, as a mere spectator, does he witness the separation of the souls and bodies of those who fall, and how does this phenomenon affect him?
- Very few deaths are altogether instantaneous. In most cases, the spirit whose body has just been mortally struck is not aware of it for the moment; it's when he begins to come to himself that his spirit can be seen moving beside his corpse. This appears so natural, that the sight of the dead body doesn't produce any disagreeable effect. All the life of the individual being concentrated in his spirit, the latter alone attracts the attention of the spirits about him. It's with him that they converse, to him that orders are given.

11 - Pacts with spirits
549 - Is there any truth in the idea that pacts can be entered into with evil spirits?
- No, there's no pact, but there's sympathy between an evil nature and evil spirits. For example, you wish to torment your neighbor, but you know not how to set about it; and you therefore call to your help some of the inferior spirits, who, like yourself, only desire to do evil, and who, in return for the help they give you in carrying out your wicked designs, expect you to help them with theirs, but it doesn't follow that your neighbor will not be able to get rid of such a conspiracy by an opposing conjuration and the action of his will.
He, who desires to do an evil deed, calls evil spirits to his assistance by that mere desire; and he is then obliged to serve them as they have served him, for they, on their side, have need of his help in the evil they desire to do. What you call a pact consists simply in this reciprocity of assistance in evil. The subjection to evil spirits, in which a man sometimes finds himself, proceeds from his abandoning himself to the evil thoughts suggested by them, and not from any sort of stipulations between them and him. The idea of a pact, in the sense commonly attached to that word, is a figurative representation of the sympathy which exists between a bad man and malicious spirits.

550 - What is the meaning of the fantastic legends of persons selling their soul to Satan in order to obtain from him certain favors?
- All fables contain a teaching and a moral; your mistake is in taking them literally. The one you refer to is an allegory that may be thus explained he, who calls evil spirits to his aid, in order to obtain from them the gifts of fortune or any other favor, rebels against Providence. He draws back from the mission he has received, and from the trials he was to have under gone, in his earthly life, and he'll reap the consequences of this rebellion in the life to come.
By this we don't mean to say that his soul is condemned to misery forever, but as, instead of detaching himself from matter, he plunges himself deeper and deeper into it, his enjoyment of earthly pleasures will only have led to his suffering in the spirit-world, until he shall have redeemed himself from the thralldom of evil by new trials, perhaps heavier and more painful than those against which he now rebels. Through his indulgence in material pleasures, he brings himself under the power of impure spirits, and thus establishes between them and him a tacit compact which leads him to his ruin, but which it's always easy for him to break with the assistance of higher spirits, if he have the firm determination to do so.

12 - Occult power, talismans and sorcerers

551 - Can a bad man, with the aid of a bad spirit who is at his orders, cause harm to his neighbor?
- No, God would not permit it.

552 - What is to be thought of the belief in the power of certain persons to throw a spell over others?
- Certain persons possess a very strong magnetic power, of which they may make a bad use if their own spirit is bad, and, in that case, they may be seconded by other bad spirits, but don't attach belief to any pretended magical power, which exists only in the imagination of superstitious people, ignorant of the true laws of nature. The facts adduced to prove the existence of this pretended power are facts which are really due to the action of natural causes that have been imperfectly observed, and above all, imperfectly understood.

553 - What is the effect of the formulas and practices by the aid of which certain persons profess to be able to control the wills of spirits?
- Their only effect is to render such persons ridiculous, if they really put faith in them; and, if they don't, they're rogues who deserve to be punished. All such formulas are mere jugglery; there is no sacramental word, no cabalistic sign, no talisman that has any power over spirits; for spirits are attracted by thought and not by anything material.
- Have not cabalistic formulas been sometimes dictated by spirits?
- Yes, there are spirits who give you strange signs and words, and prescribe certain acts, with the aid of which you perform what you call conjurations, but you may be very sure that such spirits are making game of you, and amusing themselves with your credulity.

554 - Is it not possible that he who, rightly or wrongly, has confidence in what he calls the virtue of a talisman, may attract spirit to him by that very confidence; for in that case it would be his thought that acts, the talisman being only a sign that helps to concentrate and direct his thought?
- Such an action is quite possible; but the nature of the spirit thus attracted would depend on the purity of intention and the elevation of sentiment of the party attracting him; and it rarely happens that one who is simple enough to believe in the virtue of a talisman is not actuated by motives of a material rather than of a moral character. At all events, such practices imply a pettiness and weakness of mind that would naturally give access to imperfect and mocking spirits.

555 - What meaning should we attach to the qualification of sorcerer?
- Those whom you call sorcerers are persons gifted, when they're honest, with certain exceptional faculties, like the mesmeric power or second-sight; and as such persons do things that you don't comprehend, you suppose them to be endowed with supernatural power. Have not many of your learned men passed for sorcerers in the eyes of the ignorant?

556 - Do some persons really possess the gift of healing by merely touching the sick?
- The mesmeric power may act to that extent when it's seconded by purity of intention and ardent desire to do well, for, in such a case, good spirits come to the aid of the mesmerizer, but you must be on your guard against the way in which facts are exaggerated when recounted by persons who, being too credulous or too enthusiastic, are disposed to discover something marvelous in the simplest and most natural occurrences. You must also be on your guard against the interested recitals of persons who work on credulity with a view to their own benefit.

13 - Benedictions an curses

557 - Do benedictions and curses draw down good and evil on those who are the object of them?
- God doesn't listen to an unjust malediction, and he who utters it's guilty in his eyes. As we are subjected to two opposite influences, good and evil, a curse may have a momentary action, even upon matter; but this action can never take place unless by the will of God, and as an increase of trial for him who is its object. Besides, curses are usually bestowed on the wicked, and benedictions on the good, but neither blessing nor cursing can ever turn aside the justice of Providence, which only strikes the one who is cursed if he is wicked, and only favors the one who is blessed if he merits its protection.

Chapter 10 - Occupations and missions of spirits

1 - Occupations and missions of spirits

558 - Have spirits anything else to do but to work out their own personal amelioration?
- They cooperate in the production of the harmony of the Universe by executing the volitions of God, whose ministers they're. Spirit-life is a continual occupation, hut one that has nothing in common with the painful labor of the earthly life, because there is in it neither bodily fatigue, nor the anguish of bodily wants.

559 - Do inferior and imperfect spirits also sub serve any useful end in the universe?
- All have duties to fulfill. Doesn't the lowest mason concur in the building of an edifice as really as the architect?

560 - Has each spirit special attributes?
- We all have to inhabit all regions, and to acquire knowledge of all things, by presiding successively over all the details of the Universe, but, as is said in Ecclesiastes, there's a time for everything. Thus, one spirit is accomplishing his destiny, at the present day, in your world; another will accomplish his, or has already accomplished it, at another period, upon the Earth, in the water, in the air, etc.

561 - Are the functions discharged by spirits, in the economy of things, permanent on the part of each spirit, or do they constitute the exclusive attributes of certain classes?
- All spirits have to ascend all the steps of the ladder in order to attain to perfection. God, who is just, has not willed to give science to some without labor, while others only acquire it through painful effort.

> Thus, among men, no one arrives at the highest degree of skill in any art, without having acquired the necessary knowledge through the practice of that art in all its degrees, from the lowest upwards.

562 - Spirits of the highest order having nothing more to acquire, are they in a state of absolute repose, or have they, too, occupations?
- Can you suppose that they remain idle through eternity? Eternal idleness would be eternal torture.
- What is the nature of their occupations?
- They receive orders directly from God, transmit them throughout the Universe, and superintend their execution.

563 - Are spirits incessantly occupied?
- Yes, if it be understood that their thought is always active, for they live by thought, but you must not suppose that the occupations of spirits are similar to the material occupations of men; their activity is itself a delight, through the consciousness they have of being useful.
- That is easily understood as regards good spirits, but is it the same in regard to inferior spirits?
- Inferior spirits have occupations suitable to their nature. Would you entrust intellectual undertakings to an ignorant laborer?

564 - Are there, among spirits, some who are idle, or who don't employ themselves in anything useful?
- Yes, but that idleness is only temporary and depends on the development of their intelligence. Certainly, there are among spirits, as among men, some who live only for themselves; but their idleness weighs upon them, and, sooner or later, the desire to advance causes them to feel the need of activity, and they're glad to make themselves useful. We speak of spirits arrived at the point at which they possess self-consciousness and free-will; for, at their origin, they're like new-born children, and act more from instinct than from a determinate will.

565 - Do spirits examine our works of art and take an interest in them?
- They examine whatever indicates the elevation of incarnated spirits and their progress.

566 - Does a spirit who has had a special occupation upon the Earth, as a painter or an architect, for example, take a special interest in the labors which have formed the object of his predilections during the earthly life?
- Everything blends into one general aim. A good spirit interests himself in whatever enables him to assist other souls in rising towards God, besides, a spirit who has been devoted to a given pursuit, in the existence in which you have known him, may have been devoted to some other in another existence, for, in order to be perfect, he must know everything. Thus, in virtue of his greater advancement, there may be no speciality for him, a fact to which I alluded in saying that everything blends into one general aim. Take note, also, that what seems sublime to you, in your backward world, would be mere child's play in worlds of greater advancement. How can you suppose that the spirits who inhabit those worlds, in which there exist arts and sciences unknown to you, could admire what, in their eyes, is only the work of a tyro?
- We can easily conceive that this should be the case with very advanced spirits, but our question referred to more commonplace place spirits, to those who have not yet raised themselves above terrestrial ideas.
- With them it's different; their mental outlook is narrower, and they may admire what you yourselves admire.

567 - Do spirits ever take part in our occupations and pleasures?
- Commonplace spirits, as you call them, do so; they're incessantly about you, and take, in all you do, a part which is sometimes a very active one, according to their nature; and it's necessary that they should do so, in order to push men on in the different walks of life, and to excite or moderate their passions.

> Spirits busy themselves with the things of this world in proportion to their elevation or their inferiority. The higher spirits have, undoubtedly, the power of looking into the minutest details of earthly things, but they only do so when it'll be useful to progress. Spirits of lower rank attribute to such things a degree of importance proportioned to their remembrances of the earthly life, and to the earthly ideas which are not yet extinct in their memory.

568 - When spirits are charged with a mission, do they accomplish it in the state of erraticity, or in the state of incarnation?
- They may be charged with a mission in either state. There are wandering spirits to whom such missions furnish much occupation.

569 - What are the missions with which wandering spirits may be charged?
- They're so varied that it would be impossible to describe them, and there are some of them that you could not comprehend. Spirits execute the volitions of God, and you are not able to penetrate all his designs.

> The missions of spirits have always good for their object. Whether in the spirit-state, or as men, they're charged to help forward the progress of humanity, of peoples, or of individuals, within a range of ideas more or less extensive, more or less special, to pave the way for certain events, to superintend the accomplishment of certain things. The missions of some spirits are of narrower scope, and may be said to be personal, or even local as the helping of the sick, the dying, the afflicted to watch over those of whom they become the guides and protectors, and to guide them by their counsels or by the wholesome thoughts they suggest. It may be said that there are as many sorts of spirit-missions as there are sorts of interests to watch over, whether in the physical world or in the moral world, and each spirit advances in proportion to the fidelity with which he accomplishes his task.

570 - Do spirits always comprehend the designs they're charged to execute?
- No, some of them are mere blind instruments, but others fully understand the aim they're working out.

571 - Is it only elevated spirits who have missions to fulfill?
- The importance of a mission is always proportioned to the capacities and elevation of the spirit who is charged with it; but the estafette who conveys a dispatch fulfils a mission, though one which is not that of the general.

572 - Is a spirit's mission imposed upon him, or does it depend on his own will?
- He asks for it, and is rejoiced to obtain it.
- May the same mission be demanded by several spirits?
- Yes, there are often several candidates for the same mission, but they're not all accepted.

573 - In what does the mission of incarnated spirits consists?
- In instructing men, and aiding their advancement; and in ameliorating their institutions by direct, material means. These missions are more or less general and important; but he who tills the ground accomplishes a mission as really as he who governs or instructs. Everything in nature is linked together; and each spirit, while purifying himself by his incarnation, concurs, under the human form, to the accomplishment of the providential plans. Each of you has a mission, because each of you can be useful in some way or other.

574 - What can be the mission of those who, in this life, are willfully idle?
- It's true that there are human beings who live only for themselves, and who don't make themselves useful in any way. They're much to be pitied, for they'll have to expiate their voluntary inutility by severe sufferings, and their chastisement often begins even in their present existence, through their weariness and disgust of life.
- Since they had the freedom of choice, why did they choose a life which could not be of any use to them?
- Among spirits, as among men, there are lazy ones who shrink from a life of labor. God lets them take their own way; they'll learn, by and by, and to their cost, the bad effects of their uselessness, and will then eagerly demand to be allowed to make up for lost time. It may be, also, that they had chosen a more useful life; but have subsequently recoiled from the trial, and allowed themselves to be misled by tile suggestions of spirits who encourage them in their inactivity.

575 - The common occupations of everyday life appear to us to be duties rather than missions, properly so called. A mission according to the idea we attach to this word, is characterized by au importance less exclusive, and especially less personal. From this point of view, have can we ascertain that a man has really a mission upon this Earth?
- By the greatness of the results he accomplishes, and the progress he causes to be made by his fellow-men.

576 - Are those who have received an important mission predestined thereto before their birth, and are they aware of it?
- Yes, in some cases; but, more often, they ate not aware of it. They're only vaguely conscious of an aim in coming upon the Earth; their mission reveals itself to them gradually, after their birth, through the action of circumstances. God leads them on into the road which they're to take for the accomplishment of his designs.

577 - When a man does anything useful, is it always in virtue of an anterior and predestined mission, or may he receive a mission not previously foreseen?
- Everything a man does is not the result of a predestined mission; he is often the instrument of a spirit who makes use of him in order to procure the execution of something he considers useful. For example, a spirit thinks it would be useful to publish a book which he'd write himself if he were incarnated. He seeks out the writer who will be the fittest to

comprehend and develop his idea; he suggests to him the plan of the work, and directs him in its execution in such a case, the man didn't come into the world with the mission of doing this work. It's the same in regard to various works of art or scientific discoveries. During the sleep of his body, the incarnated spirit communicates directly with the spirit in erraticity, and the two take counsel together for the carrying out of their undertaking.

578 - May spirit fail in his mission through his own fault?
- Yes, if he's not of a high degree of elevation.
- What, for him, are the consequences of such a failure?
- He's obliged to begin his task over again, this is his punishment, and, besides, he'll have to undergo the consequences of the mischief caused by his failure.

579 - Since it is from God that each spirit receives his mission, how can God have entrusted an important mission, one of general interest, to a spirit capable of failing in its discharge?
- Doesn't God foresee whether His general will be victorious or vanquished? Be sure that he foresees all things, and that the carrying out of his plans, when they're important, is never confided to those who'll leave their work half done. The whole difficulty lies, for you, in the foreknowledge of the future which God possesses, but which you can't understand.

580 - When a spirit has incarnated himself for the accomplishment of a mission, does he feel the same anxiety in regard to it as the spirit whose mission has been undertaken as a trial?
- No, for he has the results of experience to guide him.

581 - The men who enlighten the human race by their genius have certainly a mission; but there are among them many who make mistakes, and who, along with important truths, spread abroad serious errors. In what way should we regard their mission?
- As having been falsified by themselves. They're unequal to the task they have undertaken. In judging of them, however, you must take into account the circumstances in which they have been placed. Men of genius have had to speak according to their time; and teachings which appear erroneous or puerile, in the light of a later epoch, may have been sufficient for the epoch at which they were given.

582 - Can paternity be considered a mission?
- It's undeniably a mission, and also a most serious duty, the responsibilities of which will exercise a more important influence upon his future than a man is apt to suppose. God has placed the child under the tutelage of his parents, in order that they should direct his steps into the path of rectitude, and he has facilitated their task by giving to the child a frail and delicate organization, that renders him, accessible to new impressions, but there are many parents, who take more pains to train the trees in their gardens, and to make them bring forth a large crop of fine fruit, than to train the character of their child. If the latter succumbs through their fault, they'll bear the punishment of their unfaithfulness; and the sufferings of the child in a future life will come home to them, because they have not done their part towards helping him forward on the road to happiness.

583 - If a child goes wrong, notwithstanding the care of his parents, are they responsible?
- No, but the more vicious the disposition of the child, and the heavier their task, the greater will be their reward if they succeed in drawing him away from the evil road.
- If a child becomes a good man, despite the negligence or bad example of his parents, do the latter obtain any benefit therefrom?
- God is just.

584 - What can be the mission of the conqueror whose only aim is the satisfaction of his ambition, and who, in order to attain that end, doesn't shrink from inflicting the calamities he brings in his train?
- He's generally only an instrument used by God for the accomplishment of his designs; and these calamities are sometimes a means of making a people advance more rapidly.
- The good that may result from these passing calamities is foreign to him who has been the instrument in producing them, since he had only proposed to himself a personal aim; will he, nevertheless, profit by that result?
- Each one is rewarded according to his works, the good he wished to do and the guidance of his intuitions.

> Spirits, while incarnated, have occupations inherent in the nature of their corporeal existence. In the state of erraticity or of dematerialization, their occupations are proportioned to their degree of advancement. Some of them journey from world to world, acquiring instruction, and preparing for a new incarnation. Others, more advanced, devote themselves to the cause of progress by directing the course of events, and suggesting propitious ideas they assist the men of genius who help forward the advancement of the human race. Others incarnate themselves again with a mission of progress. Others take under their care individuals, families, societies, cities, countries, and peoples, and become their guardian-angels, protecting genie, and familiar spirits. Others, again, preside over the phenomena of nature, of which they're the immediate agents. The great mass of spirits of lower rank busy themselves with our occupations, and take part in our amusements. Impure and imperfect spirits wait, in sufferings and anguish, the moment when it shall please God to furnish them with the means of advancing. If they do harm, it's through spite against the happiness which they're not yet able to share.

Chapter 11 - The three reigns

1 - Minerals and plants

585 - What do you think of the division of the natural world into three reigns, the mineral, vegetable, and animal, to which some naturalists add a 4th class, the human species; or that other division of the world into two classes, the organic and the inorganic? Which of these divisions is to be preferred?
- They're all good; as to which is best, that depends on your point of view. From the point of view of matter, there are only inorganic and organic beings; from the moral point of view, there are evidently four degrees.

> These four degrees are, in fact, distinguished by well-marked characteristics, although their extremes seem to blend into each other. Inert matter, which constitutes the mineral reign, possesses only mechanical force; plants, composed of inert matter, are endowed with vitality animals, composed of inert matter, and endowed with vitality, have also a sort of instinctive intelligence, limited in its scope, but giving them the consciousness of their existence and of their individuality man, possessing all that is found in plants and animals, is raised above all the other classes by special intelligence, without fixed limits, which gives him the consciousness of his future, the perception of extra-material things, and the knowledge of God.

586 - Are plants conscious of their existence?
- No, they don't think; they have only organic life.

587 - Do plants feel sensations? Do they suffer when they're mutilated?
- Plants receive the physical impressions which act upon matter, but they have no perceptions, consequently they don't feel pain.

588 - Is the force which attracts plants towards each other independent of their will?
- Yes, for they don't think. It's a mechanical force of matter that acts upon matter; they couldn't resist it.

589 - Some plants, as, for instance, the mimosa and the dionea, have movements which give evidence of their possessing great sensitiveness, and, in some cases, a sort of will, as in the case of the latter, whose lobes seize the fly that lights on it, in order to suck its juices, and even seem to set a snare for it, in order to kill it. Are these plants endowed with the faculty of thought? Have they a will, and do they form in intermediate class between the vegetable and animal natures? Are they points of transition from the one to the other?
- Everything in nature is transition, from the very fact that everything is different, and that everything, nevertheless, is linked together. Plants don't think and have consequently no will. The oyster that opens its shell and all the zoophytes, don't think; they have only a blind natural instinct.

> The human organism furnishes us with examples of similar movements that take place without any participation of the will, as in the organs of digestion and circulation the pylorus closes itself at the contact of certain substances, as though to refuse them passage. It must be the same with the sensitive plant, the movements of which don't necessarily imply perception, and, still less, will.

590 - Is there not, in plants, an instinct of self-preservation which leads them to seek what may be useful to them, and to avoid what would do them harm?
- You may call it, if you'll, a sort of instinct: that depends on the extension you give to the word; but it's purely mechanical. When, in chemical operations, you see two bodies unite together, it's because they suit one another, that's to say, there is an affinity between them, but you don't call that instinct.

591 - In worlds of higher degree, are the plants, like the other beings, of a more perfect nature?
- Everything in those worlds is more perfect, but the plants are always plants, as the animals are always animals, and as the men are always men.

2 - Animals and men

592 - If we compare man with the animals in reference to intelligence, it seems difficult to draw a line of demarcation between them, for some animals are, in this respect, notoriously superior to some men. Is it possible to establish such a line of demarcation with any precision?
- Your philosophers are far from being agreed upon this point. Some of them will have it that man is an animal, others are equally sure that the animal is a man. They're all wrong. Man is a being apart, who sometimes sinks himself very low or who may raise himself very high. As regards his physical nature, man is like the animals and less well provided for than many of them, for nature has given to them all that man is obliged to invent with the aid of his intelligence for his needs and his preservation. His body is subject to destruction, like that of the animals, but his spirit has a destiny that he alone can understand, because he alone is completely free. Poor human beings who debase yourselves below the brutes. Do you not know how to distinguish yourselves from them? Recognize the superiority of man by his possessing the notion of the existence of God.

593 - Can the animals be said to act only from instinct?
- That, again, is a mere theory. It's very true that instinct predominates in the greater number of animals; but do you not see some of them act with a determinate will? This is intelligence; but of narrow range.

> It's impossible to deny that some animals give evidence of possessing, besides instinct, the power of performing compound acts which denote the will to act in a determinate direction, and according to circumstances. Consequently, there is in them a sort of intelligence, but the exercise of which is mainly concentrated on the means of satisfying their physical needs, and providing for their own preservation. There is, among them, no progress, no amelioration no matter what the art that we admire in their labors, what they formerly did, that they do today neither better nor worse, according to constant forms and unvarying proportions. The young bird isolated from the rest of its species none the less builds its nest on the same model, without having been taught. If some of the animals are susceptible of a certain amount of education, their intellectual development, always restricted within narrow limits, Is due to the action of man upon a flexible nature, for they themselves have no power of progressing but that artificial development is ephemeral and purely individual, for the animal, when left again to himself, speedily returns within the limits traced out for it by nature.

594 - Have animals a language?
- If you mean a language formed of words and syllables, no; but if you mean a method of communication among themselves, yes. They say much more to one another than you suppose, but their language is limited, like their ideas, to their bodily wants.
-There are animals who have no voice; have they no language?
- They understand one another by other means. Have men no other method of communicating with one another than by speech? And the dumb, what do you say of them? The animals, being endowed with the life of relation, have means of giving one another information and of expressing the sensations they feel. Do you suppose that fishes have no understanding among themselves? Man has not the exclusive privilege of language; but that of the animals is instinctive and limited to the scope of their wants and ideas, while that of man is perfectible and lends itself to all the conceptions of his intelligence.

> It's evident that fishes, emigrating in masses, like the swallows that follow the guide that leads them; they must have the means of giving one another information, of arriving at a common understanding and of concerting measures of general interest. It may be that they're gifted with a sense of vision sufficiently acute to allow of their distinguishing signs made by them to one another or the water may serve them as a vehicle for the transmission of certain vibrations. It's evident that they must have some means, whatever these may be of comprehending one another, like all other animals that have no voice and that nevertheless perform actions in common. Should it, then, be deemed strange that spirits are able to communicate among themselves without having recourse to articulate speech?

595 - Have animal's free-will in regard to their actions?
- They're not the mere machines you suppose them to be, but their freedom of action is limited to their wants and can't be compared to that of man. Being far inferior to him, they have not the same duties. Their freedom is restricted to the acts of their material life.

596 - Whence comes the aptitude of certain animals to mutate human speech and why is this aptitude found among birds, rather, for instance, than among apes, whose conformation has so more analogy to that of man?
- That aptitude results from a particular conformation of the vocal organs, seconded by the instinct of imitation. The ape imitates man's gestures; some birds imitate his voice.

597 - Since the animals have an intelligence which gives them a certain degree of freedom of action, is there, in them, a principle independent of matter?
- Yes, and that survives their body.
- Is this principle a soul, like that of man?
- It's a soul, if you like to call it so, that depends on the meaning you attach to this word, but it's inferior to that of man. There is, between the soul of the animals and that of man, as great a difference as there is between the soul of man and God.

598 - Does the soul of the animals preserve, after death, its individuality and its self-consciousness?
- It preserves its individuality, but not the consciousness of its me. The life of intelligence remains latent in them.

599 - Has the soul of the beasts the choice of incarnating itself in one kind of animal rather than in another?
- No, it doesn't possess free-will.

600 - As the soul of the animal survives its body, is it, after death, in a state of erraticity, like that of man?
- It's in a sort of erraticity, because it's not united to a body, but it's not an errant spirit. The errant spirit is a being who thinks and acts of his own free-will, but the soul of the animal has not the same faculty, for it's his self-consciousness which is the principal attribute of the spirit. The soul of the animal is classed after its death, by the spirits charged with that work, and almost immediately utilized; it has not the leisure to enter into connection with other creatures.

601 - Do animals follow a law progress like the men?
- Yes, and it's for this reason that, in the higher worlds which men are further advanced, the animals are more advanced also, and possess more developed means of communication, but they're always inferior to man, and subject to him, they're, for him, intelligent servitors.

> There's nothing unreasonable in this statement. Suppose that our most intelligent animals, the dog, the elephant, the horse, were furnished with a bodily conformation appropriate to manual labor, what could they not do under the direction of man?

602 - Do animals progress, like man, through the action of their will, or through the force of things?
- Through the force of things, this is why there is, for them, no expiation.

603 - Have the animals, in the higher worlds, a knowledge of God?
- No, man is a god for them, as spirits were formerly gods for men.

604 - The animals, even the advanced ones of the higher worlds, being always inferior to man, it would seem as though God had created intellectual beings condemned to a perpetual inferiority such an arrangement doesn't appear to be in accordance with the unity of design and of progress discernible in all his works.
- Everything in Nature is linked together by an enchaining which your intellect can't yet seize and things apparently the most discrepant have points of contact at the comprehension of which man will never arrive in his actual state. He may obtain a glimmering of them through an effort of his intelligence, but it's only when that intelligence shall have acquired its full development and shall have freed itself from the prejudices of pride and of ignorance, that he'll be able to see clearly into the work of God, until then, his narrowness of thought causes him to look at everything from a low and petty point of view. Know that God can't contradict himself and that everything in nature is harmonized by the action of general laws that never deviate from the sublime wisdom of the Creator.
- Intelligence, then, is a common property, and a point of contact, between the soul of the beast and that of man?
- Yes, but the animals have only the intelligence of material life, in man, intelligence gives moral life.

605 - Considering all the points of contact that exist between man and animals, it'd not be lawful to think that man has two souls, the animal soul and the spirit soul, and that if the latter didn't exist, just as the brute could he to live?
On the other, that the animal is a being similar to the man, having less the spiritist soul? In this way would it turn out to be the good and evil instincts of man the effect of the predominance of one or other of these souls?
- No, man hasn't two souls, but the body has its instincts resulting from the sensation of its organs. There's in him only a double nature, the animal nature and the spiritual nature. By his body he participates in the nature of the animals and their instincts, by his soul he participates in the nature of spirits.
- Thus, besides his own imperfection, which he has to get rid of, a spirit has also to struggle against the influence of matter?
- Yes, the lower a spirit's degree of advancement, the closer is the bonds which united him with matter. Do you not see that it must necessarily be so? No. man has not two souls; the soul is always one in a single being. The soul of the animal and that of man are distinct from one another, so that the soul of the one can't animate the body created for the other, but if man haven't an animal soul, placing him, by its passions, on a level with the animals, he has his body, which often drags him down to them, for his body is a being that is endowed with vitality, and that has its instincts, but unintelligent, and limited to the care of its own preservation.

> A spirit, in incarnating himself in a human body, brings to it the intellectual and moral principle that renders it superior to the animals. The two natures in man constitute for him two distinct sources of passions, one set of passions springing from the instincts of his animal nature, and the other set being due to the impurities of the spirit of which he's the incarnation and which are in sympathy with the grossness of the animal appetites. A spirit, as he becomes purified, frees himself gradually from the influence of matter. While under that influence, he approaches the nature of the brutes when delivered from that influence, he raises himself towards his true destination.

606 - Whence do the animals derive the intelligent principle that constitutes the particular kind of soul with which they're endowed?
- From the universal intelligent element.
- The intelligence of man and of the animals emanates, then, from one and the same principle?
- Undoubtedly, but, in man, it has received an elaboration which raises it above that which animates the brute.

607 - You have stated that the soul of man, at its origin, is in a state analogous to that of human infancy, that its intelligence is only beginning to unfold itself, and that it's essaying to live, where does the soul accomplish this earliest phase of its career?
- In a series of existences which precede the period of development that you call humanity.
- The soul would seem, then, to have been the intelligent principle of the inferior orders of the creation?
- Have we not said that everything in nature is linked together and tends to unity? It's in those beings, of which you're very far from knowing all, that the intelligent principle is elaborated, is gradually individualized, and made ready to live, as we have said, through its subjection to a sort of preparatory process, like that of germination, on the conclusion of which that principle undergoes a transformation and becomes spirit. It's then that the period of humanity commences for each spirit with the sense of futurity, the power of distinguishing between good and evil, and the responsibility of his actions, just as, after the period of infancy comes that of childhood, then youth, adolescence, and ripened manhood.

Is the greatest genius humiliated by having been a shapeless fetus in his mother's womb? If anything ought to humiliate him, it's his lowness in the scale of being, and his powerlessness to sound the depths of the divine designs and the wisdom of the laws that regulate the harmonies of the Universe. Recognize the greatness of God in this admirable harmony that establishes solidarity between everything in nature. To think that God could have made anything without a purpose and have created intelligent beings without a future, would be to blaspheme his goodness which extends over all his creatures.

- Does this period of humanity commence upon our Earth?
- The Earth isn't the starting-point of the earliest phase of human incarnation, the human period commences, in general, in worlds still lower than yours. This, however, isn't an absolute rule, and it may happen that a spirit, at his entrance upon the human phase, may be fitted to live upon the Earth. Such a case, however, though possible, is infrequent, and would be an exception to the general rule.

608 - Has a man's spirit, after death, any consciousness of the existences that have preceded his entrance upon the human period?
- No, for it's only with this period that his life, as a spirit, has begun for him. He can scarcely recall his earliest existences as a man, just as a man no longer remembers the earliest days of his infancy and still less the time he passed in his mother's womb. This is why spirits tell you that they don't know how they began.

609 - Does a spirit, when once he has entered upon the human period, retain any traces of what he has previously been, that is to say, of the state in which he was in what may be called the ante-human period?
- That depends on the distance which separates the two periods and the amount of progress accomplished. During a few generations there may be a reflex more or less distinct of the primitive state, for nothing in nature takes place through an abrupt transition and there are always links which unite the extremities of the chain of beings or of events, but those traces disappear with the development of free-will. The first steps of progress are accomplished slowly, because they're not yet seconded by the will, they're accomplished more rapidly in proportion as the spirit acquires a more perfect consciousness of himself.

610 - The spirits who have said that man is a being apart from the rest of creation are, then, mistaken?
- No, but the question hadn't been developed, and besides, there are things that can only be known at their appointed time. Man is, in reality, a being apart, for he has faculties that distinguish him from all others, and he has another destiny. The human species is the one which God has chosen for the incarnation of the beings that are capable of knowing him.

> Descartes taught that animals are machines, acting according to natural laws, because they have no spirit. This conception, which in the time of Kardec was still very widespread, still prevails among the majority of men. The spirits contest it, as it's seen, and their opinion is referenced by the Sciences.

3 - Metempsychosis

611 - Isn't the common origin of the intellectual principle of living beings a consecration of the doctrine of the metempsychosis?
- Two things may have the same origin and yet not resemble one another at a later period. Who could recognize the tree, with its leaves, flowers, and fruit, in the shapeless germ contained in the seed from which it has issued? From the moment when the principle of intelligence has reached the necessary degree of development for becoming spirit, and for entering upon the human phase, it has no longer any connection with its primitive state and is no more the soul of the beasts than the tree is the seed. In man there's no longer anything of the animal but his body and the passions which are the joint product of his body and of the instinct of self-preservation inherent in matter. It can't, therefore, be said that such and such a man is the incarnation of such and such an animal and consequently the doctrine of the metempsychosis, as commonly understood, isn't true.

612 - Can a spirit which has animated a human body be incarnated in an animal?
- No, for such an incarnation would be a retrogradation and a spirit never retrograde. The river doesn't flow back to his source.

613 - However erroneous, may be the idea attached to the doctrine of the metempsychosis, it mayn't that doctrine be a result of an intuitive reminiscence of the different existences of man?
- That intuitive reminiscence is seen in this belief as in many others, but, like the greater part of his intuitive ideas, man has perverted it.

> The doctrine of the metempsychosis would be true if by that word were understood the progression of the soul from a lower state to a higher state in which it acquires the new development that will transform its nature, but it's false when understood as meaning that any animal can transmigrate directly into a man and a man into an animal, which would imply the idea of a retrogradation or of a fusion. The fact that fusion isn't possible between corporeal beings of two different species is an indication of their being of degrees, that aren't assailable, and that such must be the case, also, with the spirits that animate them.

If the same spirit could animate them alternately it'd imply the existence, between them, of an identity that would manifest itself by the possibility of corporeal reproduction. Reincarnation, as now taught by spirits, is founded, on the contrary, upon the ascensional movement of nature and upon the progression of man in his own specie, which detracts nothing from his dignity. What really degrades man is the evil use he makes of the faculties which God has given him for his advancement, and, at all events, the antiquity and universality of the doctrine of the metempsychosis, and the number of eminent men who have professed it, proves that the principle of reincarnation has its roots in nature itself, a fact which, so far from diminishing the probability of its truth, must be regarded as constituting a weighty argument in its favor.

The startling-point of spirit is one of those questions which have reference to the origin of things, and to the secret designs of God. It's not given to man to comprehend them completely and he can only form, in regard to them, suppositions and theoretic systems, more or less probable. Spirits themselves are far from knowing everything and may also have, in regard to what they don't know individual opinions more or less in harmony with fact. It's thus, for example, that all spirits don't think alike in reference to the relations which exist between man and the animals. According to some, spirit only arrives at the human period after having been elaborated and individualized in the different degrees of the lower beings of the creation.

According to others, the spirit of man has always belonged to the human race, without passing through the ascensional degrees of the animal world. The first of these theories has the advantage of giving an aim to the future of animals, which are thus seen to form the earliest links in the chain of thinking beings, the 2nd theory is more consonant with the dignity of man, and may be summed up as follows: The different species of animals don't proceed intellectually from one another by road of progression. Thus the spirit of the oyster doesn't become successively that of the fish, the bird and the quadruped. Each species is a fixed type, physically and morally, each individual of which draws, from the universal source of being, the sum of the intelligent principle which is necessary to it according to the nature of its organs and the work it has to accomplish in the phenomena of nature, and which it restores to the general mass of that principle at its death.

Those of worlds more advanced than ours are also distinct races; that are fitted to the needs of those worlds and to the degree of advancement of the men of whom they're the auxiliaries, but that don't proceed, spiritually, from those of Earth. It's not the same with man. It's evident that, physically, he forms a link in the chain of living beings, but there's, morally, a solution of continuity between the animals and him, for man alone possesses the soul, or spirit, the divine spark, which gives him the moral sense and the extended vision which are wanting in the animals, and this soul, spirit, spark, is, in him, the principal being, pre-existent to, and surviving, his body, and thus preserving his Individuality.

What is the origin of spirit? What its starting-point? Is it formed by the individualizing of the intelligent principle? This is a mystery which it'd be useless to attempt to penetrate, and in regard to which, as we have said, we can do no more than build up theories. What is certain, what is indicated alike by reason and by experience, is the survival of each spirit and the persistence of his individuality after death, his faculty of progressing, the happiness or unhappiness of his next state of being, according to his advancement or his backwardness in the path of purification, and all the moral consequences which flow from this certainty, as for the mysterious kinship which exists between man and the animals, that we repeat, is God's secret, like many other matters the knowledge of which, at this time, is of little importance to our advancement, and upon which it'd be useless to insist.

3rd book - Moral laws
Chapter 1 - Divine or natural law

1 - Characteristics of natural law
614 - What is to be understood by natural law?
- The law of nature is the law of God. It's the only rule that ensures the happiness of man, for it shows him what he should or shouldn't do and he only suffers because he disobeys it.

615 - Is the law of God eternal?
- It's eternal and unchangeable as God Himself.

616 - Can God have prescribed to mankind in one age what he has forbidden in another?
- God can't be mistaken. Men are obliged to change their laws, because they're imperfect, but the laws of God are perfect. The harmony which regulates both the material Universe and the moral Universe is founded on laws established by God from all eternity.

617 - What are the objects embraced by the divine laws? Have they reference to anything, but our moral conduct?
- All the laws of nature are divine laws, since God is the author of all things. The seeker after science studies the laws of nature in the realm of matter, the seeker after goodness studies them in the soul and practices them.
- Is it given to man to fathom both these divisions of natural law?
- Yes, but a single existence doesn't suffice for doing this.

> What, indeed, are a few years for acquiring all that is necessary to constitute a perfect being, if we consider only the distance that separates the civilized man from the savage? A human life, though prolonged to its utmost possible length, is insufficient for such a work, much more is it so when cut short before its term, as is the case with so large a proportion of the human race. Some of the divine laws regulate the movements and relations of inert matter, they're termed physical laws, and their study is the domain of science, others of these laws concern man as considered in himself and in his relations to God and to his fellow, creatures, they're termed moral laws and regulate the life of relation as well as the life of the soul.

618 - Are the divine laws the same for all worlds?
- Reason tells you that they must be adapted to the special nature of each of those various worlds, and proportioned to the degree of advancement of the beings that inhabit them.

2 - Knowledge of natural law
619 - Has God given to all men the means of knowing his law?
- All may know it, but all don't understand it. Those who understand it best are they who seek after goodness. All, however, will one day understand it, for the destiny of progress must he accomplished.

> The justice of the various incarnations undergone by each human being is evident when seen in the light of the principle just enunciated, since, in each new existence, his intelligence is more developed and he comprehends more clearly what is good and what is evil. If everything had to be accomplished by each man in a single existence, what would be the fate of the many millions of human beings who die every day in the brutishness of the savage state, or in the darkness of ignorance, without having had the possibility of obtaining enlightenment?

620 - Does a spirit, before his union with the body, comprehend the law of God more clearly than after his incarnation?
- He comprehends that law according to the degree of development at which he has arrived and preserves the intuitive remembrance of it after being united with a body, but the evil instincts of man often cause him to forget it.

621 - Where is the law of God inscribed?
- In the conscience.
- Since man carries the lawn of God in his conscience, where was the need of revealing it to him?
- He had forgotten and misunderstood it; God willed that it should be recalled to his memory.

622 - Has God given to some men the mission of revealing his law?
- Yes, certainly. In every age there have been men who have received this mission, spirits of higher degree, who have incarnated themselves for the purpose of advancing human progress.

623 - Haven't those who have professed to instruct mankind sometimes made mistakes and led them astray by false reasonings?
- Those who, not being inspired by God, have arrogated to themselves, through ambition, a mission which they hadn't received, may, undoubtedly, have led them into error, nevertheless, as, after all, they were men of genius, great truths are often to be found, even in the midst of the errors they taught.

624 - What are the characteristics of the true prophet?

- The true prophet is an upright man who's inspired by God. He may be recognized both by his words and by his deeds. God doesn't employ the mouth of a liar to teach the truth.

625 - What is the most perfect type that God has offered to man as his guide and model?
- Jesus.

> Jesus is the type of the moral perfection to which man may attain upon this Earth. God offers him to our thought as our most perfect model and the doctrine taught by him is the purest expression of the divine law, because he was animated by the divine spirit, and was the purest being that has ever appeared upon the Earth. If some of those who have professed to instruct man in the law of God have, sometimes, led him astray by the inculcation of error, it's because they have allowed themselves to be swayed by sentiments of too earthly a nature, and because they have confounded the laws which regulate the conditions of the life of the soul which regulate the life of the body. Many pretended revealers have announced as divine laws what were only human laws devised by them for serving their own passions and obtaining dominion over their fellow men.

626 - Have the divine or natural laws been revealed to men by Jesus only, and had men, before his time, no other knowledge than that given them by intuition?
- Have we who told you that those laws are written everywhere? All the men who have meditated upon wisdom have therefore been able to comprehend and to teach them from the remotest times. By their teachings, imperfect though they were, they have prepared the ground for the sowing of the seed. The divine laws being written in the book of nature, it has always been possible for man to know them by searching after them. For this reason, the moral precepts they consecrate have been proclaimed, in all ages, by upright men, and, for the same reason also, the elements of the moral law are to be found among every nation above the barbarian degree, although incomplete, or debased by ignorance and superstition.

627 - Since the true laws of God have been taught by Jesus, what is the use of the teachings given by spirits? Have they anything more to teach us?
- The teachings of Jesus were often allegoric and conveyed in parables because he spoke according to the time and place in which he lived. The time has now come when the truth must be made intelligible for all. It's necessary to explain and develop the divine laws, because few among you understand them and still fewer practice them. Our mission is to strike the eyes and ears of all in order to confound pride, and to unmask the hypocrisy of those who assume the outward appearances of virtue and of religion as a cloak for their turpitudes. We're charged to prepare the reign of good announced by Jesus to furnish the explanations that will render it impossible for men to continue to interpret the law of God according to their passions, or to pervert the meaning of what is wholly a law of love and of kindness.

628 - Why hasn't the truth been always placed within reach of every one?
- Each thing can only come in its time. Truth is like light, you must be accustomed to it gradually, otherwise it only dazzles you.

> Hitherto, God has never permitted man to receive communications so full and instructive as those which he's permitted to receive at this day. There were, undoubtedly, in ancient times, as you know, individuals who were in possession of knowledge which they considered as sacred, and which they kept as a mystery from those whom they regarded as profane. You can well understand, from what you know of the laws which govern the phenomena of spirit communication, that they received only a few fragmentary truths, scattered through a mass of teachings that were generally emblematic, and often erroneous.

Nevertheless, there's no old philosophic system, no tradition, no religion, that men should neglect to study, for they all contain the germs of great truths, which, however they may seem to contradict each other perverted as they're by their mixture with various worthless accessories and may be easily coordinated, with the aid of the key that Spiritism gives you to a class of facts which have hitherto seemed to be contrary to reason, but of which the reality is irrefutably demonstrated at the present day. You should therefore not fail to make those old systems a subject of study, for they are rich in lessons and may contribute largely to your instruction.

3 - Descartes, in the third of his Metaphysical Meditations, declared that the idea of God is imprinted on man as the mark imprinted on his work. This idea of God is innate in man and impels him to perfection. Although modern schools of psychology deny the existence of innate ideas, Spiritism supports this existence through the principle of reincarnation. On the other hand, the ideas of God, of survival, of good and of evil always exist and existed among all peoples. The law of God is written in the conscience of man as the signature of the artist in his work.

4 - The sacred texts of the great religions, such as the *Bible* and the *Vedas*, the systems of ancient philosophers, the doctrines of old occult or esoteric orders, all contain great truths in their apparent contradictions. Spiritists should not retreat from these systems or see them only contradictions, when they have the key to Spiritism, with which they're able to decipher their enigmas, discovering their powerful reasons for enlightenment. Also in modern systems of philosophy or science, however contrary they may seem to spiritists, a truly Spiritist analysis may reveal the existence of great truths.

3 - Good and evil
629 - What definition can be given of the moral law?
- The moral law is the rule for acting aright, that is to say, for distinguishing practically between good and evil. It's founded on the observance of the law of God. Man acts rightly when he takes the good of all as his aim and rule of action, for he then obeys the law of God.

630 - How can we distinguish between good and evil?

- Good is whatever is in conformity with the law of God and evil is whatever deviates from it. Thus, to do right, is to conform to the law of God, to do wrong, is to infringe that law.

631 - Has man of himself the means of distinguishing what is good from what is evil?

- Yes, when he believes in God and desires to do what is right. God has given him intelligence in order that he may distinguish between them.

632 - As man is subject to error may he not be mistaken in his appreciation of good and evil and believe himself to be doing right, when, in reality, he's doing wrong?

- Jesus has said: "Whatsoever ye would that men should do unto you, do ye even so to them". The whole moral law is contained in that injunction; make it your rule of action and you'll never go wrong.

633 - The rule of good and evil, what may be called the rule of reciprocity or solidarity, can't be applied to a man's to personal conduct towards himself. Does he find, in natural law, the rule of that conduct, and a safe guide?

- When you eat too much, it hurts you. God gives you, in the discomfort thus produced, the measure of what is necessary for you. When you exceed that measure, you're punished. It's the same with everything else. Natural law traces out for each man the limit of his needs, when he oversteps that limit he's punished by the suffering thus caused. If men gave heed, in all things, to the voice which says to them enough, they'd avoid the greater part of the ills of which they accuse nature.

634 - Why does evil exist in the nature of things? I speak of moral evil. Couldn't God have created the human race in more favorable conditions?

- We have already told you that spirits are created simple and ignorant. God leaves man free to choose his road, so much the worse for him if he takes the wrong one, his pilgrimage will be all the longer. If there were no mountains, man couldn't comprehend the possibility of ascending and descending, if there were no rocks, he couldn't understand that there are such things as hard bodies. It's necessary for the spirit to acquire experience, and, to that end, he must know both good and evil. It's for this purpose that souls are united to bodies.

635 - The different social positions create new wants which aren't the same for all men; natural law would therefore appear not to be a uniform rule?

- Those different positions are in nature and according to the law of progress; they don't invalidate the unity of natural law, which applies to everything.

> The conditions of a man's existence vary according to times and places hence arise for him different wants and social positions corresponding to those wants. Since this diversity is in the order of things, it must be consonant with the law of God and this law is none the less one in principle. It's for reason to distinguish between real wants and wants that are factitious or conventional.

636 - Are good and evil absolute for all men?

- The law of God is the same for all, but evil resides especially in the desire for its commission. Good is always good and evil is always evil, whatever a man's position may be, the difference is in the degree of his responsibility.

637 - When a savage, yielding to his instinctive desire feeds on human flesh, is he guilty in so doing?

- I have said that the essence of evil is in the will; therefore a man is more or less guilty according to his light. Circumstances modify the relative intensity of good and of evil.

> A man often commits faults that are none the less reprehensible for being the consequence of the social position in which he is placed, but his responsibility is proportioned to the means he possesses of distinguishing between right and wrong. Thus the enlightened man who commits a mere injustice is more culpable in the sight of God than the ignorant savage who abandons himself to his instincts of cannibalism.

638 - Evil seems, sometimes, to be a consequence of the force of things. Such is, for instance, in some cases, the necessity of destruction, even to the extent of taking the life of a fellow creature. Can it be said that, in such cases, there's violation of the law of God?

- Evil, in such cases, is none the less evil, although necessary, but this necessity disappears in proportion as the soul becomes purified by passing from one existence to another and man then all the more culpable when he does wrong, because he comprehends more clearly the character of his action.

639 - The evil we do is often the result of the position that has been made for us by other men, where, in such a case, lies the greatest amount of culpability?

- With those who have been the cause of the wrong-doing. Thus the man who has been led into evil, by the position that his fellow-creatures have made for him, is less guilty than those who have caused him to go astray, for each has to suffer the penalty, not only of the evil he has done, but of that which he has caused another to do.

640 - Is he who profits by another's wrong doing, even though he took no part in its commission as guilty as though he had taken part in it?

- Yes, to take advantage of a crime is to take part in it. He'd, perhaps, have shrunk from committing the evil deed, but if the deed being done, he takes advantage of it, it's equivalent to doing it and proves that he'd have done it himself, if he could or if he dared.

641 - Is it as reprehensible to desire to do an evil deed as to do it?
- That's as the case may be. Voluntarily to resist the desire to do wrong, especially when there's a possibility of gratifying that desire, is virtuous, hut he, who has only not done the wrong thing because the opportunity was wanting, is as guilty as though he had done it.

642 - In order to be acceptable in the sight of God, and to insure our future happiness, is it sufficient not to have done evil?
- No, it's necessary for each to have done good also until the utmost limits of his ability, for each of you'll have to answer, not only for all the evil he has done, but also for all the good which he has failed to do.

643 - Are there persons who, through their position, have no possibility of doing well?
- There are none who can't do some good, the selfish alone find no opportunity of so doing. The mere fact of being in relation with other human beings suffices to furnish the opportunity of doing well and every day of your lives provides this possibility for everyone who isn't blinded by selfishness. For doing good isn't restricted to the giving of alms, but also comprehends being useful to the full extent of your power, whenever your assistance may be needed.

644 - For some men, isn't the medium in which they're placed the primary cause of many vices and crimes?
- Yes, but that situation is itself a part of the trial which has been chosen by his spirit in the state of freedom, he has elected to expose himself to its temptations, in order to acquire the merit of resistance.

645 - When a man is plunged, so to say, in an atmosphere of vice, doesn't the impulsion to evil become, for him, almost irresistible?
- The impulsion is strong, but not irresistible, for you sometimes find great virtues in an atmosphere of vice. Those who thus remain virtuous in the midst of incitements to evil are spirits who have acquired sufficient strength to resist temptation, and who, while thus testing that strength, fulfill the mission of exercising a beneficial influence on those around them.

646 - Is the meritoriousness of virtuous action measured by the conditions under which that action has been accomplished? In other words, are there different degrees of meritoriousness in doing right?
- The meritoriousness of virtuous action depends on the difficulty involved in it, there would be no merit in doing right without self-denial and effort God counts the sharing of his morsel of bread by the poor man, as of a higher merit than the giving of his superfluity by the rich one. Jesus told you this in his parable of the widow's mite.

> Sociological research has given rise to a reappraisal, in our time, of the traditional concept of moral. It was understood that morality is variable, because the good of one people can be bad for another and vice versa.

4 - Division of natural law
647 - Is the whole of the law of God contained in the rule of love of the neighbor laid down by Jesus?
- That rule certainly contains all the duties of men to one another, but it's necessary to show them it is various applications, or they'll continue to neglect them, as they do at the present day, besides, natural law embraces all the circumstances of life and the rule you have cited is only a part of it. Men need precise directions; general precepts are too vague and leave too many doors open to human interpretations.

648 - What do you think of the division of natural law into ten parts, the laws of adoration, labor, reproduction, preservation, society, equality, liberty, justice, love, and charity?
- The division of the law of God into ten parts is that of Moses and may be made to include all the circumstances of life, which is the essential point. You may therefore adopt it, without its being held to have any absolute value, any more than the various other systems of classification which depend on the aspect under which the subject is considered. The last of those parts is the most important because the law of charity includes all the others, and it's therefore through the observance of this law that mankind advances most rapidly in spiritual life.

Chapter 2 - The law of adoration

1 - Aim of adoration

649 - In what does adoration consist?
- In the elevation of the thought towards God. Through adoration the soul draws nearer to him.

650 - Is adoration the result of an innate sentiment or the product of exterior teaching?
- Of an innate sentiment, like the belief in the Divinity. The consciousness of his weakness leads man to bow before the being who can protect him.

651 - Are there peoples entirely without the sentiment of adoration?
- No, for there never was a people of atheists. All feel that there's, above them, a supreme being.

652 - May adoration be regarded as having its source in natural law?
- It's included in natural law, since it's the result of a sentiment innate in man, for which reason it's found among all peoples, though under different forms.

2 - External acts of adoration

653 - Are external manifestations essential to adoration?
- True adoration is in the heart. In all your actions remember that the Master's eyes is always upon you.
- Are external acts of worship useful?
- Yes, if they're not a vain pretence. It's always useful to set a good example, but those who perform acts of worship merely from affectation and for the sake of appearances, and whose conduct belies their seeming piety, set a bad example rather than a good one and do more harm than they imagine.

654 - Does God accord a preference to those who worship him according to any particular mode?
- God prefers those who worship him from the heart, with sincerity and by doing what is good and avoiding what is evil, to those who fancy they honor him by ceremonies which don't render them any better than their neighbors. All men are brothers, and children of God, he calls to him all who follow his laws, whatever may be the form under which they show their obedience. He, who has only the externals of piety, is a hypocrite, he whose worship is only pretence and in contradiction with his conduct, sets a bad example.

He who professes to worship Christ and who's proud, envious, and jealous, who's hard and unforgiving to others, or ambitious of the goods of Earth, is religious with the lips only, and not with the heart. God, who sees all things, will say to him, he who knows the truth, and doesn't follow it's a hundredfold more guilty in the evil he does than the ignorant savage, and will he treated accordingly in the day of retribution. If a blind man runs against you as he goes by, you excuse him, but if the same thing is done by a man who sees, you complain, and with reason. Don't ask, then, if any form of worship be more acceptable than another, for it's as though you asked whether it's more pleasing to God to be worshipped in one tongue rather than in another. Remember that the hymns addressed to him can reach him only through the door of the heart.

655 - Is it wrong to practice the external rites of a religion in which we don't heartily believe when this is done out of respect for those with whom we're connected, and in order not to scandalize those who think differently from us?
- In such a case, as in many others, it's the intention that decides the quality of the act. He whose only aim, in so doing, is to show respect for the belief of others, does no wrong, he does better than the man who turns them into ridicule, for the latter sins against charity, but he who goes through with such practices simply from interested motives, or from ambition, is contemptible in the sight of God and of men. God couldn't take pleasure in those who only pretend to humiliate themselves before him, in order to attract the approbation of their fellow-men.

656 - Is worship performed in common preferable to individual worship?
- When those who sympathize in thought and feeling are assembled together, they have more power to attract good spirits to them. It's the same when they're assembled for worshipping God, but you must not therefore conclude that private worship is less acceptable, for each man can worship God in his own thought.

3 - Life of contemplation

657 - Have men who give themselves up to a life of contemplation, doing nothing evil, and thinking only of God, any special merit in his eyes?
- No, for if they do nothing evil, they do nothing good, and, besides, not to do well is in itself evil. God wills that his children should think of him, but he doesn't will that they should think only of him, since he has given men duties to discharge upon the Earth. He who consumes his life in meditation and contemplation does nothing meritorious in the sight of God because such a life is entirely personal and useless to mankind and God will call him to account for the good he has failed to do.

4 - Prayer

658 - Is prayer acceptable to God?
- Prayer is always acceptable to God when dictated by the heart, for the intention is everything in his sight, and the prayer of the heart is preferable to one read from a book, however beautiful it may be, if read with the lips rather than

with the thought. Prayer is acceptable to God when it's offered with faith, fervor, and sincerity, but don't imagine that he'll listen to that of the vain, proud, or selfish man, unless it's offered as an act of sincere repentance and humility.

659 - What is the general character of prayer?
- Prayer is an act of adoration. To pray to God is to think of him, to draw nearer to him, to put one's self in communication with him. He who prays may propose to himself three things, to praise, to ask and to thank.

660 - Does prayer make men better?
- Yes, for lie who prays with fervor and confidence has more strength for withstanding the temptations of evil and for obtaining from God the help of good spirits to assist him in so doing. Such help is never refused when asked for with sincerity.
- How is it that persons who pray a great deal are sometimes very unnamable, jealous, envious, and harsh, wanting in benevolence and forbearance, and even extremely vicious?
- What is needed isn't to pray a great deal, but to pray aright. Such persons suppose that all the virtue of prayer is in its length, and shut their eyes to their own defects. Prayer, for them, is an occupation, a means of passing their time, but not a study of themselves. In such cases, it's not the remedy that's inefficacious, but the mode in which it's employed.

661 - Is there any use in asking God to forgive us our faults?
- God discerns the good and the evil, prayer doesn't hid faults from his eyes. He, who asks of God the forgiveness of his faults, obtains that forgiveness only through a change of conduct. Good deeds are the best prayers, for deeds are of more worth than words.

662 - Is there any use in praying for others?
- The spirit of him who prays exercises an influence through his desire to do well. By prayer, he attracts to himself good spirits who take part with him in the good he desires to do.

> We possess in ourselves, through our thought and our will, a power of action that extends far beyond the limits of our corporeal sphere. To pray for others is an act of our will. If our will be ardent and sincere, if calls good spirits to the aid of the party prayed for and thus helps him by the suggestion of good thoughts and by giving him the strength of body and of soul which he needs, but in his case also, the prayer of the heart is everything, that of the lips is nothing.

663 - Can we, by praying for ourselves, avert our trials, or change their nature?
- Your trials are in the hands of God and there are some of them that must be undergone to the very end, but God always takes account of the resignation with which they're borne. Prayer calls to your help good spirits who give you strength to bear them with courage, so that they seem to you less severe. Prayer is never useless when it's sincere, because it gives you strength, which is, of itself, an important result. Heaven helps him who helps himself, is a true saying. God could change the order of nature at the various contradictory demands of his creatures, for what appears to be a great misfortune to you, from your narrow point of view, and in relation to your ephemeral life on the Earth, is often a great blessing in relation to the general order of the Universe, and, besides, of how many of the troubles of his life is man himself the author, through his short-sightedness or through his wrong doing.

He's punished in that wherein he has sinned. Nevertheless, your reasonable requests are granted more often than you suppose. You think your prayer hasn't been heeded, because God hasn't worked a miracle on your behalf, while, in fact, he has really assisted you, but by means so natural that they seem to you to have been the effect of change or of the ordinary course of things, and more often still, he suggests to your minds the thought of what you must do in order to help yourselves out of your difficulties.

664 - Is it useful to pray for the dead, and for suffering spirits, and if so, in what way can our prayers soften or shorten their sufferings? Have they the power to turn aside the justice of God?
- Prayer can have no effect upon the designs of God, but the spirit for whom you pray is consoled by your prayer, because you thus give him a proof of interest, and because he who's unhappy is always comforted by the kindness which compassionates his suffering. On the other hand, by your prayer, you excite him to repentance and to the desire of doing all that in him lies to become happy and it's this way that you may shorten the term of his suffering, provided that he, on his side, seconds your action by that of his own will. This desire for amelioration, excited by your prayer in the mind of the suffering spirit, attracts to him spirits of higher degree, who come to enlighten him, console him and give him hope. Jesus prayed for the sheep that have gone astray, thereby showing you that you can't, without guilt, neglect to do the same for those who have the greatest need of your prayers.

665 - What's to be thought of the opinion which rejects the idea of praying for the dead because it's not prescribed in the gospel?
- Christ has said to all mankind: "Love one another". This injunction implies, for all men, the duty of employing every possible means of testifying their affection for each other, but without entering into any details in regard to the manner of attaining that end. If it be true that nothing can turn aside the Creator from applying, to every action of every spirit, the absolute justice of which he's the type, it's none the less true that the prayer you address to him, on behalf of a suffering spirit for whom you feel affection or compassion, is accepted by him as a testimony of remembrance that never fails to bring relief and consolation to the sufferer.

As soon as the latter manifests the slightest sign of repentance, but only then help is sent to him, but he is never allowed to remain in ignorance of the fact that a sympathizing heart has exerted itself on his behalf, and is always left under the consoling impression that this friendly intercession has been of use to him. Thus your intervention necessarily induces a feeling of gratitude and affection, on his part, to the friend who has given him this proof of kindness and of pity and the mutual affection enjoined upon all men by Christ will thereby have been developed or awakened between you and him. Both of you'll thus have obeyed the law of love and union imposed on all the beings of the Universe, that divine law which will usher in the reign of unity that's the aim and end of a spirit's education.

666 - May we pray to spirits?
- You may pray to good spirits as being the messengers of God and the executants of his will, but their power, which is always proportioned to their elevation, depends entirely on the Master of all things, without whose permission nothing takes place, for this reason, prayers addressed to them are only efficacious if accepted by God.

> Spinoza said that "God acts only according to the laws of his nature, without being constrained by anyone", and affirmed the impossibility of the miracle, because it's a violation of the laws of God. Also in regard to individual evils, he claimed that they didn't exist in the general order of the Universe.

5 - Polytheism
667 - How's it that polytheism, although it's false, is nevertheless one of the most ancient and wide-spread of human beliefs?
- The conception of the unity of God could only be, in the man the result of the development of his ideas. Incapable, in his ignorance, of conceiving of an immaterial being, without a determinate form, acting upon matter, man naturally attributed to him the attributes of corporeal nature, that is to say, a form and a face, and thenceforth everything that appeared to surpass the proportions of an ordinary human intelligence was regarded by him as a divinity. Whatever he couldn't understand was looked upon by him as being the work of a supernatural power, and, from that assumption, to the belief in the existence of as many distinct powers as the various effects which he beheld but couldn't account for, there was but a step, but there have been, in all ages, enlightened men who have comprehended the impossibility of the world's being governed by this multitude of powers, without a supreme over-ruling direction, and who have thus been led to raise their thought to the conception of the one sole God.

668 - As phenomena attesting the action of spirits have occurred in all ages of the world and have thus been known from the earliest times, may they not have helped to induce a belief in the plurality of gods?
- Undoubtedly, for, as men applied the term god to whatever surpassed humanity, spirits were, for them, so many gods. For this reason, whenever a man distinguished himself among all others by his actions, his genius, or an occult power incomprehensible by the vulgar, he was made a god of, and was worshipped as such after his death.

> The word 'god', among the Ancients, had a wide range of meaning. It didn't, as in our days, represent the Master of Nature, but was a generic term applied to all beings who appeared to stand outside of the pale of ordinary humanity and, as the manifestations that have since been known as spiritist had revealed to them the existence of incorporeal beings acting as one of the elementary powers of nature, they called them gods, just as we call them spirits. It's a mere question of words, with this difference, however, that, in their ignorance, purposely kept up by those whose interests it served, they built temples and raised altars to them, making them offerings which became highly lucrative for the persons who had charge of this mode of worship whereas, for us, spirits are merely creatures like ourselves, more or less advanced and having cast off their earthly envelope.
If we carefully study the various attributes of the pagan divinities, we shall easily recognize those of the spirits of our day, at every degree of the scale of spirit-life, their physical state in worlds of higher advancement, the part taken by them in the things of the earthly life, and the various properties of the perispirit. Christianity, in bringing its divine light to our world, has taught us to refer our adoration to the only object to which it's due, but it couldn't destroy what is an element of nature, and the belief in the existence of the incorporeal beings around us has been perpetuated under various names. Their manifestations have never ceased, but they have been diversely interpreted and often abused under the veil of mystery beneath which they were kept, while religion has regarded them as miracles, the Incredulous have looked upon them as jugglery, but, at the present time, thanks to a more serious study of the subject, carried on in the broad daylight of scientific investigation, the doctrine of spirit-presence and spirit-action, stripped of the superstitious fancies by which it had been obscured for ages, reveals to us one of the sublimest and most important principles of Nature.

6 - Sacrifices
669 - The custom of offering human sacrifices dates from the remotest antiquity, how can mankind have been led to believe that such an enormity could be pleasing to God?
- In the first place, through their not having comprehended God as being the source of all goodness. Among primitive peoples, matter predominates over spirit, their moral qualities not being yet developed; they give themselves up to the instincts of brutality. In the next place, the men of the primitive periods naturally considered that a living creature must be much more valuable in the sight of God than any merely material object, and this consideration led them to immolate, to their divinities, first animals, and afterwards men, because, according to their false ideas, they thought that the value of a sacrifice was proportioned to the importance of the victim. In your earthly life, when you wish to offer a present to any one, you select a gift, the costliness of which is proportioned to the amount of attachment or consideration that you desire to testify to the person to whom you offer it. It was natural that men who were ignorant of the Nature of the Deity should do the same.
- The sacrificing of animals, then, preceded that of human beings?
- Such was undoubtedly the case.
- According to this explanation, the custom of sacrificing human beings didn't originate in mere cruelty?

- No, but in a false idea as to what would be acceptable to God. Look, for instance, at the story of Abraham. In later times men have still farther debased this false idea by immolating their enemies, the objects of their own personal animosity, but God has never exacted sacrifices of any kind, those of animals, no more than those of men. He couldn't be honored by the useless destruction of his own creations.

670 - There are human sacrifices, when offered with a pious intention, ever been pleasing to God.
- No, never, but God always weighs the intention which dictates any act. Men, being ignorant, may have believed that they were performing a laudable deed in immolating their fellow beings, and, in such a case, God would accept their intention, but not their deed. The human race, in working out its own amelioration, naturally came to recognize its error, and to abominate the idea of sacrifices that ought never to have entered into enlightened minds. I say enlightened, because, however dense the veil of materiality in which they were enveloped, their free-will sufficed, even then to give them a glimmering perception of their origin and their destiny and many among them already understood, by intuition, the wickedness they were committing, but which they none the less accomplished for the gratification of their passions.

671 - What should be thought of the wars styled religious? The sentiment that induces a nation of fanatics to exterminate the greatest possible number of those who don't share their belief, with a view to rendering themselves acceptable to God, would seem to proceed from the same source as that which formerly led them to immolate their fellow-creatures as sacrifices.
- Such wars are stirred up by evil spirits and the men who wage them place themselves in direct opposition to the will of God, which is, that each man should love his brother as himself. Since all religions, or rather all peoples, worship the same God, whatever the name by which they call him, why should one of them wage a war of extermination against another, simply because its religion is different, or hasn't yet reached the degree of enlightenment arrived at by the aggressor?

Not to believe the word of him who was sent by God and animated by his spirit is excusable on the part of peoples who neither saw him nor witnessed the acts performed by him, and, at all events, how can you hope that they'll hearken to his message of peace, when you try to force it upon them by fire and sword? It's true that they have to be enlightened and that it's your duty to endeavor to teach them the doctrine of Christ, but this must be done by persuasion and gentleness, not by violence and bloodshed. The greater number among you don't believe in the communication we have with certain mortals, how could you expect that strangers should believe your assertions in regard to this fact if your acts belied the doctrine you profess?

672 - Was the offering of the fruits of the Earth more acceptable in the sight of God than the sacrificing of animals?
- It must evidently be more agreeable to God to be worshipped by the offering of the fruits of the Earth, than by that of the blood of victims, but I have already answered your question in telling you that God's judgment is directed to the intention, and that the outward fact is of little importance in his sight. A prayer, sent up from the depths of the heart, is a hundredfold more agreeable to God than all the offerings you could possibly make to him. I repeat it; the intention is everything, the fact, nothing.

673 - Might not these offerings be rendered more agreeable to God by consecrating them to the relief of those who lack the necessaries of life, and, in that case, might not the sacrificing of animals, accomplished in view of a useful end, be as meritorious as it's the reverse when subserving no useful end or profiting only to those who are in need of nothing? Would there not be something truly pious in consecrating to the poor the first-fruits of all that God grants to us upon the Earth?
- God always blesses those who do well, to help the poor and afflicted is the best of all ways of honoring Him. I don't mean to say that God disapproves of the ceremonies you employ in praying to him, but a good deal of the money thus spent might be more usefully employed. God loves simplicity in all things. The man who attaches more importance to externals than to the heart is a narrow-minded spirit, how, then, could it be possible for God to regard a form as of any importance in comparison with the sentiment of which it's the expression?

Chapter 3 - The law of labor

1 - Necessity of labor
674 - Is the necessity of labor a law of Nature?
- That labor is a law of Nature and is proved by the fact that it's a necessity, and that civilization obliges man to perform a greater amount of labor, because it increases the sum of his needs and of his enjoyments.

675 - Ought we to understand by "labor" only occupations of a material Nature?
- No, the spirit labors like the body. Every sort of useful occupation is a labor.

676 - Why is labor imposed upon mankind?
- It's a consequence of his corporeal nature. It's an expiation and, at the same time, a means of developing his intelligence. Without labor man would remain in the infancy of intelligence. This is why he's made to owe his food, his safety, and his well-being entirely to his labor and activity. To him who's too weak in body for the rougher kinds of work, God gives intelligence to make up for it, but the action of the intelligence is also a labor.

677 - Why does Nature herself provide for all the wants of the animals?
- Everything in Nature labors. The animals labor as really as you do, but their work, like their intelligence, is limited to the care of their own preservation and this is why labor, among them, doesn't lead to progress, while, among men, it has a double aim, the preservation of the body, and the development of thought, which is also a necessity for him, and which raises him continually to a higher level. When I say that the labor of the animals is limited to the care of their preservation, I mean that this is the aim which they propose to themselves in working, but they're also, unconsciously, and while providing only for their material needs, agents that second the views of the Creator and their labor none the less concurs to the working out of the final end of Nature, although you often fail to discover its immediate result.

678 - In worlds more advanced than Earth, is man subjected to the same necessity of labor?
- The nature of the labor is always relative to that of the wants it supplies, the less material are those wants, the less material is the labor, but you must not suppose that man, in those worlds, remains inactive and useless, idleness would be a torture instead of a benefit.

679 - Is he who possesses a sufficiency of worldly goods for his subsistence enfranchised from the law of labor?
- From material labor perhaps, but not from the obligation of rendering himself useful according to his means and of developing his own intelligence and that of others, which is also a labor. If the man, to whom God has apportioned a sufficiency of means for insuring his corporeal existence, be not constrained to win his bread by the sweat of his brow, the obligation of being useful to his fellow-creatures is all the greater in his case, because the portion appointed to him gives him a greater amount of leisure for doing good.

680 - Are there not men who are incapable of working at anything whatever and whose existence is entirely useless?
- God is just, he condemns only him who is voluntarily useless, for such a one lives upon the labor of others. He wills that each should make himself useful according to his faculties.

681 - Does the law of Nature impose upon children the obligation of laboring for their parents?
- Certainly it does, just as it imposes on parents the duty of laboring for their children. For this reason God has given a place in Nature to the sentiment of filial and paternal affection, in order that the members of a family may be led, by their mutual affection, to aid each other reciprocally a duty which is too often lost sight of in your present state of society.

2 - Limit of labor - Rest
682 - Rest being a necessity after labor, is isn't a law of Nature?
- Undoubtedly, it's. Rest serves to restore the bodily powers and is also necessary in order to give a little more freedom to the mind, enabling it to raise itself above matter.

683 - What is the limit of labor?
- The limit of strength, but God leaves man at liberty to decide this point for himself.

684 - What is to be thought of those who misuse their authority by imposing too heavy a labor on their inferiors?
- They commit one of the worst of crimes. Every man exercising authority is answerable for any excess of labor imposed by him on those who are under his orders, for he thereby transgresses the law of God.

685 - Has man a right to repose in old age?
- Yes, he's only obliged to labor according to his strength.
- But what resource is there for the old man who needs to work in order to support himself and yet is unable to do so?
- The strong should work for the weak, where family-help isn't to be had, society should supply its place; such is the law of charity.

> To say that it's necessary for man to work isn't to make a complete statement of the subject for it's also necessary that he who has to gel his bread by labor should be able to find occupation and this is far from being always the case, whenever the suspension of labor becomes general, it assumes the proportions of a famine. Economic science seeks a

remedy for this evil in the equilibrium of production and consumption, but this equilibrium, supposing it to be attainable, will always be subject to intermittences and during these intervals the laborer must live. There's an element of the question which hasn't been sufficiently considered, education, not merely the education of the intellect, not even that of the moral nature as given by books, but that which consists in the formation, of characters and habits, for education is the totality of the habits acquired.

When we consider how great a mass of individuals are thrown each day into the torrent of population abandoned, without principles or curb, to the impulsions of their animal instincts, can we wonder at the disastrous consequences thence resulting? When the art of education shall be rightly understood and practiced, each man will bring into the sphere of daily life habits of order and forethought for himself and for those dependent on him, and of respect for what is worthy of being respected, and these habits will enable him to traverse periods of difficulty with greater ease. Disorder and improvidence are social sores that can only be cured by education rightly understood; the generalization of such education is the starting-point and essential element of social wenbeing, the only pledge of security for all.

Chapter 9 - Law of reproduction

1 - Population of the globe
686 - Is the reproduction of living beings a law of Nature?
- Evidently, it's, without reproduction the corporeal world would perish.

687 - If the population of the globe goes on increasing as it has hitherto done, will it, in course of time, become too numerous?
- No, the divine overruling always provides for and maintains equilibrium. God permits nothing useless. Man sees, but a corner of the panorama of the Universe, and is therefore unable to perceive the harmony of its various departments.

2 - Succession and improvement of races
688 - There are at this moment upon the Earth races of men who're evidently and rapidly diminishing, will they eventually disappear from it?
- Yes, but it's because others will have taken their place, as your place will someday be taken by others.

689 - Are the men now upon the Earth a new creation, or the improved descendants of the primitive human beings?
- They're the same spirits, come back to improve themselves with the aid of new bodies, but who are still very far from having reached perfection. Thus the present human race, which, by its increase, tends to invade the whole Earth and to replace the races that are dying out, will have its period of decrease and disappearance. It'll be replaced by other and more perfect races that will descend from the present race, as the civilized men of the present day are descended from the rough-hewn savages of the primitive periods.

690 - Regarded from a purely physical point of view, are the bodies of the present race of men a special creation or have they proceeded from the bodies of the primitive races by reproduction?
- The origin of races is hidden in the night of time, but as they all belong to the great human family, whatever may have been the primitive root of each, they have been able to form alliances with one another and thus to produce new types.

691 - What, from a physical point of view, is the distinctive and dominant characteristic of primitive races?
- The development of brute force at the expense of intellectual power. The contrary takes place at the present day, for man now acts rather through his intelligence than through his bodily strength, and yet he accomplishes a hundred-fold more than he formerly did, because he has learned to avail himself of the forces of Nature, which the animals can't do.

692 - Is the improvement of the vegetable and animal races, through the applications of science, contrary to the law of Nature? Would it be more conformable with that law to leave them to follow their normal course?
- It's the duty of all beings to concur, in every way, in helping forward the general progress, and man himself is employed by God as an instrument for the accomplishment of his ends. Perfection being the aim towards which everything in Nature is tending, to help forward this process of improvement is to assist in working out the divine intentions.
- But man, in his efforts to ameliorate the races of the lower reigns, is generally moved by self-interest and has no other aim than the increase of his personal enjoyments; doesn't this diminish the merit of his action?
- What matters is that his merit should be null, provided the work of progress be accomplished? It's for him to render his labor meritorious by inspiring himself with a noble motive, besides, in effecting these ameliorations, he develops his intelligence and it's in this way that he derives the greatest benefit from his labor.

3 - Obstacles to reproduction
693 - Are the human laws and customs that have been established for the purpose of placing obstacles in the way of reproduction contrary to the laws of Nature?
- Whatever hinders the operations of Nature is contrary to the general law.
- But there are many species of living beings, animal and vegetable, the unlimited reproduction of which would be hurtful to other species, and would soon be destructive of the human race, is it wrong for man to arrest their reproduction?
- God has given to man, over all the other living beings of his globe, a power which he ought to use for the general good, but not to abuse. He may regulate reproduction according to his needs, but he ought not to hinder it unnecessarily. The intelligent action of mankind is a counterpoise established by God for restoring the equilibrium of the forces of Nature and herein, again, man is distinguished from the animals, because he does this understandingly, while the animals, that also concur in maintaining this equilibrium, do so unconsciously, through the instinct of destruction which has been given to them, and which causes them, while providing for their own preservation only, to arrest the excessive development of the animal and vegetable species on which they feed and which would otherwise become a source of danger.

694 - What is to be thought of usages intended to arrest reproduction in the interest of sensuality?
- They prove the predominance of the body over the soul and show how deeply man has plunged himself in matter.

4 - Marriage and celibacy
695 - Is marriage, that is to say, the permanent union of two beings, is contrary to the law of Nature?

- It's a progress arrived at by the human race.

696 - What would be the effect, upon human society, of the abolition of marriage?
- A return to the life of the beasts.

> The free and fortuitous union of the sexes is the state of Nature. Marriage is one of the first results of progress in the constitution of human society because it establishes fraternal solidarity, being found among every people, though under different conditions. The abolition of marriage would therefore be a return to the infancy of the human race and would place man even below certain animals that give him the example of constant unions.

697 - Is the absolute indissolubility of marriage to be found in the law of Nature or is it only an ordination of human law?
- It's a human law, altogether contrary to the law of Nature, but men may change their laws, those of Nature are alone unchangeable.

698 - Is voluntary celibacy meritorious in the sight of God?
- No, those who live single from selfish motives are displeasing to God, for they fail to perform their share of social duties.

699 - Isn't celibacy, on the part of some persons, a sacrifice made by them for the sake of devoting themselves more entirely to the service of humanity?
- That's a very different thing, I said from selfish motives. Every sort of personal sacrifice is meritorious when it's made for a good end and the greater the sacrifice, the greater the merit.

> God can't contradict himself nor regard as evil what he himself has made, and therefore he can't regard the violation of his law as meritorious, but although celibacy, in itself, isn't meritorious, it may become much when the renunciation of family-joys is a sacrifice accomplished in the interests of humanity. Every sacrifice of personal interests, when made for the good of others and without any reference to self, raises him who makes it above the level of his material condition.

5 - Polygamy
700 - Is polygamy or monogamy most in conformity with the law of Nature?
- Polygamy is a human institution, the abolition of which marks an era of social progress. Marriage, according to the intention of God, should be founded on the affection of the beings that enter into it. In polygamy there's no real affection, there's only sensuality.

701 - Is the almost exact numerical equality existing between the sexes an indication of the proportions according to which they ought to be united?
- Yes, for every arrangement of Nature has a specific purpose.

> If polygamy were in accordance with the law of Nature, it ought to be possible to establish it everywhere, but it'd be physically impossible to do so, owing to the numerical equality of the sexes. Polygamy must therefore be regarded as a mere custom, adapted to the present state of certain peoples and that will gradually disappear with the progress of their social improvement.

Chapter 5 - The law of preservation

1 - The instinct of self-preservation
702 - Is the instinct of self-preservation a law of Nature?
- Undoubtedly. It's given to all living creatures, whatever their degree of intelligence, in some it's purely mechanical, in others it's allied to reason.

703 - To what end has God given the instinct of self-preservation to all living beings?
- They're all necessary to the working out of the providential plans and therefore God has given them the desire to live, and besides, life is a necessary condition of the improvement of beings, they feel this instinctively, without understanding it.

2 - Means of self-preservation
704 - Has God, while giving to man the desire to live, always furnished him with the means of doing so?
- Yes, and if man doesn't always find them, it's because he doesn't know how to avail himself of the resources around him. God could not implant in man the love of life, without giving him the means of living and he has accordingly endowed the Earth with a capacity of production sufficient to furnish all its inhabitants with the necessaries of life. It's only that which is necessary that's useful, that which is superfluous is never useful.

705 - Why doesn't the Earth always produce enough to provide mankind with the necessaries of life?
- It's because man ungratefully neglects that excellent nursing-mother, moreover, he often accuses Nature of what is the result of his own unskilled fullness or want of forethought. The Earth would always produce the necessaries of life, if men could content themselves therewith. If it doesn't suffice for all his wants, it's because men employ, in superfluities, what should be devoted to the supply of necessaries. Look at the Arab in the desert, he always finds enough to live upon, because he doesn't create for himself factitious needs, but when half the products of the Earth are wasted in satisfying fanciful desires, ought man to be astonished if he afterwards runs short and has he any reason to complain if he finds himself un-provided for when a famine occurs? I repeat it, Nature isn't improvident, but man doesn't know how to regulate his use of her gifts.

706 - By the term 'fruits of the Earth', should we understand merely the products of the soil?
- The soil is the original source of all other productions, which are, in reality, only a transformation of the products of the soil, for that reason, by fruits of the Earth are to be understood everything enjoyed by man in his corporeal life.

707 - There are always persons who lack the means of existence, even in the midst of abundance. Who's to blame for this?
- In some cases, the selfishness which too often prevents men from being just to others, in other cases, and most often, themselves. Christ has said: "Seek and ye shall find". But these words don't imply that you have only to cast your eyes on the ground in order to find all that you may desire, but rather that you must seek for what you want, and not indolently, but with ardor and perseverance and without allowing yourselves to be discouraged by obstacles that are often only a means of putting your constancy, patience, and firmness to the proof.

> If civilization multiplies our needs, it also multiplies our resources and our means of existence, but it must be admitted that, in this respect, much still remains to be done, for civilization will only have accomplished its task when it shall no longer be possible for any human being to lack the necessaries of life, unless through his own fault. Unfortunately, too, many persons choose a path for which Nature hasn't fitted them and in which they necessarily fail of success. There's room in the sunshine for everyone, but on condition that each takes his own place and not that of another. Nature can't justly be held responsible for the results of defective social organization nor for those of personal selfishness and ambition.

There would, however, be blindness in denying the progress which has already been accomplished in this direction among the nations which are most advanced. Thanks to the efforts of philanthropy and of science for the amelioration of the material condition of mankind, and notwithstanding the constant increase of the population of the globe, the effects of insufficient production are considerably attenuated, so that the most unfavorable years are far less calamitous than formerly.

Hygiene, unknown to our forefathers, yet so essential a condition of public and individual health, is the object of constant and enlightened solicitude, asylums are provided for the unfortunate and the suffering and every new discovery of science is made to contribute its quota to the general weal. Far as we still are from having attained to the perfection of social arrangements, what is already accomplished gives the measure of what may be done with the aid of perseverance, if men are reasonable enough to seek after solid and practical improvements, instead of wasting their energies on utopian projects that put them back instead of helping them forward.

708 - Are there not social positions in which the will is powerless to obtain the means of existence and in which the privation of the barest necessaries of life is a consequence of the force of circumstances?
- Yes, but such a position is a trial which, however severe, the party who's subjected to it knew, in the spirit-state, that he would have to undergo. His merit will result from his submission to the will of God, if his intelligence doesn't furnish him with the means of freeing himself from his troubles. If death supervenes, he should meet it without a murmur, remembering that the hour of his deliverance is approaching, and that any yielding to despair at the last moment may cause him to lose the fruit of his previous resignation.

709 - In critical situations men have been reduced to devour their fellow men as the only means of saving themselves from starvation. Have they, in so doing, committed a crime and if so, is their crime lessened by the fact that it has been committed under the excitement of the instinct of self-preservation?
- I have already answered this question in saying that all the trials of life should be submitted to with courage and abnegation. In the cases you refer to there's both homicide and crime against Nature, a double culpability that will receive double punishment.

710 - In worlds in which the corporeal organization of living beings is of a purer nature than in the Earth, do these need food?
- Yes, but their food is in keeping with their nature. Their aliments wouldn't be substantial enough for your gross stomachs and, on the other hand, those beings could not digest your heavier food.

3 - Enjoyments of the fruits of the Earth
711 - Have all men a right to the usufruct of the products of the Earth?
- That right is a consequence of the necessity of living. God can't have imposed a duty without having given the means of discharging it.

712 - Why has God attached an attraction to the enjoyment of material things?
- In order, first, to excite man to the accomplishment of his mission, and next, to try him by temptation.
- What is the aim of temptation?
- To develop his reason, that it may preserve him from excesses.

> If man had only been urged to the using of the things of the earthly life by a conviction of their utility, his indifference to them might have compromised the harmony of the Universe. God has therefore given him the pleasurable attractions that solicit him to the accomplishing of the views of Providence, but God has also willed, through this attraction to try man by temptations that incite him to abuses against which his reason should protect him.

713 - Has nature marked out the proper limits of corporeal satisfactions?
- Yes, limits that coincide with your needs and your well-being. When you overstep them, you bring on satiety and thus punish yourselves.

714 - What's to be thought of the man who seeks to enhance corporeal enjoyments by inventing artificial excesses?
- Think of him as a poor wretch who's to be pitied rather than envied, for he is very near death.
- Do you mean to physical death, or to moral death?
- To both.

> The man who, in pursuit of corporeal satisfactions, seeks an enhancement of those satisfactions in any kind of excess, places himself below the level of the brute, for the brute goes no farther than the satisfaction of a need. He abdicates the reason given to him by God for his guidance, and the greater his excesses, the more dominion does he give to his animal nature over his spiritual nature. The maladies and infirmities, often occasioning death, that are the consequences of excess in the satisfaction of any corporeal attraction, are also punishments for thus transgressing the law of God.

4 - Necessaries and superfluities
715 - How can men know the limit of what is necessary?
- Wise men know it by intuition; others learn it through experience and to their cost.

716 - Hasn't Nature traced out the limit of our needs in the requirements of our organization?
- Yes, but man is insatiable. Nature has indicated the limits of his needs by his organization, but his vices have deteriorated his constitution and created for him wants that are not real needs.

717 - What's to be thought of those who monopolize the productions of the Earth, in order to procure for themselves superfluities, at the expense of others who lack the necessaries of life?
- They forget the law of God and will have to answer for the privations they have caused others to endure.

> There's no absolute boundary-line between the necessary and the superfluous. Civilization has created necessities that don't exist for the savage and the spirits who have dictated the foregoing precepts don't mean to assert that civilized men should live like the savage. All things are relative and the function of reason is to determine the part to be allotted to each. Civilization develops the moral sense, and, at the same time, the sentiment of charity, which leads men to give to each other mutual support. Those who live at the expense of other men's privations, monopolize the benefits of civilization for their own profit they have only the varnish of civilization as others have only the mask of religion.

5 - Voluntary privations
718 - Does the law of self-preservation make it our duty to provide for our bodily wants?
- Yes, without physical health and strength, labor is impossible.

719 - Is it blame able in a man to seek after the comforts and enjoyments of corporeal life?

- The desire of corporeal well-being is natural to man. God only prohibits excess because excess is inimical to preservation; he hasn't made it a crime to seek after enjoyment, if that enjoyment be not acquired at another's expense, and if it be riot of a Nature to weaken either your moral or your physical strength.

720 - Are voluntary privations, in view of a voluntary expiation, meritorious in the sight of God?
- Do well to others and you'll thereby acquire more merit than is to be acquired by any self-imposed privations.
- Is any voluntary privation meritorious?
- Yes, the self-privation of useless indulgences, because it loosens man's hold on matter, and elevates his soul. What's meritorious is resistance to the temptation that solicits to excess or to indulge in what is useless; it's the cutting down even of your necessaries; that you may have more to give to those who are in want. If your privations are only a vain pretence, they're a mere mockery.

721 - At every period in the past, and among all peoples, there have been men who have lived a life of ascetic mortification, is such a life meritorious from any point of view?
- Ask yourselves to whom such a life is useful and you'll have the reply to your question. If such a life is only for him who leads it and if it prevents him from doing well to others, it's only a form of selfishness, whatever the pretext with which it's colored. True mortification, according to the dictates of Christian charity, is to impose privation and labor upon yourselves for the good of others.

722 - Is there any foundation in reason for the abstinence from certain aliments practiced among various peoples?
- Whatever man can eat, without injury to his health is permitted to him. Legislators may have prohibited certain aliments for some useful end, and, in order to give greater weight to their prohibitions, have represented them as emanating from God.

723 - Is the use of animal food by man contrary to the law of Nature?
- With your physical constitution, flesh is useful for nourishing flesh, without this kind of sustenance man's strength declines. The law of preservation makes it a duty for man to keep up his health and strength that he may fulfill the law of labor. He should therefore feed himself according to the requirements of his organization.

724 - Is there any merit in abstinence from any particular kind of food, animal or other, when undergone as an expiation?
- Yes, if undergone for the sake of others, but God can't regard as meritorious any abstinence that doesn't impose a real privation and that hasn't a serious and useful aim. This is why we say that those whose fasting is only apparent are hypocrites.

725 - What's to be thought of the mutilation of the bodies of men or of animals?
- What's the use of asking such a question? Ask yourselves, once for all, whether a thing is or isn't useful. What's useless can't be pleasing to God and what is hurtful is always displeasing to him. Be very sure that God is only pleased with the sentiments that raise the soul towards him. It's by practicing his law and not by violating it, that you can shake off your terrestrial matter.

726 - If the sufferings of this world elevate us through the manner in which we beat them, are we elevated by those which we voluntarily create for ourselves?
- The only sufferings that can elevate you are those which come upon you naturally, because they're inflicted by God. Voluntary sufferings count for nothing when they're not useful to others. Do you suppose that those who shorten their lives by superhuman hardships, like the bonzes, fakirs, and fanatics of various sects, advance their progress thereby? Why do they not rather labor for the good of their fellow-creatures? Let them clothe the naked, let them comfort those who mourn, let them work for the infirm, let them impose privations upon themselves for the sake of the unfortunate and the needy and their life will be useful, and pleasing to God. When your voluntary sufferings are undergone only for yourselves, they're mere selfishness, when you suffer for others; you obey the law of charity. Such are the precepts of Christ.

727 - If we ought not to create for ourselves voluntary sufferings that are of no use to others, ought we to endeavor to ward off from ourselves those which we foresee or wit h which we are threatened?
- The instinct of self-preservation has been given to all beings to guard them against dangers and sufferings. Flagellate your spirit and not your body, mortify your pride, stifle the selfishness that eats into the heart like a devouring worm and you'll do more for your advancement than could do by any amount of macerations out of keeping with the age in which you're living.

Chapter 6 - The law of destruction

1 - Necessary destruction and unjustifiable destruction

728 - Is destruction a law of Nature?
- It's necessary that all things should be destroyed that they may be re-born and regenerated, for what you call destruction is only a transformation, the aim of which is the renewing and amelioration of living beings.
- The instinct of destruction would seem, then, to have been given to living beings for providential purposes?
- God's creatures are the instruments which he uses for working out his ends. Living beings destroy each other for food, thus maintaining equilibrium in reproduction, which might otherwise become excessive, and also utilizing the materials of their external envelopes, but it's only this envelope that's ever destroyed and this envelope is only the accessory and not the essential part of a thinking being, the essential part is the intelligent principle which is indestructible and which is elaborated in the course of the various metamorphoses that it undergoes.

729 - If destruction be necessary for the regeneration of beings, why does Nature surround them with the means of self-preservation?
- In order that their destruction may not take place before the proper time. Destruction that occurs too soon retards the development of the intelligent principle, it's for this reason that God has given to each being the desire to live and to reproduce itself.

730 - Since death is to lead us to a better life, and since it delivers us from the ills of our present existence, and is therefore to be rather desired than dreaded, why has man the instinctive horror of death which causes him to shrink from it?
- We have said that man should seek to prolong his life in order to accomplish his task. To this end God has given him the instinct of self-preservation and this instinct sustains him under all his trials, but for it, he'd too often abandon himself to discouragement. The inner voice, which tells him to repel death, tells him also that he may yet do something more for his advancement. Every danger that threatens him is a warning that bids him make a profitable use of the respite granted to him by God, but he, ungrateful, gives thanks more often to his 'star' than to his Creator.

731 - Why has Nature placed agents of destruction side by side with the means of preservation?
- We have already told you that it's in order to maintain equilibrium and to serve as a counterpoise. The malady and the remedy are placed side by side.

732 - Is the need of destruction the same in all worlds?
- It's proportioned to the more or less material state of each world, it ceases altogether in worlds of higher physical and moral purity. In worlds more advanced than yours, the conditions of existence are altogether different.

733 - Will the necessity of destruction always exist for the human race of this Earth?
- The need of destruction diminishes in man in proportion as his spirit obtains ascendancy over matter. Consequently, you see that intellectual and moral development is always accompanied by a horror of destruction.

734 - Has man, in his present state, an unlimited right of destruction in regard to animals?
- That right is limited to providing for his food and his safety, no abuse can be a matter of right.

735 - What is to be thought of destruction that goes beyond the limits of needs and of safety, of hunting, for instance, when it has no useful aim and is resorted to from no other motive than the pleasure of killing?
- It's a predominance of bestiality over the spiritual nature. All destruction that goes beyond the limits of your needs is a violation of the law of God. The animals only destroy according to the measure of their necessities, but man, who has free-will, destroys unnecessarily, he'll be called to account for thus abusing the freedom accorded to him, for, in so doing, he yields to evil, instincts from which he ought to free himself.

736 - Are those peoples especially meritorious who, in regard to the taking of animal life, carry their scrupulousness to excess?
- Their sentiment in regard to this matter, though laudable in itself, being carried to excess, becomes an abuse in its turn, and its merit, moreover, is neutralized by abuses of many other sorts. That sentiment, on their part, is the result of superstitious fear, rather than of true gentleness.

2 - Destructive calamities

737 - What is the aim of God in visiting mankind with destructive calamities?
- To make men advance more quickly. Have we not told you that destruction is necessary to the moral regeneration of spirits, who accomplish a new step of their purification in each new existence? In order to appreciate any process correctly, you must see its results. You judge merely from your personal point of view, and you therefore regard those inflictions as calamities, because of the temporary injury they cause you, but such upsetting are often needed in order to make you reach more quickly a better order of things, and to effect, in a few years, what you'd otherwise have taken centuries to accomplish.

738 - Couldn't God employ other methods than destructive calamities for effecting the amelioration of mankind?

- Yes, and He employs them every day, for he has given to each of you the means of progressing through the knowledge of good and evil. It's because man profits so little by those other means, that it becomes necessary to chastise his pride, and to make him feel his weakness.

- But the good man succumbs under the action of these scourges, as does the wicked, is this just?

- During his earthly sojourn, man measures everything by the standard of his bodily life, but, after death, he judges differently, and feels that the life of the body, as we have often told you, is a very small matter. A century in your world is but the length of a flash in eternity, and therefore the sufferings of what you call days, months, or years, are of no importance, let this he a lesson for your future use. Spirits are the real world, pre-existent to, and surviving, everything else, they're the children of God, and the object of all his solicitude, and bodies are only the disguises tinder which they make their appearances in the corporeal world. In the great calamities that decimate the human race, the sufferers are like an army that, in the course of a campaign, sees its clothing tattered, worn out, or lost. The general is more anxious about his soldiers than about their coats.

- But the victims of those scourges are none the fewer victims?

- If you considered an earthly life as it's in itself and how small a thing it's in comparison with the life of infinity, you'd attach to it much less importance. Those victims will find, in another existence, an ample compensation for their sufferings, if they have borne them without murmuring. Whether our death is the result of a public calamity or of an ordinary cause, we're none the less compelled to go when the hour of our departure has struck; the only difference is that, in the former case, a greater number go away at the same time. If we could raise our thoughts sufficiently high to contemplate the human race, as a whole, and to take in the whole of its destiny at a glance. The scourges that now seem so terrible would appear to us only as passing storms in the destiny of the globe.

739 - Are destructive calamities useful physically notwithstanding the temporary evils occasioned by them?
- Yes, they sometimes change the state of a country, but the good that results from them is often one that will be felt by future generations.

740 - May not such calamities also constitute for man a moral trial, compelling him to struggle with the hardest necessities of his lot?
- They're always trials, and, as such, they furnish him with the opportunity of, exercising his intelligence, of proving his patience and his resignation to the will of God and of displaying his sentiments of abnegation, disinterestedness, and love for his neighbor, if he be not under the dominion of selfishness.

741 - Is it in man's power to avert the scourges that now afflict him?
- Yes, a part of them, but not as is generally supposed. Many of those scourges are the consequence of his want of foresight, and, in proportion as he acquires knowledge and experience, he becomes able to avert them, that is to say, he can prevent their occurrence when he has ascertained their cause, but among the ills that afflict humanity, there are some, of a general Nature, which are imposed by the decrees of Providence and the effect of which is felt, more or less sensibly, by each individual.
- To these, man can oppose nothing bill his resignation to the divine will, though he can, and often does, aggravate their painfulness by his negligence.

> In the class of destructive calamities resulting from natural causes and independently of the action of man are to be placed pestilence, famine, inundations, and atmospheric influences fatal to the productions of the Earth, but hasn't man already found. In the applications of science, in agricultural improvements, in the rotation of crops, in the study of hygienic conditions, the means of neutralizing or at least of attenuating many of these disasters? Aren't many countries, at the present day, preserved from terrible plagues by which they were formerly ravaged? What, then, may not man accomplish for the advancement of his material well-being, when he shall have learned to make use of all the resources of his intelligence, and when he shall have added, to the care of his personal preservation, the large charity that interests itself in the well-being of the whole human race?

3 - War

742 - What is the cause that impels man to war?
- The predominance of the animal nature over the spiritual nature, and the desire of satisfying his passions. In the barbaric state, the various peoples know no other right than that of tile, strongest and their normal condition is, therefore, that of war. As men progress, war becomes less frequent, through their avoidance of the causes which lead to it, and when it becomes inevitable, they wage it more humanely.

743 - Will wars ever cease on the Earth?
- Yes, when men comprehend justice, and practice the law of God, all men will then be brothers.

744 - What has been the aim of Providence in making war necessary?
- Freedom and progress.
- If war is destined to bring us freedom, how does it happen that its aim and upshot are so often the subjugation of the people attacked?
- Such subjugation is only momentary, and is permitted in order to weary the nations of servitude, and thus to urge them forward more rapidly.

745 - What is to be thought of him who stirs up war for his own profit?

- Such a one is deeply guilty and will have to undergo many corporal existences in order to expiate all the murders caused by murder.

4 - Murder

746 - Is murder a crime in the sight of God?
- Yes, a great crime, for he who takes the life of his fellow-man cuts short an expiation or a mission, hence the heinousness of his offence.

747 - Are all murders equally heinous?
- We have said that God is just; he judges the intention rather than the deed.

748 - Does God excuse murder in cases of self-defense?
- Only absolute necessity can excuse it, but if a man can only preserve his life by taking that of his aggressor, he ought to do.

749 - Is a man answerable for the murders he commits in war?
- Not when he's compelled to fight, but he's answerable for the cruelties he commits and he'll be rewarded for his humanity.

750 - Is parricide or infanticide the greater crime in the sight of God?
- They're equally great, for all crime is crime.

751 - How is it that the custom of infanticide prevails among peoples of considerable intellectual advancement and is even recognized as allowable by their laws?
- Intellectual development isn't always accompanied by moral rectitude. A spirit may advance in intelligence and yet remain wicked for he may have lived a long time without having improved morally, and gained knowledge, without acquiring moral purification.

5 - Cruelty

752 - Is the sentiment of cruelty connected with the instinct of destruction?
- It's the instinct of destruction in its worst form, for, though destruction is sometimes necessary, cruelty never is, it's always the result of an evil nature.

753 - How comes it that cruelty is the dominant characteristic of the primitive races?
- Among the primitive races, as you call them, matter has the ascendancy over spirit. They abandon themselves to the instincts of the brute and as they care for nothing but the life of the body, they think only of their personal preservation and this generally renders them cruel. And besides, peoples, whose development is still imperfect, are under the influence of spirits equally imperfect, with whom they're in sympathy, until the coming among them of some other people, more advanced than themselves, destroys or weakens that influence.

754 - Is cruelty a result of the absence of the moral sense?
- Say that the moral sense isn't developed, but don't say that it's absent, for its principle exists in every man and is this sense which, in course of time, renders beings kind and humane. It exists, therefore, in the savage, but in him it's latent, as the principle of the perfume is in the bud, before it opens into the flowers.

> All faculties exist in man in a rudimentary or latent state; they're developed according as circumstances are more or less favorable to them. The excessive development of some of them arrests or neutralizes that of others. The undue excitement of the material instincts stifles, so to say, the moral sense, as the development of the moral sense gradually weakens the merely animal-faculties.

755 - How is it that, in the midst of the most advanced civilization, we sometimes finds persons as cruel as the savages?
- Just as on a tree laden with healthy fruit, you may find some that are withered. They may be said to be savages who have nothing of civilization about them, but the coat, they're wolves who have strayed into the midst of the sheep. Spirits of low degree and very backward, may incarnate themselves among men of greater advancement, in the hope of advancing themselves, but if the trial be too arduous, their primitive nature gets the upper hand.

756 - Will the society of the good be one day purged of evildoers?
- The human race is progressing. Those who are under the dominion of the instinct of evil, and who are out of place among good people, will gradually disappear, as the faulty grain is separated from the good when the wheat is threshed, but they'll be born again under another corporeal envelope, and, as they acquire more experience, they'll arrive at a clearer understanding of good and evil. You have an example of this in the plants and animals which man has discovered the art of improving, and in which he develops new qualities. It's only after several generations that the improvement becomes complete. This is a picture of the different existences of each human being.

6 - Dueling

757 - Can dueling be considered as coming under the head of lawful self-defense?

— No, its murder and an absurdity worthy of barbarians. When civilization is more advanced and more moral, men will see that dueling is as ridiculous as the combats which were formerly regarded as the judgment of God.

758 - Can dueling be considered as murder on the part of him who, knowing his own weakness; is pretty sure of being killed?
— In such a case it's suicide.
— And when the chances are equal, is it murder or suicide?
— It's both.

> In all cases, even in those in which the chances are equal, the duelist is guilty, in the first place, because he makes a cool and deliberate attack on the life of his fellow-man and in the second place, because he exposes his own life uselessly and without benefit to anyone.

759 - What is the real nature of what is called the point of honor in the matter of duels?
— Pride and vanity, two sores of humanity.
— But are there not cases in which a man's honor is really at stake and in which a refusal to fight would be an act of cowardice?
— That depends on customs and usages, each country and each century has a different way of regarding such matters, but when men are better and more advanced morally, they'll comprehend that the true point of honor is above the reach of earthly passions and that it's neither by killing, nor by getting themselves killed, that they can obtain reparation for a wrong.

> There's more real greatness and honor in confessing our wrongdoing, if we're in the wrong or in forgiving, if we're in the right, and, in all cases, in despising insults which can't touch those who are superior to them.

2 - Capital punishment

760 - Will capital punishment disappear some day from human legislation?
— Capital punishment will, most assuredly, disappear in course of time and its suppression will mark a progress on the part of the human race. When men become more enlightened, the penalty of death will be completely abolished throughout the Earth, men will no longer require to be judged by men. I speak of a time which is still a long way ahead of you.

> The social progress already made leaves much still to be desired, but it'd be unjust towards modern society not to recognize a certain amount of progress in the restrictions which, among the most advanced nations, have been successively applied to capital punishment and to the crimes for which it's inflicted. If we compare the safeguards with which the law, among those nations, surrounds the accused, and the humanity with which he's treated even when found guilty, with the methods of criminal procedure that obtained at a period not very remote from the present, we can't fail to perceive that the human race is really moving forwards on a path of progress.

761 - The law of Preservation gives man the right to preserve his own life; does he not make use of that same right when he cuts off a dangerous member from the social body?
— There are other means of preserving yourselves from a dangerous individual than killing him, and, besides, you ought to open the door of repentance for the criminal, and not to close it against him.

762 - If the penalty of death may be banished from civilized society, was it not a necessity in times of less advancement?
— Necessity is not the right word. Man always thinks that a thing is necessary when he can't manage to find anything better, in proportion as he becomes enlightened, he understands more clearly what is just or unjust and repudiates the excesses committed, in times of ignorance, in the name of justice.

763 - Is the restriction of the number of the cases in which capital punishment is inflicted an indication of progress in civilization?
— Can you doubt it's being so? Doesn't your mind revolt on reading the recital of the human butcheries that were formerly perpetrated in the name of justice, and often in honor of the divinity, of the tortures inflicted on the condemned and even on the accused, in order to wring from him, through the excess of his sufferings, the confession of a crime which, very often, he hadn't committed? Well, if you had lived in those times, you'd have thought all this very natural and, had you been a judge, you'd probably have done the same yourself. It's thus that what seemed to be right at one period seems barbarous at another. The divine laws alone are eternal, human laws change as progress advances and they'll change again and again until they have been brought into harmony with the laws of God.

764 - Jesus said: "He that takes the sword shall perish by the sword". Aren't these words the consecration of the principle of retaliation? And isn't the penalty of death, inflicted on a murderer, an application of this principle?
— Take care! You have mistaken the meaning of these words as of many others. The only righteous retaliation is the justice of God, because it's applied by him. You're all, at every moment, undergoing this retaliation, for you are punished in that wherein you have sinned, in this life or in another one. He who has caused his fellow-men to suffer will be placed in a situation in which he himself will suffer what he caused them to endure. This is the true meaning of the words of Jesus, for has he not also said to you: "Forgive your enemies", and has he not taught you to pray that God may forgive you

your trespasses as you forgive those who have trespassed against you, that's to say, exactly in proportion as you have forgiven? Try to take in the full meaning of those words.

765 - What is to be thought of the infliction of the penalty of death in the name of God?
- It's a usurpation of God's place in the administration of justice. Those who act thus show how far they're from comprehending God and how much they still have to expiate. Capital punishment is a crime when applied in the name of God and those who inflict it'll have to answer for it as for so many murders.

Chapter 7 - Social law

1 - Necessity of social life

766 - Is social life founded in Nature?
- Certainly, God has made man for living in society. It's not without a purpose that God has given to man the faculty of speech and the other faculties necessary to the life of relation.

767 - Is absolute isolation contrary to the law of Nature?
- Yes, since man instinctively seeks society and since all men are intended to help forward the work of progress by aiding one another.

768 - Does man, in seeking society, only yield to a personal feeling, or is there, in this feeling, a wider providential end?
- Man must progress; he can't do so alone, because, as he doesn't possess all faculties, he needs the contact of other men. In isolation he becomes brutified and etiolated.

> No man possesses the complete range of faculties. Through social union men complete one another, and thus mutually secure their well-being and progress. They need each other's help that they have been formed for living in society and not in isolation.

2 - Life of isolation

769 - We can understand that the taste for social life, as a general principle, should be founded in Nature, as are all other tastes, but why should a taste for absolute isolation be regarded as culpable if a man finds satisfaction in it?
- Such satisfaction can only be a selfish one. There are also men who find satisfaction in getting drunk, do you approve of them? A mode of life, by the adoption of which you condemn yourselves not to be useful to any one, can't be pleasing to God.

770 - What is to be thought of those who live in absolute seclusion in order to escape the pernicious contact of the world?
- The life of such persons is doubly selfish. In avoiding one evil, they fall into another, since they forget the jaw of love and charity.
- But if such seclusion is undergone as an expiation, through the imposing on one's self of a painful privation, is it not meritorious?
- The best of all expiations is to do a greater amount of good than you have done of evil.

771 - What's to be thought of those who renounce the world in order to devote themselves to the relief of the unfortunate?
- They raise themselves by their voluntary abasement. They have the double merit of placing themselves above material enjoyments and of doing well by fulfilling the law of labor.
- And those who seek in retirement the tranquility required for certain kinds of labor?
- Those that live in retirement from such a motive aren't selfish; they don't separate themselves from society since their labors are for the general good.

772 - What is to be thought of the vow of silence prescribed by certain sects from the very earliest times?
- You should rather ask yourselves whether speech is in Nature and why God has given it. God condemns the abuse, but not the use of the faculties he has given. Silence, however, is useful, for, in silence you have fuller possession of yourself, your spirit is freer and can then enter into more intimate communication with us, but a vow of silence is an absurdity. Those who regard the undergoing of such voluntary privations as acts of virtue are prompted, undoubtedly, by a good intention in submitting to them, but they make a mistake in so doing because they don't sufficiently understand the true laws of God.

> The vow of silence, like the vow of isolation, deprives man of the social relations who alone can furnish him with the opportunities of doing good, and of fulfilling the law of progress.

3 - Family - Ties

773 - Why is it that, among the animals, parents and children forgets each other, when the latter no longer need the care of the former?
- The life of the animals is material life, but not moral life. The tenderness of the dam for her young is prompted by the instinct of preservation in regard to the beings born of her. When these beings are able to take care of themselves, her task is done, Nature asks no more of her and she therefore abandons them in order to busy herself with those that come afterwards.

774 - Some persons have inferred, from the abandonment of the young of animals by their parents; that the ties of family, among mankind, are merely a result of social customs, and not a law of Nature, what is to be thought of this inference?
- Man has another destiny than of the animals, why, then, should you always be trying going to assimilate him to them? There's, in man, something more than physical wants, there's the necessity of progressing. Social ties are necessary

to progress and social ties are drawn closer by family-ties. For this reason, family-ties are a law of Nature. God has willed that men should learn, through them, to love one another as brothers.

   775 - What would be the effect upon society of the relaxation of family-ties?
 - A relapse into selfishness.

Chapter 8 - The law of progress

1 - State of Nature

776 - Are the state of Nature and the law of nature the same thing?
- No, the state of Nature is the primitive state. Civilization is incompatible with the state of nature, while the law of nature contributes to the progress of the human race.

> The state of nature is the infancy of the human race, and the starting point of its intellectual and moral development. Man, being perfectible, and containing in himself the germ of his amelioration, is no more destined to live forever in the state of nature, than he is destined to live forever in the state of infancy, the state of nature is transitory and man outgrows it through progress and civilization. The law of Nature, on the contrary, rules the human race throughout its entire career and men improve in proportion as they comprehend this law more clearly and conform their action more closely to its requirements.

777 - Man, in the state of nature, having fewer wants, escapes many of the tribulations he creates for himself in a state of greater advancement. What is to be thought of the opinion of those who regard the former state as being that of the most perfect felicity obtainable upon the Earth?
- Such felicity is that of the brute, but there are persons who understand no other, it are being happy after the fashion of the brutes. Children, too, are happier than grown-up people.

778 - Could mankind retrograde towards the slate of nature?
- No, mankind must progress unceasingly and can't return to the state of infancy. If men have to progress, it's because God so wills it, to suppose that they could retrograde towards the primitive condition would be to deny the law of progress.

2 - March of progress

779 - Does man contain in himself the force that impels him onward in the path of progress or is his progress only the product of instruction?
- Man is developed of himself, naturally, but all men don't progress at the same rate nor in the same manner and it's thus that most advances are made to help forward the others, through social contact.

780 - Does moral progress always follow intellectual progress?
- It's a consequence of the latter, but doesn't always follow it immediately.
- How can intellectual progress lead to moral progress?
- By making man comprehend good and evil, he can then choose between them. The development of free-will follows the development of the intelligence and increases the responsibility of human action.
- How comes it, then, that the most enlightened nations are often the most perverted?
- Complete and integral progress is the aim of existence, but nations, like individuals, only leach it step by step. Until the moral sense is developed in them, they may even employ their intelligence in doing evil. Moral sense and intellect are two forces which only arrive at equilibrium in the long run.

781 - Has man the power of arresting the march of progress?
- No, but he has sometimes that of hindering it.
- What is to be thought of the men who attempt to arrest the march of progress and to make the human race go backwards?
- They're wretched weaklings whom God will chastise; they'll be overthrown by the torrent they have tried to arrest.

> Progress being a condition of human nature, it's not in the power of any one to prevent it. It's a living force that bad laws may hamper, but not stifle. When these laws become incompatible with progress, progress breaks them down with all those who attempt to hold them up and it'll continue to do so until man has brought his laws into harmony with the divine justice who wills the good of all and the abolition of all laws that are made for the strong and against the weak.

782 - Are there not men who honestly obstruct progress while believing themselves to be helping it forward, because, judging the matter from their own point of view, they often regard as progress what isn't really such?
- Yes, there are persons who push their little pebbles under the great wheel, but they'll not keep it from going on.

783 - Does the improvement of the human race always proceed by slow progression?
- There's the regular slow progress that inevitably results from the force of things, but when a people doesn't advance quickly enough, God also prepares for it, from time to time, a physical or moral shock that hastens its transformation.

> Man can't remain perpetually in ignorance, because he must reach the goal marked out for him by Providence, he's gradually enlightened by the force of things. Moral revolutions, like social revolutions, are prepared, little by little, in the ideas of a people, they go on germinating for centuries and at length suddenly burst forth, overthrowing the crumbling edifice of the past, which is no longer in harmony with the new wants and new aspirations of the day. Man often perceives, in these public commotions, only the momentary disorder and confusion that affect him in his material interests, but he who raises his thoughts above his own personality admires the providential working which brings good out of evil. Such commotions are the tempest and the storm that purify the atmosphere after having disturbed it.

784 - Man's perversity is very great; does he not seem to be going back instead of advancing, at least, as regards morality?
- You're mistaken, look at the human race as a whole and you'll see that it's advancing, for it has arrived at a clearer perception of what is evil and every day witnesses the reform of some abuse. The excess of evil is required to show you the necessity of good and of reforms.

785 - What is the greatest obstacle to progress?
- Pride and selfishness. I refer to moral progress, for intellectual progress is always going on and would even seem, at the first glance, to give redoubled activity to those vices, by developing ambition and the love of riches, which, however, in their turn, stimulate man to the researches that enlighten his mind, for its thus that all things are linked together, in the moral world as in the physical world, and that good is brought even out of evil, but this state of things will only last for a time, and will change, as men become aware of that, beyond the circle of terrestrial enjoyments, there's a happiness infinitely greater and infinitely more lasting.

> There are two kinds of progress, which both support each other, but which, however, don't go hand in hand, intellectual progress and morality. Among the civilized peoples, the first has received all the incentives in the course of this century, so it has reached a degree to which it had not yet arrived before the present time. It's a long time before the latter finds himself on the same level, however, comparing today's social mores with those of a few centuries ago, only a blind man would deny the progress made. Now, if so, why should there be this ascending march to stop, with respect, preferably, to morality, rather than to the intellectual? Why is it impossible that between the 19th and the 24th century there's so much difference in this respect between the 14th and 19th centuries? To doubt whether to claim that Humanity is at the height of perfection, which would be absurd, or that it's not morally perfectable, which experience denies.

3 - Degenerate peoples
786 - History shows us many peoples who, after having been subjected to shocks that have overthrown their nationality, have relapsed into barbarism, what progress has there been made in such cases?
- When your house threatens to fall about your ears, you pull it down, in order to build another, stronger and more commodious, but until the latter is built, there's trouble and confusion in your dwelling. Comprehend this also, you're poor and live in a hovel, you become rich and quit the hovel to live in a palace, then comes a poor devil, such as you formerly were and takes possession of the hovel you have quitted, and he's a gainer by the move, for he was previously altogether without shelter. Learn from this that the spirits now incarnated in the people that you call degenerate aren't those who composed that people in the time of its splendor, those spirits, being of advanced degree, have gone to reside in nobler habitations and have progressed, while others less advanced have taken their vacated places, which they too will vacate in their turn.

787 - Are there not races that, by their nature, are incapable of progress?
- Yes, but they're day by day becoming annihilated corporeally.
- What will be the future fate of the souls that animate those races?
- They, like all others, will arrive at perfection by passing through other existences. God deprives no one of the general heritage.
- The most civilized men may, then, have been savages and cannibals?
- You, yourself, have been such, more than once, before becoming what you now are.

788 - The various peoples are collective individualities; that pass, like individuals, through infancy, manhood, and decrepitude. Doesn't this truth, attested by history, seem to imply that the most advanced peoples of this century will have their decline and their end, like those of antiquity?
- Those peoples that only live the life of the body, those whose greatness is founded only upon physical force and territorial extension, are born, grow, and die, because the strength of a people becomes exhausted like that of a man. Those whose selfish laws are opposed to the progress of enlightenment and of charity die, because light kills darkness and charity kills selfishness, but there's for nations, as for individuals, the life of the soul, and those whose laws are in harmony with the eternal laws of the Creator will continue to live and will be the guiding-torch of the other nations.

789 - Will progress ultimately unite all the peoples of the Earth into a single nation?
- No, not into a single nation, that's impossible, because the diversities of climate give rise to diversities of habits and of needs that constitute diverse nationalities, each of which will always need laws appropriate to is special habits and needs, but charity know nothing of latitudes and makes no distinction between the various shades of human color and when the law of God shall be everywhere the basis of human law, the law of charity will be practiced between nation and nation as between man and man, and all will then live in peace and happiness, because no one will attempt to wrong his neighbor, or to live at his expense.

> The human race progresses through the progress of individuals, who gradually become enlightened and improved, and who, when they constitute a majority, obtain the upper hand, and draw the rest forward. Men of genius arise from time to time and give an impulse to the work of advancement and men having authority, instruments of God, effect in the course of a few years what the race, left to itself, would have taken several centuries to accomplish. The progress of nations renders still more evident the justice of reincarnation. Through the efforts of its best men, a nation is made to advance intellectually and morally and the nation thus, advanced, is happier both in this world and in the next, but

during its slow passage through successive centuries, thousands of its people have died every day, what will be the fate of those who have thus fallen on the way?

Does their relative inferiority deprive them of the happiness reserved for those who came later? Or will their happiness be always proportioned to that inferiority? The divine justice couldn't permit so palpable an injustice. Through the plurality of existences, the same degree of happiness is obtainable by all, for no one is excluded from the heritage of progress. Those who have lived in a period of barbarism come back in a period of civilization among the same people or among another one and all are thus enabled to profit by the ascensional movement of the various nations of the Earth, from the benefits of which movement they're excluded by the theory which assumes that there is only a single life for each individual.

Another difficulty presented by the theory referred to may be conveniently examined in this place. According to that theory, the soul is crested at the same time as the body, so that, as some men are more advanced than others, it follows that God creates for some men souls more advanced than the souls he creates for other men, but why this favoritism? How can one man, who has lived no longer than another man, often not so long, have merited to be thus endowed with a soul of a quality superior to that of the soul which has been given to that other man? But the theory of the unity of existence presents a still graver difficulty. A nation, in the course of a thousand years, passes from barbarism to civilization. If all men lived a thousand years, we could understand that, in this period, they'd have the time to progress, but many die every day, at all ages and the people of the Earth are incessantly renewed, so that every day we see them appear and disappear.

Thus, at the end of a thousand years, no trace remains in any country of those who were living in it a thousand years before. The nation, from the State of barbarism in which it was, has become civilized, but what is it that has thus progressed? Is it the people who were formerly barbarian? But they died long ago. Is it the newcomers? But if the soul is created at the same time with the body, it follows that their souls weren't in existence during the period of barbarism, and we should therefore be compelled to admit that the efforts made to civilize a people have the power, net to work out the improvement of souls that are created imperfect, but to make God create souls of a better quality than these which he created a thousand years before.

Let us compare this theory of progress with the one now given by spirits. The souls that come into a nation in its period of civilization have had their infancy, like all the others, but they have lived already and have brought with them the advancement resulting from progress previously made, they come into it, attracted by a state of things with which they're in sympathy, and which is suited to their present degree of advancement, so that the effect of the efforts to civilize a people isn't to cause the future creation of souls of a better quality, but to attract to that people souls that have already progressed, whether they have already lived among that people, or whether they have lived elsewhere.

And the progress accomplished by each people, when thus explained, furnishes also the key to the progress of the human race in its entirety, by showing that when all the peoples of the Earth shall have reached the same level of moral advancement, the Earth will be the resort of good spirits only, who'll live together in fraternal union and all the bad spirits who flow infest it, finding themselves out of place among the others, and repelled by them, will go away, and will seek in lower worlds the surroundings that suit them, until they have rendered themselves worthy of coming back into our transformed and happier world.

The theory commonly received leads also to this other consequence, that the labor of social amelioration is profitable only to present and future generations, its result is null for the generations of the past, who made the mistake of coming into the world too soon and who have to get on as they can, weighted, as they're through the faults of their barbarian epoch. According to the doctrine now set forth by spirits, the progress accomplished by later generations is equally beneficial to the generations that preceded them, and who re-living, upon the Earth under improved conditions, are thus enabled to improve themselves in the focus of civilization.

4 - Civilization

790 - Is civilization a progress, or, according to some philosophers, a decadence, of the human race?
- A progress, but incomplete. Mankind doesn't pass suddenly from infancy to the age of reason.
- Is it reasonable to condemn civilization?
- You should condemn those who misuse it, rather than condemn the work of God.

791 - Will civilization be eventually purified, so that the evils caused by it'll disappear?
- Yes, when man's moral nature shall be as fully developed as his intelligence. The fruit can't come before the flower.

792 - Why doesn't civilization produce at once all the good it's capable of producing?
- Because men aren't as yet either ready or disposed to obtain that good.
- May it not be also because in creating new wants it excites new passions?
- Yes, and because all the faculties of a spirit don't progress together, everything takes time. You can't expect perfect fruit from a civilization that is still incomplete.

793. By what signs shall we know when a civilization has reached its apogee?
- You'll know it by its moral development. You believe yourselves to be considerably advanced because you have made great discoveries and wonderful inventions, because you're better lodged and better clothed than the savages, but you'll only have the right to call yourselves civilized when you have banished from your society the vices that dishonor it and when you live among yourselves like brothers, practicing Christian charity, until then, you're merely enlightened nations, having traversed only the first phase of civilization.

> Civilization has its degrees like everything else. An incomplete civilization is a state of transition which engenders special evils unknown to the primitive state, but it none the less constitutes a natural and necessary progress, which

brings with it the remedy for the evils it occasions. In proportion as civilization becomes perfected, it puts an end to the ills it has engendered and these ills disappear altogether with the advance of moral progress.

Of two nations which have reached the summit of the social scale, that one may be called the most advanced in which is found the smallest amount of selfishness, cupidity and pride, in which the habits are more moral and intellectual than material, in which intelligence can develop Itself most freely, in which there's the greatest amount of kindness, good faith and reciprocal benevolence and generosity, in which the prejudices of caste and of birth are the least rooted, for those prejudices are incompatible with the true love of the neighbor, in which tree laws sanction no privilege and are the same for the lowest as for the highest, in which justice is administered with the least amount of partiality, in which the weak always finds support against the strong, in which human life, beliefs, and opinions are most respected, in which there's the smallest number of the poor and the unhappy, and finally, in which every man who is willing to work is always sure of the necessaries of life.

5 - Progress of human legislation

794 - Would the laws of Nature be sufficient for the regulation of human society without the help of human laws?
- If the laws of Nature were properly understood and if men were willing to practice them, they'd be sufficient, but society has its exigencies and requires the cooperation of special laws.

795 - What is the cause of the instability of human laws?
- In times of barbarism the laws were made by the strongest, who framed them to their own advantage. It has therefore become necessary to modify them, as men have acquired a clearer comprehension of justice. Human laws will become more stable in proportion as they approach the standard of true justice, that's to say, in proportion as they're made for all and become identified with natural law.

> Civilizations have created for men new wants and these wants are relative to the social state he has made for himself. He has found it necessary to regulate by human laws the rights and duties appertaining to this state but, influenced by his passions, he has often created rights and duties that are merely imaginary that are contrary to natural law and that every nation effaces from its code in proportion as it progresses. Natural law is immutable and the same for all, human law is variable and progressive, it alone could consecrate, in the infancy of human societies, the right of the strongest.

796 - Isn't tile severity of penal legislation a necessity in the present state of society?
- A depraved state of society requires severe laws, but your laws, unhappily, aim rather at punishing wrong doing when done, than at drying-up the fountain-head of wrong doing. It's only education that can reform mankind, when that is done, you'll no longer require laws of the same severity.

797 - How can the reform of human laws be brought about?
- It'll be brought about by the force of things and by the influence of the men of greater advancement who lead the world onward in the path of progress. It has already reformed many abuses and it'll reform many more. Wait!

6 - Influence of Spiritism on progress

798 - Will Spiritism become the general belief or will its acceptance remain confined to the few?
- It'll certainly become the general belief and will mark a new era in the history of the human race, because it belongs to the natural order of things and because the time has come for it to be ranked among the branches of human knowledge. It'll nevertheless have to withstand a good many violent attacks, attacks that will be prompted rather by interest than by conviction, for you must not lose sight of the fact that there are persons whose interest is to combat this belief, some from self-conceit, others from worldly considerations, but its opponents, finding themselves in a decreasing minority, will at length be obliged to rally to the general opinion, on pain of rendering themselves ridiculous.

> Ideas are only transformed in the long run, never suddenly. Erroneous ideas become weakened in the course of successive generations and finish by disappearing, little by little, with those who professed them, and who are replaced by other individuals imbued with new ideas, as is the case in regard to political principles. Look at paganism, there's certainly no one, in our day, who professes the religious ideas of pagan times, and yet, for several centuries after the advent of Christianity, they left traces that could only be effaced by the complete renovation of the races that held them. It'll be the same with Spiritism, it'll make considerable progress, but there will remain, during two or three generations, a leaven of incredulity that only time will be able to destroy. Nevertheless, its progress will be more rapid than that of Christianity, because it's Christianity itself that opens the road for it and furnishes its basis and support. Christianity had to destroy; Spiritism has only to build up.

799 - In what way can Spiritism contribute to progress?
- By destroying materialism, which is one of the sores of society and thus making men understand where their true interest lies. The future life being no longer veiled by doubt, men will understand more clearly that they can insure the happiness of their future by their action in the present life. By destroying the prejudices of sects, castes and colors, it teaches men the large solidarity that will, one day, unite them as brothers.

800 - Is it not to be feared that Spiritism may fail to triumph over the carelessness of men and their attachment to material things?
- To suppose that any cause could transform mankind as by enchantment would show a very superficial knowledge of human nature. Ideas are modified little by little, according to the differences of individual character and several

generations are needed for the complete effacing of old habits. The transformation of mankind can therefore only be effected in the course of time, gradually, and by the contagion of example. With each new generation, a part of the veil is melted away, Spiritism is come to dissipate it entirely, but, meantime, if it should do no more than cure a man of a single defect, it'd have led him to take a step forward and would thus have done him great good, for the taking of this first step will render all his subsequent steps easier.

801 - Why haven't spirits taught, from the earliest times, what they're teaching at the present day?

- You don't teach to children what you teach to adults and you don't give to a new-born babe the food which he couldn't digest, there's a time for all things. Spirits have taught many things that men have not understood or have perverted, but that they're now capable of understanding aright. Through their teaching in the past, however incomplete, they have prepared the ground to receive the seed which is now about to fructify.

802 - Since Spiritism is to mark a progress on the part of tile human race, why don't spirits hasten this progress by manifestations so general and so patent as to carry conviction to the most incredulous?

- You always want miracles, but God sows miracles by handfuls under your feet and yet you still have men who deny their existence. Did Christ himself convince his contemporaries by the prodigies he accomplished? Do you not see men, at this day, denying the most evident of facts, though occurring under their very eyes? Have you not among you some who say that they'd not believe, even though they saw? No, it's not by prodigies that God wills to bring men back to the truth, he wills, in his goodness, to leave to them the merit of convincing themselves through the exercise of their reason.

Chapter 9 - The law of equality

1 - Natural equality
803 - Are all men equal in the sight of God?
- Yes, all tend towards the same goal and God has made his laws for the equal good of all. You often say, "The sun shines for all", and, in saying this, you enunciate a truth much broader and of more general application than you think.

> All men are subjected to the action of the same natural laws. All are born in the same state of weakness and are subject to the same sufferings and the body of the rich is destroyed like that of the poor. God hasn't given to any man any natural superiority in regard either to birth or to death all are equal in his sight.

2 - Inequality of aptitudes
804 - Why has God not given the same aptitudes to all men?
- All spirits have been created equal by God, but some of them have lived more and others less, and have consequently acquired more or less development in their past existences. The difference between them lies in their various degrees of experience and in the training of their will, which constitutes their freedom, and in virtue of which some improve themselves more rapidly, hence the diversity of aptitudes that you see around you. This medley of aptitudes is necessary in order that every man may concur in working out the designs of Providence, within the limits of the development of his physical and intellectual strength. What one can't do, another does, and thus each contributes his share of usefulness to the general work, besides, all the words of the Universe being united by solidarity, it's necessary that the inhabitants of the higher worlds, most of which were created before yours, should come and dwell in it, in order to set you an example.

805 - Does a spirit, in passing from a higher world to a lower one, preserve, in their integrity, the faculties he had previously acquired?
- Yes, we have already told you that a spirit who has progressed can't again fall back. He may choose, in his spirit-state, a corporeal envelope more benumbing or a position more precarious than those he quits, but all this is so combined as to teach him some new lesson and thus to aid his future progress.

> The diversity of human aptitudes is thus seen to be the result, not of any diversity in the creation of men, but of the various degrees of advancement attained to by the spirits who are incarnated in them. God, then, hasn't created the inequality of human faculties, but he has permitted spirits of different degrees of development to be thus brought into contact with each other, in order that the more forward may aid the more backward and also in order that all men, having need of one another's help, may arrive at the practical comprehension of the law of charity that is destined to unite them.

3 - Social Inequalities
806 - Is the inequality of social conditions a law of Nature?
- No, it's the work of man, not of God.
- Will this inequality eventually disappear?
- Nothing is eternal but the laws of God. Do you not see that it's being effaced little by little every day? Your present inequalities will disappear with the disappearance of pride and selfishness, the only inequality that will remain is that of desert, when the members of the great family of God will no longer regard themselves as being of blood more or less pure, they'll know that it's only the spirit that is more or less pure and that this doesn't depend on social position.

807 - What should one think of those who abuse the superiority of their social positions for their own benefit, to oppress the weak?
- They deserve anathema! Woe to them! They'll, in turn, be oppressed; they'll be born reborn in a life in which they'll have to suffer everything that they have made to suffer to the others.

4 - Inequality of riches
808 - Isn't the inequality of riches a result of the inequality of faculties, which gives to some persons more means of acquiring than are possessed by others?
- Yes, and no, and knavery and robbery? What do you say of them?
- But hereditary riches aren't the fruit of evil passions?
- How do you know that? Go back to their source and you'll see whether it's always pure. How do you know whether they weren't, in the beginning, the fruit of a spoliation or an injustice? But without speaking of their origin, which may have been bad, do you think that the hankering after wealth, even when most honestly acquired, the secret longings to possess it more quickly, are laudable sentiments? These are what God judges and his judgment is often more severe than that of men.

809 - If a fortune has been ill-gotten in the beginning, are those who subsequently inherit it responsible for this?
- Most certainly they're not responsible for the wrong that may have been done by others and of which they may be altogether ignorant, but you must understand that a fortune is often sent to such and such an individual for the sole purpose of giving him the opportunity of repairing an injustice. Happy for him if he comprehends this. If he does it in the name of him who committed the injustice, the reparation will be counted to both of them, for it's often the latter that has endeavored to bring it about.

810 - We may, without infringing legality, dispose of property more or less equitably, are we held responsible, after death, for the disposition we have made of it?
- Every seed bears its fruit, the fruit of good deeds is sweet that of others is always bitter, always remember that.

811 - Is an absolute equality of riches possible? And has it ever existed?
- No, it's not possible. The diversity of faculties and characters is opposed to it.
- There are men, nevertheless, who believe it to be the remedy for all the ills of society. What do you think of them?
- They're framers of systems or moved by ambition and jealousy; they don't understand that the equality they dream of would be speedily broken up by the force of things. Combat selfishness, for that is your social pest and don't run after chimeras.

812 - Why equality of wealth isn't possible, will it be the same with well-being?
- No, but well-being is relative and everyone could enjoy it if they understood it properly, because true well-being consists in each employing his time as he pleases, not in the performance of works for which no taste is felt. As each has different skills, no useful work would be left to do. In everything there's balance; man is the one who disturbs you.
- Is it possible that everyone understands?
- Men will understand each other when they all practice the law of justice.

813 - There are men who fall into misery through their own fault; surely society isn't responsible in such cases?
- Yes, we have already said that society is often the primary cause of such failures, and besides, is it not the duty of society to watch over the moral education of all its members? Society often perverts their judgment through a bad education instead of correcting their evil tendencies.

5 - Trials of riches an of poverty
814 - Why has cod given wealth and power to some and poverty to others?
- In order to try them in different ways, moreover, as you know, it's the spirits themselves who have selected those trials, under which they often succumb.

815 - Which of the two kinds of trial, poverty or riches, is the most to be dreaded by man?
- They're equally dangerous. Poverty excites murmurings against Providence, riches excite to all kinds of excesses.

816 - If the rich suffer more temptations, does he also have more means to do well?
- And precisely what he doesn't always do, he becomes selfish, proud and insatiable, his needs increase with fortune and he thinks he doesn't have enough for himself.

> Worldly grandeur and authority over our fellow-creatures are trials as great and as slippery as misfortune, for the richer and more powerful we're, the more obligations we have to fulfill, and the greater are our means of doing both good and evil. God tries the poor through resignation and the rich through the use he makes of his wealth and power.

6 - Equality of rights of men and of women
817 - Are men and women equal in the sight of God and have they the same rights?
- Hasn't God given to them both the knowledge of good and evil and the faculty of progressing?

818 - Whence come the moral inferiority of women in some countries?
- From the cruel and unjust supremacy which man has usurped over her. It's a result of social institutions and of the abusive exercise of strength over weakness. Among men but little advanced morally, might is mistaken for right.

819 - For what purpose is woman physically weaker than man?
- In order that to her may be assigned certain special functions. Man is made for rough work, as being the stronger; woman, for gentler occupations and both are differenced that they may aid each other in passing through the trials of a life full of bitterness.

820 - Doesn't woman's physical weakness make her naturally dependent on man?
- God has given strength to the one sex in order that it may protect the other, but not to reduce it to servitude.

> God has fitted the organization of each being for the functions which it has to discharge. If God has given less physical strength to woman, he has, at the same time, endowed her with a greater amount of sensibility, in harmony with the delicacy of the maternal functions and the weakness of the beings confided to her care.

821 - The functions to which the woman is destined by Nature will have as great importance as the functions deferred to the man?
- Yes, and even bigger. It's she who gives you the first notions of life.

822 - All men being equals according to the law of God, ought they also to be such according to the law of men?
- Such equality is the very first principle of justice. Don't unto others what you wouldn't that others should do unto you.
- In order to be perfectly just, ought legislation to proclaim an equality of rights between men and women?

- Equality of rights, yes, but not of functions. Each should have a specified place. Let man busy himself with the outer side of life and woman with its inner side, each sex according to its special aptitude. Human law, in order to be just, should proclaim the equality of rights of men and women. Every privilege accorded to either sex is contrary to justice. The emancipation of woman follows the progress of civilization; her subjection is a condition of barbarism. The sexes, moreover, exist only through the physical organization. Since spirits can assume that of either sex, there's no difference between them in this respect and them ought consequently to enjoy the same rights.

7 - Equality before the grave

823 - Where does man's desire to perpetuate his memory through funeral monuments arise?
- Last act of pride.
- But the sumptuousness of the funeral monuments isn't due, more often than not, to the relatives of the deceased, who wish to honor the memory, than to the deceased himself? Pride of relatives, desirous of glorifying themselves. Oh! Yes, it's not always for the dead that all these demonstrations are made. They're made for self-love and for the world, as well as for ostentation of wealth. Suppose, perhaps, that the memory of a loved one lasts less in the heart of the poor, who can't put him on the grave but a simple flower? Do you suppose that marble saves from oblivion the one that on Earth was useless?

824 - Is funeral pomp blame able under all circumstances?
- No, when displayed in honor of a noble life, it's just and conveys a useful lessens.

> The grave is the place of meeting for all men, the inevitable end of all human distinctions. It's in vain that the rich man seeks to perpetuate his memory by stately monuments; time will destroy them like his body nature has so willed it. The remembrance of his deeds, whether good or bad, will be less perishable than his tomb; the pomp of his funeral will neither cleanse away his turpitudes nor raise him a single step on the ladder of the spirit-hierarchy.

Chapter 10 - The law of liberty

1 - Natural liberty

825 - Are there any positions in life in which a man may flatter himself that he enjoys absolute freedom?
- No, because all of you, of greatest as well as the least, have need of one another.

826 - In what condition of life could a man enjoy absolute freedom?
- That of a hermit in a desert. As soon as two men find themselves together, they have reciprocal rights and duties to respect, and are, therefore, no longer absolutely free.

827 - Does the duty of respecting the rights of others deprive a man of the right of belonging to himself?
- In nowise, for he holds that right from Nature.

828 - How can we reconcile the liberal opinions professed by some persons with the despotism they themselves sometimes exercise in their own houses and among their subordinates?
- Their intelligence is aware of the law of Nature, but this perception is counterbalanced by their pride and selfishness. When their profession of liberal principles is not hypocrisy, they know what ought to be done, but do it not.
- Will their profession of liberal principles, in the earthly life, be of any avail to such persons in the other life?
- The more clearly a principle is understood by the intellect, the more inexcusable is the neglect to put it into practice. He, who is sincere, though simple, is farther advanced on the divine road than he who tries to appear what he's not.

2 - Slavery

829 - Are any men intended by Nature to be the property of other men?
- The absolute subjection of any man to another man is contrary to the law of God. Slavery is an abuse of strength; it disappears with progress, gradually, as all other abuses will disappear.

> The human law which sanctions slavery is a law against Nature, because it assimilates man to the brute and degrades him physically and morally.

830 - When slavery is already established in the habits of a people, are those who profit by that institution to blame for conforming to a usage which appears to them to be natural?
- What is wrong is always wrong and no amount of sophistry can change a bad deed into a good one, but the responsibility of wrong-doing is always proportional to the means of comprehending it possessed by the wrong-doer. He, who profits by the institution of slavery, is always guilty of a violation of natural law, but in this, as in everything else, the guilt is relative. Slavery having become rooted in the habits of certain peoples, men may have taken advantage of it without seeing it to be wrong and as something which appeared to them altogether natural, but when their reason, more developed and enlightened by the teachings of Christianity has, shown them that their slave is their equal in the sight of God, they're no longer excusable.

831 - Doesn't the inequality of natural aptitudes place some of the human races under the sway of other races of greater intelligence?
- Yes, in order that the latter may raise them to a higher level, but not that they may brutify them still more by slavery. Men have too long regarded certain human races as working animals furnished with arms and hands, which they have believed themselves to have the right of using and selling like beasts of burden. They fancy themselves to be of purer blood, fools, who see only matter. It isn't the blood that is more or less pure, but only the spirit.

832 - There are men who treat their slaves humanely, who let them want for nothing, and who think that freedom would expose them to greater privations, what do you say of such persons?
- I say that they have a better understanding of their own interests than those who treat them cruelly; they take the same care of their cattle and horses, in order to get a better price for them at market. They're not so guilty as those who treat them badly, but they none the less treat them as merchandise, by depriving them of the right of belonging to themselves.

3 - Freedom of thought

833 - Is there in man something that escapes constraint and in regard to which he enjoys absolute liberty?
- Yes, in his thought man enjoys unlimited freedom, for thought knows no obstacles. The action of thought may be hindered, but not annihilated.

834 - Is man responsible for his thoughts?
- He's responsible for them to God. God alone can take cognizance of thought and condemns or absolves it according to his justice.

4 - Freedom of conscience

835 - Is freedom of conscience the natural consequence of freedom of thought?
- Conscience is an inner thought that belongs to man, like all his other thoughts.

836 - Has man tile right to set up barriers against freedom of conscience?

- No more than against freedom of thought, for God alone has the right to judge the conscience. If man, by his laws, regulates the relations between men and men, God, by the laws of Nature, regulates the relations between men and God.

837 - What is the effect of the hindrances opposed to freedom of conscience?
- To constrain men to act otherwise than as they think and thus to make hypocrites of them. Freedom of conscience is one of the characteristics of true civilization and of progress.

838 - Is every honest belief to be respected, even when completely false?
- Every belief is worthy of respect when it's sincere and when it leads to the practice of goodness. Blame able beliefs are those which lead to the practice of evil.

839 - Is it wrong to scandalize those whose belief is not the same as our own?
- To do so is to fail in charity and to infringe on freedom of thought.

840 - Is it an infringement of the freedom of conscience to place hindrances in the way of beliefs that are of a Nature cause social disturbance?
- You can only repress action, belief is inaccessible.

> The repression of the external acts of a belief, when those acts are injurious to others isn't an infringement of the freedom of conscience, for such repression leaves the belief itself entirely free.

841 - Ought we, out of respect for freedom of conscience, to allow of the propagation of pernicious doctrines, or may we, without infringing upon that freedom, endeavor to bring back into the path of truth those who are led astray by false principles?
- Most certainly you not only may, but should, do so, but only by following the example of Jesus, by employing gentleness and persuasion and not by resorting to force, which would be worse than the false belief of those whom you desire to convince. Conviction can't be imposed by violence.

842 - All doctrines claiming to be the sole expression of the truth, by what signs can we recognize the one which has the best right to call itself such?
- The truest doctrine will be the one which makes the fewest hypocrites and the greatest number of really virtuous people, that's to say, of people practicing the law of charity in its greatest purity and in its widest application. It's by this sign that you may recognize a doctrine as true, for no doctrine, of which the tendency to make divisions and demarcations among the children of God, can be anything but false and pernicious.

5 - Free-will
843 - Has man freedom of action?
- Since he has freedom of thought, he has freedom of action. Without free-will man would be a machine.

844 - Does man posses free-will from his birth?
- He possesses free-will from the moment when lie possesses the will to act. In the earliest portion of a lifetime free-will is almost null, it's developed and changes its object with the development of the faculties. The child, having thoughts in harmony with the wants of his age, applies his free-will to the things which belong to that age.

845 - Aren't the instinctive predispositions that a man brings with him at birth an obstacle to the exercise of his free-will?
- A man's instinctive predispositions are those which belonged to his spirit before his incarnation. If he's but little advanced, they may incite him to wrongdoing, in which he'll be seconded by spirits who sympathize with that wrong-doing, but no incitement is irresistible when there's a determination to resist, remember that to will is to be able.

846 - Hasn't our organism an influence on the acts of our life, and if so, doesn't this influence constitute an infringement of our free-will?
- Spirits are certainly influenced by matter, which may hamper them in their manifestations, this is why, in worlds in which the body is less gross than upon the Earth, the faculties act more freely, but the instrument doesn't give the faculty. In considering this question, you must also distinguish between moral faculties and intellectual faculties. If a man has the instinct of murder, it's assuredly his spirit that possesses this instinct and not his organs. He, who annihilates his thought, in order to occupy himself only with matter, becomes like the brute and still worse, for he no longer endeavors to preserve himself from evil and it's this which constitutes his culpability, because he does so of his own free-will.

847 - Does aberration of the mental faculties deprive man of free-will?
- He whose intelligence is deranged by any cause whatever is no longer master of his thoughts and thenceforth is no longer free. Mental aberration is often a punishment for the spirit who, in another existence, has been vain or haughty, or has made a bad use of his faculties. He may be re-born in the body of an idiot, as the despot may be re-born in the body of a slave and the hard-hearted possessor of riches, in that of a beggar, but the spirit suffers from this constraint, of which he is fully conscious and it's in this constraint that you see the action of matter.

848 - Is the aberration of the mental faculties produced by drunkenness an excuse for the crimes committed in that state?

- No, for the drunkard has voluntarily deprived himself of his reason in order to satisfy his brutish passions. He thus commits, not one crime, but two.

849 - What is the dominant faculty of man in the savage state? Is it instinct or free-will?
- Instinct, which, however, doesn't prevent his acting with entire freedom in certain things, but, like the child he uses his freedom for the satisfaction of his needs and obtains its development only through the development of his intelligence. Consequently, you, who are more enlightened than the savage, are more blame able than a savage if you do wrong.

850 - Doesn't social position sometimes place obstacles in the way of free action?
- Society has, undoubtedly, its exigencies. God is just and takes everything into account, but he'll hold you responsible for any lack of effort on your part to surmount such obstacles.

6 - Fatality
851 - Is there a fatality in the events of life, in the sense commonly attached to that word, that's to say, are the events of life ordained beforehand, and, if so, what becomes of free-will?
- There's no other fatality than that which results from the determination of each spirit, on incarnating himself, to undergo such and such trials. By choosing those trials he makes for himself a sort of destiny which is the natural consequence of the situation in which he has chosen to place himself. I speak now of physical trials only, for, as regards moral trials and temptations, a spirit always preserves his freedom of choice between good and evil and is always able to yield or to resist. A good spirit, seeing a man hesitate, may come to his aid, but can't influence him to the extent of mastering his will. On the other hand, a bad spirit that is to say, a spirit of inferior advancement may trouble or alarm him by suggesting exaggerated apprehensions, but the will of the incarnated spirit retains, nevertheless, its entire freedom of choice.

852 - There are persons who seem to be pursued by a fatality independent of their own action. Aren't their misfortunes, in such cases, the result of predestination?
- They may be trials which those persons are compelled to undergo because they have been chosen by them in the spirit-state, but you often set down to destiny what is only the consequence of your own faults. Try to keep a clear conscience and you'll be consoled for the greater part of your afflictions.

> The true or false view we take of the things about us causes us to succeed or to fail in our enterprises, but it seems to us easier and less humiliating to our self-love, to attribute our failures to fate or to destiny, than to cur mistakes. If the influence of spirits sometimes contributes to our success, it's none the less true that we can always free ourselves from their influence, by repelling the ideas they suggest when they're calculated to mislead us.

853 - They're persons who escape one danger only to fall into another, it seems as though it had been impossible for them to escape death. Is there not a fatality in such cases?
- There's nothing fatal, in the true meaning of the word, but the time of death. When that time has come, no matter under what form death presents itself, you can't escape it.
- If so, whatever danger may seem to threaten us, we shall not die if our hour hasn't come?
- No, you'll not be allowed to die-and of this you have thousands of examples, but when your hour has come, nothing can save you. God knows beforehand the manner in which each of you'll quit your present life and this is often known also to your spirit, for its revealed to you when you make choice of such and such existence.

854 - Does it follow, from the inevitability of the hour of death, that the precautions we take in view of apparent danger are useless?
- No, for those precautions are suggested to you in order that you may avoid the dangers with which you are threatened. They're one of the means employed by Providence to prevent death from taking place prematurely.

855 - What is the aim of providence in making us incur dangers that are to be without result?
- When your life is imperiled, it's a warning which you yourself have desired, in order to turn you from evil and to make you better. When you escape from such a peril and while still feeling the emotion excited by the danger you had incurred, you think, more or less seriously, according to the degree in which you are influenced by the suggestions of good spirits, of amending your ways. The bad spirit returning to his former post of temptation, you flatter yourself that you'll escape other dangers in the same way and you again give free scope to your passions. By the dangers you incur, God reminds you of your weakness and of the fragility of your existence. If you examine the cause and the Nature of the peril you have escaped, you'll see that in many cases its consequences would have been the punishment of some fault you have committed or of some duty you have neglected. God thus warns you to look into your hearts and to pursue the work of your self-amendment.

856 - Does a spirit know beforehand the kind of death to which he'll succumb in the earthly life?
- He knows that he has exposed himself by the life he has chosen to die in some particular manner rather than in another, but he also foresees the efforts he'll have to make in order to avoid the danger and he knows that, if God so permit, he'll escape it.

857 - There are men who brave the perils of the battlefield with the full persuasion that their hour is not come; is there any foundation for such confidence?

- A man often has a presentiment of his end, he may, in the same way, have a presentiment that his time for dying has not yet come. These presentiments are due to the action of his spirit-protectors, who may wish to lead him to hold himself ready to go away, or to raise his courage in moments when he has especial need of it. They may also come to him from the intuition he has of the existence he has chosen, or of the mission he has accepted, and which he knows, as a spirit, that he has to fulfill.

858 - How is it that those who have a presentiment of their death generally dread it less than others?
- It's the man and not spirit, who dreads death, he who has the presentiment of his death thinks of it rather as a spirit than as a man. He understands that it'll be a deliverance and awaits it calmly.

859 - If death is inevitable when the time appointed for it has arrived, is it the same in regard to all the accidents that may happen to us in the course of our life?
- They're often small enough to permit of our warning you against them and sometimes of enabling you to avoid them by the direction we give to your thoughts, for we don't like physical suffering, but all this is of little importance to the life you have chosen. The true and sole fatality consists in the hour at which you have to appear in, and disappear from, the sphere of corporeal life.
- Are there incidents which must necessarily occur in a life and that spirits will not avert?
- Yes, but those incidents you, in your spirit-state, foresaw when you made your choice, but, nevertheless, you must not suppose that everything which happens to you was written, as people express it. An event is often the consequence of something you have done by an act of your free-will, so that, had you not done that thing, the event would not have taken place. If you burn your finger, it's not because such an incident was preordained, for it's a trifling inconvenience resulting from your own carelessness, and a consequence of the laws of matter. It's only the great sorrows, the events of serious importance and capable of influencing your moral state, that is foreordained by God, because they'll be useful to your purification and instruction.

860 - Can a man, by his will and his efforts, prevent events that were to have occurred from taking place and vice-versa?
- He can do so if this seeming deviation is compatible with the life he has chosen, and in order to do good, which should be, and is, the sole end of life, he may prevent evil, especially that which might contribute to a still greater evil.

861 - Did the man who commits a murder know, in choosing his existence, that he'd become a murderer?
- No, he knew that, by choosing a life of struggle, he incurred the risk of killing one of his fellow-creatures, but he didn't know whether he'd or would not, do so, for there is, almost always, deliberation in the murderer's mind before committing the crime and he who deliberates is, evidently, free to do or not to do. If a spirit knew beforehand that he'd commit a murder, it'd imply that he was predestined to commit that crime. No one is ever predestined to commit a crime and every crime, like every other action, is always the result of determination and free-will.
- You're all too apt to confound two things essentially distinct the events of material life and the acts of moral life. If there's, sometimes, a sort of fatality, it's only in those events of your material life of which the cause is beyond your action and independent of your will. The acts of the moral life, they always emanate from the man himself, who, consequently, has always the freedom of choice, in those acts, therefore, there's never fatality.

862 - There are persons who never succeed in anything and who seem to be pursued by an evil genius in all their undertakings, is there not, in such cases, something that may be called a fatality?
- It's certainly a fatality, if you like to call it so, but it results from the choice of the kind of existence made by those persons in the spirit-state, because they desired to exercise their patience and resignation by a life of disappointment, but you must not suppose that this fatality is absolute, for its often the consequence of a man's having taken a wrong path, one that isn't adapted to his intelligence and aptitudes. He who tries to cross a river without knowing how to swim stands a very good chance of drowning and the same may be said in regard to the greater part of the events of your life. If a man undertook only the things that are in harmony with his faculties, he'd almost always succeed.
What causes his failure is his conceit and ambition which draws him out of his proper path and makes him mistake for a vocation what is only a desire to satisfy those passions. He fails and through his own fault, but, instead of blaming himself, he prefers to accuse his star. One who might have been a good workman and earned his bread honorably in that capacity prefers to make bad poetry and dies of starvation. There would be a place for every one if everyone put himself in his right place.

863 - Don't social habits often oblige a man to follow one road rather than another and isn't his choice of occupation often controlled by the opinion of those about him? Isn't the sentiment which leads us to attach a certain amount of importance to the judgment of others an obstacle to the exercise of our free-will?
- Social habits are made, not by God, but by men, if men submit to them, it's because it suits them to do so and their submission is therefore an act of their free-will, since, if they wished to enfranchise themselves from those habits, they could do so. Why, then, do they complain? It's not social habits that they should accuse, but their pride, which makes them prefer to starve rather than to derogate from what they consider being their dignity. Nobody thanks them for this sacrifice to opinion, though God would take note of the sacrifice of their vanity. We don't mean to say that you should brave public opinion unnecessarily, like certain persons who possess more eccentricity than true philosophy, there's as much absurdity in causing yourself to be pointed at as an oddity or stared at as a curious animal, as there's wisdom in descending, voluntarily and unmurmuring, when you are unable to maintain yourself at the top of the social ladder.

864 - If there are persons to whom fate is unpropitious, there are others who seem to be favored by fortune, for they succeed in everything they undertake. To what is this to be attributed?
- In many cases, to their skilful management of their affairs, but it may also be a species of trial. People are often intoxicated by success, they put their trust in their destiny and pay in the curl for their former successes by severe reverses, which greater prudence would have enabled them to avoid.

865 - How can we account for the run of luck that sometimes favors people under circumstances with which neither the will nor the intelligence have anything to do, in games of hazard, for instance?
- Certain spirits have chosen beforehand certain sorts of pleasure; the luck that favors them is a temptation. He, who wins as a man often loses as a spirit, such kick is a trial for his vanity and his cupidity.

866. The fatality which seems to shape our material destinies is, then, a result of our free-will?
- You, yourself, have chosen your trial, the severer it's, and the better you bear it, the higher you do raise yourself. Those who pass their lives in the selfish enjoyment of plenty and of human happiness are cowardly spirits who remain stationary. Thus the number of those who are unfortunate is much greater, in your world, than of those who are fortunate, because spirits generally make choice of the trial that will be most useful to them. They see too clearly the futility of your grandeurs and your enjoyments, besides, the most fortunate life is always more or less agitated, more or less troubled, if only by the absence of sorrow.

867 - Whence conies the expressions "born under a lucky star"?
- From an old superstition that connected the stars with the destiny of each human being a figure that some people are silly enough to take for literal truth.

7 - Foreknowledge

868 - Can the future be revealed to man?
- As a rule, the future is hidden from him; it's only in rare and exceptional cases that God permits it to be revealed.

869 - Why is the future hidden from man?
- If man knew the future, he'd neglect the present and would not act with the same freedom, because he'd be swayed by the thought that, if such and such a thing is to happen, there's no need to occupy one's self about it or else he'd seek to prevent it. God has willed that it should not be thus, in order that each may concur in the accomplishment of the designs of Providence, even of those which he'd desire to thwart and thus you, yourselves, often prepare the way, without your knowing it, for the events that will occur in the course of your life.

870 - Since it's useful that the future should be hidden, why does God sometimes permit it to be revealed?
- Because in such cases this foreknowledge, instead of hindering the accomplishment of the thing that's to be, will facilitate it, by inducing the person to whom it's revealed to act in a different way from that in which he'd otherwise have acted, and, besides, it's often a trial. The prospect of an event may awaken thoughts more or less virtuous. If a man becomes aware, for instance, that he'll succeed to an inheritance which he hadn't expected, he may be tempted by a feeling of cupidity, by elation at the prospect of adding to his earthly pleasures, by a desire for the death of him to whose fortune he'll succeed, in order that he may obtain possession of it more speedily or, on the other hand, this prospect may awaken in him only good and generous thoughts. If the prediction be not fulfilled, it's another trial, that of the way in which he'll bear the disappointment, but he'll none the less have acquired the merit or the blame of the good or bad thoughts awakened in him by his expectation of the event predicted.

871 - Since God knows everything, he knows whether a nun will or will not fail in a given trial, where then is the use of this trial, since it can show God nothing that he doesn't already know in regard to that man?
- You might as well ask why God didn't create man accomplished, perfect, or why man has to pass through childhood before arriving at adult age. The aim of trial isn't to enlighten God in regard to man's deserts, for God knows exactly what they're, but to leave to man the entire responsibility of his conduct, since he's free to do or not to do. Man having fret choice between good and evil, trial serves to bring him under the action of temptation, and thus to give him the merit of resistance, for God, though knowing beforehand whether he'll triumph or succumb, can't, being just, either reward or punish him otherwise than according to the deeds he has done.

> The same principle is practically admitted among men. Whatever may be the qualifications of a candidate for any distinction, whatever may be our confidence of his success, no grade can be conferred on him without his having undergone the prescribed examination, that's to say, without his desert having been tested by trial, just as a judge only condemns the accused for the crime he has actually committed and not on the presumption that he could or would commit such crime. The more we reflect on the consequences that would result from our knowledge of the future, the more clearly do we see the wisdom of Providence in hiding it from us. The certainty of our future good fortune would render us inactive that of coming misfortune would plunge us in discouragement in both cases our activities would be paralyzed. For this reason, the future is only shown to man as end which he's to attain through his own efforts, but without knowing the sequence of events through which he'll pass in attaining it. The foreknowledge of all the incidents of his journey would deprive him of his initiative and of the use of his free-will, he'd let himself be drawn, passively, by the force of events, down the slope of circumstances, without any exercise of his faculties. When the success of a matter is certain, we no longer busy ourselves about it.

Theoretic summary of the springs of human action

872 - The question of free-will may be thus summed up, Man isn't fatally led into evil, the acts he accomplishes aren't written down beforehand, the crimes he commits aren't the result of any decree of destiny. He may have chosen, as trial and as expiation, an existence in which, through the surroundings amidst which he's placed or the circumstances that supervene, he'll be tempted to do wrong, but he always remains free to do or not to do. Thus a spirit exercises free-will, in the spirit-life, by choosing his next existence and the kind of trials to which it'll subject him, and, in the corporeal life, by using his power of yielding to, or resisting, the temptations to which he has voluntarily subjected himself. The duty of education is to combat the evil tendencies brought by the spirit into his new existence duty which it'll only be able to thoroughly fulfill when it shall be based on a deeper and truer knowledge of man's moral nature.

Through knowledge of the laws of this department of his nature education will be able to modify it, as it already modifies his intelligence by instruction and his temperament by hygiene. Each spirit, when freed from matter, and in the state of erraticity, chooses his future corporeal existences according to the degree of purification to which he has already attained and it's in the power of making this choice, as we have previously pointed out, that his free-will principally consists. This free-will isn't annulled by incarnation, for, if the incarnated spirit yields to the influence of matter, it's always to the very trials previously chosen by him that he succumbs and he's always free to invoke the assistance of God and of good spirits to help him to surmount them.

Without free-will, there would be for man neither guilt in doing wrong, nor merit in doing right, a principle so fully recognized in this life, that the world always apportions its blame or its praise of any deed to the intention, that is to say, to the will of the doer and will is but another term for freedom. Man, therefore, couldn't seek an excuse for his misdeeds in his organization without abdicating his reason and his condition as a human being and assimilating himself to the condition of the brute. If he could do so in regard to what is wrong, he'd have to do the same in regard to what is right, but whenever a man does what is right, he takes good care to claim the merit of his action and never thinks of attributing that merit to his organs, which proves that he instinctively refuses to renounce, at the bidding of certain theory-builders, the most glorious privilege of his species, freedom of thought.

Fatality, as commonly understood, supposes an anterior and irrevocable ordaining of all the events of human life, whatever their degree of importance. If such were the order of things, man would be a machine, without a will of his own. Of what use would his intelligence be to him, seeing that he'd be invariably overruled in all his acts by the power of destiny? Such pre-ordination, if it took place, would be the destruction of all moral freedom, there would be neither such thing as human responsibility and consequently neither good nor evil, neither virtues nor crimes. God, being sovereignty just, couldn't chastise his creatures for faults which they hadn't the option of not committing, nor could he reward them for virtues which would constitute for them no merit. It'd be, moreover, the negation of the law of progress, for, if man were thus dependent on fate, he'd make no attempt to ameliorate his position, since his action would be both unnecessary and unavailing.

On the other hand, fatality isn't a mere empty word, it really exists in regard to the position occupied by each man upon the Earth and the part which he plays in it, as a consequence of the kind of existence previously made choice of by his spirit, as trial, expiation, or mission, for in virtue of that choice, he's necessarily subjected to the vicissitudes of the existence he has chosen and to all the tendencies, good or bad, inherent in it, but fatality ceases at this point, for it depends on his will to yield or not to yield, to those tendencies. The details of events are subordinated to the circumstances to which man himself gives rise by his action and in regard to which he may be influenced by the good or bad thoughts suggested to him by spirits.

There's a fatality, then, in the events which occur independently of our action, because they're the consequence of the choice of our existence made by our spirit in the other life, but there can be no fatality in the results of those events, because we're often able to modify their results by our own prudence. There's no fatality in regard to the acts of our moral life. It's only in regard to his death that man is placed under the law of an absolute and inexorable fatality, for he can neither evade the decree which has fixed the term of his existence, nor avoid the kind of death which is destined to interrupt its course. According to the common belief, man derives all his instincts from himself, they proceed either from his physical organization, for which he's not responsible, or from his own nature, which would furnish him with an equally valid excuse for his imperfections, as, if such were the case, he might justly plead that it's through no option of his own that he has been made what he is.

The doctrine of Spiritism is evidently more moral. It admits the plenitude of man's free-will, and, in telling him that, when he does wrong, he yields to an evil suggestion made by another spirit, it leaves him the entire responsibility of his wrong-doing, because it recognizes his power of resisting that suggestion, which it's evidently more easy for him to do than it'd be to fight against his own nature. Thus, according to Spiritist Doctrine, no temptation is irresistible. A man can always close his mental ear against the occult voice which addresses itself to his inner consciousness, just as he can close it against a human voice. He can always withdraw himself from the suggestions that would tempt him to evil, by exerting his will against the tempter, asking of God, at the same time, to give him the necessary strength and calling on good spirits to help him in vanquishing the temptation.

This view of the exciting cause of human action is the natural consequence of the totality of the teaching now being given from the spirit-world. It's not only sublime in point of morality; it's also eminently fitted to enhance man's self-respect. For it shows him that he's as free to shake off the yoke of an oppressor, as lie is to close his house against unwelcome intrusion, that he's not a machine, set in motion by an impulsion independent of his will, that he's a reasoning being, with the power of listening to, weighing, and choosing freely between, two opposing counsels. Let us add that, while thus counseled, man isn't deprived of the initiative of his action, what he does, he does of his own motion, because he's still a spirit, though incarnated in a corporeal envelope, and still preserves, as a man, the good and bad qualities he possessed as a spirit.

The faults we commit have their original source, therefore, in the imperfection of our own spirit, which hasn't yet acquired the moral excellence it'll acquire in course of time, but which, nevertheless, is in full possession of his free-will. Corporeal life is permitted to us for the purpose of purging our spirit of its imperfections through the trials to which we are thus subjected and it's precisely those imperfections that weaken us and render us accessible to the suggestions of other imperfect spirits, who take advantage of our weakness in trying to make us fail in the fulfillment of the task we have imposed upon ourselves. If we issue victorious from the struggle, our spirit attains a higher grade, if we fail, he remains as it was, no better and no worse, but with the unsuccessful attempt to be made over again, a repetition of the same trial that may retard our advancement for a very long period, but in proportion as we effect our improvement, our weakness diminishes and we give less and less handle to those who'd tempt us to evil, and as our moral strength constantly increases, bad spirits cease at length to act upon us.

The totality of spirits, good and bad, constitute by their incarnation the human race and as our Earth is one of the most backward worlds, more bad spirits than good ones are incarnated in it, and a general perversity is visible among mankind. Let us, then, do our utmost not to have to come back to it, but to merit admission into a world of higher degree, one of those happier worlds in which goodness reigns supreme and in which we shall remember our sojourn in this lower world only as a period of exile.

Chapter 11 - The law of justice, of love and of charity

1 - Natural rights and justice

873 - Is the sentiment of justice natural or the result of acquired ideas?

- It's so natural that your feeling spontaneously revolts at the idea of an injustice. Moral progress undoubtedly develops this sentiment, but it doesn't create it. God has placed it in the heart of man and for this reason you often find, among simple and primitive people, notions of justice more exact than those of others who are possessed of a larger amount of knowledge.

874 - If justice be a law of Nature, how is it that man understands it so differently, and that the same thing appears just to one, and unjust to another?

- It's because your passions often mingle with this sentiment and debase it, as they do with the greater part of the natural sentiments, causing you to see things from a false point of view.

875 - How should justice be defined?

- Justice consists in respect for the rights of others.
- What determines those rights?
- Two things, human law and natural law. Men having made laws in harmony with their character and habits, those laws have established rights that have varied with the progress of enlightenment. Your laws, at this day, though still far from perfect, no longer consecrate what were considered as rights in the Middle Ages, those rights, which appear to you monstrous, appeared just and natural at that epoch. The rights established by men aren't, therefore, always conformable with justice, moreover, they only regulate certain social relations, while in private life there are an immense number of acts that are submitted only to the tribunal of conscience.

876 - Independently of the right established by human law, what is the basis of justice according to natural law?

- Christ has told you: "Do unto others whatsoever you'd that others should do unto you". God has placed in the heart of man, as the true rule of all justice, the desire which each of you feels to see his own rights respected. When uncertain as to what he should do in regard to his fellow-creature in any given conjuncture, let each man ask himself what he'd wish to have done to himself under the same circumstances, God couldn't give him a safer guide than his own conscience.

> The true criterion of justice is, in fact, to desire for others what one would desire for one's self, not merely to desire for one's self what one would desire for others, which isn't precisely the same thing. As it not natural to desire harm for one's self, we are sure, in taking our personal desires as the type of our conduct towards our neighbors, never to desire anything but good for them. In all ages and in all beliefs, man has always sought to enforce his personal rights; the sublime peculiarity of the Christian religion is its taking of personal right as the basis of the right of the neighbor.

877 - Does the necessity of living in society impose any special obligations on mankind?

- Yes, and the first of these is to respect the rights of others, he, who respects those rights will always be just. In your world, where so many neglect to practice the law of justice, you have recourse to reprisals and this causes trouble and confusion in human society. Social life gives rights and imposes corresponding duties.

878 - It's possible for a man to be under an illusion as to the extent of his rights, what is there that can show him their true limit?

- The limit of the right which he'd recognize on the part of his neighbor towards himself under similar circumstances, and vice-versa.
- But if each attributes to himself the rights of his fellow-creatures, what becomes of subordination to superiors? Wouldn't such a principle be anarchical and destructive of all power?
- Natural rights are the same for all men, from the smallest to the greatest, God hasn't fashioned some men from a finer clay than others and all are equals in his sight. Natural rights are eternal, the rights which man has established perish with his institutions, but each man feels distinctly his strength or his weakness, and will always be conscious of a sort of deference towards him whose wisdom or virtue entitles him to respect. It's important to mention this, in order that those who think themselves superior may know what are the duties that will give them a right to deference. There will be no insubordination when authority shall be attributed only to superior wisdom.

879 - What would be the character of the man who should practice justice in all its purity?

- He'd be truly righteous, after the example of Jesus, for he'd practice the love of the neighbor and charity, without which there can be no real justice.

2 - Right of property - Robbery

880 - Which is the first of all the natural rights of man?

- The right to live and therefore no one have the right to take the life of his fellow creature or to do anything that may compromise his personal existence.

881 - Does the right to live give to man the right to amass the means of living, in order that he may repose when no longer able to work?

- Yes but he should do this in concert with his family, like the bee, by honest labor and not by amassing in solitary selfishness. Certain animals, even, set man an example of this kind of fore-sight.

882 - Has man the right to defend what he has amassed by his labors?
- Hasn't God said: "Thou shalt not steal"? And didn't Jesus say: "Render unto Caesar the things that are Caesar's"? What a man has amassed by honest labor is a legitimate property that he has a right to defend for possession of the property which is the fruit of labor is a natural right as sacred as the right to labor or to live.

883 - Is the desire to posses natural to man?
- Yes, but when it's simply for himself and for his personal satisfaction, it's selfishness.
- But isn't the desire to possess a legitimate one, since he who has enough to live upon isn't a burden to others?
- Some men are insatiable and accumulate without benefit to any one, merely to satisfy their passions. Do you suppose that this can be pleasing to God? He, on the contrary, who amasses through his labor, in order to have the means of assisting his fellow creatures, practices the law of love and of charity, and his labor, receives the blessing of God.

884 - What is the characteristic of legitimate property?
- No property is legitimate unless acquired without injury to others.

> The law of love and of justice, forbidding us to do to others what we'd not that others should do to us, implicitly condemns every means of acquiring which would be contrary to that law.

885 - Is the right of property unlimited?
- Everything that has been legitimately acquired is undoubtedly a property, but, as we have said, human legislation, being imperfect, frequently sets up conventional rights opposed to natural justice. For this reason, men reform their laws in proportion as progress is accomplished and as they obtain a better notion of justice. What appears right in one century appears barbarous in another.

3- Charity and love of the neighbor
886 - What is the true meaning of the word charity as employed by Jesus?
- Benevolence for everyone, indulgence for the imperfections of others, forgiveness of injuries.

> Love and charity are the complement of the law of justice; for, to love our neighbor is to do him all the, good in our power, all that we should wish to have done to ourselves. Charity, according to Jesus, is not restricted to alms-giving, but embraces all our relations with our fellow-men whether our inferiors, our equals, or our superiors. It prescribes indulgence on our part because we need the same ourselves; it forbids us to humiliate the unfortunate, as is too often done. How many, who are ready to lavish respect and attentions on the rich, appear to think it not worth their while to be civil to the poor, and yet, the more pitiable the situation of the latter, the more scrupulously should we refrain from adding humiliation to misfortune. He, who is really kind, endeavors to raise his inferior in his own estimation, by diminishing the distance between them.

887 - Jesus has also said, "Love your enemies", but would it not be contrary to our natural tendencies to love our enemies and doesn't unfriendliness proceed from a want of sympathy between spirits?
- It'd certainly be impossible for a man to feel tender and ardent affection for his enemies, and Jesus didn't intend to prescribe anything of the kind. To love your enemies means to forgive them, and to return good for evil. By so doing, you become their superior, by vengeance, you place yourselves beneath them.

888 - What is to be thought of alms-giving?
- To be reduced to beg degrades a man morally as well as physically, it brutifies him. In a state of society based on the law of God and justice, provision would be made for assisting the weak without humiliating them; the means of living would be insured to all who are unable to work, so as not to leave their life at the mercy of chance and of individual good-will.
- Do you blame alms-giving?
- No, it's not the giving of alms that is reprehensible, but the way in which it's too often done. He, who comprehends charity as inculcated by Jesus, seeks out the needy, without waiting for the latter to hold out his hand.

> True charity is always gentle as well as benevolent, for it consists as much in the manner of doing a kindness as in the deed itself. A service, if delicately rendered, has a double value, but if rendered with haughtiness, though want may compel its acceptance, the recipient's heart isn't touched by it. Remember, also, that ostentation destroys, in the sight of God, the merit of beneficence. Jesus has said: "Let not your left hand knows what your right hand does", teaching you, by this injunction, not to tarnish charity by pride and vanity. You must distinguish between giving, properly so called, and beneficence. The most necessitous isn't always he who begs by the wayside. Many, who are really poor, are restrained from begging by the dread of humiliation and suffer silently and in secret, he, who's really humane, seeks out this hidden misery and relieves it without ostentation.

"Love one another", such is the divine law by which God governs all the worlds of the Universe. Love is the law of attraction for living and organized beings; attraction is the law of love for inorganic matter. Never lose sight of the fact that every spirit, whatever his degree of advancement, or his situation in reincarnation or in erraticity, is always placed between a superior who guides and improves him, and an inferior towards whom he has the same duties to fulfill. Be therefore charitable, not merely by the cold bestowal of a coin on the mendicant who ventures to beg it of you, but by seeking out the poverty that hides itself from view. Be indulgent for the defects of those about you, instead of despising the ignorant and the vicious, instruct them, and make them better, be gentle and benevolent to your inferiors, he the same for the humblest creatures of the lower reigns and you'll have obeyed the law of God. Saint Vincent of Paul

889 - Are there not men who are reduced to beggary through their own fault?

- Undoubtedly there are, but if a sound moral education had taught them to practice the law of God, they'd not have fallen into the excesses which have caused their ruin. It's mainly through the generalization of such education that the improvement of your globe will be ultimately accomplished.

4 - Maternal and filial affection

890 - Is maternal affection a virtue or is it an instinctive feeling common to men and to animals?

- It's both. Nature has endowed the mother with the love of her offspring in order to ensure their preservation. Among the animals, maternal affection is limited to the supply of their material needs, it ceases when this care is no longer needed. In the human race, it lasts throughout life and assumes a character of unselfish devotion that raises it to the rank of a virtue; it even survives death and follows the career of the child from beyond the grave. You see, therefore, that there's in this affection, as it exists in man, something more than as it exists among the animals.

891 - Since maternal affection is a natural sentiment, why is it that mothers often hate their children, and even, in some cases, before their birth?

- The absence of maternal affection is sometimes a trial chosen by the spirit of the child or an expiation for him if he have been a bad father, a bad mother or a bad son, in some previous existence. In all cases, a bad mother can only be the incarnation of a bad spirit, who seeks to throw obstacles in the path of the child, in order to make him succumb in the trial he has chosen, but such a violation of the laws of Nature will not remain unpunished and the spirit of the child will be rewarded for surmounting the obstacles thus thrown in his way.

892 - When parents have children who cause them sorrow, are they not excusable for not feeling for them the same tenderness they'd have felt had their conduct been different?

- No, for the training of their children is a task that has been confided to them, and their mission is to make every possible effort to bring them back into the right road. Besides, the sorrows of parents are often the consequence of the bad habits they have allowed their children to contract from the cradle, a reaping of the evil harvest of which they themselves have sown the seeds.

Chapter 12 - Moral perfection

1 - Virtues and vices

893 - Which is the most meritorious of all the virtues?

- All virtues are meritorious, for all of them are signs of progress on the upward road. There's virtue in every act of voluntary resistance to the seductive influence of evil tendencies, but the sublimity of virtue consists in the sacrifice of self-interest to the good of others. The highest of all virtues is that which takes the form of the widest and most disinterested kindness.

894 - There are persons who do good from a spontaneous impulse, without having to overcome any opposite feeling, is there as much merit in their action as in that of others who, in doing good, have to struggle with their own nature, and to surmount an opposing impulse?

- Those that have no longer to struggle against selfishness are those who have already accomplished a certain amount of progress. They have struggled and triumphed in the past and their generosity, therefore, no longer costs them any effort. To do well seems to them to be perfectly natural because they have acquired the habit of kindness. They should be honored as veterans, who have won their grades on the field of battle.

> As you're still far from perfection, such persons strike you with astonishment, because their action contrasts so strongly with that of the rest of mankind, and you admire it in proportion to its rarity, but you must know that what is the exception in your world is the rule in worlds of more advanced degree. In those worlds goodness is everywhere spontaneous, because they're inhabited only by good spirits, among who even an evil intention would be considered as an exceptional monstrosity. It's this general prevalence of goodness that constitutes the happiness of those worlds, it'll be the same in your Earth when the human race shall have been transformed and shall rightly comprehend and practice the law of charity.

895 - Besides the defects and vices in regard to which no one can be mistaken, what is the most characteristic sign of imperfection?

- Selfishness. Virtuous appearances are too often like gilding upon copper, that can't stand the application of the touchstone. A man may possess good qualities which make him pass in the eyes of the world for virtuous, but those qualities, though proving him to have made a certain amount of progress, may not be capable of standing trial and the slightest disturbance of his self-love may suffice to show his real character. Absolute disinterestedness is indeed so rare a thing in your Earth, that you may well regard it with wonder, as something phenomenal.

896 - There are persons who are generous, but without discernment and who lavish their money without doing any real good, from the want of a reasonable plan for its employment, is there any merit in their action?

- Such persons have the merit of disinterestedness, but they haven't that of the good they might do. If disinterestedness be a virtue, thoughtless prodigality is always, to say the least of it, a want of judgment. Fortune is, no more given to some persons to be thrown away than to others to be locked up in a safe, it's a deposit of which they'll have to render an account, for they'll have to answer for all the good they might have done, but failed to do, for all the tears they might have dried with the money they have wasted on those who had no need of it.

897 - Is he to blame who does good, not with a view to obtaining any reward upon the Earth, but in the hope that he'll be rewarded for it in the other life and that his situation there will be the better for having done it? And will such a calculation act unfavorably on his advancement?

- You should do well from charity, that is to say, disinterestedly.

- But it's very natural that we should desire to advance, in order to emerge from, so painful a state as our present life, spirits themselves tell us that we should practice rectitude in order to attain this end. Is it wrong, then, to hope that, through doing good, we way be better off than we are upon the Earth?

- Certainly, not, but he, who does good spontaneously, without even thinking of its result, for himself and simply for the sake of pleasing God and relieving his suffering neighbor, has already reached a higher degree of advancement and is nearer to the summit of happiness, than his brother who, more selfish, does good from calculation, instead of being impelled to it solely by the sentiment of charity already naturalized in his heart.

- No, no, by doing well we merely meant being charitable. He, who calculates, in every charitable deed he does, how much interest it'll pay him, in the present life or in the next one, acts selfishly, but there is no selfishness in working out one's own improvement in the hope of bringing one's self nearer to God, which should be the aim of every effort.

898 - The corporeal life being only a temporary sojourn in a bluer state of existence and our future life being therefore what we should mainly care for, is there any use in trying to acquire scientific knowledge that only bears upon the objects and wants of corporeal life?

- Undoubtedly there is, for such knowledge enables you to benefit your brethren, and beside, your spirit, if it have already progressed in intelligence, will ascend more rapidly in the other life and will learn in an hour what it'd take you years to learn upon the Earth. No kind of knowledge is useless; all knowledge contributes more or less to your advancement because the perfected spirit must know everything, and because progress has to be made in every direction, so that all acquired ideas help forward his development.

899 - Of two men, equally rich, and both of whom employ their wealth solely for their personal satisfaction, but one of whom was born in opulence and has never known want, while the other owes his fortune to his labor, which is the more culpable?

- He who has known what it's to want, for he has felt the suffering which he doesn't relieve.

900 - Can he who constantly accumulates, without doing well to any one, find an excuse in the fact that he'll thus leave t larger fortune to his heirs?

- Such an excuse would only be a compromise with a bad conscience.

901 - Of two miserly men, one denies himself the necessaries of life and dies of want in the midst of his treasure, the other is stingy in regard to others, but is lavish in his outlay for himself, and, while he recoils from making the smallest sacrifice to render a service to his neighbor or to subserve a noble cause, is regard less of expense in the gratification of his tastes or passions. If a kindness is asked of him, he's always short of funds, but for the satisfying of any fancy of his own, he has always plenty of money. Which of them is the guiltier of the two and which of them will be the worse off in the spirit-word?

- He who spends on his own enjoyment, for he's more selfish than miserly. The other is already undergoing a part of his punishment.

902 - Is it wrong to desire riches as a means of doing well?

- Such a desire is laudable when it's pure, but is it always quite disinterested and does it, never cover any secret thought of self? Is not the first person to whom one wishes to do good too often one's self?

903 - Is it wrong to study other people's defects?

- To do so merely for the sake of criticizing or divulging them is very wrong, for it's a want of charity. To do so with a view to your own benefit, through your consequent avoidance of those defects in your own person, may sometimes be useful, but you must not forget that indulgence for the faults of others is one of the elements of charity. Before reproaching others with their imperfections, you should see whether others might not reproach you with the same defects. The only way to profit by such a critical examination of your neighbor's faults is by endeavoring to acquire the opposite virtues. Is he miserly? Be generous. Is he proud? Be humble and modest. Is he harsh? Be gentle. Is he shabby and petty? Be great in all you do. In a word, act in such a way as that it may not be said of you, in the words of Jesus, that you see the mote in your brother's eye, but don't see the beam in your own eye.

904 - Is it wrong to probe the sores of society for the purpose of rendering them evident?

- That depends on the motive from which it's done. If a writer's only object be to create a scandal, it's a procuring of a personal satisfaction for himself by the presentation of pictures that are corrupting rather than instructive. The mind necessarily perceives the evils of society, but the observer who takes pleasure in portraying evil for its own sake will be punished for doing so.

- How can we judge, in such a case, of the purity of intention and the sincerity of an author?

- It's not always necessary to do so. If he writes good things, profit by them, if bad ones, it's a question of conscience that concerns himself, but if he desires to prove his sincerity, he must do so by the excellence of his own example.

905 - There are books that are very fine, full of moral teachings front which, though they have aided the progress of the human race, their authors have not derived much moral profit. Will the good those authors have done by their writings be counted to them as spirits?

- The principles of morality, without a corresponding practice, are the seed without the sowing. Of what use is the seed, if you don't make it fructify and feed you? Such men are all the more guilty, because they possess the intelligence which enables them to comprehend. By not practicing the virtues they recommend to others, they fail to secure the harvest they might have reaped for themselves.

906 - Is it wrong for him who does good to be conscious of the goodness of his deed, and to acknowledge that goodness to himself?

- Since a man is conscious of the evil he does, he must also be conscious of the good he accomplishes, it's only by this testimony of his conscience that he can know whether he has done ill or well. It's by weighing all his actions in the scales of God's law and especially of the law of justice, love and charity; that he can decide whether they're good or bad, and can thus approve or disapprove of them. It can't, therefore, be wrong in him to recognize the fact that he has triumphed over his evil tendencies and to rejoice in having done so, provided he doesn't make this recognition a subject of vanity, for, in that case, he'd be giving way to a tendency as reprehensible as any of those over which he has triumph.

2 - The passions

907 - As our passions have their roots in Nature, are they evil in themselves?

- No, it's only their excess that is evil, for excess implies a perversion of the will, but the principle of all his passions has been given to man for his good and they may all spur him on to the accomplishment of great things. It's only their abuse that does harm.

908 - How can we define the limit at which the passions cease to be good or bad?

- The passions are like a horse that is useful when under control, but dangerous when it obtains the mastery. A passion becomes pernicious the moment when you cease to govern it and when it causes an injury to yourselves or to others.

> The passions are levers that Increase man's powers tenfold and aid him in the accomplishment of the designs of Providence, but if instead of ruling them, he allows himself to be ruled by them, he falls into every sort of excess and the same force which, held well in hand, would have been useful to him, falls upon and crushes him. All the passions have their source in a natural sentiment or a natural want. They're therefore not evil in themselves, since they constitute one of the providentially, appointed conditions of our existence, what is usually meant by "passion" is the exaggeration of a need or a sentiment. But this exaggeration is the excessive action of a motive power and not the power itself, it's this excessive action which becomes an evil and leads to evil consequences of every kind. Every passion that brings man nearer to the nature of the animals takes him further from the spiritual nature. Every sentiment that raises man above the nature of the animals is evidence of the predominance of his spiritual nature over his animal nature and brings him nearer to perfection.

909 - Would a man's own efforts always suffice to enable him to vanquish his evil tendencies?
- Yes, very slight ones are often all that is needed; it's the will that is wanting. Alas! How few of you make any serious efforts to vanquish those tendencies.

910 - Can a man obtain efficacious help from spirits in overcoming his passions?
- If he addresses a sincere prayer for such help to God and to his good Genius, good spirits will certainly come to his aid, for it's their mission to do so.

911 - Isn't the action of the passions sometimes so violent that the will is powerless to withstand them?
- There are many who say I'll, but whose willing is only on their lips and who aren't sorry that what they declare themselves to will doesn't take place. When a man is unable to vanquish his passions, it's because, through the backwardness of his spirit, he takes pleasure in yielding to them. He, who controls his passions comprehends his spiritual nature, he knows that every victory over then is a triumph of his spirit over matter.

912 - What is the most efficacious means of combating the predominance of the corporeal nature?
- The practice of abnegation.

3 - Selfishness

913 - Which, among the vices, may be regarded as the root of the others?
- Selfishness, as we have repeatedly told you, for it's from selfishness that everything evil proceeds. Study all the vices and you'll see that selfishness is at the bottom of them all. Combat them as you'll, you'll never succeed in extirpating them until attacking the evil in its root, you have destroyed the selfishness which is their cause. Let all your efforts tend to this end, for selfishness is the veritable social gangrene. Whoever would make, even in his earthly life, some approach towards moral excellence, must root out every selfish feeling from his heart, for selfishness is incompatible with justice, love and charity, it neutralizes every good quality.

914 - Selfishness having its root in the sentiment of personal interest, it'd seem that, to extirpate pate it entirely from the human heart, must be a very difficult matter. Is it possible to do so?
- In proportion as men become enlightened in regard to spiritual things, they attach less value to material things and as they emancipate themselves from the thralldom of matter, they reform the human institutions by which selfishment is fostered and excited. Such should be the aim of education.

915 - Selfishness being inherent in the human race, will it not always constitute an obstacle to the reign of perfect goodness upon the Earth?
- It's certain that selfishness is your greatest evil, but it belongs to the inferiority of the spirits incarnated upon the Earth and not to the human race as such, and consequently, those spirits, in purifying themselves by successive incarnations, get rid of their selfishness as they do of their other impurities. Have you, upon the Earth, none who have divested themselves of selfishness and who practice charity? There are more of such than you think, but they're little known, for virtue doesn't seek to display itself in the glare of popularity. If there's one such among you, why should there not be ten? If there are ten, why should there not be a thousand? And so on.

916 - Selfishness, so far from diminishing, increases with the civilization that seems to strengthen and intensify it, how can the effect be destroyed by the cause?
- The greater the development of an evil, the more hideous is it seen to be. It was necessary for selfishness to do a vast amount of harm in order that you might see the necessity of extirpating it. When men shall have divested themselves of selfishness, they'll live like brothers, doing each other no harm, but mutually aiding each other from a sentiment of solidarity. The strong will then be the support and not the oppressor, of the weak, and none will lack the necessaries of life, because the law of justice will be obeyed by all. It's of this reign of justice that spirits are now charged to prepare the advent.

917 - By what means can selfishness be destroyed?
- Of all human imperfections, the most difficult to root out is selfishness, because it's connected with the influence of matter, from which man, still too near his origin, hasn't yet been able to enfranchise himself and which his laws, his social organization, his education, all tend to maintain. Selfishness will be gradually weakened as your moral life obtains predominance ever your material life, through the knowledge which Spiritism gives you of the reality of your future state, stripped of allegoric fables. Spiritism, when it comes to be rightly understood and identified with the beliefs and habits of

the human race, will transform all your customs, usages and social relations. Selfishness is based on the importance you attribute to your own personality, Spiritism, on the contrary, when rightly understood, causes you to look at everything from a point of view so elevated that the sentiment of personality is lost, so to say, in the contemplation of immensity. In destroying the sentiment of self-importance, by showing its real nature, Spiritism necessarily combats selfishness.

> Man is often rendered selfish by his experience of the selfishness of others, which makes him feel the need of defending himself against them. Seeing that others think of themselves and not of him, he's led to think of himself rather than of others, but let the principle of charity and fraternity become the basis of social institutions, of the legal relations between nation and nation and between man and man and each individual will think less of his own personal interests, because he'll see that these have been thought of by others, he'll experience the moralizing influence of example and of contact. Amidst the present overflow of selfishness, much virtue is needed to enable a man to sacrifice his own interests for the sake of others, who often feel, but little gratitude for such abnegation, but it's above all to those who possess this virtue that the Kingdom of Heaven is opened and the happiness of the elect assured, while, at the day of judgment, whoever has thought only of himself will be set aside and left to suffer from his loneliness. Fénélon

4 - Characteristics of the virtuous man
918 - By what signs can we recognize a man as having accomplished the progress that will raise him in the spirit-hierarchy?
- The elevation of an incarnated spirit is proved by the conformity of all the acts of his corporeal life with the law of God, and by his comprehension of spiritual life.

> The truly virtuous man is he who practices the law of justice, love and charity, in its greatest purity. If he interrogates his conscience in regard to the acts accomplished by him, he'll ask himself whether he has done nothing wrong, whether he has done all the good in his power, whether no one has cause to complain of him and whether he has done to others all that he'd wish others to do to him. Being filled with the sentiment of charity and kindness for all, he does well for its own sake, without hope of reward and sacrifices his own interest to justice. He's kind, benevolent, humane, for all, because he sees a brother in every man, whatever his race or his belief. If God has given him power and riches, he considers them as a trust confided to him for the general good, he's not vain of them, for he knows that God. Who has given them to him can take them from him.

If the constitution of society has made other men dependent on him, he treats them with kindness and benevolence, as being his equals in the sight of God, he uses his authority to raise them morally and not to crush them by his pride. He's indulgent for the weaknesses of others, knowing that he too needs indulgence, and remembering the Words of Christ: "Let him that is without sin cast the first stone". He's not vindictive, but remembers only benefits, following the example of Jesus; he forgives all offences, for he knows that he'll only obtain forgiveness in proportion as he has forgiven. He respects the rights of others, as established by the law of Nature, as scrupulously as he desires those rights to be respected in his own case.

5 - Self-knowledge
919 - What is the most efficacious method of ensuring one's own moral improvement in the present life and resisting the attraction of evil?
- One of the sages of antiquity has told you: "Know thyself".
- We fully admit the wisdom of the maxim, but this self-knowledge is just what it's most difficult to acquire, by what means can we acquire it?
- Do what I myself used to do during my life upon the Earth. At the close of each day I examined my conscience, reviewed all that I had done and asked myself whether I hadn't failed in some duty, whether someone might not have reason to complain of me. It was in this way that I succeeded in obtaining a know-ledge of myself and in ascertaining what there was in me that needed reforming.

He, who, every evening, should thus recall all the actions of the day, asking himself whether he has done ill or well and praying God and his guardian angel to enlighten him would acquire great strength for self-improvement, for, believe me, God would assist him. Ask yourself these questions, inquire of yourself what you have done and what was your aim in such and such a manner, whether you have done anything that you'd blame in another, whether you have done anything that you'd be ashamed to avow. Ask yourself also this question, if it pleased God to call me back, at this moment, into the other life, should I, on returning into the world of spirits, in which nothing is hidden, have to dread the sight of any one?

> Examine what you may have done, first, against God, next, against your neighbor and lastly, against yourself. The answers to these questions will either give repose to your conscience or show you some moral malady of which you'll have to cure yourself. Self-knowledge is, therefore, the key to individual improvement, but you'll ask, how is one to judge one's self? Isn't each man subject to the illusions of self-love, which diminish his faults in his own eyes and find excuses for them? The miser thinks himself to be merely practicing economy and foresight; the proud man thinks his pride to be only dignity. This is true, but you have a means of ascertainment that can't deceive you. When you're in doubt as to the quality of any one of your actions, ask yourself what would be your judgment in regard to it if it were done by another?

If you'd blame it in another, it can't be less blamable when done by you, for God's justice has neither two weights nor two measures. Endeavour also to learn what is thought of it by others and don't overlook the opinion of your enemies, for they have no interest in disguising the truth and God often places them beside you as a mirror, to warn you more frankly than would be done by a friend. Let him, then, who is firmly resolved on self-improvement examine his conscience in order to root out his evil tendencies, as he roots out the weeds from his garden, let him every night, cast up his moral accounts for the day, as the tradesman counts tip his profit and loss, he may be sure that the former will be a more profitable operation than the latter.

He, who, after this footing tip of his day's doings, can say that the balance of the account, is in his favor, may sleep in peace and fearlessly wait the moment of his awaking in the other life. Let the questions you address to us be clear and precise and don't hesitate to multiply them, you may well devote a few minutes to the securing of a happiness that will last forever. Do you not labor every day with a view to insuring repose for your old age? Isn't this repose the object of your desires, the aim that prompts your endurance of the fatigues and privations of the moment? But what comparison is there between a few days of rest, impaired by the infirmities of the body and the endless rest that awaits the virtuous? And isn't this latter worth the making of a few efforts? I know that many will say, the present is certain, and the future uncertain, but this is precisely the error we are charged to remove from your minds, by showing you your future in such a way as to leave no doubt in your minds concerning it.

This is why, having begun by producing phenomena calculated to arrest your attention through their appeal to your senses, we now give you the moral teachings that each of you is charged to spread abroad in his turn. It's to this end that we have dictated *The Spirits' Book*. Saint Augustine.

4th book - Hopes and consolations
Chapter 1 - Earthly joys and sorrows

1 - Happiness and unhappiness

920 - Is it possible for man to enjoy perfect happiness upon the Earth?
- No, for corporeal life has been appointed to him either as a trial or an expiation, but it depends upon himself to lighten the evils of his lot and to render it as happy as life can be upon the Earth.

921 - We can conceive that man will be happy upon the Earth when the human race shall have been transformed, but, meanwhile, is it possible for each man to ensure for himself a moderate amount of happiness?
- Man is more often the artisan of his own unhappiness. If he obeyed the law of God, he'd not only spare himself much sorrow, but would also procure for himself all the felicity that is compatible with the grossness of earthly existence.

> He, who is perfectly sure that the future life is a reality regards his corporeal life as being merely a traveler's momentary halt in a wayside inn and easily consoles himself for the passing annoyances of a journey which is bringing him to a new and happier position, that will be all the more satisfactory in proportion to the completeness of the preparations he has made for entering upon it. We're punished, even in the present life, for our infraction of the laws of corporeal existence, by the sufferings which are the result of that infraction and of our own excesses. If we trace what we call our earthly ills back to their origin, we shall find them to be, for the most part, the result of a first deviation from the straight road. This deviation caused us to enter upon a wrong path and each subsequent step brought us more and more deeply into trouble.

922 - Earthly happiness is relative to the position of each person, what suffices for the happiness of one would be misfortune for another. Is there, nevertheless, a common standard of happiness for all men?
- As regards material existence, it's the possession of the necessaries of life, as regards moral existence; it's a good conscience and the belief in a future state.

923 - Doesn't that which is a superfluity for one become a necessary of life for another and vice versa according to differences of position?
- Yes, according to your material ideas, your prejudices, your ambition and all your absurd notions that you'll gradually get rid of as you come to understand the truth of things. Undoubtedly, he who, having possessed an income of thousands, becomes reduced to as many hundreds, looks upon himself as being very unfortunate, because he can no longer cut so great a figure in the world, maintain what he calls his rank, keep horses, carriages and lackeys, and gratify all his tastes and passions. He appears to himself to lack the very necessaries of life, but is he really so much to be pitied while, beside him, so many others are dying of cold and hunger, and haven't even where to lay their head? He, who is wise, compares himself with what is below him, never with what is above him, unless it be to raise his soul towards the Infinite.

924 - There are misfortunes which come upon men independently of their own conduct and that befall even the most upright, is there no way of preserving one's self from them?
- Such misfortunes must be borne with resignation and without murmuring, if you'd progress, but you may always derive consolation from the hope of a happier future, provided you do what is needed to obtain it.

925 - Why does God so often bestow the gifts of fortune on men who don't appear to have deserved such a favor?
- Wealth appears to be a favor to those who see only the present, but you must remember that fortune is often a more dangerous trial than poverty.

926 - Doesn't civilization, by creating new wants, become the source of new afflictions?
- The ills, of your world are proportional to the factitious wants that you create for yourselves. He, who is able to set bounds to his desires and to see without envy what, is above him, spares himself many of the disappointments of the earthly life, the richest of men is he who has the fewest needs.
- You envy the enjoyments of those who appear to you to be the favorites of fortune, but do you know what is in store for so many of them? If they use their wealth only for themselves, they're selfish, and, in that case, a terrible reverse awaits them, instead of envying, you should pity them. God sometimes permits the wicked to prosper, but his prosperity is, not to be envied, for he'll pay for it with weeping and gnashing of teeth. If a righteous man undergoes misfortune, it's a trial from which, being bravely borne, he'll reap a rich reward. Remember the words of Jesus: - Blessed are they that mourn, for they shall be comforted.

927 - Superfluities are certainly not indispensable to happiness, but it's otherwise in regard to the necessaries of life. Is it not, then, really a misfortune to be deprived of these?
- A man is really unfortunate only when deprived of what is necessary to life and to bodily health. If this privation be the result of his own misconduct, he has only himself to blame for it, if it be the fault of others, a heavy responsibility will rest with those who have caused it.

928 - By our special aptitudes, God evidently shows to each of us our special vocation, aren't many of the ills of life attributable to our not following that vocation?

— Yes. It often happens that parents, through pride or avarice, force their children from the path traced out for them by Nature, but they'll be held responsible for the results of this misdirection.

— You'd then approve of the son of some high personage making himself a cobbler, for instance, if he were endowed with a natural aptitude for cobbling?

— You must not go off into absurdities and exaggerations. Civilization has its necessities. Why should the son of a man occupying a high position make himself a cobbler, if able to do something more important? Such a one might always make himself useful, according to the measure of his faculties, without running counter to common sense. For instance, if he were not fitted to make a good lawyer, he might be a good engineer, a mechanician, etc.

> The placing of people in positions for which they're naturally unfit is assuredly one of the most frequent causes of failure and disappointment. Want of aptitude for the career on which one has entered is an inexhaustible source of reverses, and as he who has thus failed in one career in often prevented by pride front seeking a resource in some humbler avocation, he's often tempted to commit suicide in order to escape what he regards as a humiliation, whereas, if a sound moral education had raised him above the stupid prejudices of pride, he'd have been at no loss to obtain the means of subsistence.

929 - There are persons who, being utterly without resources, though surrounded by abundance, have no other prospect than starvation. What course should they take under such circumstances? Ought they to allow themselves to die of hunger?

— No one should ever admit into his mind the idea of allowing himself to die of hunger, a man could always find the means of obtaining food if pride didn't interpose itself between want and work. It has often been said that no work is dishonorable it honestly done, but this is one of the aphorisms that each man is more prompt to apply to his neighbor than to himself.

930 - It's evident that, were it not for the social prejudices by which we allow ourselves to be swayed, a man would always be able to find some sort of work that would enable him to gain a living, even though he thus took a humbler position, but among those who have no such prejudices or who put them aside, are there not some who are really unable to provide for their wants, through illness, or through other circumstances independent of their will?

— In a society organized according to the law of Christ, no one would die of hunger.

> Were society organized with wisdom and forethought, no one could lack the necessaries of life unless through his own fault, but a man's faults themselves are often the result of the circumstances in which he finds himself placed. When men shall have advanced sufficiently to practice the law of God, they'll not only be better intrinsically and as individuals, but will organize their social relations on a basis of justice and charity.

931 - Why is it that, in our world, the classes that suffer are so much more numerous than those that are prosperous?

— None of you are perfectly happy and what the world regards as prosperity often hides the most poignant sorrows. Suffering is everywhere. However, by way of replying to the thought which prompted your question, I answer, that what you call the suffering classes are the most numerous, because the Earth is a place of expiation. When mankind shall have made it the sojourn of goodness and of good spirits, there will be no more unhappiness in the Earth, which will then be a terrestrial paradise for all its inhabitants.

932 - How is it that, in this world, the wicked so often has power over the good?

— That is a consequence of the weakness of the good. The wicked are intriguing and audacious, the good are often timid, when the latter shall be determined to have the upper hand they'll have it.

933 - Men are often the artisans of their own worldly sufferings, are they also the artisans of their moral sufferings?

— Even more so, for their worldly sufferings are often independent of their action, but it's wounded pride, disappointed ambition, the anxieties of avarice, envy, jealousy, all the passions, in short, that constitute the torments of the soul. Envy and jealousy! Happy are they who know not those two gnawing worms. Where envy and jealousy exist, there can be no calm, no repose. Before him who's the slave of those passions, the objects of his longings, of his hatreds, of his anger, stand like so many phantoms, pursuing him without respite, even in his sleep. The envious and jealous are always in a fever, is such a state a desirable one? Can you not understand that, with such passions, man creates for himself the most terrible tortures and that the Earth really becomes a Hell for him?

> Many of our colloquial expressions present vivid pictures of the effects of the different passions. We say, puffed up with pride, dying with envy, bursting with spite, devoured by jealousy, etc., pictures that are only too true to their originals. In many cases, these evil passions have no determinate object. There are persons, for instance, who are naturally jealous of everyone who rises, of everything that oversteps the common line, even when their own interest is in no way concerned and simply because they're not able to command a similar success. Every manifestation of superiority on the part of others is regarded by them as an offence to themselves, for the jealousy of mediocrity would always, if it could, bring everyone down to its own level.

Much of the unhappiness of human life is a result of the undue importance attached by man to the things of this world, vanity, disappointed ambition and cupidity, make up no small part of his troubles. If he placed his aims beyond the narrow circle of his outer life, if he raised his thoughts towards the infinitate that is his destiny, the vicissitudes of human existence would seem to him as petty and puerile as the broken toy over the loss of which the child weeps so bitterly. He, who finds his happiness only in the satisfaction of pride and of gross material appetites, is unhappy when he can't satisfy them, while he who asks for no superfluities is happy under circumstances that would be deemed calamitous by others. We're now speaking of civilized people, for the savage, having fewer wants, hasn't the same incitements to envy and anxiety, his way of looking at things is altogether different.

In the civilized state, many reasons upon and analyses his unhappiness and is therefore all the more painfully affected by it, but he may also reason upon and analyze the means of consolation within his reach. This consolation is furnished him by Christianity, which gives him the hope of a better future and by Spiritism, which gives him the certainty of that future.

2 - Loss of those we love

934 - Isn't the loss of those who are dear to us a legitimate source of sorrow, seeing that this loss is both irreparable and independent of our action?

- This cause of sorrow, which acts alike upon rich and poor, is the common law of humanity, for it's either a trial or an expiation, but you have the consolation of holding communication with your friends through the means already possessed by you, while awaiting other means that will be more direct and more accessible to your senses.

935 - What is to be thought of the opinion which regards communication with those who are beyond the grave as a profanation?

- There can be no profanation where there is reverent concentration of thought and sympathy and when the evocation is made with fitting respect, and the proof of this is found in the fact the spirits who love you take pleasure in coming to you, they rejoice in being remembered by you and in being able to converse with you, but there would be profanation in this communication if carried on in a spirit of frivolity.

> The possibility of entering into communication with spirits is most consoling, since it gives us the means of holding converse with those of our relatives and friends who have quitted the earthly life before us. By our evocation, we draw them nearer to us they come to our side, hear us, and reply to us there is, so to say, no longer any separation between them and us. They aid us with their counsels and assure us of the pleasure afforded them by our remembrance It's a satisfaction for us to know that they're happy, to learn from themselves the details of their new existence and to acquire the certainty of our rejoining them in our turn.

936 - What effect has the inconsolable sorrow of survivors upon the spirits who are the object of that sorrow?

- A spirit is touched by the remembrance and regrets of those he has loved, but a persistent and unreasonable sorrow affects him painfully, because he sees, in this excessive grief, a want of faith in the future and confidence in God, and, consequently, an obstacle to the advancement of the mourner, and, perhaps, to their reunion.

> A spirit, when disincarnated, being happier than he was upon the Earth, to regret his change of life is to regret his being happy. Two friends are prisoners, shut up in the same dungeon both of them are some day to be set at liberty, but one of them obtains his deliverance before the other. Would it be kind on the part of him who remains in prison to regret that his friend has been set at liberty before him? Would there not be on his part more selfishness than affection in wishing his friend to remain in captivity and suffering as long as himself?

It's the same with two persons who love one another upon the Earth, he who quits it first is the first delivered and the other ought to rejoice in his deliverance, while awaiting with patience the moment when he shall he delivered in his turn. We may illustrate this subject by another comparison. You have a friend whose situation, while remaining near you, is a painful one, his health or his interests require that he should go to another country, where he'll be better off in every respect. He'll no longer be near you at every moment, but you'll still be in correspondence with him the separation between you'll be only in your daily life. Should you grieve for his removal, since it's for his good?

By the evident proofs which it gives us of the reality of the future life and of the presence about us and the continued affection and solicitude of those we have loved, as well as by the relations which it enables us to keep up with them, Spiritism offers us the most effectual consolation under the greatest and most painful of earthly sorrows, it does away with solitude and separation, for it shows us that the most isolated of human beings is always surrounded by a host of friends, with whom he can hold affectionate converse. We're often impatient under the tribulations of life, they seem to us so intolerable that we can't believe it to be possible for us to bear up under them, and yet, if we have borne them with courage, if we have been able to silence our murmurings, we shall rejoice to have undergone them, when we have finished our earthly career, as the patient rejoices, when convalescent, to have resigned himself to the painful course of treatment that has cured him of his malady.

3 - Disappointments, ingratitude, blighted affections

937 - Aren't the disappointments that are caused by ingratitude and by the fragility of earthly friendships, also a source of bitterness of the human heart?

- Yes, but we teach you to feel pity for the ungrateful and for faithless friends; their unkindness will do more harm to them-selves than to you. Ingratitude comes of selfishness and he who is selfish will meet, sooner or later, with hearts as hard as his own has been. Think of all those who have done more good than you have done, who are more worthful than you are and whose kindness has been repaid with ingratitude. Remember that Jesus himself, during his life, was scoffed at, despised and treated as a knave and an impostor, and don't be surprised that you should be treated in the same way. Let the consciousness of the good you have done be your recompense in your present life and don't trouble yourself about those to whom you have done it. Ingratitude serves to test your persistence in doing well, it'll be counted to you hereafter and those who have been unmindful of your kindness will be punished and all the more severely, the greater has been their ingratitude.

938 - Aren't the disappointments caused by ingratitude calculated to harden the heart and render it unfeeling?

- It'd be wrong to let them do so, for the generous man is always glad to have done well. He knows that, if those whom he has benefited don't remember his kindness in the present life, they'll remember it in a future one and will then feel shame and remorse for their ingratitude.

- But this knowledge will not prevent him from being acutely pained by ingratitude in the present life, might not this pain lead him to think that he'd be happier if he possessed less sensibility?

- Yes, if he preferred a selfish happiness, but that sort of happiness is a very pitiable one. Let such a man try to understand that the ungrateful friends who desert him are unworthy of his friendship and that he has been mistaken in his estimate of them, and he'll no longer regret their loss. Their place will by and by be filled by others who're better able to understand him. You should pity those from whom you have received ill-treatment that you have not deserved, for a heavy retribution will overtake them, but you should not allow yourselves to be painfully affected by their misconduct. Your indifference to their ill-treatment will place you above them.

> Nature has implanted in man the need of loving of being loved. One of the greatest enjoyments accorded to him upon the Earth is the meeting with hearts that sympathize with his own. This sympathy gives him a foretaste of the happiness that awaits him in the world of perfected spirits, where all is love and kindness a happiness that is refused to the selfish.

4 - Antipathetic unions

939 - Since spirits who are sympathetic to one another are spontaneously attracted to each other, how is it that, among incarnated spirits, the love is often only on one side, that the most sincere affection is met with indifference or even with repulsion, and that, moreover, the liveliest affection of two persons for one another may be changed into dislike, and even into hatred?

- Such a contrariety of feeling is a punishment, but only a passing one. Besides, how many are there who imagine themselves to be desperately in love with each other, because they judge one another from appearances only, but who, when obliged to live together, soon discover that their affection was nothing more than a passing caprice? It's not enough to be taken with someone who pleases you and whom you imagine to be gifted with all sorts of good qualities; it's only by living together that you can ascertain the worth of the appearances that have captivated you.

On the other hand, how many of those unions that seem, at first, as though they never could become sympathetic, grow, in time, into a tender and lasting affection, founded upon the esteem that has been developed between the parties by a better and more complete acquaintance with each other's good qualities? You must not forget that it's the spirit which loves and not the body, and that, when the illusion of corporeal attractions is dissipated, the spirit perceives the real quality of the union into which it has entered.

- There are two kinds of affection, that of the body and that of the soul, and these are often mistaken for one another. The affection of the soul, when pure and sympathetic, is lasting, that of the body is perishable this is why those who fancied that they loved each with an eternal affection often detest one another when their illusion has vanished.

940 - Isn't the lack of sympathy between persons destined to live together also a source of sorrow and one that is all the more bitter because it poisons an entire existence?

- Very bitter it's, undoubtedly, but it's usually a misfortune of your own causing. In the first place, your laws are in fault, for how can you suppose that those who dislike one another can be intended by God to live together? In the next place, you yourselves are to blame, for you often seek, in those unions, the satisfaction of your pride and ambition rather than the happiness of a mutual affection and, in such cases; you undergo the natural consequences of your prejudices.

- But in such cases, is there not generally an innocent victim?

- Yes, one for whom it's a heavy expiation, but the responsibility of such unhappiness will, nevertheless, be brought home to those who caused it. If the light of truth has reached the soul of the victim, faith in the future will give consolation under present suffering, but the causes of these private misfortunes will disappear in proportion as your prejudices are dissipated.

5 - Fear of death

941 - The fear of death causes perplexity to many persons, whence comes this fear in the case of those who believe in a future life?

- Such fear is altogether misplaced, but when people have been, in their youth, thoroughly indoctrinated into the belief that there is a Hell as well as a Heaven, and that they'll most likely go to the former, because whatever belongs to human life is a mortal sin for the soul, they're naturally afraid, if they have retained their religious belief, of the fire that is to burn them for ever without destroying them, but most of those who are thus indoctrinated in their childhood, if possessed of judgment, throw aside that belief when they grow up, and, being unable to assent to such a doctrine, become atheists or materialists, so that the natural effect of such teaching is to make them believe that there is nothing beyond this present life.

- Death has no terrors for the righteous man, because, with faith, he has the certainty of a future life, hope leads him to expect an existence happier than his present one and charity, which has been the law of his action, gives him the assurance that, in the world which he's about to enter, he'll meet with no one whose recognition he'll have reason to dread.

> The carnally minded man, more attracted by corporeal life than by the life of the spirit, knows only the pains and pleasures of terrestrial existence. His only happiness is in the fugitive satisfaction of his earthly desires, his mind, constantly occupied with the vicissitude, of the present life, and painfully affected by them, is tortured with perpetual anxiety. The thought of death terrifies him, because he has doubts about his future and because he has to leave all his affections and all his hopes behind him he leaves the Earth. The spiritually minded man, who has raised himself above

the factitious wants created by the passions, has, even in this lower life, enjoyments unknown to the carnally-minded. The moderation of his desires gives calmness and serenity to his spirit. Happy in the good he does, life has no disappointments for him and its vexations pass lightly over his consciousness, without leaving upon it any painful impress.

942 - Will not these counsels, as to the way to be happy in the present life be considered by many persons as somewhat commonplace, will they not be looked upon as truisms and will it not be said that, after all, the true secret of happiness is to be able to bear up under one's troubles?
- A good many people will take this view of the matter, but, of these, not a few will be like the sick man, for whom the physician prescribes dieting, but who demands to be cured without changing his habits and while continuing the indulgences of the table that keep up his dyspepsia.

6 - Weariness of life - Suicide

943 - What is the cause of the weariness of life which sometimes takes possession of people without any assignable reason?
- Idleness, lack of conviction, sometimes, satiety. For him who employs his faculties in the pursuit of some useful aim in harmony with his natural aptitudes, exertion isn't disagreeable, his time passes quickly in congenial occupation and he's able to bear the vicissitudes of life with patience and resignation, because he looks forward to a more solid and lasting happiness in the future.

944 - Has a man the right to dispose of his life?
- No, that right belongs to God alone. He, who voluntarily commits suicide, contravenes the providential ordering which sent him into the earthly life.
- Isn't suicide always voluntary?
- The madman who kills himself doesn't know what he is doing.

945 - What is to be thought of those who commit suicide because they're sick of life?
- Fools! Why did they not employ themselves in some useful work? Had they done so, life would not have been a weariness to them.

946 - What is to be thought of those who resort to suicide in order to escape from the troubles and disappointments of this world?
- They're weaklings who lack courage to bear the petty annoyances of existence. God helps those who suffer bravely, but not those who have neither strength nor courage. The tribulations of life are trials or expiations, happy are those who bear them without murmuring, for great will be their reward. Unhappy, on the contrary, are those who expect their well-being from what they impiously call chance or luck. Chance or luck, to borrow their own expressions, may favor them for a time, but only to make them feel, afterwards, and all the more bitterly, the emptiness of those words.
- Will not those who have driven an unhappy fellow-creature to this deed of despair be held responsible for the consequences of their action?
- Yes, and heavy indeed will be their punishment, for they'll have to answer for those consequences as for a murder.

947 - Can we consider as having committed suicide the man who, becoming disheartened in his struggle with adversity, allows himself to die of despair?
- Such self-abandonment is suicide, but those who had caused the crime or might have prevented it, would be more to blame for it than the one by whom it had been committed and the latter would therefore be judged leniently, but, nevertheless, you must not suppose that he'd be entirely absolved if he had been wanting in firmness and perseverance or had failed to make the best use of his intelligence to help himself out of his difficulties. And it'd go still harder with him if he had been one of those whose intelligence is paralyzed by pride, who'd blush to earn their living by manual labor and would rather die of starvation than derogate from what they call their social position. Is there not a hundred fold more nobleness and true dignity in bearing up against adversity, in braving the ill-natured remarks of the futile and selfish, whose goodwill is only for those who are in want of nothing and who turn the cold shoulder to all who are in need of help? To throw away one's life on account of such people is doubly absurd, seeing that they'll be perfectly indifferent to the sacrifice.

948 - Is suicide as blamable, when committed in order to escape the disgrace of having done wrong, as when it's prompted by despair?
- A fault isn't effaced by suicide, which, on the contrary, is a second fault added to the first. He, who has had the courage to do wrong, should have the courage to bear the consequences of his wrong doing. God is the sole judge and sometimes diminishes the penalty of wrongdoing in consideration of the circumstances which led to it.

949 - Is suicide excusable wizen committed in order to avoid bringing disgrace on one's children or family?
- He who has recourse to such an expedient does wrong, but, as he believes his action to be for the best, God takes note of his intention, for his suicide is a self-imposed expiation, his fault is extenuated by his intention, but it's none the less a fault, but when you have got rid of your social prejudices and abuses, you'll have no more suicides.

> He, who takes his own life in order to escape the disgrace of a bad action proves that he attaches more value to the estimation of men than to that of God, for the goes back into the spirit-world laden with his iniquities, of the means of atoning for which, during his earthly life, he has thus deprived himself. God is less inexorable than men often are; he

pardons those who sincerely repent and takes account of sill our efforts to repair what we have done amiss, but nothing is repaired by suicide.

950 - What is to be thought of him who makes away with himself in the hope of arriving sooner at a happier state of existence?
- Another piece of folly. Let a man do well, and he'll be much surer of reaching such a state. His suicide will delay his entrance into a better world, for be himself will ask to be allowed to come back to the Earth, in order to complete the life that he has cut short in pursuit of a mistaken idea. The sanctuary of the good is never opened by a fault, no matter what may have been its motive.

951 - Isn't the sacrifice of one's life meritorious when it's made in order to save the lives of others, or to be useful to them?
- Incurred for such an end, its sublime, but such a voluntary sacrifice of life is not suicide. It's the useless sacrifice that is displeasing to God and also that which is tarnished by pride. A sacrifice is only meritorious when disinterested, if accomplished in view of a selfish end, its value is proportionally lessened in the sight of God.

> Every sacrifice of our interest or enjoyment made for the sake of others is supremely meritorious in the sight of God for it's the fulfilling of the law of charity. Life being, of all earthly possessions, the one to which men attach the greatest value, he, who renounces it for the good of his fellow creatures doesn't commit a crime he accomplishes a sacrifice, but before accomplishing it, he should consider whether his life might not be more useful than his death.

952 - Does he commit suicide who falls a victim to the excessive indulgence of passions which he knows will hasten his death, but which habit has converted into physical necessities that lie is unable to control?
- He commits moral suicide. Do you not see that a man, in such a case, is trebly guilty? For he is guilty of a want of firmness, of the sin of bestiality and of forgetfulness of God.
- Is such a man more or less guilty than he, who kills himself from despair?
- He's guiltier, because he has had time to reflect on the suicidal nature of the course he was pursuing. In the case of him who commits suicide on the spur of the moment, there is sometimes a degree of bewilderment not unallied to madness. The former will be punished much more severely than the latter; for the retributive penalties of crime are always proportioned to the consciousness of wrong doing that accompanied its commission.

953 - Is it wrong on the part of him who finds himself exposed to some terrible and inevitable death to shorten his sufferings by killing himself?
- It's always wrong not to await the moment of dissolution appointed by God. Besides, how can a man tell whether the end of his life has really come or whether some unexpected help may not reach him at what he supposes to be his last moment?
- We admit that suicide is reprehensible under ordinary circumstances, but we are supposing a case in which death is inevitable and in which life is only shortened by a few instants?
- There is always in such a case a want of resignation and of submission to the will of the Creator.
- What in such a case are the consequences of suicide?
- The same as in all other cases, an expiation proportioned to the gravity of the fault, according to the circumstances under which it was committed.

954 - Is there guilt in the imprudence which has accidentally caused a loss of life?
- There's no guilt where there's no positive intention or consciousness of doing harm.

955 - Are the women who, in some countries, voluntarily burn themselves to death with the body of their husband, to be considered as committing suicide, and have they to undergo the punishment of that crime?
- They obey the dictates of a superstitious prejudice, and, moreover, are often the victims of force rather than of their own free-will. They believe themselves to be accomplishing a duty, and such an act doesn't partake of the character of suicide. Their excuse is found in the moral nullity and ignorance of the greater number of them. All such barbarous and stupid customs will disappear with the development of civilization.

956 - Do those persons attain the end they have in view, who, unable to bear the loss of the objects of their affection, kills themselves in the hope of rejoining them in the other life?
- In such cases the result of suicide is the opposite of what was hoped for. Instead of being reunited to the object of their affection, those who have made this sad mistake find themselves separated and for a very long time, from the being they hoped to rejoin, for God can't recompense, by the granting of a favor, an act which is at once a proof of moral cowardice and an insult offered to himself in distrusting his providence. They'll pay for their folly with sorrows still greater than those they fancied they were about to shorten and for which they'll not be compensated by the satisfaction they hoped do obtain.

957 - What are in general the effects of suicide on the state of the spirit by whom it has been committed?
- The consequences of suicide vary in different cases, because the penalties it entails are always proportioned to the circumstances which, in each case, have led to its commission. The one punishment which none can escape who have committed suicide is disappointment; the rest of their punishment depends on circumstances. Some of those who have killed themselves expiate their fault at once; others do so in a new earthly life harder to bear than the one whose course they have interrupted.

> Observation has confirmed the statement that the consequences of suicide are not the same in all cases, but it has also shown us that some of those consequences, resulting from the sudden interruption of life, are the same in all cases of violent death. Foremost among these is the greater tenacity and consequent persistence of the link that unites the spirit and the body, which link. In nearly all such cases, is in its full strength at the moment when it's broken, whereas, when death is the result of natural causes, that link has been gradually weakened and is often severed before life is completely extinct. The consequences of violent death are, first, the prolongation of the mental confusion which usually follows death, and, next, the illusion which causes a spirit, during a longer or shorter period, to believe himself to be still living in the earthly life.

Chapter 2 - Future joys and sorrows

1 - Annihilation - Future life
958 - Why has man an instinctive horror of the idea of annihilation?
- Because there's no such thing as nothingness.

959 - Whence does man derive the instinctive sentiment of a future life?
- From the knowledge of that life possessed by his spirit previous to his incarnation, the soul retaining a vague remembrance of what it knew in its spirit-state.

> In all ages, man has occupied himself with the question of a future beyond the grave and it's natural that he should have done so. Whatever importance he may attach to the present life, he can't help seeing how brief it's and how precarious, since it may be cut short at any moment, so that he's never sure of the morrow. What becomes of him after death? The query is a serious one, for it refers, not to time, but to eternity. He, who is about to spend many years in a foreign country endeavors' to ascertain beforehand what will be his position there, how, then, is it possible for us not to inquire what will be our state on quitting our present life since it'll be forever?

The idea of annihilation is repugnant to reason. The most thoughtless of men, when about to quit this life, asks himself what is going to become of him and involuntarily indulges in hope. To believe in God without believing in a future life would be illogical. The presentiment of a better life is in the inner consciousness of all men. God can't have placed it there for nothing. The idea of a Nature life implies the preservation of our individuality after death, for what good would it do us to survive our body, if our moral essence were to be lost in the ocean of infinity? Such a result would be, for us, the same as annihilation.

2 - Intuition of future joys and sorrows
960 - Whence comes the belief in future rewards and punishments which is found among all nations?
- It's a presentiment of the reality imparted to each man by the spirit incarnated in him. This internal voice doesn't speak to him without a purpose; he's wrong in giving so little heed to it. If he listened to it more often and more heedfully, it'd be better for him.

961 - What's the predominant sentiment at the moment of death is it doubt, fear, or hope?
- Doubt with the skeptical, fear with the guilty, hope with the good.

962 - How is it that there are skeptics, since the soul imparts to each man the sentiment of spiritual things?
- There are fewer skeptics than you suppose. Many of those who, from pride, affect skepticism during life, are a good deal less skeptical when they come to die.

> The doctrine of moral responsibility is a consequence of the belief In a future life. Reason and our sense of justice tell us that, in the apportionment of the happiness to which all men aspire, the good and the wicked could not be confounded together. God could not will that some men should obtain, without effort, blessings which others only obtain through persevering exertion. Our conviction of the justice and goodness of God, as evidenced by the justice and goodness of his laws, forbids us to suppose that the good and the bad can occupy the same place in his sight, or to doubt that, sooner or later, the former will receive a reward and the latter a chastisement, for the good and the evil they have done, and thus, from our Innate sense of justice, we derive our intuition of the rewards and punishments of the future.

3 - Intervention of God in rewards and punishments
963 - Does God concern himself personally about each man? Is he not too great and are we not too small, for each individual to be of any importance in his sight?
- God concerns himself about all the beings he has created, however small they may be, nothing is too minute for his goodness.

964 - Has God to concern himself about each of our actions in order to reward or to punish us?
- God's laws apply to all your actions. When a man violates one of those laws, God doesn't pronounce sentence on him by saying, for example: "You have been gluttonous and I shall punish you for it". But he has traced a limit to appetite. Maladies and even death are the consequence of overstepping that limit. Punishment, in all cases, is a result of the infraction of a law.

> Is it not true that the land thus given will produce exactly in the ratio of the skill and care bestowed on its cultivation and that any mistake or negligence on the part of the son will have an injurious effect on its productiveness? The son will therefore be well or ill off in his old age, according as he has followed or neglected the directions given to him by his father. God is still more provident than the earthly father, for he tells us, every moment, whether we're doing right or doing wrong, through the spirits whom he constantly sends to counsel us, though we don't always heed them. There's also this further difference, that, if the son of whom we have been speaking has misemployed or wasted his time, he has no opportunity of repairing his past mistakes, whereas, God always gives to man the means, through new existences, of doing this.

4 - Nature of future joys and sorrows
965 - Is there anything of materiality in the joys and sorrows of the soul after death?

- Common sense tells you that they can't be of a material nature, because the soul isn't matter. There's nothing carnal in those joys and sorrows and yet they're a thousand times more vivid than those you experience upon the Earth, because the spirit when freed from matter is more impressionable, matter deadens its sensibility.

966 - Why does man often form to himself so gross and absurd an idea of the joys and sorrows of the future life?
- Because his intelligence is still but imperfectly developed. Does the child comprehend as does the adult? Besides, his idea of a future life is often a result of the teachings to which he has been subjected teachings that are urgently in need of reform.

> Your language being too incomplete to express what lies beyond the range of your present existence, it has been necessary to address you through comparisons borrowed from that existence and you have mistaken the images and figures thus employed for realities, but, in proportion as man becomes enlightened, his thought comprehends much that his language is unable to express.

967 - In what does the happiness of perfected spirits consist?
- In knowing all things, in feeling neither hatred, jealousy, envy, ambition, nor any of the passions that make men unhappy. Their mutual affection is for them a source of supreme felicity. They have none of the wants, sufferings, or anxieties of material life, they're happy in the good they do, for the happiness of spirits is always proportioned to their elevation. The highest happiness, it's true, is enjoyed only by spirits who are perfectly purified, but the others are not unhappy. Between the bad ones and those who have reached perfection, there is an infinity of gradations of elevation and of happiness, for the enjoyments of each spirit are always proportioned to his moral state.
Those who have already achieved a certain degree of advancement have a presentiment of the happiness of those who are further on than themselves, they aspire after that higher happiness, but it's for them an object of emulation, and not of jealousy. They know that it depends on themselves to attain to it and they labor to that end, but with the calmness of a good conscience and they're happy in not having to suffer what is endured by evil spirits.

968 - You place the absence of material wants among the conditions of happiness for spirits, but isn't the satisfaction of those wants a source of enjoyment for mankind?
- Yes, of animal enjoyment, but when men can't satisfy those wants, they're tortured by them.

969 - What are we to understand when it's said that the purified spirits are gathered into the bosom of God, and employed in singing his praises?
- The statement is an allegorical picture of the knowledge they possess of the perfections of God, because they see and comprehend him, but you must not take it literally, any more than other statements of a similar character. Everything in Nature, from the grain of sand upwards sings, that's to say, proclaims the power, wisdom, and goodness of God, but you must not suppose that spirits of the highest order are absorbed in an eternal contemplation, which would be a monotonous and stupid would be a perpetual uselessness. They have no longer to undergo the tribulations of corporeal life, an exemption which is itself an enjoyment, and, besides, as we have told you, they know and comprehend all things and make use of the intelligence they have acquired in aiding the progress of other spirits and they find enjoyment in this order of occupation.

970 - In what do the sufferings of inferior spirits consist?
- Those sufferings are as various as are the causes by which they're produced, and are proportioned to the degree of inferiority of each spirit, as the enjoyments of the higher spirits are proportioned to their several degrees of superiority. They may be summed up thus, the sight of happiness to which they're unable to attain, envy of the superiority which renders other spirits happy and which they seem to be lacking in themselves, regret, jealousy, rage, despair, in regard to what prevents them from being happy, remorse and indescribable moral anguish. They long for all sorts of enjoyments and are tortured by their inability to satisfy their cravings.

971 - Is the influence exercised by spirits over one another always good?
- It's always good on the part of good spirits, but perverse spirits endeavor to draw aside from the path of repentance and amendment those whom they think are susceptible of being misled and whom they have often led into evil during their earthly life.
- Death, then, doesn't deliver us from temptation?
- No, but the action of evil spirits is much less powerful over other spirits than over men, because they no longer have the material passions of the tempted for auxiliaries.

972 - In what way do evil spirits bring temptation to bear upon other spirits, since they haven't the passions to work upon?
- If the passions no longer exist materially, they still exist in thought, on the part of spirits of slight advancement and the evil ones keep up impure thoughts in their victims by taking them to places where they witness the exercise of those passions and whatever tends to excite them.
- But what end do those passions subserve, since they have no longer any real object?
- That is just what constitutes the tortures of the spirit life. The miser sees gold which he can't possess, the debauchee, orgies in which he can take no part, the haughty, honors which he envies, but can't share.

973 - What are the greatest sufferings that can be endured by wicked spirits?

- It's utterly impossible to describe the mental tortures that are the punishment of some crimes, even those by whom they're experienced would find it difficult to give you an idea of them, but, assuredly, the most frightful of them all is the sufferer's belief that his condemnation is unchangeable and for all eternity.

> Men form to themselves, in regard to the joys and sorrows of the soul after death, a conception more or less elevated according to the state of their intelligence. The greater a man's degree of development, the more refined and the more divested of materiality is his idea of them, the more rational is the view he takes of the subject and the less literally does he understand the images of figurative language in regard to them. Enlightened reason, in teaching us that the soul is an entirely spiritual being, teaches us also that it can't be affected by impressions that act only upon matter, but it doesn't follow there from that's exempt from suffering or that it doesn't undergo the punishment of its wrongdoing.

3 - The communications made to us by spirits show us the future state of the soul, no longer as a matter of theory, but as a reality. They bring before us all the incidents of the life beyond the grave, but they also show us that they're the natural consequences of the terrestrial life and that, although divested of the fantastic accompaniments created by the imagination of men, they're none the less painful for those who, in this life, have made a bad use of their faculties. The diversity of those consequences is infinite, but may be summed up by saying that each soul is punished by that wherein it has sinned. It's thus that some are punished by the incessant sight of the evil they have done, others, by regret, fear, shame, doubt, isolation, darkness, separation from those who are dear to them, etc.

974 - Whence comes the doctrine of eternal fire?
- From taking a figure of speech for a reality, as men have done in so many instances.
- But may not this fear lead to a useful result?
- Look around you and see whether there are many who are restrained by it, even among those by whom it's inculcated. If you teach what is contrary to reason, the impression you make will be neither durable nor salutary.

> Human language being powerless to express the Nature of the sufferings of spirit life, man has been unable to desvise any more appropriate comparison for them than that of flee, because, for him, fire is at once the type of the most excruciating torture and the symbol of the most energetic action. It's for this reason that the belief in everlasting burning has been held from the earliest antiquity and transmitted by succeeding generations to the present day and it's for this reason, also, that all nations speak, in common parlance of fiery passions, of burning love, burning hate, burning with jealousy, etc.

975 - Do inferior spirits comprehend the happiness of the righteous?
- Yes, and that happiness is a source of torment for them, for they understand that they're deprived of it through their own fault, but it also leads a spirit, when freed from matter, to aspire after a new corporeal existence, because every such existence, if well employed, will shorten the duration of that torment. It's thus that he makes choice of the trials through which he'll be enabled to expiate his faults, for you must remember that each spirit suffers for all the evil he has done or of which he has been the voluntary cause, for all the good which he might have done and which he didn't do and for all the evil that has resulted from his having failed to do the good he might have done.

> In the state of erraticity, a spirit's sight is no longer veiled, it's as though he had emerged from a fog and saw the obstacles that intervene between him and happiness and he therefore suffers all the more, because he understands the full extent of his culpability. For him, illusion is no longer possible; he sees things as they really are.

3 - A spirit, when errant, embraces, on the one hand, all his past existences at a glance, on the other, he foresees the future promised to him, and comprehends what he lacks for its attainment. He's like a traveler who, having reached the top of a hill, beholds both the road over which he has already travelled and that by which he has still to go in order to reach the end of his journey.

976 - Isn't the sight of spirits who suffer a cause of affliction for the good ones? And, if so, what becomes of the happiness of the latter, that happiness being thus impaired?
- Good spirits aren't distressed by the suffering of those who are a lower point than themselves, because they know that it'll have an end, they aid those who suffer to become better, and lend them a helping hand. To do this is their occupation and is a joy for them when they succeed.
- This is comprehensible on the part of spirits who are strangers to them and who take no special interest in them, but doesn't the sight of their sorrows and sufferings disturb the happiness of the spirits who have loved them upon the Earth?
- If spirits didn't see your troubles, it'd prove that they become estranged from you after death, whereas all religions teach you that the souls of the departed continue to see you, but they regard your afflictions from another point of view. They know that those sufferings will aid your advancement if you bear them with resignation and they're consequently more pained by the want of fortitude which keeps you back, than by sufferings which they know to be only temporary.

977 - Spirits being unable to hide their thoughts from one another and all the acts of their lives being known, does it follow that those who have wronged their fellows are always in presence of their victims?
- Common sense might suffice to tell you that it can't be otherwise.
- Is this divulging of all his evil deeds and the perpetual presence of those who have been the victims of them, it's a chastisement for the guilty spirit?
- Yes, and a heavier one than you may suppose it to be, but it only lasts until he has expiated his wrong doing, either as a spirit or as a man in new corporeal existences.

> When we find ourselves in the world of spirits, all our past will be brought into view and the good the evil that we have done will be equally known. In vain would the malefactor seek to avoid the sight of his victims, their presence, from which he cannot possibly escape, will be for him a punishment and a source of remorse until he has expiated the wrongs he has done them, while the spirit of the upright man will find himself constantly surrounded by kindness and good-will. Even upon the Earth there's no greater torment for the wicked man than the presence of his victims, whom he does his utmost to avoid. What will it be when, the illusions of the passions being dissipated, he comprehends the evil he has done, sees his most secret actions brought to light and his hypocrisy unmasked and perceives that he cannot hide himself from the sight of those he has wronged? But while the soul of the wicked is thus a prey to shame, regret and remorse, that of the righteous enjoys perfect peace.

978 - Doesn't the remembrance of the faults committed by the soul, during its state of imperfection, disturb its happiness even after it has attained to purity?
- No, because it has redeemed its faults and has come forth victorious from the trials to which it had submitted for that purpose.

979 - Doesn't the prevision of the trials it has still to undergo, in order to complete its purification, excite in the soul a painful apprehension that must lessen its happiness?
- Yes, in the case of a soul who is still soiled by evil and therefore it can only enjoy perfect happiness when it has become perfectly pure, but for souls who have attained to a certain degree of elevation, the thought of the trials they have still to undergo has in it nothing painful.

> The soul, arrived at a certain degree of purification, has already a foretaste of happiness. It's pervaded by a feeling of satisfaction and is happy in all that it sees, in all that surrounds it. The veil which covers the marvels and mysteries of creation being already partially raised for it, the divine perfections begin to be perceived by it in their splendor.

980 - Is the sympatric link which unites spirits of the same order a source of felicity for them?
- The union of spirits who sympathize in the love of goodness is one of their highest enjoyments, for they have no fear of seeing that union disturbed by selfishness. In worlds altogether spiritual, they form families animated by the same sentiment and this union constitutes the happiness of those worlds, as in your world you group yourselves into categories and experience pleasure in being thus brought together. The pure and sincere affection felt by elevated spirits and of which they're the object, is a source of felicity, for there are neither false friends nor hypocrites among them.

> Man enjoys the first fruits of this felicity upon the Earth when he meets with those with whom he can enter into cordial and noble union. In a life of greater purity than that of the Earth, this felicity becomes ineffable and unbounded because their inhabitants meet only with sympathetic souls whose affection will not be chilled by selfishness. For love is life, its selfishness that kills.

981 - Is there, as regards the future state of spirits, any difference between him who, during his earthly life, was afraid of death, and him who looked forward to it with indifference or even with joy?
- There may be a very considerable difference between them, though this is often obliterated by the causes which gave rise to that fear or that desire. Those who dread death and those who desire it, may be moved by very different sentiments and it's those sentiments which determine the state of a spirit. For instance, it's evident that, if a man only desires death because it'll put an end to his tribulations, that desire is, in reality, a sort of murmuring against providence and against the trials which lie has to undergo.

982 - Is it necessary to make a profession of Spiritism and to believe in spirit manifestations in order to ensure our well-being in the next life?
- If it were so, it'd follow that those who don't believe in them or who haven't even had the opportunity of learning anything about them, will be disinherited, which would be absurd. Its right doing that ensures future well being and right-doing is always right doing, whatever may be the path that leads to it.

> Belief in Spiritism aids our self improvement by clearing our ideas in regard to the future; it hastens the progress and advancement of individuals and of the masses because it enables us to ascertain what we shall someday be and is at once a beacon and a support. Spiritism teaches us to bear our trials with patience and resignation, turns us from the wrong-doing that would delay our future happiness and contributes to our attainment of that happiness, but it doesn't follow that we may not attain to that happiness without it.

5 - Temporal sorrows

983 - Doesn't a spirit, when expiating its faults in a new existence, undergo material suffering, and, that being the case, is it correct to say that, after death, the soul experiences only moral sufferings?
- It's very true that, when the soul is reincarnated, it's made to suffer by the tribulations of corporeal life, but it's only the body that undergoes material suffering.

> You often say, of one who is dead, that he's released from suffering, but this is not always true. As a spirit, he has no more physical sufferings, but, according to the faults he has coinmitted, he may have to bear moral sufferings still more severe, and, in a new existence, he may be still unhappy. He, who has made a selfish use of riches will have to beg his bread and will be a prey to all the privations of poverty, the proud will undergo humiliations of every kind, he who has

misused his authority and treated his subordinates with disdain and harshness, will be forced to obey a master still harder than himself. All the tribulations of life are the expiation of faults committed in a preceding existence, when they're not the consequence of faults committed in the present one. When you have quitted your present life, you'll understand this.

3 - He, who, in the earthly life, esteems himself happy because he is able to satisfy his passions, makes few efforts at self-improvement. Such ephemeral happiness is often expiated in the present life, but will certainly be expiated in another existence equally material.

984 - Are the troubles of our earthly life always the punishment of faults committed by us in our present lifetime?
- No, we have already told you that they're trials imposed on you by God or chosen by you in the spirit state and before your reincarnation, for the expiation of faults committed by you in a former existence, for no infraction of the laws of God and especially of the law of justice, ever remains unpunished and if it be not expiated in the same life, it'll certainly be so in another. This is why persons whom you regard as excellent are so often made to suffer, they're stricken in their present life for the faults of their past existences.

985 - When a soul is reincarnated in a world less gross than the Earth, is such a reincarnation a reward?
- It's a consequence of its higher degree of purification, for, in proportion as spirits become purified, they reincarnate themselves in worlds of progressively higher degrees, until, having divested themselves of all materiality and washed themselves clean of all stains, they enter on the eternal felicity of the fully purified spirits in the presence of God.

> In worlds in which the conditions of existence are less material than in ours, the wants of their inhabitants are less gross and their physical sufferings are less acute. The men of those worlds no longer possess the evil passions which, in lower worlds, make them each other's enemies. Having no motives for hatred or jealousy, they live in peace with one another, because they practice the law of justice, of love and of charity and they therefore know nothing of the worries and anxieties that come of envy, pride, and selfishness and that make the torment of our terrestrial existence.

986 - Can a spirit who has progressed in his terrestrial existence be reincarnated in the same world?
- Yes, and if he haven't been able to accomplish his mission, he may himself demand to complete it in a new existence, but, in that case, it's no longer an expiation for him.

987 - What becomes of the man who, without doing evil, does nothing to shake off the influence of matter?
- Since he has made no progress towards perfection, he has to begin a new existence of the same Nature as the one he has quitted. He remains stationary and thus prolongs the sufferings of expiation.

988 - There are persons whose life flows on in a perfect calm, who, having nothing to do for themselves, are exempt from all cares. Is their good fortune a proof that they have nothing to expiate from any former existence?
- Do you know many such? If you think you do, you are mistaken. Such lives are often only calm in appearance. A spirit may have chosen such an existence, but he perceives, after quitting it, that it has not served to bring him on and he then regrets the time he has wasted in idleness. Bear well in mind that a spirit can only acquire knowledge and elevation through activity, that, if he supinely falls asleep, he doesn't advance. He's like one who needs to work, but who goes off for a ramble or goes to bed, with the intention of doing nothing. Bear well in mind, also, that each of you'll have to answer for voluntary uselessness on your part and that such uselessness is always fatal to your future happiness. The sum of that happiness is always exactly proportioned to the sum of the good that you have done, the sum of your unhappiness is always proportioned to the sum of the evil that you have done and to the number of those whom you have rendered unhappy.

989 - There are persons who, without being positively wicked, render all about them unhappy by their ill temper, what is for them the consequence of this?
- Such persons are assuredly not good and they will expiate this wrong by the sight of those whom they have rendered unhappy, which will be a constant reproach for them, and then, in another existence, they'll endure all that they have caused to be endured by others.

6 - Expiation and repentance
990 - Does repentance take place in the corporeal state or in the spiritual state?
- In the spiritual state, but it may also take place in the corporeal state, when you clearly comprehend the difference between good and evil.

991 - What is the consequence of repentance in the spiritual state?
- The desire for a new incarnation, in order to become purified. The spirit perceives the imperfections which deprive him of happiness and he therefore aspires after a new existence in which he'll be able to expiate his faults.

992 - What is the consequence of repentance in the corporeal state?
- The spirit will advance even in his present life, if he have the time to repair his faults. Whenever your conscience reproaches you or shows you an imperfection, you may always become better.

993 - Are there not men who have only the instinct of evil and are inaccessible to repentance?

- I have told you that progress must be incessant. He who, in his present life, has only the instinct of evil, will have the instinct of goodness in another one and it's to effect this end that he's re-born many times, for all must advance, all must reach the goal, but some do this more quickly, others more slowly, according to the energy of their desire. He, who has only the instinct of good, is already purified, for he may have had that of evil in an anterior existence.

994 - Does the perverted spirit who hasn't recognized his faults during his life always recognize them after his death?
- Yes, he always does so and lie then suffers all the more, for he feels all the evil he has done or of which he has been the voluntary cause. Nevertheless, repentance isn't always immediate. There are spirits who obstinately persist in doing wrong, notwithstanding their sufferings, but, sooner or later, they'll see that have taken the wrong road and repentance will follow this discovery. It's to their enlightenment that the efforts of the higher spirits are directed and that you may usefully direct your own.

995 - Are there spirits who, without being wicked, ape indifferent about their own fate?
- There are spirits who don't occupy themselves with anything useful, but are in a state of expectancy. In such cases they suffer in proportion to their inactivity, for all states and conditions must conduce to progress and with them, this progress is effected by the suffering they experience.
- Have they no desire to shorten their sufferings?
- They have that desire, undoubtedly, but they have not sufficient energy to do what would give them relief. Are there not among you many who prefer to starve rather than to work?

996 - Since spirits see the harm that is done them by their imperfections, how is it that any of them persist in aggravating their position and prolonging their state of inferiority, by doing evil, as spirits, in turning men aside from the right road?
- It's those whose repentance is tardy that act thus. A spirit who repents may afterwards allow himself to be drawn back into the wrong road by other spirits still more backward than himself.

997 - We sometimes find that spirits, who are evidently of very he who, urged on by pride, revolts against God, persisting in his touched by the prayers offered for them. How is it that others, whom we have reason to believe are more enlightened, show a hardness and a cynicism that no efforts can vanquish?
- Prayer is only efficacious in the case of spirits who repent, he who, urged on by pride, revolts against God, persisting in his wrong doing and perhaps going even more widely astray, can't be acted upon by prayer and can only derive benefit there from when a glimmering of repentance shall have shown itself in him.

> We must not lose sight of the fact that a spirit, after the death of his body isn't suddenly transformed. If his life has been reprehensible, it has been so because he was imperfect, but death doesn't render him perfect all at once he may in his wrong doing, his false ideas, his prejudices, until he has become enlightened by study, reflection and suffering.

998 - Is expiation accomplished in the corporeal state, or in the spirit state?
- Expiation is accomplished during the corporeal existence, through the trials to which the spirit is subjected, and, in the spirit state, through the moral sufferings belonging to the spirit's state of inferiority.

999 - Does sincere repentance during the earthly life suffice to efface the faults of that life and to restore the wrong doer to the favor of God?
- Repentance helps forward the amelioration of the spirit, but all wrongdoing has to be expiated.
- That being the case, if a criminal should say, "Since I must necessarily expiate my past, I have no need to repent", what effect would it have upon him?
- If he hardens himself in the thought of evil, his expiation will be longer and more painful.

1000 - Can we, in the present life, redeem our faults?
- Yes, by making reparation for them, but don't suppose that you can redeem them by a few trifling privations, or by giving, after your death, what you can no longer make use of. God doesn't value a sterile repentance, a mere smiting of the breast, easily done. The loss of a little finger in doing well to others effaces more wrong doing than any amount of self torture undergone solely with a view to one's own interest. Evil can only be atoned for by good and attempts at reparation are valueless if they touch neither a man's pride nor his worldly interests. How can his rehabilitation be sub served by the restitution of ill gotten wealth after his death, when it has become useless to him and when he has already profited by it? What benefit can he derive from the privation of a few futile enjoyments and of a few superfluities, if the wrong he has done to others isn't undone? What, in truth, is the use of his humbling himself before God, if he keeps up his pride before men?

1001 - Is there no merit in ensuring the useful employment, after our death, of he property possessed by us?
- To say that there's no merit so doing wouldn't be correct, it's always better than doing nothing, but the misfortune is, that he who only gives after his death is often moved rather by selfishness than by generosity, he wishes to have the honor of doing good without its costing him anything. He, who imposes privation upon himself during his life reaps a double profit the merit of his sacrifice and the pleasure of witnessing the happiness he has caused, but selfishness is apt to whisper, whatever you give away is so much cut off from your own enjoyments and as the voice of selfishness is usually more persuasive than that of disinterestedness and charity, it too often leads a man to keep what he has, under pretext of the necessities of his position. He's to be pitied who knows not the pleasure of giving, for he's deprived of one of the purest and sweetest of enjoyments. In subjecting a man to the trial of wealth, so slippery and so dangerous for his future,

God placed within his reach, by way of compensation, the happiness which generosity may procure for him, even in his present life.

1002 - What will become of him who, in the act of dying, acknowledges his wrong-doing, but hasn't time to make reparation? Does repentance suffice in such a case?
- Repentance will hasten his rehabilitation, but it doesn't absolve him. Has he not the future, which will never be closed against him?

7 - Duration of future penalties

1003 - Is the duration of the sufferings of the guilty, in the future life, arbitrary or subordinate to a low?
- God never acts from caprice; everything in the Universe is ruled by laws which reveal his wisdom and his goodness.

1004 - What decides the duration of the sufferings of the guilty?
- The length of time required for his amelioration. A spirit's state of suffering or of happiness being proportioned to tile degree of his purification, the duration of his sufferings, as well as their nature, depends on the time it takes him to become better. In proportion as he progresses and his sentiments become purified, his sufferings diminish and change their nature.

1005 - Does time appear, to the suffering spirit, longer or shorter than in the earthly life?
- It appears longer, sleep doesn't exist for him, it's only for spirits arrived at a certain degree of purification that time is merged, so to say with infinity.

1006 - Could a spirit suffer eternally?
- Undoubtedly, if he remained eternally wicked, that's to say, if he were never to repent nor to amend, he'd suffer eternally, but God hasn't created beings to let them remain forever a prey to evil, he created them only in a state of simplicity and ignorance and all of them must progress, in a longer or shorter time, according to the action of their will. The determination to advance may be awakened more or less tardily, as the development of children is more or less precocious, but it'll he stimulated, sooner or later, by the irresistible desire of the spirit himself to escape from his state of inferiority and to be happy. The law which regulates the duration of a spirit's sufferings is, therefore, eminently wise and beneficent, since it makes that duration to depend on his own efforts, he's never deprived of his free-will, but, if he makes a bad use of it, he'll have to bear the consequences of his errors.

1007 - Are there spirits who never repent?
- There are some whose repentance is delayed for a very long time, but to suppose that they'll never improve would be to deny the law of progress and to assert that the child will never become a man.

1008 - Does the duration of a spirit's punishment always depend on his own will and is it never imposed on him for a given time?
- Yes, punishment may be imposed on him for a fixed time, but God, who wills only the good of his creatures, always welcomes his repentance and the desire to amend never remains sterile.

1009 - According to that, the penalties imposed on spirits are never eternal?
- Interrogate your common sense, your reason, and ask yourself whether an eternal condemnation for a few moments of error would not be the negation of the goodness of God? What, in fact, is the duration of a human life, even though prolonged to a hundred years, in comparison with eternity? ETERNITY! Do you rightly comprehend the word? Sufferings, tortures, without end, without hope, for a few faults! Doesn't your judgment reject such an idea? That the ancients should have seen, in the Master of the Universe, a terrible, jealous, vindictive God, is conceivable, for, in their ignorance, they attributed to the divinity the passions of men, but such isn't the God of the Christians, who places love, charity, pity, the forgetfulness of offences, in the foremost rank of virtues, and who could not lack the qualities which he has made it the duty of his creatures to possess.
Is it not a contradiction to attribute to him infinite love and infinite vengeance? You say that God's justice is infinite, transcending the limited understanding of mankind, but justice doesn't exclude kindness, and God would not be kind if he condemned the greater number of his creatures to horrible and unending punishment. Could he make it obligatory on his children to be just, if his own action towards them didn't give them the most perfect standard of justice? And is it not the very sublimity of justice and of kindness to make the duration of punishment to depend on the efforts of the guilty one to amend and to mete out the appropriate recompense, both for good and for evil, to each, according to his works?
Saint Augustine

> Set yourselves, by every means in your power, to combat and to annihilate the idea of eternal punishment, which is a blasphemy against the justice and goodness of God and the principal source of the skepticism, materialism and indifferentism that have invaded the masses since their intelligence has begun to be developed when once a mind has received enlightenment, in however slight a degree, the monstrous injustice of such an idea is immediately perceived, reason rejects it and rarely fails to confound, in the same ostracism, the penalty against which it revolts and the God to whom that penalty is attributed.
Hence the numberless ills which have burst upon you and for which we come to bring you a remedy. The task we point out to you'll be all the easier because the defenders of this belief have avoided giving a positive opinion in regard to it, neither the Councils nor the Fathers of the Church have definitely settled this weighty question. If Christ, according to the Evangelists and the literal interpretation of his allegorical utterances, threatens the guilty with a fire that is

unquenchable, there's absolutely nothing in those utterances to prove that they're condemned to remain in that fire eternally.

3 - Hapless sheep that have gone astray, behold, advancing towards you, the Good Shepherd who, so far from intending to drive you forever from his presence, comes himself to seek you, that he may lead you back to the fold. Prodigal children, renounce your voluntary exile and turn your steps towards the paternal dwelling. Your Father, with arms already opened, to receive you, is waiting to welcome you back to your home. Lamennais.

4 - Wars of words! Wars of words! Hasn't enough blood been already shed for words and must the fires of the stake be rekindled for them? Men dispute about the words eternal punishments, everlasting burnings, but do you not know that what you now understand by eternity wasn't understood in the same way by the ancients? Let the theologian consult the sources of his faith and he, like the rest of you, and will see that, in the Hebrew text, the word which the Greeks, the Latin's and the moderns, have translated as endless and irremissibly punishment, has not the same meaning. Eternity of punishment corresponds to eternity of evil.

Yes, so long as evil continues to exist among you, so long will punishment continue to exist, it's in this relative sense that the sacred texts should be interpreted. The eternity of punishments, therefore, is not absolute, but relative. Let a day come when all men shall have donned, through repentance, the robe of innocence, and, on that day, there will be no more weeping, wailing or gnashing of teeth.

Your human reason is, in truth, of narrow scope, but, such as it's, it's a gift of God and there is no man of right feeling who, with the aid of that reason, can understand the eternity of punishment in any other sense. If we admit the eternity of punishment, we must also admit that evil will be eternal, but God alone is eternal and he could not have created an eternal evil, without plucking from his attributes the most magnificent of them all, his sovereign power, for he who creates an element destructive of his works is not sovereignty powerful. Plunge no more thy mournful glance, human race, into the entrails of the Earth, in search of chastisements. Weep, but hope, expiate, but take comfort in the thought of a God who is entirely loving, absolutely powerful, essentially just. Plato.

5 - Union with the Divine Being is the aim of human existence. To the attainment of this aim three things are necessary knowledge, love justice; three things are contrary to this aim ignorance, hatred, injustice. You're false to these fundamental principles when you falsify the idea of God by exaggerating his severity, thus suggesting to the mind of the creature that there is in it more clemency, long suffering, love, and true justice, than you attribute to the Creator. You destroy the very idea of retribution by rendering it as inadmissible, by your minds, as is, by your hearts, the policy of the middle Ages, with its hideous array of torturers, executioners, and the stake. When the principle of indiscriminating retaliation has been banished for ever from human legislation, can you hope to make men believe that principle to be the rule of the Divine Government?

Believe me, brothers in God and in Jesus Christ, you must either resign yourselves to let all your dogmas perish in your hands rather than modify them or you must revivify them by opening them to the beneficent action that good spirits are now bringing to bear on them. The idea of a Hell full of glowing furnaces and boiling cauldrons might be credible in an age of iron, in the 19th century it can be nothing more than an empty phantom, capable, at the utmost, of frightening little children and by which the children themselves will no longer be frightened when they're a little bigger.

By your persistence in upholding mythic terrors, you engender incredulity, source of every sort of social disorganization and I tremble at beholding the very foundations of social order shaken, and crumbling into dust for want of an authoritative code of penalty. Let all those who are animated by a living and ardent faith, heralds of the coming day, unite their efforts, not to keep up antiquated fables now fallen into disrepute, but to resuscitate and revivify the true idea of penalty, under forms in harmony with the usages, sentiments, and enlightenment of your epoch.

6 - What in fact is a sinner? One who, by a deviation from the right road, by a false movement of the soul, has swerved from the true aim of his creation, which consists in the harmonious worship of the beautiful, the good, as embodied in the archetype of humanity, the divine exemplar, Jesus Christ. What is chastisement? The natural, derivative consequence of that false movement, the amount of pain necessary to disgust the sinner with his departure from rectitude, by his experience of the suffering caused by that departure. Chastisement is the goad which, by the smarting it occasions, decides the soul to cut short its wanderings and to return into the right road. The sole aim of chastisement is rehabilitation and therefore, to assume the eternity of chastisement is to deprive it of all reason for existing.

7 - Cease, I beseech you, the attempt to establish a parallelism of duration between good, essence of the Creator, and evil, essence of the creature, for, in so doing, you establish a standard of penalty that's utterly without justification. Affirm, on the contrary, the gradual diminution of imperfections and of chastisements through successive existences and you consecrate the doctrine of the union of the creature with the Creator by the reconciliation of justice with mercy. Paul, Apostle.

8 - It's desired to stimulate men to the acquisition of virtue and to turn them from vice, by the hope of reward and the fear of punishment, but, if the threatened punishment is represented under conditions repugnant to reason, not only will it fail of its aim, but it'll lead men, in rejecting those conditions, to reject the very idea of punishment itself, but let the idea of future rewards and punishments be presented to their mind under a reasonable form and they'll not reject it. This reasonable explanation of the subject is given by the teachings of Spiritism.

9 - The doctrine of eternal punishment makes an implacable God of the Supreme Being. Would it be reasonable to say of a sovereign that he's very kind, very benevolent, very indulgent, that he only desires the happiness of all around him, but that he is, at the same time, jealous, vindictive, inflexibly severe and that he punishes three quarters of his subjects

with the most terrific tortures, for any offence or any infraction of his laws, even when their imputed fault has resulted simply from their ignorance of the laws they have transgressed? Would there not be an evident contradiction in such a statement of the sovereign's character? And can God's action be less consistent than that of a man?

10 - The doctrine in question presents another contradiction. Since God for knows all things, he must have known, in creating a soul, that it'd transgress his laws and it must therefore have been, from its very formation, predestined by him to eternal misery, but is such an assumption reasonable or admissible? The doctrine of punishment proportioned to wrongdoing is, on the contrary, entirely consonant with reason and justice. God undoubtedly foresaw, in creating a given soul, that, in its ignorance, it'd do wrong, but he has ordained that its very faults themselves shall furnish it with the means of becoming enlightened through its experience of the painful effects of its wrong doing he'll compel it to expiate that wrong doing, but only in order that it may be thereby more firmly fixed in goodness thus the door of hope is never closed against it, and the moment of its deliverance from suffering is made to depend on the amount of effort it puts forth to achieve its purification. If the doctrine of future punishment had always been presented under this aspect, very few would ever have doubted its truth.

11 - The word eternal is often figuratively employed, in common parlance, to designate any long period of duration of which the end isn't foreseen, although it's known that it'll come in course of time. We speak, for instance, of the eternal snows of mountain peaks and polar regions, although we know, on the one hand, that our globe will come to an end, and, on the other hand, that the state of those regions may be changed by the normal displacement of the Earth's axis or by some cataclysm. The word eternal, therefore, in this case, doesn't mean infinitely perpetual. We say, in the suffering of some long illness, that our days present the same eternal round of weariness, is it strange, then, that spirits who have suffered for years, centuries, thousands of ages even, should express themselves in the same way? Moreover, we must not forget that their state of backwardness prevents them from seeing the other end of their road and that they therefore believe themselves to be destined to suffer forever, a belief which is itself a part of their punishment.

12 - The doctrine of material fire, of furnaces and tortures, borrowed from the pagan Tartarus, is completely given up by many of the most eminent theologians of the present day, who admit that the word "fire" is employed figuratively in the *Bible* and is to be understood as meaning moral fire. Those who, like ourselves, have observed the incidents of the life beyond the grave, as presented to our view by the communications of spirits, have had ample proof that its sufferings are none the less excruciating for not being of a material nature and even as regards the duration of those sufferings, many theologians are beginning to admit the restriction indicated above and to consider that the word eternal may be considered as referring to the principle of penalty in itself, as the consequence of an immutable law and not to its application to each individual. When religious teaching shall openly admit this interpretation, it'll bring back to a belief in God and in a future life many who are now losing themselves in the mazes of materialism.

8 - Resurrection of the body

1010 - The dogma of the resurrection of the flesh will be the consecration of the reincarnation taught by the spirits?

- How could you have it any other way? As with so many others, these words only seem to be unreasonable, in the opinion of some people, because they take them to the letter. They lead, therefore, to unbelief. Give them a logical interpretation and those whom you call free thinkers will admit them without difficulties, precisely for the reason that they reflect. Because, don't be deceived, these free thinkers what they ask and wish most is to believe. They have, like others, or perhaps more than others, the seat of the future, but they can't admit what science denies. The doctrine of the plurality of existences is consistent with the justice of God; it alone explains what, without it, is inexplicable. How could you pretend that your principle was not in your own religion?

- Thus, by the dogma of the resurrection of the flesh, does the Church itself teach the doctrine of reincarnation?

- It's evident, too, that this doctrine stems from many things that have gone unnoticed and will soon be understood in this sense. It'll be recognized soon that Spiritism stands out at every step of the very text of the sacred writings. Spirits, therefore, don't come to subvert religion as some claim. They come, on the contrary, to confirm it, to sanction it by irrefutable evidence, but as time has come for them to no longer employ figurative language, they express themselves without allegory and give things a clear and precise sense, which can't be subjected to any false interpretation. That's why, in a while, much greater than today is the number of sincerely religious and believing people.

1011 - The Church, then, in the dogma of the resurrection of the body, really teaches the doctrine of reincarnation?

- That is evident, but it'll soon be seen that reincarnation is implied in every part of Holy Writ. Spirits, therefore, don't come to overthrow religion, as is sometimes asserted, they come, on the contrary, to confirm and sanction it by irrefragable proofs, but as the time has arrived to renounce the use of figurative language, they speak without allegories and give to every statement a clear and precise meaning that obviates all danger of false interpretation. For this reason there will be, ere long, a greater number of persons sincerely religious and really believing than are to be found at the present day.

> Physical science demonstrates the impossibility of resurrection according to the common idea. If the relics of the human body remained homogeneous, even though dispersed and reduced to powder, we might conceive the possibility of their being reunited at some future time, but such isn't the case. The body is formed of various elements, oxygen, hydrogen, azote, carbon, etc., and these elements, being dispersed, serve to form new bodies, so that the same molecule of carbon, for example, will have entered Into the composition of many thousands of different bodies, such and such an individual may have, in his body, molecules that were in the bodies of the men of the earliest ages and the very same organic molecules that you have this day absorbed in your food may have come from the body of someone whom you

have known and so on, matter being finite in quantity and its transformations being infinite in number, how is it possible that the innumerable bodies formed out of it should be reconstituted with the same elements?

Such a reconstruction is a physical impossibility. The resurrection of the body can, therefore, be rationally admitted only as a figure of speech, symbolizing the fact of reincarnation, thus interpreted; it has in it nothing repugnant to reason, nothing contrary to the data of physical science. It's true that, according to theological dogma, this resurrection isn't to take place until the Last Day, while, according to spiritist doctrine, it takes place every day, but isn't this picture of the Last Judgment a grand and noble metaphor, implying, under the veil of allegory, one of those immutable truths that will no longer be met with incredulity when restored to their true meaning?

To those who carefully ponder the spiritist theory of the future destiny of souls and of the fate that awaits them as the result of various trials they have to undergo, it'll be apparent that, with the exception of the condition of simultaneousness, the judgment which condemns or absolves them is not a fiction, as is supposed by unbelievers. It's also to be remarked that the judgment which assigns to each soul its next place of habitation is the natural consequence of the plurality of worlds, now generally admitted, while, according to the doctrine of the Last Judgment, the Earth is supposed to be the only inhabited world.

8 - Paradise, Hell and Purgatory

1012 - There will be in the Universe circumscribed places for the pains and joys of the spirits according to their merits?

- We have already answered this question. Feathers and joys are inherent in the degree of perfection of the spirits. Each one takes from himself the principle of his happiness or his misfortune and as they're everywhere, no enclosed or enclosed place exists especially destined to one or another thing. As for the incarnated, these are more or less happy or miserable, as the world in which they dwell is more or less advanced.

- Accordingly, then, with what you have come to say, Hell and Heaven don't exist, as man imagines them?

- They're simple allegory; everywhere there are spirits who are happy and kind. However, as we have also said, spirits of the same order are gathered together by sympathy, but may gather where they please, when they're perfect.

> The localization of rewards and punishments in fixed places exists only in man's imagination; it proceeds from his tendency to materialize and to circumscribe the things of which he can't comprehend the essential infinitude.

1013 - What is to be understood by Purgatory?

- Physical and moral suffering, the period of expiation, it's almost always upon the Earth that you're made by God to undergo your Purgatory and to expiate your wrong doing.

> What men call Purgatory is also a figure of speech, that should be understood as signifying, not any determinate place, but the state of imperfect spirits who have to expiate their faults until they have attained the complete purification that will raise them to the state of perfect blessedness. As this purification is effected by means of various incarnations, Purgatory consists in the trials of corporeal life.

1014 - How is it that spirits who, by their language, would seem to be of high degree, have replied according to the commonly received ideas to those who have questioned them in the most serious spirit concerning Hell and Purgatory?

- They speak according to the comprehension of those who question them, when the latter are too fully imbued with preconceived ideas, in order to avoid any abrupt interference with their convictions. If a spirit should tell a Muslim, without proper precautions, that Mahomet wasn't a true prophet, he'd not he listened to with much cordiality.

- Such precautions are conceivable on the part of spirits who wish to instruct us, but how is it that others, when questioned as to their situation, have replied that they were suffering the torture's of Hell or of Purgatory?

- Spirits of inferior advancement, who are not yet completely dematerialized, retain a portion of their earthly ideas and describe their impressions by means of terms that are familiar to them. They're in a state that allows of their obtaining only a very imperfect foresight of the future, for which reason it often happens that spirits in erraticity or, but recently freed from their earthly body, speak just as they'd have done during their earthly life. Hell may be understood as meaning a life of extremely painful trial; with uncertainty as to the future attainment of any better state and Purgatory as a life that is also one of trial, but with the certainty of a happier future. Do you not say, when undergoing any very intense physical or mental distress, that you're suffering the tortures of the damned? But such an expression is only a figure of speech and is always employed as such.

1015 - What is to be understood by the expression a soul in torment?

- An errant and suffering soul, uncertain about its future and to whom you can render, in its endeavor to obtain relief, an assistance that it often solicits at your hands by the act of addressing itself to you.

1016 - In what sense should the word Heaven be understood?

- Do you think it's a place, like the Champs Elysees of the ancients, where all good spirits are promiscuously clustered, with no other concern than to enjoy, for all eternity, a passive happiness? No, it's the universal space; it's the planets, the stars and all the higher worlds, where spirits enjoy their faculties fully, without the tribulations of material life, nor the anguish peculiar to inferiority.

1017 - Spirits have said that they inhabited the 3rd, 4th and 5th Heaven, etc., what did they mean in saying this?

- You ask them which Heaven they inhabit, because you have the idea of several Heavens, placed one above the other, like the stories of a house and they therefore answer you according to your own ideas, but, for them, the words 3rd, 4th or 5h Heaven express different degrees of purification and consequently of happiness. It's the same when you ask a spirit whether he's in Hell, if he's unhappy, he'll say yes because, for him, Hell is synonymous with suffering, but he knows very well that it isn't a furnace. A Pagan would have replied that lie was in Tartarus.

> The same may be said in regard to other expressions of a similar character, such as "the city of flowers", "the city of the elect", the 1st, 2nd or 3rd "sphere", etc., which are only allegorical and employed by some spirits figuratively, by others from ignorance of the reality of things, or even of the most elementary principles of natural science. According to the restricted idea formerly entertained in regard to the localities of rewards and punishments and to the common belief that the earth was the centre of the universe, that the sky formed a vault overhead and that there was a specific region of stars. Men placed Heaven up above and Hell down below, hence the expressions to "ascend into Heaven", to be in "the highest Heaven" to be "cast down into Hell", etc.

Now that Astronomy, having traced up the Earth's history and described its constitution, has shown us that it's one of the smallest worlds that circulate in space and devoid of any special importance, that space is infinite and that there is neither "lip" nor "down" in the universe, men have been obliged to cease placing Heaven above the clouds and Hell in the "lower parts of the Earth". As for Purgatory, no fixed place was ever assigned to it. It was reserved for Spiritism to give, in regard to all these points, an explanation which is at once and in the highest degree, rational, sublime and consoling, by showing us that we have in ourselves our "Hell" and our "Heaven", and that we find our "Purgatory" in the state of incarnation, in our successive corporeal or physical lives.

1018 - In what sense should we understand the words of Christ, "My kingdom isn't of this world"?
- Christ, in replying thus, spoke figuratively. He meant to say that he reigned only over pure and unselfish hearts, he's wherever the love of goodness holds sway, but they who are greedy for the things of this world and attached to the enjoyments of Earth, aren't with him.

1019 - Will the reign of goodness ever be established upon the Earth?
- Goodness will reign upon the Earth when, among the spirits who come to dwell in it, the good shall be more numerous than the bad, for they'll then bring in the reign of love and justice, which are the source of good and of happiness. It's through moral progress and practical conformity with the laws of God, that men will attract to the Earth good spirits, who'll keep bad ones away from it, but the latter will not definitively quit the Earth until its people shall be completely purified from pride and selfishness.

> The transformation of the human race has been predicted from the most ancient times and you're now approaching the period when it's destined to take place. All those among you who are laboring to advance the progress of mankind are helping to hasten this transformation, which will be effected through the incarnation, in your Earth, of spirits of higher degree, who'll constitute a new population, of greater moral advancement than the human races they'll gradually have replaced. The spirits of the wicked people who are mowed down each day by death and of all who endeavor to arrest the onward movement, will be excluded from the Earth and compelled to incarnate themselves elsewhere, for they'd be out of place among those nobler races of human beings, whose felicity would be impaired by their presence among them.

They'll be sent into never worlds; less advanced than the Earth and will therein fulfill hard and laborious missions, which will furnish them with the means of advancing, while contributing also to the advancement of their brethren of those younger worlds, less advanced than themselves. Do you not see, in this exclusion of backward spirits from the transformed and regenerated Earth, the true significance of the sublime myth of the driving out of the first pair from the Garden of Eden?

And do you not also see, in the advent of the human race upon the Earth, under the conditions of such an exile and bringing within, itself the germs of its passions and the evidences of its primitive inferiority, the real meaning of that other myth, no less sublime, of the fall of those first parents, entailing the sinfulness of their descendants? Original sin, considered from this point of view, is seen to consist in the imperfection of human nature and each of the spirits subsequently incarnated in the human race is therefore responsible only for his own imperfection and his own wrong doing and not for those of his forefathers.

3 - Devote yourselves, then, with zeal and courage to the great work of regeneration, all you who are processed of faith and good will, you'll reap a hundredfold for all the seed you sow. Woe to those who close their eyes against the light, for they'll have condemned themselves to long ages of darkness and sorrow. Woe to those who centre their enjoyment in the pleasures of the earthly life, for they'll undergo privations more numerous than their present pleasures; and woe, above all, to the selfish, for they'll find nobody to aid them in bearing the burden of their future misery.

Conclusion

1 - He who, in regard to terrestrial magnetism, knows only the little figures of ducks which, with the aid of a magnet, are made to swim about in a basin of water, would find it difficult to understand that those toy figures contain the secret of the mechanism of the Universe and of the movement of worlds, he, whose knowledge of Spiritism is confined to the table turning which was the starting point of the modern manifestations, is in a similar position, he regards it merely as an amusement, a social pastime and can't understand how a phenomenon so simple and so common, known to antiquity and even to savage tribes, can be connected with the weightiest questions of psychology and of human life, for the superficial observer, what connection can exist between a table that turns and the morality and future destiny of the human race?

But as, from the simple pot which, in boiling, raises its lid, there has issued the potent motor with whose aid man transports himself through space and suppresses distance, so, be it known to you, ye who believe in nothing beyond the world material. There has issued, from the table-turning, which provokes your disdainful smiles, a new philosophy that furnishes the solution of problems which no other has been able to solve, I appeal to all honest adversaries of Spiritism, and I adjure them to say whether they have taken the trouble to study what they criticize, reminding them that criticism is necessarily of no value unless the critic knows what he is talking about, to ridicule that of which we know nothing, which we have not made the subject of conscientious examination, isn't to criticize, but to give proof of frivolity and want of judgment.

Assuredly, if we had present this philosophy as being the product of a human brain, it'd have met with less disdain and would have had the honor of being examined by those who profess to be the leaders of opinion, but it claims to be derived from spirits, what an absurdity. It's scarcely held to deserve a single glance by those who judge it merely by its title, as the monkey in the fable judged of the nut by its husk, but put aside all thought of the origin of this book, suppose it to be the work of a man and say, in truth and honesty, whether, after having carefully read it, you find in it anything to laugh at?

2 - Spiritism is the most formidable opponent of materialism and it's therefore not surprising that it should have the materialists for adversaries, but as materialism is a doctrine which many of those who hold it hardly dare to avow, they cover their opposition with the mantle of reason and science, their shafts are especially aimed at the marvelous and the supernatural, which they deny and as, according to them, Spiritism is founded on the marvelous and the supernatural, they declare that it can be nothing more than a ridiculous delusion. Strange to say, some of those who are most incredulous in regard to Spiritism deny the possibility of its phenomena in the name of religion, of which they often know as little as they do of Spiritism.

They don't reflect that, in denying, without restriction, the possibility of the "marvelous" and the "supernatural", they deny religion, for religion is founded on revelation and miracles and what is revelation if not extra human communications? All the sacred writers, from Moses downwards, have spoken of this order of communications, and what are miracles if not facts of a character emphatically marvelous and super natural, since they are, according to liturgical acceptation, derogations from the laws of Nature, so that, in rejecting the marvelous and the supernatural, they reject the very basis of all religions? But it's not from this point of view that we have to consider the subject. Belief in spirit manifestation doesn't necessarily settle the question of miracles, that is to say, whether God does or doesn't, in certain cases, derogate from the eternal laws that regulate the Universe, it leaves, in regard to this question, full liberty of belief to all.

Spiritism says and proves that the phenomena on which it's based are supernatural only in appearance, that they only appear to some persons to be such, because they're unusual and out of the pale of facts hitherto known and that they're no more supernatural than all the other phenomena which the science of the present day is explaining, though they appeared to be "miraculous" in the past. All spiritist phenomena, without exception, are the consequence of general laws, they reveal to us one of the powers of Nature, a power hitherto unknown, or rather that has not hitherto been understood, but which observation shows us to be included in the scheme of things. Spiritism, therefore, is founded less on the marvelous and the supernatural than is religion itself and those who attack it on this score do so because they know not what it really is. As for those who oppose it in the name of science, we say to them, be they ever so learned, if your science, which has taught you so many things, has not taught you that the domain of Nature is infinite, you are scientific to very little purpose.

3 - You say that you wish to cure your age of a malady of credulity that threatens to invade the world. Would you prefer to see the world invaded by the incredulity that you seek to propagate? Is it not to the absence of all belief that is to be attributed the relaxing of familyties and the greater part of the disorders that are undermining society? By demonstrating the existence and immortality of the soul, Spiritism revives faith in the future, raises the courage of those who are depressed and enables us to bear the vicissitudes of life with resignation.

Do you call this an evil? Two doctrinal theories are offered for our acceptance, one of them denies the existence of a future life, the other proclaims and proves it, one of them explains nothing, the other explains everything, and, by so doing, appeals to our reason, one of them is the justification of selfishness, the other gives a firm basis to justice, charity and the love of one's fellow-creatures, one of them shows only the present and annihilates all hope, the other consoles us by showing the vast field of the future, which of the two is the more pernicious?

There are some, among the most skeptical of our opponents, who give themselves out as apostles of fraternity and progress, but fraternity implies disinterestedness and abnegation of one's own personality and by what right do you impose such a sacrifice on him to whom you affirm that, when be is dead, everything will be over for him, that soon, perhaps tomorrow, he'll be nothing more than a worn out machine, out of gear and thrown aside as so much rubbish?

Why, in that case, should he impose on himself any privation? Is it not more natural that he should resolve to live as agreeably as possible during the few brief instants you accord to him? And would not such a resolve naturally suggest to him the desire to possess largely in order to secure the largest amount of enjoyment? And would not this desire naturally give birth to jealousy of those who possess more than he does? And, from such jealousy to the desire to take from them what they possess, is there more than a single step?

What is there, in fact, to restrain him from doing so? The law? But the law doesn't reach every case. Conscience? The sense of duty? But what, from your point of view, is conscience? And upon what do you base the sense of duty? Has that sense any motive or aim if it be true that everything ends for us with our present life? In connection with such a belief, only one maxim can be reasonably admitted, every man for himself. Fraternity, conscience, duty, humanity, progress even, are but empty words. Ah! You who proclaim such a doctrine, you know not how much harm you do to society nor of how many crimes, do you incur the responsibility. But why do we speak of responsibility? Nothing of the kind exists for the materialist; he renders homage only to matter.

4 - The progress of the human race results from the practical application of the law of justice, love and charity. This law is founded on the certainty of the future, take away that certainty and you take away its corner stone. It's from this law that all other laws are derived, for it comprises all the conditions of human happiness, it alone can cure the evils of society and the improvement that takes place in the conditions of social life, in proportion as this law is better understood and better carried out in action, becomes clearly apparent when we compare the various ages and peoples of the Earth. And if the partial and incomplete application of this law has sufficed to produce an appreciable improvement in social conditions, what will it not effect when it shall have become the basis of all social institutions? Is such a result possible? Yes, for as the human race has already accomplished ten steps, it's evident that it can accomplish twenty and so on.

We can infer the future from the past. We see that the antipathies between different nations are beginning to melt away, that the barriers which separated them are being overthrown by the progress of civilization and that they're joining hands from one end of the world to the other. A larger measure of justice has been introduced into international law, wars occur less frequently and don't exclude the exercise of humane sentiments, uniformity is being gradually established in the relations of life, the distinctions of races and castes are being effaced and men of different religious beliefs are imposing silence on sectional prejudices, that they may unite in adoration of one and the same God.

We speak of the nations who are at the head of civilization. In all these relations, men are still far from perfection and there are still many old ruins to be pulled down before the last vestiges of barbarism will have been cleared away, but can those ruins withstand the irresistible action of progress, that living force which is itself a law of Nature? If the present generation is more advanced than the last, why shouldn't the next be more advanced than the present one? It'll necessarily be so through the force of things, in the first place, because each generation, as it passes away, carries with it some of the champions of old abuses and society is thus gradually reconstituted with new elements that have thrown aside antiquated prejudices, in the second place, because, when men have come to desire progress, they study the obstacles which impede it and set themselves to get rid of them.

The fact of the progressive movement of human society being incontestable, there can be no doubt that progress will continue to be made in the future. Man desires to be happy; it's in his nature so to do. He only he has not obtained complete happiness and that this happiness, but for which result progress would have no object, for where would be the value of progress for him if it didn't improve his position? But when he shall have obtained all the enjoyments that can be afforded by intellectual progress, he'll perceive that he has not obtained complete happiness and that this happiness is impossible without security in the social relations, and as he can only obtain this security through the moral progress of society in general, he'll be led, by the force of things, to labor for that end, to the attainment of which, Spiritism will furnish him with the most effectual means.

5 - Those who complain that spiritist belief is spreading in all directions and threatening to invade the world, thereby proclaim its power, for no opinion that isn't founded on reason and on fact could become general, therefore, if Spiritism is taking root everywhere, making converts in every rank of society, and especially among the educated classes, as is admitted by all to be the case, it's evident that it must founded in truth. That being so, all the efforts of its detractors will be made in vain, an assertion borne out by the fact that the ridicule attempted to be heaped upon it by those who have hoped thereby to arrest its march seems only to have given it new life.

This result fully justifies the assurances that have been so constantly given us by our spirit friends, who have repeatedly said to us; don't allow yourself to be made uneasy by opposition. Whatever is done against you'll turn to your advantage and your bitterest opponents will serve you in spite of themselves. Against the will of God, the ill will of men is of no avail. Through the moral teachings of Spiritism, the human race will enter upon a new phase of its destiny, that of the moral progress which is the inevitable consequence of this belief.

The rapid spread of spiritist ideas should cause no surprise, being due to the profound satisfaction they give to those who adopt them with intelligence and sincerity, and as happiness is what men desire above all things, it's not surprising that they should embrace ideas which impart so much happiness to those who hold them. The development of these ideas presents three distinct periods: The 1st is that of curiosity, excited by the strangeness of the phenomena produced, the 2nd, that of reasoning and philosophy, the 3rd, that of application and consequences. The period of curiosity is gone by, for curiosity has only a brief existence, the mind, when satisfied in regard to any novelty, quitting it at once for another, as isn't its habit in regard to subjects that awaken graver thought and that appeal to the judgment.

The 2nd period has already begun, the 3rd will certainly follow. The progress of Spiritism has been specially rapid since its essential nature and its scope have been more correctly understood, because it touches the most sensitive fiber of the human heart, the desire of happiness, which it augments immeasurably, even in the present world, this, as previously remarked, is the cause of its wide acceptance, the secret of the force that will make it triumph. It renders happy those who understand it, while awaiting the extension of its influence over the masses. How many a spiritist, who has never witnessed any of the physical phenomena of spirit manifestation, says to himself, besides the phenomena of Spiritism, there's its philosophy, which explains what no other has ever explained.

That philosophy furnishes me, through arguments draw from reason only and independently of any sanction but that of reason, with a rational solution of problems that are of the most vital importance to my future, it gives me calmness, security, confidence, it delivers me from the torments of uncertainty. In comparison with results so valuable, the question of the physical phenomena is of secondary importance. To those who attack this philosophy, we reply, would you like to have a means of combating it successfully? If so, here it's, bring forward something better in its place, find a more philosophic solution of the problems it solves, give to man another certainty that shall render him still happier, but you must thoroughly understand the meaning of the word certainty, for man only accepts as certain what appears to him to be reasonable.

You must not content yourselves with saying that the thing isn't so, which is a mode of proceeding altogether too easy. You must prove, not by negation, but by facts, that what we assert to exist has no existence, has never been, and can't be and above all, having shown that it has no existence, you must show what you have to offer in its place and you must prove that the tendency of Spiritism isn't to make men better, and consequently happier, by the practice of the purest morality, that sublime and simple morality of the Gospels which men praise so much and practice so little. When you have done all this, you'll have a right to attack it. Spiritism is strong because its bases are those of religion itself, God, the soul, the rewards and punishments of the future, because it shows those rewards and punishments to be the natural consequences of the earthly life, and because, in the picture it presents of the future, there is nothing which the most logical mind could regard as contrary to reason.

What compensation can you offer for the sufferings of the present life, you whose whole doctrine consists in the negation of the future? You base your teachings on incredulity, Spiritism is based on confidence in God, while the latter invites all men to happiness, to hope, to true fraternity, you offer them, in prospect, annihilation and in the present, by way of consolation, selfishness, it explains everything and you explain nothing, it proves by facts, while your assertions are devoid of proof. How can you expect that the world should hesitate between these two doctrines? To suppose that Spiritism derives its strength from the physical manifestations and that it might therefore be put an end to by hindering those manifestations, is to form to one's self a very false idea of it. Its strength is in its philosophy, in the appeal it makes to reason, to common sense. In ancient times it was the object of mysterious studies, carefully hidden from the vulgar; at the present day it has no secrets, but speaks clearly, without ambiguity, mysticism or allegories susceptible of false interpretations.

The time having come for making known the truth, its language is such as all may comprehend. So far from being opposed to the diffusion of the light, the new revelation is intended for all mankind, it doesn't claim a blind acceptance, but urges everyone to examine the grounds of his belief and as its teachings are based upon reason, it'll always be stronger than those who base their arguments upon annihilation. Would it be possible to put a stop to spirit manifestations, by placing obstacles in the way of their production? No, for such an attempt would have the effect of all persecutions, that of exciting curiosity and the desire of making acquaintance with a forbidden subject.

Were spirit manifestations the privilege of a single individual, it'd undoubtedly be possible, by preventing his action, to put an end to them, but unfortunately for our adversaries, those manifestations are within everybody's reach and are being obtained by all, from the highest to the lowest, from the palace to the cottage. It might be possible to prevent their production in public, but, as is well known, it's not in public, but in private, that they're most successfully produced and as any one may be a medium, how would it be possible to prevent each family in the privacy of its home, each individual in the silence of his chamber, each prisoner, even, in his cell, from holding communication with the invisible beings around them, in the very presence of those who should endeavor to prevent them from doing so?

If mediums were forbidden to exercise their faculty in one country, how would it be possible to hinder them from doing so elsewhere throughout the rest of the world, since there isn't a single country, in either continent, in which mediums aren't to be found? In order to shut up all the mediums, it'd be necessary to incarcerate half the human race and even if it were possible, which would scarcely be easier, to burn all the spiritist books in existence, they'd at once be reproduced, because the source from which they emanate is beyond the reach of attack and it's impossible to imprison or to burn the spirits who are their real authors.

Spiritism isn't the work of any man; no one can claim to have created it, for it's as old as creation itself. It's to be found everywhere, in all religions and in the Catholic religion even more than in the others, and with more authoritative inculcation, for the Catholic dogma contains all that constitutes Spiritism, admission of the existence of spirits of every degree, their relations, occult and patent, with mankind, guardian-angels, reincarnation, the emancipation of the soul during the present life, second-sight, visions and manifestations of every kind, including even tangible apparitions, as for demons, they're nothing else than bad spirits and with the exception of the belief that the former are doomed to evil forever, while the path of progress isn't closed against the others, there is, between them, only a difference of name.

What is the special and peculiar work of modern Spiritism? To make a coherent whole of what has hitherto been scattered, to explain, in clear and precise terms, what has hitherto been wrapped up in the language of allegory, to eliminate the products of superstition and ignorance from human belief, leaving only what is real and actual, this is its mission, but that of a founder doesn't belong to it. It renders evident that which already exists, it coordinates, but it creates nothing, for its elements are of all countries and of every age. Who, then, could flatter himself with the hope of being able to stifle it, either by ridicule or by persecution? If it were possible to proscribe it in one place, it'd reappear in another, or on the very spot from which it had been banished, because it exists in the constitution of things and because no man can annihilate that which is one of the powers of Nature, or veto that which is in virtue of the Divine decrees.

But what interest could any Government have in opposing the propagation of spiritist ideas? Those ideas, it's true, is a protest against the abuses that spring from pride and selfishness, but although such abuses are profitable to the few, they're injurious to the many and Spiritism would therefore have the masses on its side, while its only adversaries would be those who profit by the abuses against which it protests. So far from Governments having anything to dread from the spread of spiritist ideas, the tendency of those ideas being to render men more benevolent towards one another, less greedy of material things and more resigned to the orderings of Providence, they constitute, for the State, a guarantee of order and of tranquility.

6 - Spiritism presents three different aspects, viz., the facts of spirit manifestation, the philosophic and moral principles deducible from those facts and the practical applications of which those principles are susceptible, hence three classes into which its adherents are naturally divided, or rather, three degrees of advancement by which they're distinguished: 1st, those who believe in the reality and genuineness of the spirit manifestations, but confine themselves to the attestation of these and for whom Spiritism is merely an experimental science; 2nd, those who comprehend its moral bearings; and 3rd, those who put in practice, or, at least, endeavor to put in practice, the system of morality which it's the mission of Spiritism to establish.

Whatever the point of view experimental, scientific or moral, from which these strange phenomena are considered, every one perceives that they're ushering in an entirely novel order of ideas, which must necessarily produce a profound modification of the state of the human race and everyone who understands the subject also perceives that this modification can only be for good. As for our adversaries, they may also be grouped into three categories:1st, those who systematically deny whatever is new or doesn't proceed from themselves, and who speak without knowing what they're talking about. To this class belong all those who admit nothing beyond the testimony of their senses they have not seen anything, don't wish to see anything and are still more unwilling to go deeply into anything, they'd, in fact, be unwilling to see too clearly, for fear of being obliged to confess that they have been mistaken, they declare that Spiritism is chimerical insane, utopian, and has no real existence, as the easiest way of settling the matter, they're the willfully incredulous.

With them may be classed those who have condescended to glance at the subject, in order to be able to say, I have tried to see something of it, but I have not been able to succeed in doing so, and who don't seem to be aware that half an hour's attention isn't enough to make them acquainted with a new field of study. 2nd, those who, although perfectly aware of the genuineness of the phenomena, oppose the matter from interested motives. They know that Spiritism is true, but being afraid of consequences, they attack it as an enemy, and 3rd, those who dread the moral rules of Spiritism as constituting too severe a censure of their acts and tendencies.

A serious admission of the truth of Spiritism would be in their way, they neither reject nor accept it, but prefer to close their eyes in regard to it. The 1st class is swayed by pride and presumption, the 2nd by ambition, the 3rd by selfishness. We should seek in vain for a fourth class of antagonists, viz., that of opponents who, basing their opposition on a careful and conscientious study of Spiritism, should bring forward positive and irrefutable evidence of its falsity. It'd be hoping too much of human nature to imagine that it could be suddenly transformed by spiritist ideas. The action of these undoubtedly isn't the same nor is it equally powerful, in the case of all those by whom they're professed, but their result, however slight it may be, is always beneficial, if only by proving the existence of an extracorporeal world and thus disproving the doctrines of materialism. This result follows from a mere observation of the phenomena of Spiritism, but, among those who, comprehending its philosophy, see in it something else than phenomena more or less curious, it produces other effects.

The 1st, and most general of these, is the development of the religious sentiment, even in those who, without being materialists, are indifferent to spiritual things and this sentiment leads to contempt of death, we don't say to a desire for death, for the spiritist would defend his life like anyone else, but to an indifference which causes him to accept death, when inevitable, without murmuring and without regret, as something to be welcomed rather than feared, owing to his certainty in regard to the state which follows it. The 2nd effect of spiritist convictions is resignation under the vicissitudes of life. Spiritism lead us to consider everything from so elevated a point of view that the importance of terrestrial life is proportionally diminished, and we're less painfully affected by its tribulations, we have consequently more courage under affliction, more moderation in our desires, and also a more rooted repugnance to the idea of shortening our days, Spiritism showing us that suicide always causes the loss of what it was intended to obtain.

The certainty of a future which it depends on ourselves to render happy the possibility of establishing relations with those who are dear to us in the other life, offer the highest of all consolations to the spiritist and his field of view is widened to infinity by his constant beholding of the life beyond the grave, and his growing acquaintance with conditions of existence hitherto veiled in mystery. The third effect of spiritist ideas is to induce indulgence for the defects of others, but it must be admitted that, selfishness being the most tenacious of human sentiments, it's also the one which it's most difficult to extirpate. We're willing to make sacrifices provided they cost us nothing and provided especially that they impose on us no privations, but money still exercises an irresistible attraction over the greater number of mankind and very few understand the word "superfluity" in connection with their own personality. The abnegation of our personality is, therefore, the most eminent sign of progress.

7 - Do spirits, it's sometimes asked, teach us anything new in the way of morality, anything superior to what has been taught by Christ? If the moral code of Spiritism be no other than that of the gospel, what is the use of it? This mode of reasoning is singularly like that of the Caliph Omar, in speaking of the Library of Alexandria: - *If it contains only what is found in the Koran, it's useless and in that case must be burned, and if it contains anything that isn't found in the Koran, it's bad, and in that case, also, it must be burned.*

No, the morality of Spiritism isn't different from that of Jesus, but we have to ask, in our turn, whether, before Christ, men had not the law given by God to Moses? Isn't the doctrine of Christ to be found in the Decalogue? But will it therefore be contended that the moral teaching of Jesus is useless? We ask, still further, of those who deny the utility of the moral teachings of Spiritism, why it's that the moral teachings of Christ are so little practiced and why it's that those who rightly proclaim their sublimity are the first to violate the first of his laws, viz., that of universal charity Spirits now come not only to confirm it, but also to show us its practical utility, they render intelligible, patent, truths that have hitherto been taught under he form of allegory, and, with this reinculcation of the eternal truths of morality, they also give us the solution of the most abstract problems of psychology.

Jesus came to show men the road to true goodness. Since God sent him to recall to men's mind the divine law they had forgotten. Why should he not send spirits to recall it to their memory once again and with still greater precision, now that they're forgetting it in their devotion to pride and to material gain? Who shall take upon himself to set bounds to the power of God or to dictate his ways? Who shall say that the appointed time has not arrived, as it's declared to have done by spirits, when truths hitherto unknown or misunderstood are to be openly proclaimed to the human race in order to hasten its advancement?

Is there not something evidently providential in the fact that spirit manifestations are being made on all points of the globe? It's not a single man, an isolated prophet, who comes to arouse us, light is breaking forth on all sides and a new world is being opened out before our eyes. As the invention of the microscope has revealed to us the world of the infinitely little, the existence of which was unsuspected by us and as the telescope has revealed to us the myriads of worlds the existence of which we suspected just as little, so the spirit communications of the present day are revealing to us the existence of an invisible world that surrounds us on all sides, that is incessantly in contact with us and that takes part, unknown to us, in everything we do. Yet a short time and the existence of that world, which is awaiting every one of us, will be as incontestable as is that of the microscopic world and of the infinity of globes in space.

Is it nothing to have made known that new world, to have initiated us into the mysteries of the life beyond the grave? It's true that these discoveries, if such they can he called, are contrary to certain received ideas, but have not all great scientific discoveries modified and even overthrown, ideas as fully received by the world, and has not our pride of opinion had to yield to evidence? It'll be the same in regard to Spiritism, which are long, will have taken its place among the other branches of human knowledge. Communication with the beings of the world beyond the grave enables us to see and to comprehend the life to come, initiates us into the joys and sorrows that await us therein according to our deserts and thus brings back to spiritualism those who had come to see in man only matter, only an organized machine, we're therefore justified in asserting that the facts of Spiritism have given the death blow to materialism.

Had Spiritism done nothing more than this, it'd be entitled to the gratitude of all the friends of social order, but it does much more than this, for it shows the inevitable results of evil, and, consequently, the necessity of goodness. The number of those whom it has brought back to better sentiments, whose evil tendencies it has neutralized and whom it has turned from wrongdoing, is already larger than is usually supposed and is becoming still more considerable every day, because the future is no longer for them a vague imagining, a mere hope, but a fact, the reality of which is felt and understood when they see and hear those who have left us lamenting or rejoicing over what they did when they were upon the Earth. Whoever witnesses these communications begins to reflect on the reality thus brought home to him and to feel the need of self examination, self judgment and self amendment.

8 - The fact that differences of opinion exist among spiritists in regard to certain points of doctrine has been used by opponents as a handle against it. It's not surprising that, in the beginning of a new science, when the observations on which it's based are still incomplete, the subjects of which it treats should have been regarded by its various adherents from their own point of view and that contradictory theories should thus have been put forth. But a deeper study of the facts in question has already overthrown most of those theories, and, among others, that which attributed all spirit communications to evil spirits, as though it were impossible for God to send good spirits to men, a supposition that is at once absurd, because it's opposition to the facts of the case, and impious, because it's a denial of the power and goodness of the Creator.

Our spirit guides have always advised us not to trouble ourselves about divergences of opinion among spiritists, assuring us that unity of doctrine will eventually be established and we accordingly see that this unity has already been arrived at in regard to the major part of the points at issue, and that divergences of opinion, in regard to the others, are disappearing day by day. To the question, while awaiting the establishment of doctrinal unity, upon what basis can an impartial and disinterested inquirer arrive at a judgment as to the relative merits of the various theories put forth by spirits? The following reply was given, the purest light is that which isn't obscured by any cloud, the most precious diamond is the one which is without a flaw, judge the communications of spirits, in like manner, by the purity of their teachings. Don't forget that there are, among spirits, many who have not yet freed themselves from their earthly ideas.

Learn to distinguish them by their language, judge them by the sum of what they tell you, see whether there is logical sequence in the ideas they suggest, whether there is, in their statements, nothing that betrays ignorance, pride or malevolence, in a word, whether their communications always bear the stamp of wisdom that attests true superiority. If your world were inaccessible to error, it'd be perfect, which it's far from being, you have still to learn to distinguish error from truth, you need the lessons of experience to exercise your judgment and to bring you on. The basis of unity will he found in the body of doctrine among the adherents of which good has never been mixed with evil, men will rally spontaneously to that doctrine, because they'll judge it to be the truth. But what matter a few dissidences of opinion, more apparent than real?

The fundamental principles of Spiritism are everywhere the same and should unite you all in a common bond, that of the love of God and the practice of goodness. Whatever you suppose to be the mode of progression and the normal conditions of your future existence, the aim proposed is still the same, viz., to do right and there is but one way of doing that. If there be, among spiritists, differences of opinion in regard to some points of theory, all of them are agreed in regard to the fundamentals of the matter, unity, therefore, already exists among them, with the exception of the very small number of those who don't yet admit the intervention of spirits in the manifestations and who attribute these either to purely physical causes, which is contrary to the axiom, every intelligent effect must have an intelligent cause, or to a reflex action of our own thought, which is disproved by the facts of the case.

There may, then, be different schools, seeking light in regard to the points of spiritist doctrine that are still open to controversy, there ought not to be rival sects, making opposition to one another. Antagonism should only exist between those who desire goodness and those who desire or do evil, but no one who has sincerely adopted the broad principles of morality laid down by Spiritism can desire evil or wish ill to his neighbor, whatever may be his opinions in regard to points of secondary importance. If any school be in error, it'll obtain light, sooner or later, if it seeks honestly and without prejudice and all schools possess, meanwhile, a common bond that should unite them in the same sentiment. All of them have a common aim, it matters little what road they take, provided it leads to the common goal. None should attempt to impose their opinion by force, whether physical or moral and any school that should hurl its anathema at another would be clearly in the wrong, for it would evidently be acting under the influence of evil spirits.

The only force of an argument is its intrinsic reasonableness and moderation will do more to ensure the triumph of the truth than diatribe envenomed by envy and jealousy. Good spirits preach only union and the love of the neighbor and nothing malevolent or uncharitable can ever proceed from a pure source. As bearing on the subject of the foregoing remarks and also as a fitting termination of the present work, we subjoin the following message from the spirit of Saint Augustine, a message conveying counsels well worthy of being laid to heart by all who read it. Long enough have men torn one another to pieces, anathematizing each other in the name of a God of peace and of mercy, whom they insult by such a sacrilege. Spiritism will eventually constitute a bond of union among them, by showing what is truth and what is error, but there will still be, and for a long time to come, scribes and Pharisees who'll reject it, as they rejected Christ.

Would you know the quality of the spirits who influence the various sects into which the world is divided? Judge them by their deeds and by the principles they profess. Never did good spirits instigate to the commission of evil deeds, never did they counsel or condone murder or violence, never did they excite party hatreds, the thirst for riches and honors or greed of earthly things. They alone who are kind, humane, benevolent, to all, are counted as friends by spirits of high degree, they alone are counted as friends by Jesus, for they alone are following the road which he has shown them as the only one which leads to him. Saint Augustine.

Sociedade Armônica - The best for the world.
Do what you like, that allows you to evolve and live well anywhere; that harms no one and always brings happiness.

Printed in Great Britain
by Amazon